TESTING ACCOMMODATIONS FOR STUDENTS WITH DISABILITIES

SCHOOL PSYCHOLOGY BOOK SERIES

TESTING ACCOMMODATIONS FOR STUDENTS WITH DISABILITIES

RESEARCH-BASED PRACTICE

Benjamin J. Lovett and
Lawrence J. Lewandowski

American Psychological Association • Washington, DC

Published by
American Psychological Association
750 First Street, NE
Washington, DC 20002
www.apa.org

To order
APA Order Department
P.O. Box 92984
Washington, DC 20090-2984
Tel: (800) 374-2721; Direct: (202) 336-5510
Fax: (202) 336-5502; TDD/TTY: (202) 336-6123
Online: www.apa.org/pubs/books
E-mail: order@apa.org

In the U.K., Europe, Africa, and the Middle East, copies may be ordered from
American Psychological Association
3 Henrietta Street
Covent Garden, London
WC2E 8LU England

Typeset in Goudy by Circle Graphics, Inc., Columbia, MD

Printer: United Book Press, Baltimore, MD
Cover Designer: Mercury Publishing Services, Inc., Rockville, MD

The opinions and statements published are the responsibility of the authors, and such opinions and statements do not necessarily represent the policies of the American Psychological Association.

Library of Congress Cataloging-in-Publication Data

Lovett, Benjamin J.
  Testing accommodations for students with disabilities : research-based practice / Benjamin J. Lovett and Lawrence J. Lewandowski. — First edition.
      pages cm. — (School psychology book series)
  Includes bibliographical references and index.
  ISBN-13: 978-1-4338-1797-7
  ISBN-10: 1-4338-1797-7
  1. Testing accommodations--United States. 2. Students with disabilities—Services for—United States. I. Lewandowski, Lawrence J. II. Title.
  LB3060.59.L68 2014
  371.26–dc23
                                    2014009734

British Library Cataloguing-in-Publication Data
A CIP record is available from the British Library.

Printed in the United States of America
First Edition

http://dx.doi.org/10.1037/14468-000

To my mother, on the occasion of her retirement from a career spent
helping children with special needs.
—*Benjamin J. Lovett*

To Fran and Diane for their constant commitment, support, patience,
and inspiration.
—*Lawrence J. Lewandowski*

CONTENTS

SERIES FOREWORD

Outside of their homes, children spend more time in schools than in any other setting. Tragedies such as Sandy Hook and Columbine and more hopeful developments such as the movement toward improved mental health, physical health, and academic achievement all illustrate the ongoing need for high-quality writing that explains how children, families, and communities associated with schools worldwide can be supported through the application of sound psychological research, theory, and practice.

Thus, for the past several years the American Psychological Association (APA) Books Program and APA Division 16 (School Psychology) have partnered to produce the School Psychology Book Series. The mission of this series is to increase the visibility of psychological science, practice, and policy for children and adolescents in schools and communities. The result has been a strong collection of scholarly work that appeals not only to psychologists but also to individuals from all fields who have reason to seek and use what psychology has to offer in schools.

Many individuals have made significant contributions to the School Psychology Book Series. First, we would like to acknowledge the dedication of past series editors: Sandra L. Christensen, Jan Hughes, R. Steve McCallum,

LeAdelle Phelps, Susan Sheridan, and Christopher H. Skinner. Second, we would like to acknowledge the outstanding editorial vision of the scholars who have edited or authored books for the series. The work of these scholars has significantly advanced psychological science and practice for children and adolescents worldwide.

We welcome your comments about this volume and other topics you would like to see explored in this series. To share your thoughts, please visit the Division 16 website at http://www.apadivisions.org/division-16.

Linda A. Reddy, PhD
Series Editor

PREFACE

In many school districts and postsecondary settings, testing accommodations are a controversial topic. To take just the news stories going on as we wrote this preface, the Oklahoma Department of Education had been investigated by the Office of Civil Rights for having inappropriate policies on testing accommodations (Archer, 2013), and the Law School Admission Council was being sued by plaintiffs whose requests for accommodations on the Law School Admission Test (LSAT) were denied (Dotinga, 2014). Many stories similar to these simply fail to make the news, and then there are the countless disputes over accommodations that happen at individualized education program (IEP) meetings and less formally in school building hallways and disability service office meeting rooms throughout the country.

Although neither of us initially intended to become a testing accommodations researcher, we were driven to investigate the topic after seeing frequent disputes over testing accommodations and hoping that empirical research could test some of the claims being made by disputants. There is still much research to be done, but we are now at the point, about 20 years after the first empirical studies began, at which we can say some things about accommodations with confidence, and we can evaluate claims made by advocates and critics of accommodations by testing those claims against research. We have spent many years bringing research to individual schools, school districts, testing agencies, and student services offices, and we hope that this book will serve as a resource for the many more testing entities that we cannot reach personally.

This book displays and continues our efforts to strengthen the bidirectional relationship between research and practice. The practice-to-research direction is easy to see: Our own research studies, and those of other scholars, have been guided by specific concerns that arise in real accommodations cases. The research-to-practice direction is still in its infancy, but it is our aim to make accommodation decisions in schools and other testing settings that are based directly on research findings like those reviewed in this book. We see many reasons to be optimistic that this can happen; when we present to school psychologists at conventions, or to K–12 teachers at in-service workshops, we are pleased by the enthusiastic responses of audience members who are excited to learn that researchers have actually tried to investigate empirically the dilemmas that they, as practitioners, deal with every day. Often audience members interrupt our presentations to ask, "What would you do with a kid who . . ." and we are always eager to try to apply research to a new real-life situation. Sometimes, we find it difficult to answer, and then the audience member's question prompts a new empirical study!

It is therefore a genuine pleasure to present this book, which covers those empirical studies, to readers who can then actually implement research-based accommodations decisions. And we're very grateful to the teachers, psychologists, school administrators, college and university employees, and testing agency professionals who have invited us to consult, thus giving us access to a much wider number of accommodations cases than we could ever have seen while working in any one of those positions. We also thank Kathleen Dickinson for her help with references, and we thank the editorial staff at APA Books for their help throughout the publication process. Finally, we thank Linda Reddy for coordinating the initial book proposal and for her faith in the book from the start.

TESTING ACCOMMODATIONS FOR STUDENTS WITH DISABILITIES

1

INTRODUCTION

As standardized testing becomes an ever more widespread feature of education, training, and selection, testing accommodations also are becoming increasingly prevalent. Part of the growth in accommodations comes from legal changes ensuring that individuals with disabilities have the right to demonstrate their skills and compete fairly with nondisabled individuals. In addition, educational systems have recently been given the responsibility to ensure that all students, including those with disabilities, are making appropriate academic progress. Testing accommodations are part of these shifts, and are generally viewed as a welcome development.

However, the professionals charged with making decisions about testing accommodations often come to different conclusions regarding which accommodations (if any) are appropriate in each case. Therefore, it is not surprising that we see great inconsistency in when students are given accommodations, and this sometimes leads to confusion and frustration when

http://dx.doi.org/10.1037/14468-001
Testing Accommodations for Students With Disabilities: Research-Based Practice, by B. J. Lovett and L. J. Lewandowski

students do not receive the accommodations that they and their families think are appropriate. Consider the following cases.

Tyler, an 8-year-old in second grade, has just received a diagnosis of attention-deficit/hyperactivity disorder (ADHD). One of the problems that prompted his parents to take him for an ADHD assessment was his poor performance in school, and now his parents are meeting with school staff to determine whether he needs an accommodations plan or even special education services. Tyler's classroom teacher suggests that he be given extended-time accommodations when he takes the state exams that spring. His parents are skeptical about his need for extra time and instead request that a proctor be available to keep him on task during the exam.

Maria is a 17-year-old high school senior preparing to take two college admission tests, the SAT and the ACT. She has a history of a mild hearing loss, first diagnosed in infancy, and although she does not receive special education, she has been informally given certain accommodations, such as preferential classroom seating, throughout her school career. She applies to the testing agencies requesting that she take the test in a separate room, saying that one of the symptoms accompanying her hearing loss is a hyper-sensitivity to sudden noises that might distract her during the exams. Both testing agencies deny her request, citing insufficient documentation of her accommodation needs.

Cases like Tyler's and Maria's happen every day in schools and post-secondary settings, and although they are typical, they raise difficult and complex questions. Scientific research can help answer these questions and guide decision makers in determining the appropriate accommodations for testing.

In this book, we provide a research-based approach to determining which (if any) testing accommodations are appropriate for students with disabilities. Specifically, we offer practical decision-making strategies for different types of accommodation (timing/scheduling, response format, setting, and presentation) and apply the strategies to hypothetical case studies of students with various disability diagnoses. We base our recommendations on research, ethical and legal requirements, and psychometric properties of the test. Also, we consider a range of disabilities—from low-incidence disabilities such as blindness and cerebral palsy to high-incidence disabilities such as ADHD. We stress the importance of using relevant research evidence when making decisions that can at times be quite controversial.

This book was initially written for those who make decisions about testing accommodations—school psychologists, educators, and other mental health clinicians who work in the schools or with school-age clients. However, the book will also benefit disability services professionals at colleges and testing agencies, along with mental health professionals who diagnose and manage learning and attention disorders in adults. Given the range of training and experience in these different audiences, we make no assumptions about the reader's background in psychometric theory, clinical skills, research design, or knowledge of special education; rather, we aim for maximum accessibility, not unlike the goal that we promote for tests. Our hope is that members of all audiences will be better equipped to make decisions about accommodations and be able to defend these decisions on solid grounds of empirical evidence.

In the remainder of this chapter, we introduce the concept of testing accommodations and differentiate it from similar concepts, such as alternate assessment and instructional accommodations. We also review research describing how accommodations are currently used. Finally, we explain how the rest of this book is organized.

WHAT IS AN ACCOMMODATION?

We define a *testing accommodation* as an alteration to the test administration procedure that does not change the test content. Admittedly, when certain intensive accommodations are provided, there may be disagreement over whether the test content has been changed, but we believe that the distinction between testing procedure and test content is a meaningful one, despite the existence of borderline cases. In addition, note that this definition deliberately lacks any evaluation of the appropriateness of an accommodation; in any particular case, for a particular student on a particular test at a particular time, an accommodation may be appropriate or inappropriate.

As we discuss in more detail in later chapters, testing accommodations are often needed because students with disabilities may not be able to demonstrate their skills under typical testing conditions. They may not have sufficient time to consider all of the test items, or they may misunderstand what test items are asking them to do, or they may find that making the desired test responses is too difficult physically. Without accommodations, then, we are left with inaccurate inferences about a student's skill levels, threatening the appropriateness of any decisions that we make regarding that student.

Thurlow, Elliott, and Ysseldyke (2003) offered a useful taxonomy of testing accommodations, classifying them into five rough categories. *Setting accommodations* include taking a test in a separate location from other students—either with fewer students or in a setting with special characteristics, such as fewer distractions. *Presentation accommodations* include presenting test instructions and/or items using a different medium (e.g., through an audio tape rather than in written form) or with additional aids (e.g., highlighting key words in each test item). *Scheduling accommodations* include taking a test at a specific time in the day or taking parts of the test in a different order than usual. *Timing accommodations* include having additional time to take a test or being permitted to take additional breaks during a test. Finally, *response accommodations* include responding to test items using alternative means (e.g., reporting answers to a scribe) or having access to special equipment (e.g., a dictionary) when responding. Most, but not all, accommodations fit into these categories.

Accommodations Versus Modifications?

Some researchers contrast *accommodations* with *modifications*. For instance, Mather and Wendling (2011) reported that "accommodations do not alter the essential elements of the task, whereas modifications alter the task demands in some way" (p. 250). Similarly, Hollenbeck (2002) wrote that accommodations "must not change the assessment construct(s) of interest," whereas a modification "changes the construct being assessed" (pp. 396–397). However, in the present book, we refer to both of these kinds of alterations as *accommodations*, and we are skeptical of the use of two distinct terms for several reasons.

First, many test format alterations that are typically classified as accommodations (e.g., taking a test in a separate room) change the test in some way, and so they change the construct being measured to some degree. So long as an alteration is only available to some examinees, there is some difference in testing conditions across examinees. Alterations, then, are best placed on a continuum that indexes the degree to which each construct that the test measures is altered. The use of two terms suggests an inappropriate, dichotomous "either/or" conceptualization of the issue.

Second, the degree to which an alteration changes the constructs being measured depends on the test. Obviously, a read-aloud alteration would not be appropriate on a test of decoding skills, whereas it may be appropriate on a test of mathematics reasoning skills. But the accommodation/modification distinction tempts school-based professionals as well as scholars to determine, in a rigid way, which alterations are "always" or "usually" accommodations and which are modifications. Indeed, after making the distinction, Mather and Wendling (2011) went on to list extended time as an accommodation, even as Hollenbeck (2002) gave an example in which extended time is a modification.

Finally, the accommodation/modification distinction assumes that test developers and test users have a clear sense of which constructs they wish to measure and which constructs are ancillary and irrelevant. On certain high-stakes standardized tests, this assumption may be accurate, but on teacher-made classroom tests, it is unlikely to be accurate. Teachers rarely consider which precise set of constructs a test is developed to assess and which ancillary skills the test will require. Even on high-stakes tests, test users may make inferences about scores on the basis of aspects of the testing format that the test developers consider to be irrelevant. For instance, even though the developers and administrators of the SAT do not explicitly view the test as a measure of test-taking speed, users of the scores (e.g., college admissions officers) may make inferences about the examinees' ability to complete problems under time pressure.

For all of these reasons, the accommodation/modification distinction is dubious, and it may even be pernicious if it leads to premature and overly general lists of accommodations and modifications. Perhaps the most dangerous consequence would be assuming that accommodations (as opposed to modifications) are, by definition, appropriate; as we discuss in Chapter 3, whether an alteration alters the constructs measured by a test is just one of the relevant questions to consider when making decisions about the appropriateness of the alteration.

Accommodations Versus Alternate Assessments

We do make a distinction between test accommodations and alternate assessments (also called *alternative assessments*). An *alternate assessment* is "a method of measuring the performance of students unable to participate in the typical district or state assessment" (Thurlow et al., 2003, p. 78). Characterized as "the ultimate accommodation" by Roach (2005), alternate assessments are typically in K–12 schools where they are often given to students with significant cognitive disabilities. Extensive and frequently changing legal regulations permit a certain proportion of students who score well on alternate assessments to count toward the school's total number of proficient students (Umpstead, 2009).

Alternate assessments are classified into several kinds (see Bolt & Roach, 2009, Chapter 5 for a helpful overview), and currently the most prevalent kind are alternate assessments based on alternate achievement standards (AA-AAS). These assessments require students to demonstrate skills that are relevant to the curricular objective for all students, but they "typically cover a *narrowed range of content* . . . and *performance levels that are substantially different from grade level*" (emphasis in original; Wakeman, Browder, Flowers, & Karvonen, 2011, p. 155). AA-AAS methods can include portfolios of student work and teacher-completed checklists that describe what academic skills a student displays. For instance, the state of Iowa uses a rating scale to document reading skills of certain students with severe cognitive disabilities; the rating scale for students in Grades 3 through 5 includes items such as "identifies text as fiction or nonfiction" and "identifies warning labels" (Iowa Department of Education, 2013).

Although we occasionally refer to research on alternate assessments, we do not discuss them in detail in the present book. They come with a set of unique challenges (Hess, Burdge, & Clayton, 2011), and the procedures for developing alternate assessments and deciding which students should take them are significantly different from procedures for accommodations. Moreover, even if alternate assessments become more prevalent (as is likely to happen), accommodations are likely to remain far more common and to be present in far more settings.

Instructional Versus Testing Accommodations

Testing accommodations should be distinguished from the accommodations that students with disabilities access during instruction, such as preferential seating (e.g., near the front of the room) and alterations to materials provided (e.g., access to class notes ahead of time). Students' instructional accommodations will not always be appropriate in testing situations, and so research finding imperfect matches between students' instructional and testing accommodations (e.g., Ysseldyke et al., 2001) is not necessarily worrisome. However, often a match is expected; as Bolt (2011) noted, having access to accommodations prior to the test ensures that students understand how to use the accommodations, and it increases the chance that students have been able to access the taught content that the test is based on. We would add that it is always worth asking why a student is receiving a testing accommodation when that student does not use (or apparently need) the accommodation during instruction.

We should also distinguish between testing accommodations and what are sometimes called *grading adaptations* (e.g., Silva, Munk, & Bursuck, 2005). Sometimes students with disabilities are graded using different practices: Compared with peers, their grades may be based more on improvement, or on effort, on different assignments or even on different grading scales (e.g., whereas 85% correct is typically needed for a grade of B, a student with a disability may only need to obtain 75% correct answers for a B). Grading adaptations are understandably controversial, and they are more a feature of special education than typical disability-related accommodations; we do not discuss them further.

Accommodations Versus Comfort Measures

We wish to make a final distinction between testing accommodations and what we call *comfort measures*; the latter are small test administration alterations that are done to satisfy students' preferences or test-taking styles, and they are available to all test takers, regardless of disability status. For instance, a teacher may permit students to access water bottles on their desks during an exam or to mark their answers to multiple-choice items in the exam booklet rather than on a cover sheet. If these alterations are made available to all students (by request), and they are not done to specifically remedy the effects of a disability condition, they do not constitute testing accommodations.[1]

In postsecondary settings, comfort measures may need to be formally requested, just so that test proctors will be aware of them. For instance, it is not uncommon for a pregnant examinee to request additional bathroom breaks or for a new mother to request a break to be able to express milk; access to pillows for back pain or access to prescribed medication during the exam are common requests that do not usually fall under "disability accommodations" but still constitute alterations to the test administration procedure.

We make this distinction because comfort measures can mask the need for accommodations. A student whose health problem requires frequent drinking of water will not require accommodations when all students are permitted to access water bottles, but she may require accommodations on a later exam where this is not permitted. On the other hand, use of comfort measures can also lead to a history of "accommodations" that are not actually needed. For instance, if a teacher permits students to write answers to multiple-choice items either in an exam booklet or on a cover sheet, a student may choose the former (because it is easier), but he may be perfectly able to do the latter if required to do so. We should, then, inquire about the use of comfort measures, but testing entities should not be bound to necessarily provide previously accessed comfort measures later as accommodations. Moreover, some comfort measures should be available as part of universal design (see Chapter 10), so that all students are able to access the test under "standard" conditions.

TESTING ACCOMMODATIONS IN CURRENT PRACTICE

As we discuss in more detail in Chapter 2, the use of testing accommodations has grown along with other inclusive features of special education. When students with disabilities were not educated in the same schools as

---

[1]We should note that on certain high-stakes standardized tests, especially in postsecondary settings, even small changes such as access to water bottles may be considered an accommodation and would only be permitted to students who have documentation showing that they have a unique need for the alteration.

nondisabled students, there was no need for accommodations. During the past half-century, the rights of students with disabilities were increasingly recognized, along with society's responsibility to ensure that these students were making progress in academic skills. Therefore, more emphasis was placed on students with disabilities participating in the full educational programming of their nondisabled peers, and accommodations were recognized as needed to fairly test these students. A similar process has happened with regard to postsecondary settings; as adults with disabilities have been included in more settings (e.g., college, employment), accommodations have been recognized as a necessary component to their participation.

Prevalence of Testing Accommodations

How common is it for a student to receive testing accommodations? There is no quick and simple answer to this question. However, a variety of research studies have investigated the prevalence of accommodations for specific samples taking specific tests. One relatively comprehensive survey of accommodations use was recently undertaken by the U.S. Government Accountability Office (2011); it asked selected high-stakes testing agencies (mainly those who coordinate admissions and professional certification testing) about their most frequently requested and granted accommodations. Extended time accounted for almost three quarters of requested and granted accommodations, followed in frequency by adjustments in the testing environment (e.g., distraction-reduced setting). In addition, almost half of testing accommodations were for students with learning disabilities, followed in frequency by those with ADHD; only 10% of accommodations cases involved students with physical or sensory disabilities. Finally, on these tests, approximately 2% of test administrations on average were given with accommodations. This report has a good deal of useful information, but the data are unlikely to generalize to K–12 settings because fewer students with disabilities are represented in some of the settings where this survey was conducted (e.g., medical school students taking licensure exams).

At the K–12 level, much relevant information is tracked by the National Center on Educational Outcomes at the University of Minnesota, whose website (http://www.cehd.umn.edu/NCEO) includes a database containing statistics on accommodations from various states in various years. Some of these data were summarized in a recent study by Vang, Thurlow, and Altman (2012), who investigated the prevalence of accommodations by students with disabilities taking statewide assessments during the 2008–2009 school year. The prevalence varied widely across different states and also depended on grade level and test subject area (reading vs. mathematics). In some states (California, Minnesota, New York), accommodations were consistently given to fairly few students (at times fewer than 10% of students with disabilities), whereas in other states (Delaware, Louisiana, Massachusetts, New Jersey), accommodations were given to the vast majority of students with disabilities (at times over 90% of students received accommodations in some of these states).[2] In general, the prevalence of accommodations on reading and mathematics tests was similar, but in some states the two rates were quite different; for instance, for eighth graders, Idaho had the largest gap: Over 60% of students with disabilities received accommodations on the statewide mathematics assessment, whereas fewer than 1% of students with disabilities received accommodations on the statewide reading assessment. Such variability in accommodations use stems from states having wide authority over accommodations policies, a point that we discuss in more detail in Chapter 2.

Even these statistics do not address what happens when accommodations are implemented outside of the statewide assessments. A study by Bottsford-Miller, Thurlow, Stout, and Quenemoen (2006) found substantial divergence between the accommodations given on in-class versus standardized assessments for K–12 students. For instance, in their sample of students with disabilities, 75.6% of students were given extended time on in-class tests, but only 53.3% were given the accommodation on standardized assessments. Similarly, 51.5% of students were given read-aloud accommodations on in-class tests, but only 40.6% were given this accommodation on standardized assessments. In contrast, setting accommodations (e.g., being tested in a private room) were given more frequently on standardized assessments (39.5%) than on in-class tests (24.5%). We should note that there may be valid reasons for the divergences observed here; state regulations govern the provision of specific accommodations on statewide standardized assessments, and these assessments may at times even measure different constructs than in-class tests. However, the divergences still show why describing the prevalence of accommodations is so difficult.

Finally, we conclude our discussion of prevalence by noting that testing accommodations have become a global phenomenon in recent years. Pepper's (2007) international survey documented a remarkably wide range of procedures for assessing the educational progress of students with disabilities. Most of the 25 countries surveyed permitted at least certain types of testing accommodations, although the specific accommodations permitted varied greatly. In certain countries, especially controversial procedures were allowed, such as in Hungary, where students with disabilities would actually receive eight additional points on their exam.

---

[2]Further complicating matters, a proportion of students with disabilities were not included in the accommodations prevalence because they received alternate assessments.

Perspectives on Accommodations: Controversy and Consensus

Providing testing accommodations is a practice fraught with polarized perspectives, ranging from advocates who passionately argue for their necessity and see no disadvantages to their use (e.g., Shaywitz, 2003) to critics who view the use of accommodations as akin to cheating on the part of undeserving students and their pushy parents (e.g., Tapper, Morris, & Setrakian, 2006). Researchers who study accommodations are usually somewhere in the middle, stressing the need for accommodations in some cases, while noting the need for improvements in the way that accommodation decisions are made (Koretz & Barton, 2004; Pitoniak & Royer, 2001).

A sizeable body of research has examined the perspectives of what is perhaps the most important group of stakeholders: the students who receive the accommodations (see Lovett & Leja, 2013, for a comprehensive review of this research). This literature has yielded two general findings that are especially important. First, the most typical response of students with disabilities to testing accommodations is a positive one. On average, students report being pleased to have accommodations, and when they are tested both with and without accommodations, they report less anxiety and less discomfort during the testing with accommodations (Lang, Elliott, Bolt, & Kratochwill, 2008). For instance, Kosciolek and Ysseldyke (2000) administered two alternate forms of a reading comprehension test (one with accommodations, one without) to elementary school students with disabilities and found that 75% of these students preferred the test with accommodations. Recent research has suggested that accommodations may also increase students' motivation and self-efficacy (Feldman, Kim, & Elliott, 2011).[3]

A second common finding provides a counterpoint to the first: Students' responses to accommodations vary, depending on the student, the accommodation in question, and the climate in which the accommodation is provided. For instance, several studies have found that some students dislike read-aloud accommodations, or at least prefer to take tests without them (Nelson, Jayanthi, Epstein, & Bursuck, 2000; Rickey, 2005). In addition, a study of students in the United Kingdom with ADHD found that most were ambivalent about receiving accommodations, expressing concern that they would be held to higher standards of performance because of the accommodations and that their peers would perceive the accommodations as unfair (Taylor & Houghton, 2008). Therefore, accommodations should never be

---

[3]Students' generally positive reaction to accommodations should not mask concerns that some students have about stigma related to receiving accommodations (see e.g., Taylor & Houghton, 2008). Staff development should include training staff in awareness of students' potential concerns on this point.

presumed to be a positive addition to a student's testing experience, and they may even have the potential to bother students.

The Need for Research-Based Practice

By *research-based practice*, we mean decisions about testing accommodations that are informed by the results of empirical research on the accommodations' efficacy and appropriateness, as well as empirical findings on other relevant topics. The need for research-based practice is founded in part on the ethical obligations of school psychologists. For instance, the National Association of School Psychologists' (2010) *Principles for Professional Ethics* states that "school psychologists must . . . use scientific knowledge from psychology and education to help clients and others make informed choices" (p. 6). Similarly, the American Psychological Association's (2010) *Ethical Principles of Psychologists and Code of Conduct* requires that "psychologists' work is based on established scientific and professional knowledge" (Sec. 2.04). But the need for explicit research-based practice guidelines is also founded in the following sobering findings about current testing accommodations practice:

1. *Teachers are often ignorant of which accommodations are even permissible on high-stakes tests.* Siskind (1993) surveyed 60 South Carolina teachers (most of them special education teachers) about which of 51 accommodations were permitted on a state exam. Out of a possible score of 51 on the survey (for 100% correct answers), the average score was 28.52, which would be (as Siskind noted) a failing grade. A later study in Oregon (Hollenbeck, Tindal, & Almond, 1998) yielded similar findings; the average "score" on the survey of permissible accommodations was again quite low (54.8%), leading the researchers to conclude that "teachers' knowledge of allowable accommodations was limited enough to jeopardize the validity of score interpretation" (p. 181) for students with disabilities. Most recently, Lazarus, Thompson, and Thurlow (2006) replicated this finding; these investigators surveyed 798 special education teachers in four states and found that more than half of the teachers were unable to accurately characterize common accommodations (including read aloud, spell checker/dictionary access, and calculator access) as permitted or not permitted on their states' exams.
2. *Teachers' interpretations and implementation of accommodations vary.* Byrnes (2008) asked teachers for their interpretations of

three common accommodations: extended time, scribing, and preferential seating. Some teachers reported that extended time meant unlimited time limits or additional wait time to respond to oral questions from the teacher. Some teachers reported that scribing meant that another student could scribe for the target student or that the student could also have access to a computer to write. Finally, although preferential seating is less of a testing accommodation than an instructional accommodation, teachers' interpretations were diverse there as well, including seating the child close to the teacher, in the front of the room, away from distractions, close to the board, and near a peer role model (among other interpretations).

3. *Teacher-recommended accommodations are less helpful and less efficient than accommodations suggested by objective testing.* In a set of studies, Lynn and Doug Fuchs and their colleagues (L. S. Fuchs, Fuchs, Eaton, Hamlett, Binkley, & Crouch, 2000; L. S. Fuchs, Fuchs, Eaton, Hamlett, & Karns, 2000) compared teachers' judgments about appropriate accommodations with judgments made using an objective procedure (the procedure determined whether students benefited more than their peers from an accommodation, as measured on a brief diagnostic test). The teachers' judgments were made about their individual students, and this simulates well how teachers contribute to multidisciplinary team decisions about accommodations. Accommodations recommended by the objective procedure led to greater benefits than teacher-recommended accommodations, and this result was found across both reading and mathematics tests. Moreover, teachers recommended more accommodations than the objective procedure did, suggesting that they tend to be less efficient than an objective procedure in allocating accommodation resources. A more recent study (Ketterlin-Geller, Alonzo, Braun-Monegan, & Tindal, 2007) cast further doubt on the quality of teacher-recommended accommodations, finding that teacher recommendations did not even predict which accommodations had been approved by the individualized education programs (IEPs) of a sample of third-grade students in special education.

4. *School-based teams make accommodations decisions on the basis of comfort and other affective factors, rather than on the basis of students' disability-related functional impairments.* In a fascinating study, Rickey (2005) used observations and interviews to make a detailed examination of the testing accommodations process at three middle schools in Iowa. Surprisingly, she found

that the primary factor considered in making accommodation decisions was not a student's ability to access a test or even more general concerns about score validity. Instead, it was the student's affective state. Decision makers mentioned students' self-esteem, as well as their frustration and anxiety levels, but it was rare to hear mention of anything having to do with students' inability to access a test because of disability-related functional impairments. In fact, at one of the three schools, students' stress during exams was the only reason given for the use of testing accommodations. Although Rickey's study was limited to three schools, its findings certainly confirm our own experiences when consulting with school districts.

5. *Diagnosticians are not sufficiently knowledgeable about standards for determining disability status and accommodations eligibility.* A variety of studies have shown that although diagnostic evaluations often conclude with testing accommodations, diagnosticians often fail to recognize key considerations in what makes an accommodation appropriate or even what determines someone's disability status for legal purposes. For instance, Gordon, Lewandowski, Murphy, and Dempsey (2002) asked 147 diagnosticians to complete a survey about standards for accommodation eligibility under the Americans With Disabilities Act of 1990 (ADA). These investigators found that many diagnosticians believed that their job as evaluators was to help clients secure testing accommodations, and that the appropriateness of accommodations depended in large part on their clients' ability to benefit from the accommodations. In a second study, Joy, Julius, Akter, and Baron (2010) reviewed disability documentation submitted by 50 medical students requesting testing accommodations on the basis of an ADHD diagnosis. Although ADHD documentation typically includes psychological evaluations, these investigators found that only 14% of the applicants had documentation that established that the applicant met the official diagnostic criteria for ADHD. These two studies are representative of a diverse literature, more of which is reviewed in Chapter 4.

Why Is Research-Based Practice so Rare?

The apparent lack of research-based practice is, of course, not limited to the testing accommodations process. The helping professions, including school psychology and special education, are rife with practices that have meager scientific support (M. Burns & Ysseldyke, 2009; Gambrill, 2006;

Lilienfeld, Lynn, & Lohr, 2003). In the case of testing accommodations, research-based practice is especially difficult to promote because advocacy for individuals with disabilities tends toward an easy answer: Accommodations are good, because they have the possibility to allow students with disabilities to reach their potential. This perspective is grounded in the noblest of intentions; as we discuss in Chapter 2, the ethical foundations of testing accommodations are deep. However, the ease with which advocates uncritically endorse accommodations makes an objective evaluation more difficult.

Admittedly, advocacy is generally a positive force, and it has been instrumental in advancing the rights of individuals with disabilities. However, there is a necessary tension between science and advocacy. In their discussion of the distinction between science and advocacy in special education, Brigham, Gustashaw, and Brigham (2004) noted that "for many advocates, the starting point is the conclusion, and any evidence that points away from the conclusion is likely to be ignored or suppressed" (p. 201). In the case of testing accommodations, this means that advocates know what the correct decisions are, whether or not the research is present to support them. This happens on both sides of testing accommodations disputes; advocates for students with disabilities may insist on accommodations without a clear rationale, whereas testing entities may deny accommodations summarily, also without a clear rationale. In our consulting work, we frequently see advocacy and rarely see research-based practice. We have consulted with teachers and school administrators who are resistant to the use of accommodations that were clearly justified under the circumstances, and we have often met clinicians who recommend accommodations that are clearly not justified under the circumstances. Our aim in this book is to provide an approach to accommodations practice grounded in research rather than advocacy.

In addition to an advocacy mind-set, a second reason why research-based practice is rare involves professionals' lack of exposure to these practices. Not only is measurement/assessment training generally lacking in teacher training programs (e.g., Plake, Impara, & Fager, 1993; Stiggins, 1999), but teachers appear to have little exposure to research-based training in accommodations decision making. We devote Appendix B to discussing this problem in further detail and describing approaches to professional development training in accommodations practices.

A PREVIEW OF COMING ATTRACTIONS

Chapters 2 and 3 focus on preliminary material that affects all accommodations. In Chapter 2, we focus on legal and ethical issues associated with testing accommodations. What regulations govern which accommodations can and should be given when? What are the ethical precepts that motivate accommodations in the first place, and what are the ethical concerns raised by that the use of accommodations? Finally, what are the implications of these legal and ethical cornerstones for procedures for approving the use of accommodations? Chapter 3 shifts the focus to psychometric issues, detailing the conceptual logic underlying accommodations and posing five questions that should be considered when deciding if a particular accommodation should be given to a particular examinee. The chapter concludes with a guide to common research designs in studies of testing accommodations.

Chapter 4 covers the nature of disability conditions that lead to testing accommodations consideration. We discuss the difference between disability diagnoses and the determination of functional impairments that keep a student from accessing a test under standard testing conditions. We review research on which functional impairments are associated with which disability conditions, and we suggest assessment strategies for measuring impairment directly. We also discuss research on the reliability and accuracy of the diagnoses themselves, because a diagnosis is usually a precondition for accommodation eligibility.

Chapters 5 through 7 cover various specific accommodations. In each of these chapters, we begin by describing relevant features of tests (e.g., time pressure) as well as examinee traits (e.g., distractibility) that can influence test scores. We then review the results of any empirical research studies on the accommodations. We conclude each of these chapters by offering practical decision strategies for each type of accommodations and applying the strategies to hypothetical case studies of students with various disability diagnoses.

Chapters 8 and 9 zoom out from specific accommodations, back to more general issues. Chapter 8 discusses the relationship between accommodations and interventions. Even though accommodations and special education services are linked legally (i.e., many students receive testing accommodations as part of an IEP), the possibility of using interventions to make accommodations unnecessary has been largely neglected. In Chapter 8, we describe a general conception of intervention based on behavior analysis, and we discuss research on particular interventions that address specific functional impairments relevant to accommodations use. Chapter 9 continues the theme of planning for students' independent living, by considering the transition from high school to postsecondary education and employment. There we discuss differences in legal requirements, administrative guidelines, and available accommodations.

The final two chapters take an even broader perspective. Chapter 10 is a primer on Universal Design for Assessment (UDA). UDA is a set of principles that guides the development of student assessment tools that are accessible to all learners, resulting in tools that make accommodations easier to implement, while simultaneously making accommodations necessary for fewer students. Finally, in Chapter 11, we offer conclusions about the practice of testing accommodations, as well as some discussion of the most recent trends in accommodations, including technology-assisted testing and individualized assessment.

Two appendices follow the 11 regular chapters. Appendix A provides specific guidelines for documenting relevant disability conditions when students request testing accommodations in postsecondary settings. We hope that this appendix will be helpful to disability service office staff who review documentation as well as test agency administrators who develop accommodations policies. Appendix B describes professional development applications for K–12 teachers and college-level instructors. We cover ways in which psychologists and others with expertise in accommodations can work with educators to help them design widely accessible exams and decide when accommodations are appropriate on exams.

There are three topics related to the book that we do not discuss in detail. The first topic was already mentioned: alternate assessments, which are sufficiently different from accommodations that they are beyond our scope. The second topic is accommodations for English language learners (ELLs), a growing population containing some students who need accommodations because of their limited English proficiency preventing their demonstration of skills (Abedi, Hofstetter, & Lord, 2004; Bolt & Roach, 2009). Much of the psychometric framework that we develop in Chapter 3 applies to ELLs as well, and many of the accommodations discussed in Chapters 5 through 7 are used with ELLs, but we do not review research that focuses specifically on accommodations for ELLs. Although detailed coverage of this topic is beyond the scope of our book, practitioners should keep in mind that some ELLs also have disabilities and may need accommodations because of their ELL-related language deficiencies, their disabilities, or both.

The final related topic is accommodations for students with disabilities who are taking diagnostic tests—for instance, adapting an intelligence test for a blind student to obtain a more accurate gauge of her intellectual abilities. Accommodations are used far less often on diagnostic tests and tend to be given only to students with relatively low-incidence disabilities; moreover, there is very little empirical research on accommodations in these situations.

We conclude our introduction by calling the reader's attention to two features of the book that cut across all of the chapters. First, we take as our topic testing accommodations across all settings and tests. We use examples from different kinds of assessment situations and quite varied populations, from kindergarteners to medical students and beyond. Increasingly, school psychologists are involved in testing accommodations decisions that have implications for postsecondary decisions, if only because an established history of accommodations is weighed heavily when making subsequent decisions. We believe that the commonalities of testing are greater than the differences, and we try to emphasize the underlying principles of accommodation appropriateness to allow readers to apply our recommendations to new situations and examples that we cannot cover. In addition, in the book's central chapters on specific accommodations, we have included a diverse set of case studies to help readers see the process of applying research to a wide range of accommodations decisions.

The book's second general theme may surprise some readers, and that is our pairing of celebration of accommodations with criticism of certain current practices. It seems to us that many articles and books on accommodations minimize the disadvantages (psychometric ones as well as others) of accommodations while overplaying their virtues. To be clear, we are very much in favor of testing accommodations; as we discuss in detail in Chapter 2, in many cases we believe them to be vital. However, we find accommodations to be proffered too often in some settings, and we worry about their unintended effects. We hope, then, that this book provides a balanced perspective on an important practice and avoids both the dismissive tone of certain critics as well as the uncritical acceptance of certain advocates.

2

LEGAL, PROCEDURAL, AND ETHICAL FOUNDATIONS

Providing testing accommodations is a practice, like any other, subject to legal regulation and based in ethical principles. Understanding the legal, ethical, and procedural foundations of testing accommodations allows for improved accommodation decision making, especially in cases in which controversy exists.

LEGAL FOUNDATIONS OF TESTING ACCOMMODATIONS

Two sets of laws with overlapping coverage define the legal framework for testing accommodations:[1] *education* laws and *disability discrimination* laws. The former set applies to school students; the later set of laws applies to all

---

[1]We offer the standard caveat that comes with coverage of legal principles: Readers should not interpret anything in this chapter—or the rest of the book—as legal advice, and readers are instead encouraged to contact a licensed attorney with questions about the specific cases that they must address.

http://dx.doi.org/10.1037/14468-002
Testing Accommodations for Students With Disabilities: Research-Based Practice, by B. J. Lovett and L. J. Lewandowski

citizens with disabilities. Historically, both sets have grown in the past half-century to be ever more inclusive and to ensure that individuals with disabilities can increasingly participate in education and in society more generally. We discuss each set of laws in turn, focusing on statutes passed by legislative bodies, although we occasionally note holdings in court cases, as well as regulations promulgated by administrative agencies (e.g., the U.S. Department of Education).

Education Laws

The primary law regulating special education is the Individuals With Disabilities Education Act (IDEA). Passed in 1975 as the Education for All Handicapped Children Act, the IDEA protects the rights of certain children with disabilities: those who fit into one or more of 13 disability categories and only if their disability impinges on their ability to benefit from education. The IDEA requires that schools perform comprehensive evaluations to determine if a child has a relevant disability condition and, if so, that the school develop an individualized education program (IEP) that specifies individualized goals and objectives for the child, as well as the special education and related services that the child requires to receive an appropriate education (Yell, 2012).

When the IDEA first became law, testing accommodations were not explicitly mentioned. However, in a landmark case, *Board of Education of the Hendrick Hudson Central School District v. Rowley* (1982; hereafter, simply *Rowley*), the U.S. Supreme Court set a standard for interpreting the IDEA that has important implications for testing accommodations. Amy Rowley was a deaf student who was succeeding in school under an IEP, but her parents requested more services than the IEP was providing. The Supreme Court ruled against the Rowley family, ruling that the IDEA does not require that a student be given all possible services. As Yell (2012) explained the *Rowley* standard, "students with disabilities do not have a right to the best possible education or an education that allows them to achieve their maximum potential. Rather they are entitled to an education that is reasonably calculated to confer educational benefit" (p. 192). When a student is succeeding academically without testing accommodations, then there appears to be no legal requirement that accommodations be given just to maximize performance.

Another important provision in the original IDEA has important implications for accommodations: the requirement that "to the maximum extent appropriate, children with disabilities . . . are educated with children who are not disabled" through "the use of supplementary aids and services" if necessary. This is often known as the "least restrictive environment" provision of the

IDEA. Testing accommodations, when they are used appropriately, are part of the apparatus that allows students with disabilities to be educated with their peers. However, when used unnecessarily, testing accommodations can actually create a more restrictive environment than is appropriate for a student; for instance, a high school student with an attention-deficit/hyperactivity disorder (ADHD) diagnosis who takes all of the tests for her classes in a separate location is being educated (because assessment is part of education) in a more restrictive environment than may be necessary. A desire for full inclusion (at least for students with milder high-incidence disabilities) is another reason to not use testing accommodations when they are not needed.

When the IDEA was amended in 1997, the amendments required that students with disabilities be included in large-scale assessment programs that states and school districts use to monitor student progress (except in very rare exceptions). The rationale for this change was that school districts needed to ensure that all students were making progress toward academic goals and should not forget about students with disabilities on this point. Moreover, the 1997 amendments charged the IEP team with the responsibility of determining what accommodations, if any, would be needed to allow each student to participate in large-scale assessments. IEP teams must include, at minimum, a parent, a special and general education teacher, an administrator, and the student (when appropriate). Someone on the IEP team must be able to "interpret the instructional implication of the evaluation results," (§300.321) and this role is often filled by school psychologists, giving them input into testing accommodation decisions.

In 2001, the No Child Left Behind (NCLB) Act was passed. Despite its initial bipartisan support, NCLB is a controversial law, perhaps most famous for its requirement that all American students be proficient in reading and mathematics by the 2013–2014 school year and that schools show that they are making "adequate yearly progress" toward this outcome. (NCLB concerns all education, not just special education.) As part of this initiative, schools were required to administer more frequent statewide assessments in selected grades, and at least 95% of students with disabilities must be assessed. To this end, under NCLB, schools must provide whatever accommodations are needed to allow students with disabilities to participate in these assessments.[2] It is important that although NCLB places a cap on the proportion of students who can be classified as proficient on the basis of alternate assessments, there is no such cap for test scores obtained with accommodations (Shriner & Ganguly, 2007). This can lead to unnecessary accommodations; there is

---

[2]Under NCLB, at least 95% of all students in tested grades must be assessed, and at least 95% of students in certain groups (including students with identified disabilities) in tested grades must be assessed (Yell, 2012).

no downside to schools (other than logistical complexities during state exam administration), and the benefits seem obvious (e.g., possible increases in scores; parents who feel that the students' needs have been recognized and that the school is committed to student success).

In 2004, the IDEA was amended (by the Individuals With Disabilities Education Improvement Act, sometimes called IDEIA), leading to further changes in special education procedures. Nothing was explicitly changed about testing accommodations; the provisions of IDEA 1997 and NCLB requiring inclusion of students with disabilities in large-scale assessments, and requiring that these students be given needed testing accommodations, were retained. However, the 2004 IDEA amendments also had two important general themes that bear on the provision of accommodations. First, IDEA 2004 encouraged schools to find ways to reduce the numbers of students labeled as having disabilities. Consistent with this goal, the criteria for classifying students in the largest IDEA category, specific learning disability, were changed to encourage schools to test out different academic intervention strategies before labeling a child with a learning disability. We discuss the implications of this change more in Chapter 4, but we mention it here because this apparently small legal change may have a large impact on students' qualification for testing accommodations, because accommodations are provided far less frequently to students who are accessing academic interventions without a disability label. Second, IDEA 2004 also emphasized the importance of scientific research in special education practice. Specifically, the amendments require that judgments about the special education services provided to a student be "based on peer-reviewed research to the extent practicable" (Etscheidt & Curran, 2010). Although accommodations are not mentioned specifically here, we interpret this provision to mean that accommodation decisions should also be based on peer-reviewed research. We hope that practitioners will be able to use the peer-reviewed research reviewed in the current text to explain decisions about accommodations, as well as to defend decisions if challenged.

Disability Discrimination Laws

In 1973, Section 504 of the Rehabilitation Act was enacted to protect individuals with disabilities from being discriminated against by any entity receiving federal funding (including public K–12 schools as well as the vast majority of colleges and universities). Unlike IDEA, Section 504 does not provide for IEPs, but its scope is wider because it goes well beyond educational agencies, applies to adults as well as children, and is not limited to students who fit into the 13 IDEA disability categories but applies to anyone with a condition that "substantially limits" a major life activity, including learning.[3] Moreover, Section 504 requires entities that receive federal funding to provide "reasonable accommodations" to individuals who are disabled under the law, and testing accommodations fall under this law. As Phillips (2011) noted, in the context of testing, "a *reasonable accommodation* must be *needed* by a disabled person to *access* the test while ensuring *construct preservation* and *score comparability*" (p. 38, emphasis in original). Section 504, then, makes it possible for a wide variety of individuals to receive testing accommodations, provided that the accommodations are deemed to be "reasonable."

Many children who only receive accommodations (instructional as well as testing accommodations) but no special education services per se receive their accommodations through Section 504 (under a "504 plan" or "individualized accommodation plan") rather than through the IDEA. Some of these students have very little disability documentation because the school has never conducted a comprehensive evaluation under the IDEA. For instance, a student may receive testing accommodations under Section 504 based on a physician's letter diagnosing ADHD and recommending the accommodations. In theory, cases of students like this one would be reviewed to determine whether they are substantially limited in a relevant major life activity and whether the accommodations were truly reasonable, but when the diagnoses and recommendations are made by outside entities, schools may be hesitant to question the need for accommodations. This may be a further source of unnecessary testing accommodations because it is doubtful that many of the external professionals making diagnoses have expertise in testing accommodations.[4]

In 1990, the Americans With Disabilities Act (ADA) was signed into law, demonstrating a clear federal commitment to protecting the rights of individuals with disabilities. First and foremost, the ADA extended the provisions of Section 504 to private entities that serve the public, including private and parochial schools and the few colleges and universities that receive no federal funding. The range of protected individuals is very similar to Section 504, as is the emphasis on reasonable accommodations. Public schools have largely ignored the ADA with regard to students with disabilities, because Section 504 and the IDEA already defined their responsibilities in this regard.

However, for certain entities, such as private schools and testing agencies (e.g., for admission, certification, and licensure), the ADA has changed

---

[3]This is somewhat oversimplified. Some of the Section 504 provisions also protect individuals who are not disabled, but who have suffered disability-related discrimination anyway (e.g., because they were perceived to have a disability by a discriminating employer). Similar provisions are found in the Americans With Disabilities Act (ADA) discussed next.
[4]We expand on this point in Chapter 9, where we review research in postsecondary settings showing that external evaluators do not understand the ADA or make recommendations consistent with the law.

responsibilities. These entities do not receive federal funding, but they are required by the ADA to provide reasonable accommodations for students with disabilities. In addition, the law specifically addressed testing accommodations in certain settings in one passage ("Examinations and Courses"):

> Any person that offers examinations or courses related to applications, licensing, certifications, or credentialing for secondary or postsecondary education, professional, or trade purposes shall offer such examinations or courses in a place and manner accessible to persons with disabilities or offer alternative accessible arrangements for such individuals. (Sec. 12189)

The law also stated the following:

> The examination is selected and administered so as to best ensure that when the examination is administered to an individual with a disability that impairs sensory, manual, or speaking skills, the examination results accurately reflect the individual's aptitude or achievement level or whatever other factor the examination purports to measure, rather than reflecting the individual's impaired sensory, manual, or speaking skills (except where those skills are the factors that the examination purports to measure). (Sec. 12189)

In 2008, the ADA was amended in important ways. The Supreme Court had, in a series of rulings, interpreted the ADA in a relatively narrow way, so as to apply the label *disabled* to fewer people. In the ADA Amendments Act of 2008 (ADAAA), Congress clearly rebuked the Supreme Court and made clear that the ADA was to be interpreted more broadly (Rozalski, Katsiyannis, Ryan, Collins, & Stewart, 2010). However, certain key features of the original law were retained; perhaps most important, disability status is still determined though a substantial limitations test where the comparison group is a general population or "most people" standard.

More recently, in 2010, the Department of Justice released guidelines for implementing the ADA (as amended), specifically with regard to testing accommodations. Interestingly, the "Examinations and Courses" guideline cited previously was amended with the following language:

> When considering requests for modifications, accommodations, or auxiliary aids or services, the entity gives considerable weight to documentation of past modifications, accommodations, or auxiliary aids or services received in similar testing situations, as well as such modifications, accommodations, or related aids and services provided in response to an Individualized Education Program (IEP) provided under the Individuals with Disabilities Education Act or a plan describing services provided pursuant to Section 504 of the Rehabilitation Act of 1973, as amended (often referred as a Section 504 plan). (28 C.F.R. § 36.309)

Although the ADAAA itself appears to be sound, we have significant concerns about these regulations for its implementation. The passage just cited means that K–12 entities' decisions about testing accommodations are to be given "considerable weight" in postsecondary settings. Of course, this is problematic, because as we discussed in Chapter 1, a variety of research studies have found that K–12 accommodation decisions are based on inadequate procedures (for more details on the weak empirical basis for the ADA amendments on this point, see Burgoyne & Mew, 2011; Lovett, in press). If giving substantial weight to past decisions to grant accommodations amounts to "rubber stamping" subsequent accommodation requests, a single inappropriate decision to grant an accommodation binds all future testing entities to that decision. This seems inappropriate; if an IEP team decides to grant a second-grade student accommodations on a state exam, should the College Board be bound by this decision a decade later? Should the National Board of Medical Examiners be bound by the decision 2 decades later when the student takes her final licensure exam? Because of these kinds of problems, it is our hope that the regulations will be revised at some point to reflect these concerns. Certainly, there is nothing in the revised ADA statute itself that requires testing entities to rely on past accommodations decisions when the past decisions are in error. Even so, practitioners must understand the Department of Justice regulations as they exist currently (even as we point out their limitations).

PROCEDURAL IMPLICATIONS OF LEGAL REQUIREMENTS

Despite the several laws that apply, directly or indirectly, to testing accommodations, the details of individual accommodations decisions are not covered by these laws. Formal regulations and informal guidance at the state level, as well as individual instructors' decisions regarding accommodations on classroom tests, begin where the laws leave off.

State Regulations and Guidance

As with many education-related responsibilities, states have wide latitude in determining regulations for the use of testing accommodations, at least on statewide assessments. States have only developed such regulations relatively recently, as noted by Lazarus, Thurlow, Lail, and Christensen (2009), who examined how regulations for accommodations on high-stakes K–12 tests changed between 1993 and 2005. These investigators found that in 1993, fewer than half of states explicitly listed any accommodations as permitted, but by 2001, all did. As of 2005, the most common accommodations allowed were either for visual disabilities (large print was permitted by 48 states and Braille by 45 states) or else were low-intensity accommodations that were unlikely to compromise score validity (individual and small-group test administration were each permitted by 45 states). Over the 1993–2005 period, fewer and fewer accommodations were explicitly prohibited; in 2005, only spell checker and multiple-day administration were prohibited, and only in two states and one state, respectively.

This report was recently updated by Christensen, Braam, Scullin, and Thurlow (2011), who conducted an analysis of state policies on accommodations as of 2009. Their report is so comprehensive that we discuss it in some detail. As Christensen et al. noted, allowing accommodations is not a yes/no issue; state policies regarding a given accommodation might involve (a) allowing the accommodation without any restrictions; (b) allowing the accommodation under certain circumstances, such as on reading assessments but not mathematics assessments; (c) allowing the accommodation but taking it into account when scoring the assessment; or (d) explicitly prohibiting the accommodation. Further complicating matters, states are not all required to make policies for an exhaustive list of accommodations, and each state's policies are silent about certain accommodations.

With regard to presentation accommodations, Christensen et al. (2011) found that almost all states allowed large print and Braille test formats, usually without any restrictions. Read-aloud accommodations were somewhat different; although most states permitted that test directions be read aloud without any restrictions, states generally put restrictions on when test questions and passages could be read aloud, and nine states explicitly prohibited reading passages aloud. About one third of states (17) permitted a "familiar examiner" accommodation without any restrictions, and slightly fewer states (14) permitted students to read their own test aloud.

The data for response accommodations were similar. Christensen et al. (2011) found that almost all states permitted use of a scribe or word processor, although some of these states put various restrictions on their use. Most states also permitted students to write their answers in test booklets (rather than on separate sheets). Many states did not have explicit guidelines for some of the response accommodations, such as signing test responses to an interpreter and pointing to answers. The only response accommodation that was frequently explicitly prohibited was access to a spell checker (16 states forbade this).

Finally, with regard to timing and scheduling accommodations, most states allowed extended time, breaks during tests, and scheduling test administration at a time "most advantageous to the student," and generally these were all allowed without any restrictions. In contrast, most states did not have explicit policies regarding the reordering of test subtests or the administration of tests over multiple sessions or multiple days. Multiple-day administration was the only timing/scheduling accommodation that was explicitly prohibited, and only by two states.

In addition to examining which accommodations were permitted, Christensen et al. (2011) noted which states had policies allowing groups other than those with disabilities to access accommodations. One state (Kansas) had the most liberal policy, allowing any student access to appropriate accommodations without any restrictions, and 14 more states permitted all students to receive certain accommodations on certain tests. In addition, 42 states permitted students served under Section 504 to receive accommodations, and the same number permitted English language learners to receive them.

Finally, Christensen et al. (2011) examined state documents that discussed the process for determining appropriate accommodations in individual cases. Often, states specified factors that could and could not be used by IEP teams and similar bodies to make accommodation decisions. Almost all states (45 of them) noted that the nature of the accommodations that the student used outside of statewide tests (e.g., on teacher-made classroom tests) could be used as a factor. Interestingly, far fewer states (25) mentioned the degree to which proposed accommodations maintained validity of the test and its resulting scores. More states than this (37) noted, appropriately, that individual student needs and characteristics could play a role in decision making. At times, states explicitly mentioned factors that could not be used, most commonly administrative convenience (12 states) and the student's disability (10 states).[5] Presumably, the latter prohibition refers to using the student's disability category rather than the individual student's needs (e.g., not all cases of a given disability are alike).

In sum, Christensen et al.'s (2011) report shows both consensus and divergence in state policies. We should note that there are no similar reports for tests in postsecondary settings. Many higher education institutions and standardized testing agencies do include lists of possible accommodations as part of the applications that students complete when requesting accommodations, and presumably an accommodation's presence on the list suggests that it is permitted, at least under certain circumstances (although the lists are generally not intended to be exhaustive). Research is needed to determine if accommodations that students have access to in K–12 education would

---

[5]It may seem odd that a student's disability could *not* be used when making accommodations decisions. This only means that the student's official disability label or category cannot be used. Instead, team members must look at the individual student's skills and abilities. For instance, a student identified as having a specific learning disability may or may not need a read-aloud accommodation, depending on that particular student's reading skills.

be likely to transfer to other settings (e.g., college admission tests, classroom exams in college). Contacting individual testing agencies and college offices of disability services would be more difficult than contacting the 50 state offices of education, but such research would be invaluable to successful post-secondary transition.

Less Regulation of Classroom Assessments

Although most codified guidelines for accommodations pertain to high-stakes standardized tests, students take far more tests in classroom settings, and especially for younger students, the classroom is the setting where students often become accustomed to test accommodations. Part of the reason (and a partial justification) for the lack of formal guidelines here is that the standard administration procedures for classroom exams are at the instructor's discretion and vary widely. As we discuss in more detail elsewhere, we encourage teachers to develop, in consultation with colleagues and administrators, guidelines for which accommodations would be appropriate on various classroom assessments. At the very least, this should be done for the accommodations that are relevant to students in a teacher's current classes who have IEPs or 504 plans. (To address every possible accommodation for a wide variety of disabilities would be unnecessary.) The accommodations guidelines would be based on factors discussed in more detail in Chapter 3 (e.g., that the accommodations should preserve a test's essential features and increase the validity of interpretations based on the student's test scores).

At the postsecondary level, college and university faculty often have very little formal training in the construction and administration of assessment tools.[6] As such, when students with disabilities take their classes and request accommodations, faculty members are often unsure as to the appropriateness of the accommodations and have rarely thought about how to determine their appropriateness. At some research institutions, undergraduate teaching is not the primary responsibility of faculty members, and they may even be confused by requests for accommodations. We encourage disability services office personnel to reach out to faculty (through academic department offices) to help faculty understand the importance of accommodations as well as how to determine which accommodations should be permitted on particular exams. It is especially important to have clear policies for exams in large courses, where informal decisions could easily lead to unfairness.

---

[6]This is changing, with the advent of outcomes assessment in higher education (e.g., Suskie, 2009). However, instruments used for outcomes assessment are often distinct from the assessments used to determine students' grades.

ETHICAL ISSUES ASSOCIATED WITH
TESTING ACCOMMODATIONS

In psychology, *ethics* often refers to formalized codes of professional behavior that psychologists are expected to follow, and indeed, such codes do bear on the practice of making decisions about accommodations. However, we begin our discussion of ethical issues by taking a step back to consider a more general perspective on the moral basis of accommodations. Simply put, society is filled with relatively arbitrary requirements that have the unintended effect of excluding individuals with disabilities. Curbs on streets were not built to discriminate against individuals who cannot step up and down, and tests of history knowledge were not designed to discriminate against students with visual disabilities, but without proper accommodations, discriminatory effects are still present.

Accommodations equalize access by "not sweating the small stuff," to borrow a phrase from a series of popular self-help books. When we do not wish to measure vision skills, we allow students with visual disabilities to take a history test administered orally or in a large print or Braille format. By not "sweating" the administration delivery mode of the test, we allow students with disabilities to access the test. Many features of a given test's administration—time limits, scheduling, response modes, and others—may be present primarily for administrative convenience, and so these features are among the "small stuff" that can be accommodated, permitting variability in the ways that examinees access test content. Used well, testing accommodations—like all disability accommodations—allow for a more humane and just world without compromising standards or allowing an unfair advantage to anyone. To the extent that test accommodations reach these goals, their provision is not only ethically acceptable but also ethically required.

An additional ethical foundation of accommodations, at least in the K–12 arena, is the full inclusion of students with disabilities in public education. In an era of high-stakes testing for school accountability, when incentives for high scores are substantial, schools are tempted to exclude students whose scores would lead the school's performance to suffer as a whole. More generally, students with disabilities are at risk of being designated less likely to profit from instructional resources. By allowing students with disabilities to participate in testing programs, testing accommodations can help to ensure that these students are not neglected. As mentioned earlier, it was this rationale that led testing accommodations to be explicitly mentioned in IDEA 1997 and other laws. Of course, the pressure for high scores can also lead schools to overaccommodate students with disabilities in the hopes of increasing performance, but even so, the goal of increased inclusion in the school community is certainly a positive one.

Ethical Guidelines Applied to Testing Accommodations

In addition to these general ethical foundations of accommodations, formalized professional ethics codes apply as well. For instance, the American Psychological Association's (APA; 2010) *Ethical Principles of Psychologists and Code of Conduct* influences the provision of testing accommodations in two ways. First, one of the five general principles in the code is "Respect for People's Rights and Dignity," in which the code notes that "Psychologists are aware of and respect" individual differences, including disability status. Second, the Code's Standard 9 (Assessment) makes a variety of statements about using assessment methods appropriately, especially 9.02(a): "Psychologists administer, adapt, score, interpret, or use assessment techniques, interviews, tests, or instruments in a manner and for purposes that are appropriate in light of the research and proper application of the techniques" (p. 12). Note the use of the word *adapt*, suggesting that changes, including accommodations, may be needed. Moreover, this standard suggests that psychologists need to be familiar with relevant research on testing accommodations.

In addition to the Code, APA (2012) recently released the *Guidelines for Assessment and Intervention With Persons With Disabilities*, and Guideline 15 reads: "Psychologists strive to determine whether accommodations are appropriate for clients to yield a valid test score." The discussion accompanying this standard notes the following: "It is expected that for many kinds of tests, an accommodated measure would yield more valid results than the same measure without such accommodations. Still, validation research is always appropriate." We generally endorse this guideline and accompanying discussion, although it is limited in that it does not distinguish between clinical assessment (which psychologists are likely to engage in) and educational/occupational testing (for which psychologists are likely to make accommodation recommendations, after diagnosing a client with a disability condition). In clinical assessment situations, it is usually clear what constructs are being measured (e.g., intelligence, personality), and the psychologist is in a relatively good position to distinguish between appropriate and inappropriate accommodations. However, when psychologists make recommendations about educational/occupational tests to be conducted at a later date (e.g., the SAT), they may not have sufficient information to know how the scores from those tests will be interpreted and used, threatening the presumption that accommodated test administrations will generally yield more valid inferences about the examinee's skill levels.

The APA *Guidelines* also refer to the *Standards for Educational and Psychological Testing*, authored jointly by APA and two other professional associations—the American Educational Research Association (AERA) and the National Council on Measurement in Education (NCME)—in 1999.

The *Standards for Educational and Psychological Testing* (hereafter referred to as the *Standards*) are currently under revision, but in the most recent released version (1999), there is considerable discussion of accommodations. Standard 5.1 states that "test administrators should follow carefully the standardized procedures for administration and scoring, unless the situation or a test taker's disability dictates that an exception be made" (p. 63) and the accompanying discussion notes that "a test taker with a disabling condition may require special accommodation" (p. 63). Unfortunately, these comments do not help to determine when accommodations are appropriate or which accommodations would be appropriate in a given case.

Later comments in the *Standards* do help clarify the implications for practice. Chapter 10 of the volume is devoted entirely to testing examinees with disabilities, and the opening discussion clearly notes that disability conditions should not always lead to accommodations:

> First, the disability may, in fact, be directly relevant to the focal construct. . . . Second, an accommodation for a particular disability is inappropriate when the purpose of a test is to diagnose the presence and degree of that disability. . . . Third, it is important to note that not all individuals with disabilities require special provisions when taking tests. Many individuals have disabilities that would not influence their performance on a particular test, and hence no modification is needed. (pp. 101–102)

The specific standards in this chapter go on to detail the relevant features when deciding whether and how to use accommodations. Space prevents us from discussing each standard in turn, but especially important points are that decision makers should know relevant research on how disabilities affect test performance; empirical research should optimally determine the length of modified time limits; and when enough examinees with disabilities are present, research should be done to establish reliability and validity of a test with individuals from disability groups. More generally, the *Standards* notes repeatedly the dilemma that accommodations may be needed to make valid inferences on the basis of test scores, but that accommodations can also compromise validity.

Finally, in addition to APA's documentation and the *Standards*, the National Association of School Psychologists' (2010) *Principles for Professional Ethics* addresses testing accommodations, at least indirectly. Standard II.3.5 reads, in part: "School psychologists conduct valid and fair assessments . . . They actively pursue knowledge of the student's disabilities . . . and then select, administer, and interpret assessment instruments and procedures in light of those characteristics" (p. 7). Again, like the APA guidelines, this standard appears to apply more to clinical assessment than to the recommendations that school psychologists may make regarding accommodations on classroom and high-stakes educational tests. Even so, the standard suggests that school psychologists should be familiar with thinking about accommodations, if only for the assessments that they perform themselves.

Ethical Concerns Regarding Testing Accommodations

Although the ethical principles reviewed previously show that there is a clear ethical basis for the provision of testing accommodations, many scholars have also expressed ethical concerns about the practice of providing accommodations to students with disabilities. We should preface our discussion of these concerns by noting that they are primarily directed at the provision of accommodations to students with high-incidence, "mild" disabilities, rather than those with low-incidence, "severe" disabilities. Whereas it is clear that students with (for instance) severe visual impairments will be unable to access a test in the standard format, it is less clear if students with (for instance) learning disabilities will be unable to access a test under standard timing conditions. When there is no clear inability to access tests under standard conditions, several ethical concerns should be considered.

The first concern is that, in practice, accommodations tend to be used to benefit students who are already doing well. Lichtenberg (2004) considered testing accommodations, obtained through dubious disability diagnoses, to be one of the ways in which "the academically rich get richer" (p. 19), and Lerner (2004) used the even more colorful phrase of "affirmative action for elites" (p. 1041). Both of these authors argued that affluent students are more likely to have parents and school districts that are aware of the services available for students with disability diagnoses and that are willing to push hard to obtain every possible advantage for their children. News stories have provided largely anecdotal evidence on this topic (e.g., Tapper, Morris, & Setrakian, 2006), but critics also point to wide disparities in rates of identification of disabilities across states, regions, and other demographic groups (Vickers, 2010). Thus, although social justice concerns animate much contemporary support for testing accommodations, in some cases, their effects can backfire, providing a score boost to those students who need it least.

Of course, this first concern can, at least in theory, be remedied by more careful attention to who receives diagnoses and accommodations, ensuring that lower socioeconomic status (SES) students with disabilities and accommodation needs are identified, while more closely monitoring the provision of accommodations to higher SES students who have been inappropriately identified as needing them. In addition, this concern applies more in the settings of college admissions testing and beyond than in typical K–12 settings. Indeed, in these latter settings, disability diagnosis and special education services are generally associated with lower SES and minority status (for a review and discussion, see Skiba et al., 2008).

A second, more radical concern notes that providing accommodations to students with disabilities can serve to mask deficiencies in assessment programs more generally. Earle and Sharp (2000; see also Sharp & Earle, 2000) noted that when we exempt students with disabilities from taking tests under particular conditions, we conveniently avoid asking whether those conditions are appropriate (or sufficient) for measuring nondisabled students' skills. Earle and Sharp gave the example of final exams taken in sociology classes: "It is very difficult to see how the skills and knowledge required by a practicing sociologist could justify the requirement that graduates must demonstrate these in 3-hour examinations, without recourse to sources, discussion or extended thought" (p. 544). We would soften this criticism somewhat, to merely note that when testing accommodations are given to students with disabilities, test administrators should consider why they are necessary and if their necessity suggests that an aspect of the testing procedure is not appropriate for nondisabled students either. Moreover, we would note that in many settings, being able to perform tasks quickly and without referring to sources is important, especially when basic academic skills are being trained; in these settings, the accommodations rather than the tests should be questioned.

A third, related concern is that accommodations discriminate against nondisabled students, who would benefit from accommodations but cannot obtain them. In Chapter 3 and Chapters 5 through 7, we compare the effects of accommodations on the test performance of students with and without disabilities; here we merely note that many nondisabled students indicate that they would like the opportunity to take tests with accommodations. For instance, in a survey conducted by Lewandowski, Lambert, Lovett, Panahon, and Sytsma (in press) of over 600 college students, a majority of the nondisabled students reported believing that extended time, additional breaks, and separate room accommodations would increase their performance on high-stakes exams. Given the varying criteria for disability diagnosis (and therefore accommodation access), at least some students who could benefit from accommodations as much as students with identified disabilities are denied them (see Elliott & Marquart, 2004, for an example of such findings).

A fourth concern has to do with the potential for accommodations to signal competence in examinees who actually lack that competence, by inappropriately boosting scores. This concern applies primarily to certification and licensure tests, which have the role of protecting the public from dangerously incompetent professionals (Melnick, 2011; Sireci & Hambleton, 2009). Some accommodations would clearly be absurd, such as "a student pilot who, as a consequence of defective vision, is excused landings" (Sharp

& Earle, 2000, p. 196), whereas other cases are tougher, such as a physician-in-training who is granted additional time to make diagnoses during a licensure examination. These examples can be extended, with some modification, to K–12 assessments—if students who are certified as "proficient" in mathematics are actually not, but accommodations boosted their score above the cutoff for proficiency. Such a case would not be dangerous for society, but the consequences for the student and his or her future teachers may be significant. We spend much of the book trying to address this concern, by considering when testing accommodations lead to more appropriate inferences about a student's skills and when they actually lead to less warranted inferences.

We add a final concern that goes to the heart of testing accommodations. One hallmark of skilled performance is the ability to perform under varied conditions (response generalization; Martin & Pear, 2007). As Stokes and Baer (1977) noted in their seminal article on generalization, to be truly helpful, a behavior change usually "must occur over time, persons, and settings, and the effects of the change sometimes should spread to a variety of related behaviors" (p. 350). This is especially true with regard to academic skills; for instance, instructors do not use paper-and-pencil tests because life consists largely of these tests, but because it is hoped that the behaviors displayed on these tests will generalize to other situations. Training for generalization requires practice with "diverse materials, persons, and settings" (Martens & Witt, 2004, p. 24). But testing accommodations, especially when used incautiously, can keep students with disabilities from having to perform under diverse conditions, leaving them with narrow skills that only appear when a very precise stimulus causes the student to emit the appropriate response. A student may become accustomed to always responding under untimed conditions, or having test items read aloud, or having rest breaks whenever they are requested, or receiving prompts to keep focused on the exam. Situations outside of tests come with fewer ready accommodations, and a student whose skills were only assessed in rarefied conditions may find those skills to be of little value elsewhere. It is a sad irony that although testing accommodations are based in a desire to help students with high-incidence disabilities to participate fully and meaningfully in education, they have the potential to keep those students from fully benefiting from that education. Obviously, there are times when accommodations are needed for access; no one would suggest that a blind student was being held back when provided with accommodations on a written, teacher-made U.S. history test. However, for many students with high-incidence disabilities, it is less clear whether accommodations are aiding or hindering skill development. We have no immediate reply to this concern, and it relates to the more general problem in special education of making standards for students that are both challenging and reasonable (Kauffman, McGee, & Brigham, 2004). We discuss this issue further in Chapter 8, on the relationship between accommodations and interventions.

SCORE FLAGGING: A SPECIAL LEGAL/ETHICAL ISSUE

We conclude our consideration of the legal and ethical foundations of testing accommodations by discussing a special issue that is particularly controversial at the postsecondary level. When a student takes a high-stakes test with one or more accommodations, the score report may contain a *flag*, or an indication that the test score was obtained under nonstandard conditions and that any comparisons with other examinees' scores are to be made with caution (Heaney & Pullin, 1998). Most frequently, the flag does not describe the specific nature of the accommodations, only saying that accommodations were given.

Until recently, most large-scale tests flagged scores obtained with accommodations, but in 2000 an examinee with a physical disability, after taking the Graduate Management Admission Test (GMAT) with accommodations, sued the Educational Testing Service (ETS) over the resulting score flag (Sireci, 2005). ETS agreed to stop flagging scores on certain tests, including the GMAT. The College Board appointed an independent committee to determine if flags should also be removed from score reports from their exams (such as the SAT). The committee of six voting members split four to two in favor of removing the flags. Psychometrician Stephen Sireci was in the majority, but in a thoughtful and balanced discussion of flagging (Sireci, 2005), he admitted that "an 'accommodated standardized test' is the ultimate psychometric oxymoron," and so "those on both sides of the flagging debate have much fuel for their fire" (p. 4). Ultimately, the College Board followed the recommendations of the committee majority and dropped flags from the score reports for its tests.

One's perspective on flagging is likely to be influenced by one's vantage point in the process of testing. During the period of heated debate a decade ago, the College Board completed a study in which a variety of stakeholders completed surveys and interviews about flagging scores (Mandinach, Cahalan, & Camara, 2002). Most admission officers and guidance counselors who were surveyed recommended that the flagging of scores continue. The admission officers in particular expressed concern that flags allow colleges to make admission decisions that are ultimately more helpful to applicants (because the decisions are based on the applicant's predicted chance of success at the institution). In contrast, a slight majority of disability service providers (54%) recommended that flags be dropped; many of these individuals are likely to see themselves as advocates for students with disabilities.

For their part, the *Standards* (AERA, APA, & NCME, 1999) directs the following:

> When there is credible evidence of score comparability across regular and modified administrations, no flag should be attached to a score. When such evidence is lacking, specific information about the nature of the modification should be provided, if permitted by law, to assist test users properly to interpret and act on test scores. (p. 108)

Although these guidelines suggest that the default decision should be flagging scores, critics of flags note several problems with the practice. First, flags let score users know the examinee's disability status, which is otherwise a protected piece of information in many situations (e.g., college admissions, professional licensure). Score users might then discriminate against an examinee because of his or her disability status, and so flags have a dubious legal status (APA, 2012). Second, and relatedly, score flags can lead students to feel stigmatized, because not only has their general disability status been disclosed but also they may worry that anyone reading the score report will doubt their skills in areas relevant to test taking (e.g., reading skills). Third, flags do not give enough detail (compared with what the *Standards* recommend) to allow score users to make individualized interpretations of examinee's scores. Scores from students who receive additional time, who dictate their answers to a scribe, and who are permitted access to a calculator are all treated the same way, with a generic flag. Fourth, at least some accommodations (e.g., taking a test in a private room) seem unlikely to have significant effects on the validity of the scores, even though no validity studies have been conducted. Finally, at least in the case of extended time on the SAT, the existing evidence suggests that effects on score validity are relatively small and inconsistent (Sireci, 2005).

However, other scholars support flagging scores obtained with accommodations. For instance, Abrams (2005) argued that the dropping of flagging, at least for the SAT, has actually resulted in a less equitable system of accommodations because when flags were dropped, the system for requesting accommodations was tightened as well. According to Abrams, this has led more affluent students with well-connected and knowledgeable parents to constitute the pool of students who are able to obtain professional evaluations that meet the guidelines of the new request system. As evidence, he noted that after flags were dropped, the proportion of students receiving SAT accommodations went down, but (at least in one city) the SAT scores of students receiving accommodations had increased, suggesting that higher achieving students were now the ones receiving the accommodations.

At the very least, we would agree that flagging scores takes away some of the incentive to obtain accommodations; if examinees believe that their scores will be weighted less or viewed with skepticism because of the flag, they are less likely to seek accommodations when they are unnecessary or inappropriate. (Many of the respondents to the survey by Mandinach et al., 2002, expressed concern over the possibility of fraud in the accommodations system.) Testing agencies may feel that they do not need to review applications and accompanying disability documentation as carefully, because students who are willing to assume the burden of the flag are welcome to the accommodations that they request. Of course, this same mechanism could discourage truly needy students from using the accommodations that they require, out of the fear of their scores being misinterpreted.

Perhaps more to the point, supporters of flags note that there is not strong evidence of comparability of exams administered with and without accommodations. For instance, Freedman (2003) averred that "the SAT taken by disabled students with extended time *is a different test*. That's why their scores are flagged" (p. 42, emphasis added). This may be even truer of other accommodations, such as read aloud. Ultimately, though the question of whether a given accommodation makes a given test "a different test" is an empirical question. At least large-scale tests such as the SAT have a sizeable research base on this point (for certain widely used accommodations, e.g., extended time). In contrast, for most accommodations on most exams, there is not sufficient research to scientifically conclude that scores are comparable across standard and accommodated conditions.

In any case, certain high-stakes standardized tests (e.g., the Medical College Admission Test) continue to flag scores obtained with accommodations. Moreover, even for the exams that do not flag scores, there are scholars who call for the flags' reinstatement. As Sireci (2005) noted, there are fair points made on both sides of the flagging debate. Therefore, we expect that flagging will continue to be a hot issue in the accommodations world.

CONCLUSIONS FOR PRACTITIONERS: THE IMPORTANCE OF INDIVIDUAL CASE REVIEW

Some readers may feel overwhelmed by the complex web of laws and ethical guidelines governing the provision of testing accommodations; in this final section, we provide a synopsis of the most important points. Two sets of laws are relevant here. Special education laws apply to students in K–12 education (and younger children, too) who have been identified as having a disability condition that affects their ability to benefit from education, and testing accommodations may be part of the IEP that is developed to ensure that they receive an appropriate educational program. Disability discrimination laws apply more widely (e.g., covering adults as well as children) but apply more conservative criteria, defining disability in terms of substantial limitations relative to the general population and mandating only those accommodations needed to access an opportunity such as a test.

Accommodations regulations at the state level must not violate these laws, but the regulations still vary widely in terms of which accommodations are appropriate and which student factors may be used to make decisions about accommodations; practitioners should therefore check with state guidelines, and external evaluators should be mindful of these guidelines when making accommodations recommendations. These guidelines usually apply only to the official exams used by the state for accountability purposes; exams made by teachers in K–12 classrooms and instructors in postsecondary settings are governed by local norms and individual teacher/instructor decisions, which are only bound by the special education and disability discrimination laws.

Professional ethics codes provide a final source of information about accommodations, but these codes generally discuss accommodations on tests administered by psychologists (e.g., diagnostic tests). An exception is the *Standards*, which note both the advantages and disadvantages of accommodations, suggesting that accommodations decisions must be made very carefully without a "default" to provide or not provide them, but rather a careful review in every case. Interestingly, this individualized case-by-case decision process is exactly the process mandated by law for all special education and disability accommodation decisions. It is a process that all laws and ethics codes agree on, and so we conclude on this point of apparent consensus: Accommodation decisions should be made with great care, without a bias toward either providing or proscribing them, based on the individual student's characteristics and the test to be taken. The recent regulations developed to implement the ADA/ADAAA make careful initial decisions even more important because these regulations require testing entities to give substantial weight to past decisions.

This guidance, to review each accommodations case carefully before making a decision, may seem anticlimactic, even vacuous. However, we see many schools, postsecondary institutions, and testing agencies that do not heed it. Instead, we see many school districts that provide accommodations (at least low-intensity accommodations) almost reflexively to students with certain disability conditions, and we occasionally see testing agencies that seem unwilling to grant certain accommodations without even considering the necessarily unique features of an individual applicant and his or her request. Careful review of each decision is actually, therefore, a strict standard, and it would be a great step forward. In the next chapter, we discuss the questions that should be asked when that review is undertaken.

3

PSYCHOMETRIC FOUNDATIONS

The logic behind testing accommodations can be better understood through an appreciation of psychometrics, the theory of psychological measurement. Although the technical sophistication of psychometrics often scares psychologists away (for a discussion, see Borsboom, 2006), the psychometric concepts that are most relevant to testing accommodations can be understood in a relatively nontechnical fashion, and the official *Standards for Educational and Psychological Testing* (hereafter, the *Standards*; American Educational Research Association [AERA], American Psychological Association [APA], & National Council on Measurement in Education [NCME], 1999) reflect this. Moreover, even a basic familiarity with psychometrics is very helpful when examining research on accommodations.

In this chapter, we review basic psychometric concepts before considering one concept (construct-irrelevant variance) in some detail. We then present a psychometric framework for determining the appropriateness of

http://dx.doi.org/10.1037/14468-003
Testing Accommodations for Students With Disabilities: Research-Based Practice, by B. J. Lovett and L. J. Lewandowski

accommodations. We conclude with a primer on the research designs used most frequently in empirical studies on accommodations. Because we intend this book to be a practical "user's guide" to accommodations rather than a researcher's manual, statistical and design concepts are generally covered without technical details, and readers are referred to other sources for more advanced treatments.

RELIABILITY AND VALIDITY

As Suen (1990) observed, all psychological measurement begins in recording someone's response to a stimulus (or set of stimuli). For instance, we observe a child's response to the stimulus "What is two plus two?" or a job applicant's response to the stimulus "Have you ever stolen from an employer?" We then convert the person's responses to a test score (through the process of *scaling*), and we can ask two questions about that score. First, is the score *reliable*? Second, what *valid* inferences can we draw based on that score?

Reliability

Synonyms for reliability include consistency and dependability, and the essence of reliability involves the tendency of a test score to replicate (Brennan, 2001). Many factors keep a test score from replicating perfectly (e.g., how an examinee is feeling on a particular day, whether a slightly different wording is used in a test item), and a score is reliable to the extent that it is relatively unaffected by these factors. A highly reliable test score will be very similar regardless of, for instance, how someone is feeling on the day that the exam is taken; a test score with low reliability will be more influenced by such factors.

There are a variety of ways that test developers and researchers estimate the reliability of a test score (for more details and technical considerations, see Furr & Bacharach, 2008; R. J. Gregory, 2011). To determine the test–retest reliability of a test score, we would give a set of examinees the same test twice, yielding two sets of test scores (one from the first administration and one from the second administration). The two sets of scores are correlated to determine whether examinees who obtained higher scores during the first administration also obtained higher scores during the second administration of the test. If the correlation is strong and positive, the test score has high test–retest reliability, and we can predict how a given examinee will perform on a second administration of the test, on the basis of how he or she performed on a first administration; this is one type of replicability.

We can also use *alternate form reliability* by devising two different forms of the same test. For instance, the Peabody Picture Vocabulary Test (the PPVT-4; Dunn & Dunn, 2007b) has two forms (A and B), and we can determine the test score's alternate form reliability by giving a set of examinees both forms of the test and correlating the resulting two sets of test scores (one set from Form A and one set from Form B). Again, a strong positive correlation represents high alternate form reliability because we can predict someone's test score on one form of the test by looking at their score on the other form, another type of replicability.

Many tests do not have alternate forms. Therefore, we more commonly estimate reliability by determining a test score's *internal consistency*. The simplest type of internal consistency involves making two quasi-alternate forms, by splitting a test in half (*split-half reliability*) and correlating the scores from the two test halves. Of course, a test can be split in half in many ways (e.g., the even-numbered test items vs. the odd-numbered test items; the first 50% of items on a test form vs. the latter 50% of items), and so psychometricians have devised estimates of internal consistency that tell us what would happen if we divided a test into two halves in all of the possible ways and took the average of all of the resulting split-half correlations. The most commonly used estimate is Cronbach's alpha (Cronbach, 1951); these estimates are interpreted in much the same way as other reliability estimates: Higher reliability represents a greater tendency of a score to replicate, this time across the different items on a test. That is, on a test with higher internal consistency, an examinee is more likely to perform similarly on different items of the test.

All of these different types of reliability estimates are quantified through the use of a *reliability coefficient* that varies between 0 and 1. Values closer to 1 represent greater score reliability. The minimum reliability needed for a test score to be used depends on precisely how it will be used; frequently used rules of thumb include requiring a reliability of 0.90 or more to make important decisions about individuals, 0.80 or more for screening instruments that will determine if further testing should be done, and 0.70 or more for research purposes. Test users should keep two things in mind when evaluating reliability coefficients. First, a given test often yields many scores, each with its own reliability coefficient. For instance, the Wechsler Intelligence Scale for Children, Fourth Edition (WISC–IV; Wechsler, 2003), yields a score for each individual task (subtest) as well as several composite scores. Therefore, it is more precise to refer to the reliability of a particular test score rather than to the reliability of a test itself. Second, reliability estimates are always based on a particular sample and may not generalize to other samples. For instance, if a published reliability coefficient is based on the data of nondisabled students, the score reliability for students with a particular disability may be different.

Accommodations can affect reliability in a variety of ways, either for good or for ill. As E. Burns (1998) noted, some disability conditions may undermine a test's reliability, and appropriate accommodations can restore that reliability. For instance, if visually impaired students are given a written test in a standard test format, their score may be determined by guessing (i.e., random chance), leading to low reliability estimates (e.g., the test–retest reliability coefficient may be close to zero). However, if these students are given a presentation accommodation (e.g., large print, Braille), the test's reliability would be restored. Importantly, misapplied accommodations can reduce reliability by introducing random error. For instance, in many K–12 schools, when annual state exams are given, students in a given grade are separated into separate rooms, so that students receiving a given accommodation or set of accommodations can all be administered the exam together. The variability in testing rooms (e.g., physical environment, competence and attitude of proctor) can introduce many additional sources of error. This would lead to lower reliability (consider how the students' scores might not replicate if they were to take the test in a different room).

Validity

Validity is perhaps the most important consideration in measurement. The *Standards* define it as "the degree to which evidence and theory support the interpretations of test scores entailed by proposed uses of tests" (AERA, APA, & NCME, 1999, p. 9). Validity, then, always refers to specific interpretations and uses of tests and test scores. For instance, a certain state mathematics test may lead to valid inferences about the mathematics skills of fourth graders in Kentucky, but not to valid inferences of the quality of the students' teachers. Similarly, an occupational interest inventory may lead to valid inferences about examinees' likelihood of enjoying being a physician, but invalid inferences about examinees' likelihood of success in medical school.

Traditionally, evidence for validity has been classified into three (admittedly overlapping) categories: *content*, *criterion related*, and *construct* (R. J. Gregory, 2011). Content validity evidence would include any evidence that a test covers the different areas of the domain being assessed, without covering anything outside the domain. For instance, an exam designed to measure the general mathematics skills of incoming college freshmen should include items measuring skills in several areas (e.g., algebra, geometry), and it should not require significant nonmathematics skills. Criterion-related validity evidence includes any evidence that the test's scores predict an outcome (criterion); for instance, the main validity evidence supporting the SAT is its prediction of student's GPAs during their first year in college.

Criterion-related validity evidence usually comes in the form of correlation coefficients or other indices of the strength of an association between variables.

Construct validity evidence includes any evidence that the test measures an underlying trait (the construct) that it was designed to measure. For instance, an IQ test is designed to predict intelligence, and so it should correlate with traits that are theoretically related to intelligence while not correlating substantially with theoretically unrelated traits. Similarly, a test designed to measure law students' knowledge of contract law should yield higher scores in a group of law students who have taken the class, compared with a group of students whose contract law class has not yet begun. Construct validity evidence comes in a wide variety of forms and actually encompasses the other forms of validity evidence, because validity is fundamentally about the relationship between a test score and the construct that the test is designed to measure (Messick, 1989). Often, the most important inferences that we make on the basis of test scores rest on interpreting the scores with reference to constructs. For instance, when we provide special education services to a student with a developmental disability, we may make inferences on the basis of scores from tests of intelligence and adaptive functioning; we first interpret the scores as indicating the student's levels of these underlying traits and then make an inference about what services are likely to be most appropriate.

Validity is closely connected to the appropriateness of testing accommodations. Accommodations are appropriate when giving a particular student a test under standard testing conditions leads to invalid inferences, but the same test given under altered conditions leads to (increasingly) valid inferences. For instance, consider a student with a mild hearing impairment who takes an orally administered spelling test with his classmates. The student's hearing impairment may prevent him from adequately hearing the teacher's speech, leading to invalid inferences about the student's spelling knowledge. A variety of accommodations could help increase the validity of these inferences; the student could be given preferential seating next to the teacher, or the teacher could wear a microphone with speakers sitting on the student's desk.

Unfortunately, cases are often not so clear-cut. Consider a student with a recent attention-deficit/hyperactivity disorder (ADHD) diagnosis who is being given an initial individualized education program (IEP). Members of the IEP team note that other students with ADHD have been given extended-time testing accommodations and consider giving the newly diagnosed student the same accommodations. It is unclear whether administering tests to the student with standard time allotments leads to invalid inferences about his skill levels. Moreover, it is unclear whether extended-time accommodations would increase the validity of these inferences. For instance, even if the teacher reports that the student often turns in exams in which the answer areas for test items have been left blank, it is unclear if the student would use the additional time to answer these items. In later chapters, we describe accommodation decision-making procedures designed to maximize validity, with special attention to these kinds of difficult cases.

Construct-Irrelevant Variance

The validity concept most relevant for understanding testing accommodations is *construct-irrelevant variance* (Haladyna & Downing, 2004). According to psychometric theory, test scores vary due to three sources. First, examinees vary in their levels of the trait being examined; for instance, when taking a reading comprehension test, students' reading comprehension skills vary, leading to variability in their scores on the test. Second, chance factors such as transient illness or guessing the answers to items correctly affect test scores; these factors are said to constitute *random error*, and they decrease reliability by making a test score less likely to replicate. Finally, examinees vary in skills that affect test scores inappropriately—that is, examinees vary in qualities that the test is not designed to measure, but which it measures anyway. For instance, students vary in anxiety when taking the SAT, and this is likely to affect their scores; even though the SAT is not designed to measure anxiety, individual differences in anxiety likely contribute to the variability in obtained SAT scores. This last factor, sometimes called *systematic error*, causes construct-irrelevant variance. Construct-irrelevant variance is a significant threat to validity, because it decreases the confidence with which we can use test scores to make inferences about the traits that we are trying to measure.

Haladyna and Downing (2004) described four categories of sources of construct-irrelevant variance in educational assessment. First, students vary widely in the preparation for tests that they receive; some students undergo extensive test preparation for college admissions tests, whereas other students arrive to take the test without any preparation. Second, variability in test development, administration, and scoring matters; for instance, some students take high-stakes achievement tests in their own classrooms, whereas others are relocated for logistical reasons, and it is possible that this variability affects scores. Third, students vary in traits other than what the tests are meant to assess; for instance, English vocabulary skills affect test scores substantially, leading to potentially invalid inferences about English language learners (ELLs) and students from certain cultural backgrounds. Finally, cheating is a variable impacting scores; some students cheat, whereas others do not, and cheaters differ in the extent of their cheating. These examples highlight the range of factors impacting test scores in a systematic way, leading to systematic underestimates or overestimates of students' skills.

Students' disability conditions can also contribute to construct-irrelevant variance, because of the interaction of certain functional skill deficits with certain test administration conditions and task requirements. For instance, most tests of college students' writing skills are not designed to test motor skills, but if some examinees have physical disabilities that lead to deficits in motor stamina or endurance, variability in motor skills may account for a portion of the variability in students' writing test scores. Similarly, most paper-and-pencil classroom tests in high schools are not explicitly designed to measure reading speed. However, if students with reading disabilities are among the examinees taking these tests, and their reading speed is too slow to finish the items and check their work in the allotted time, some of the variability in the resulting set of test scores will be due to students' variability in reading speeds—variance that is irrelevant to the constructs that the classroom teacher is intending to measure.

In cases such as these, accommodations are designed to reduce construct-irrelevant variance, thus enhancing validity. By allowing certain students with physical disabilities to dictate their test responses to a scribe and allowing certain students with reading disabilities additional time to take the test, we would keep the tests from measuring construct-irrelevant factors such as motor skill and reading speed. This would lead to test scores with a higher proportion of score variance due to actual variability in the constructs of interest. All testing accommodations, despite the superficial diversity in their implementation and in the populations that use them, work on this logic: They reduce variability in construct-irrelevant factors, "leveling the playing field" so that students with disabilities can have as much opportunity as nondisabled students to show their skills.

Unfortunately, testing accommodations do not always reduce construct-irrelevant variance, and they have the potential to increase it. Test scores are not supposed to be indices of how the test was administered, and so variability in administration conditions is an important source of construct-irrelevant variance in its own right (McCallin, 2006). If different examinees have different time allotments, time allotment (a construct-irrelevant factor) varies, which may lead to increases in construct-irrelevant variance in scores. The same is true of variability in presentation format, or response format, or administration setting; these factors are usually not part of the target construct, but when they are permitted to vary, they can lead test scores' construct-irrelevant variance to increase. This decreases validity, of course, because test users are then apt to infer that a student's high score is due to the student's skill levels, when actually it may be due to the student receiving more time on the test than other examinees (or some other dispensation).

The potential for accommodations to threaten validity should not be surprising, when one considers the importance of standardization in testing. Indeed, the introduction of standardization in measurement is bound up with the transition to psychology as a science; the pioneers of scientific psychology emphasized that stimuli must be presented to participants in a reliable manner and their responses recorded objectively (Richards, 2002). Since then, tests have been distinguished from other procedures (e.g., interviews, behavioral observation) by their standardized nature. The *Standards*, therefore, observe that standardization regarding "instructions to test takers, time limits, the form of item presentation or response, and test materials or equipment should be strictly observed" (AERA, APA, & NCME, 1999, p. 63). They go on to note that exceptions may be needed for examinees with disabilities as well as other situations, but conclude that a need for flexibility in special cases "should be tempered by the consideration that departures from standard procedures may jeopardize the validity of the test score interpretations" (p. 63).

A FRAMEWORK FOR EVALUATING ACCOMMODATIONS: PHILLIPS'S FIVE QUESTIONS

Our discussion of construct-irrelevant variance demonstrated that testing accommodations are a double-edged sword, necessary as well as dangerous, able to both enhance and threaten validity. How, then, can we know whether a particular accommodation for a particular student on a particular test is likely to enhance or threaten the validity of inferences about that student's skills?

Two decades ago, Phillips (1994) proposed a set of five questions that she suggested be answered before standardization is broken and a testing accommodation is given:

1. Will format changes or alterations in testing conditions change the skill being measured?
2. Will the scores of examinees tested under standard conditions have a different meaning than scores for examinees tested with the requested accommodation?
3. Would nondisabled examinees benefit if allowed the same accommodation?
4. Does the disabled examinee have any capability for adapting to standard test administration conditions?
5. Is the disability evidence or testing accommodations policy based on procedures with doubtful validity and reliability? (p. 104)

She argued that "answering 'yes' to any of these questions suggests that an accommodation is not appropriate" (p. 104).

In the years since Phillips's article, relatively few researchers have formally adopted her framework, and we suspect that few applied practitioners keep her questions on hand. But these five questions are nonetheless the key issues to consider when determining if a particular accommodation decision is likely to enhance or threaten validity. In each of our chapters on particular accommodations, we consider these questions as we discuss the research and draw conclusions about when each accommodation is appropriate.

In this section, we consider the logic behind each question. But first we pause to note that in practice, these questions should be considered for each individual student on each test (or test type). That is, rather than deciding that additional testing time is an appropriate (or an inappropriate) accommodation per se, the accommodation may be appropriate for a particular student on a particular test, but inappropriate for the same student on a different test. The need for accommodations always depends on an interaction between a student's characteristics (the pattern of unimpaired skills and functional deficits that accompany the student's disability condition) and the characteristics of a test (e.g., the presentation format, the standard time allotment, the constructs that the test is designed to measure, the scoring procedures). Therefore, accommodation decisions should always be an individualized process and one that is repeated each time that there is a new test on which to consider accommodating the student.

Task Alterations and Construct Validity

Phillips (1994) suggested that we ask first whether accommodations would "change the skill being measured" by a test. This concern goes to the heart of construct validity because accommodations have the power to change which constructs affect someone's test performance. At times, this type of change will be obvious, making accommodations inappropriate. For instance, access to calculators is sometimes a permitted accommodation on tests of mathematics reasoning, but it would generally be inappropriate on tests of arithmetic computation, where it would change the construct from "computational skills" to "calculator use skills." Similarly, orally administering a reading comprehension test makes it a test of *listening* comprehension skills.

In other cases, it is more difficult to determine whether a construct has been changed when accommodations are present. The essential problem is that any test requires a variety of skills, and any accommodation involves some change to the skills that are required, or else the accommodation would have no purpose. Extended-time accommodations keep tests from measuring speed of performance, and dictionary accommodations keep tests from measuring spelling skills; these accommodations (and others) are given when test administrators are uninterested in these kinds of skills—when they are considered ancillary rather than the targets of assessment.

Sometimes the distinction between ancillary and target skills is clear; for instance, although standard paper-and-pencil tests require visual skills, a high school history exam is not designed to measure visual skills, and accommodations for students with vision problems (e.g., large-text fonts, Braille forms) would generally be available for such an exam. At other times, the distinction is less clear. Consider again the high school history exam; say that an essay item on the exam requires students to analyze a passage from the U.S. Constitution. A student with a diagnosis of dyslexia may have an IEP that makes him or her eligible for read-aloud accommodations, except where reading skills are being measured. Should high school students be able to read and analyze a passage, and should a student with poor reading skills receive accommodations that obviate the need for reading? Does this particular teacher wish to measure reading skills? Is listening comprehension close enough to reading comprehension that we can say that the target skill is analytical thinking, regardless of visual or oral presentation of the material to be analyzed? These are difficult questions. In Chapter 10, we discuss how to help assessment developers (including classroom teachers) determine which skills are target skills and how to make decisions about accommodations accordingly.

Accommodations and Score Comparability

As Phillips's second question notes, test scores obtained with accommodations by examinees with disabilities should be comparable to scores obtained by nondisabled examinees under standard conditions. We interpret *comparability* in two ways. First, the scores obtained with accommodations should have the same reliability and validity evidence (see Willingham, 1989). For instance, if a mathematics test yields scores with a lower reliability coefficient when the test is read orally to examinees, the scores obtained with a read-aloud accommodation are not comparable to scores obtained under standard conditions. Similarly, if scores on the ACT do not predict performance in college classes as well when the ACT is taken in a separate room (i.e., lowered criterion-related validity), the scores from group and individual administrations of the ACT are not comparable.

A second, and more controversial, meaning of *comparable* is that we should be able to directly compare test scores obtained on a test across different examinees, regardless of whether the test was taken with accommodations. That is, if student A scores significantly higher than student B, we should be able to say confidently that student A has stronger skills in the area measured by the test, without considering if either student received testing accommodations. To understand the controversy over this kind of comparability, we must consider the distinction between *norm-referenced* and *criterion-referenced* testing (R. J. Gregory, 2011). Norm-referenced testing involves calculating or interpreting an examinee's test score by comparing it to the scores of other examinees. For instance, the scores yielded by IQ tests are directly calculated by comparing someone's performance with other people at the same age. Similarly, if a corporation has 10 openings for a particular job position and decides to offer the job to the 10 applicants with the highest scores on a personnel selection test (out of 50 applicants), a decision about any given applicant is being made on the basis of where he or she falls in the distribution of other examinees' performance. Norm-referenced testing requires the highest level of evidence of comparability across different testing conditions because examinees from different conditions must be compared directly to interpret their test scores or take actions (e.g., admission to college) on the basis of the scores.

Criterion-referenced testing involves giving the score of an individual examinee some kind of direct meaning, without needing to consider how other examinees performed. For instance, if a student answers 24 items correctly on a given high-stakes mathematics achievement test used for school accountability, the student might be judged as being within the "proficient" range. This judgment has nothing to do with how other examinees performed; it is possible for all of the students (or none) to be in the proficient range. It is sometimes argued that criterion-referenced testing does not require comparability across accommodated and standard testing conditions, because examinees from these conditions are being scored separately and are not directly compared with each other. If this is the case, accommodations could be used much more liberally in criterion-referenced testing situations.

Unfortunately, this logic is superficially appealing but flawed, as shown by Haertel and his colleagues (Haertel, 2003; Haertel & Lorié, 2004; Haertel & Wiley, 2003). These scholars began by distinguishing between several types of criterion-referenced score interpretation. First, Haertel (2003) gave the example of a typing test; the tasks on the test are taken to be a "direct, representative sample from a domain of criterion-task performances of interest to the test user" (p. 3) The test score has a direct meaning, because the typing speed demonstrated on the test is an estimate of the typing speed that the examinee will have in a different context (e.g., employment) with a large range of material to be typed. In this type of criterion-referenced score interpretation (which Haertel called *criterion-referenced direct sample* interpretation), comparability between standard and accommodated conditions can only be assumed if the accommodations would also be given on the real-world tasks that the test is designed to be an index of performance on. For instance, if nursing students are asked to calculate dosage equivalents by hand on a final exam in a nursing pharmacology course, a calculator accommodation would not be appropriate unless a calculator would also be provided in real-world settings.

A second type of interpretation, *criterion-referenced construct-based* interpretation, includes the high-stakes achievement tests that yield score ranges indicating "basic" or "proficient" skill levels; scores have a direct meaning in that they indicate the examinee's level of some construct (e.g., knowledge of eighth-grade science). As Haertel (2003) noted, setting cut scores for descriptors such as "proficient" requires a judgment process. For instance, judges with expertise in middle school science curriculum may be asked to indicate which items from an item pool would be answered correctly by an eighth grader who is proficient in science. In criterion-referenced, construct-based interpretation, comparability can only be assumed if the judgment process is repeated when the judges consider the accommodation. In the science test example, the judges would need to be asked to consider the items again, and say which items a proficient eighth grader would answer correctly when the items are read aloud (or when some other accommodation is given).

Finally, in *criterion-referenced expectancy table* interpretation, an expectancy table links past examinees' test scores to performance on a criterion variable (e.g., an SAT verbal score of 700 is linked to a 90% chance of getting a first-year college GPA of 3.0 or above). Because this kind of inference is based on the performance of past examinees, there is a type of comparison across examinees implicit in the inference, and therefore any accommodations would need evidence of comparability.

In sum, then, regardless of whether a score is interpreted in a norm-referenced or criterion-referenced fashion, evidence of score comparability across standard and accommodated conditions is always helpful, and it is often vital. Moreover, additional evidence may be important, such as evidence that accommodations will be available on relevant real-world tasks. In short, Phillips was right to place the burden on accommodations proponents to show evidence of comparability.

Differential Benefits for Examinees With Disabilities

Testing accommodations are thought of as special exceptions, made for the minority of examinees who cannot access the test under standard conditions. This implies that the majority of examinees, who are not eligible for accommodations, are able to take the test with valid results. Phillips (1994) argued, therefore, that if a given accommodation is appropriate on a given test, nondisabled examinees should not be able to benefit from the accommodation. Zuriff (2000) agreed and called this the *maximum potential thesis* (MPT): An accommodation is appropriate if and only if nondisabled examinees are able to perform up to their maximum potential on the test under standard conditions. MPT proponents often consider everyday life accommodations as analogies; for instance, curb cuts are of great benefit to people who use wheelchairs, but they are of negligible benefit to people who walk.

The MPT is a strict, uncompromising standard; if nondisabled examinees could benefit at all from an accommodation, the accommodation is inappropriate. Still, it appears that many accommodations advocates believe that common testing accommodations meet this standard. For instance, Shaywitz (2003) claimed that in research, "only students diagnosed as learning-disabled showed a significant improvement in test scores with additional time" (p. 337).

Unfortunately, the research has suggested otherwise. Sireci, Scarpati, and Li (2005) reviewed the extant research on the effects of accommodations on students with and without disabilities, testing the MPT, which they called the *interaction hypothesis*. They concluded the following:

> The vast majority of studies relating to the interaction hypothesis showed that *all* student groups (SWD [students with disabilities] and their general education peers) had score gains under accommodation conditions. Moreover, in general, the gains of SWD were *greater* than those of their general education peers under accommodation conditions. (p. 481, emphasis in original)

Sireci et al. argued that the data supported a weaker claim, the differential boost hypothesis (DBH), which claims that students both with and without disabilities benefit from accommodations, but students with disabilities receive a differentially large boost in their scores (see also L. S. Fuchs & Fuchs, 2001).

Interestingly, Sireci et al. (2005) went on to argue that support for the DBH (and not the MPT) was sufficient to "suggest that many accommodations are justified and are effective for reducing construct-irrelevant barriers to students' test performance" (p. 481). They explicitly argued against the standard set by the MPT, stating that so long as the DBH is satisfied, "the fact that the general education students achieved higher scores with an accommodation condition does not imply that the accommodation is unfair. It could imply that the standardized test conditions are too stringent for *all* students" (p. 481, emphasis in original).

Elliott, Kettler, and McKevitt (2002) went even further than Sireci et al. (2005), arguing that even if the DBH is *not* satisfied, accommodations may be appropriate. Their standard is whether an accommodation changes the construct designed to be measured by the test (see Questions 1 and 2 discussed previously); if it does not, the accommodation is appropriate for any students with disabilities who would benefit from it. Elliott et al. admitted that it may seem unfair that nondisabled students are not permitted to access the accommodations as well, but it is simply what regulations often allow.

We understand the positions of Sireci et al. (2005) and Elliott et al. (2002), but we nonetheless support the MPT, for two reasons. First, in certain testing settings (e.g., college admissions), examinees are competing against each other, and so receiving an accommodation that would have helped your competitors is patently unfair to your competitors. Second, as we discussed previously, we believe that it is often difficult to say precisely which traits and skills are central to what a test is supposed to measure, and which traits and skills are ancillary. We agree, though, with these other scholars, that when all students are capable of benefiting from an accommodation, test developers should investigate whether the standard testing conditions are too strict; we return to this point in Chapter 10, with our discussion of universal design for assessment.

We conclude this section by noting that it is too often assumed, without evidence, that nondisabled students would not benefit from an accommodation, and so "small" alterations to a testing procedure should be permitted informally. This is assuredly not the case, as a body of research reviewed by D. Lee, Reynolds, and Wilson (2003) shows; these investigators described studies finding that apparently small alterations (e.g., asking examinees to be "thoughtful" when answering test items) had significant effects on scores. D. Lee et al. noted, appropriately, that "test users should be very cautious in making any change in standardized administration, even when [the changes] are intended to accommodate individuals with disabilities" (p. 75).[1]

Examinees' Capacity for Adaptation to Standard Conditions

Test accommodations are designed, again, to be used for students who cannot access a test under standard conditions. In theory, this is an easily comprehensible point, but in practice it can be difficult to tell if a disability condition leads to a true inability to access a test or just a less pleasant testing experience. Admittedly, we should not ignore examinees' comfort; as the *Standards* notes, "The testing environment should furnish reasonable comfort with minimal distractions" (AERA, APA, NCME, 1999, p. 63). On the

---

[1]Although differential benefits are an important factor in determining accommodation appropriateness, it could be argued that this is too "outcome-focused" a criterion because accommodations are supposed to increase access to a test rather than performance per se. We discuss this issue further in Chapter 10 on universal design.

other hand, the examinees' experience of testing need not be an especially pleasurable one to obtain valid results; Phillips (1994) was simply arguing that accommodations are not necessary if an examinee is able to adapt to the standard testing conditions. An accommodation is not appropriate just because it increases comfort.

Advocacy literature has presumed that the answer to Phillips's (1994) question is no, that students with disabilities cannot adapt to standard test conditions, and this literature therefore encourages students and their families to seek whatever accommodations may be beneficial. But there is no empirical evidence to support this default position of requesting many accommodations.

Indeed, very little direct research has explored whether students with disabilities are capable of adapting, so as to reduce their need for accommodations. However, a variety of studies bear on this question indirectly. In an especially relevant study, Rickey (2005) explored the process of accommodation decision making at three middle schools in Iowa, observing multidisciplinary team meetings and interviewing a variety of stakeholders in the accommodations process. She found, perhaps surprisingly, that at all three schools the primary reason for justifying accommodations was to reduce students' frustration with testing and improve their ability to emotionally handle the testing experience. At one of the schools, this was the only justification given. At the other two schools, validity of test results was occasionally considered, but generally, decision makers at these schools recommended accommodations for reasons such as maintaining the students' self-esteem. If the results found by Rickey are typical of many schools, this would suggest that accommodation decisions are not based on proper foundations (i.e., to increase the validity of inferences about students' skills based on their test scores).

A second source of evidence comes from research on students' perceptions of testing accommodations. Research by Elliott and his colleagues has found that students with disabilities perceive tests as easier, experience less test anxiety and greater self-efficacy, and more generally prefer testing when accommodations are provided (e.g., Elliott & Marquart, 2004; Feldman, Kim, & Elliott, 2011; Lang, Elliott, Bolt, & Kratochwill, 2008). However, these studies have also found that, on average, nondisabled students have an improved testing experience as well when they receive accommodations. Of course, there is nothing wrong with testing accommodations improving students' testing experiences; appropriate accommodations keep examinees from being unduly hindered by their disability conditions and would improve the testing experience. However, if even nondisabled students perceive accommodations as beneficial, we must consider whether we are giving them to particular students for the right reasons. These perceived benefits also make unnecessary accommodation requests more likely because anxiety before and during tests, especially high-stakes tests, is a common experience.

A third source of evidence on this point comes from research on interventions. If testing accommodations are given because of students' deficits in construct-irrelevant skills that keep them from accessing a test under standard conditions, it may be possible to alter their skill levels, obviating the need for accommodations. Some construct-irrelevant skills are not amenable to intervention (e.g., visual skills in blind individuals), but others (e.g., test anxiety, reading fluency) are often modifiable. Accommodations are a consequence of accepting that something about the examinee cannot be changed, but this acceptance can be premature in the case of students with high-incidence disabilities. Therefore, multidisciplinary teams might insist that students receive interventions along with testing accommodations, in the hopes of removing the need for the accommodations. In postsecondary settings, this approach may be less relevant, but in K–12 settings, there is a need to tie accommodations and interventions more closely than they are currently. In Chapter 8, we discuss the research on several types of interventions that are relevant to common accommodation needs, offering practical advice for professionals working in K–12 settings as well as those in counseling/clinical settings who work with students preparing for exams.[2]

A fourth source of evidence comes from postsecondary settings, where it is not uncommon for students to request accommodations for the first time, even though they may have no history of low scores on standardized tests. When this happens, it suggests that the students may be able to adapt to standard conditions. Obviously, one could always argue that high scores obtained without accommodations would have been even higher had accommodations been given, but this is an unfalsifiable claim, and it also raises concerns that the individual may not be disabled relative to the general population. We discuss these issues more fully in Chapter 9 but mention them briefly here for their connection to the issue of adaptation.

A final source of evidence on this point comes from work examining whether students with disabilities actually need the accommodations that have been granted to them. Most of this research has examined extended-time accommodations. For instance, Cahalan-Laitusis, King, Cline, and Bridgeman (2006) found that students with learning disabilities and ADHD who used extended time accommodations on SAT items generally used

---

[2]Taking tests is itself a set of skills that students with high-incidence disabilities are often deficient in, and that can be remedied through deliberate interventions. It is not uncommon for older, high-functioning students with high-incidence disabilities to report that the primary setting in which they experience trouble is high-stakes test taking, but it is rare that these students are given high-quality, research-based test-taking interventions. In Chapter 8, we review the literature on test-taking skills and programs for increasing them in more detail.

very little of the extended time that they were granted. Of course, even the relatively small amount of additional time taken may have been used because it was available, without providing any benefit; that is, we do not know if the students with disabilities could have worked faster if they needed to. Pariseau, Fabiano, Massetti, Hart, and Pelham (2010) examined this possibility in a sample of children with ADHD; students given less time to complete work-sheets worked at a faster rate and answered more items correctly per unit of time. These studies simply suggest that Phillips's (1994) question about adaptation is very much a live issue; we should not assume that students are unable to complete tests under standard conditions.

Reliability and Validity of Decision Procedures

Phillips's (1994) final question asks whether the procedures that we use to make two kinds of decisions (diagnoses of disability conditions and proffering accommodations) are sufficiently reliable and valid. The first type of decision has generally been ignored by accommodation researchers; the students' diagnoses have been taken as a given. But this is hardly justifiable when the types of disability classifications that are most commonly associated with provision of accommodations have criteria that are hotly contested. In Chapter 4, we discuss disability conditions in detail, but just as an example, consider the perennial debates over the definition of *specific learning disability* and the identification of children who have learning disabilities. Because a disability classification is generally a prerequisite for receiving accommoda-tions, and different schools often use different criteria for identifying students with learning disabilities, whether a student receives accommodations may depend on where he or she goes to school.

The same is true for students who receive private evaluations and are in the gray area between "normal" and "disordered" with regard to a variety of disorders. For instance, whether a high-functioning student has an autism spectrum disorder (or Asperger's) diagnosis depends on which diagnostician evaluated the child. Because mild cases of a disorder are gen-erally the most common (just considering the mathematics of the normal distribution of any relevant variable), reliability of diagnosis will often be suboptimal.

Reliability is generally considered to be a precondition for validity (R. J. Gregory, 2011), but even if disability diagnoses are reliable, they may not be valid. For instance, IQ-achievement discrepancy criteria for diagnosing learning disabilities may be easy to apply reliably (e.g., if a reading composite score must be 22 points below a full-scale IQ, different evaluators should calculate the discrepancy identically, clerical errors notwithstanding), but discrepancy criteria are widely believed to be invalid indicators of learning disabilities (e.g., Sternberg & Grigorenko, 2002). The criteria for other disorders are generally less contested, but controversies remain, and these controversies have an impact on who is eligible for testing accommodations.

Of course, the actual procedures for making accommodation decisions do not rest solely on disability diagnoses; a diagnosis is generally necessary but not sufficient to receive a given accommodation. The process of accommodation decisions must, then, be examined separately for its reliability and validity. Unfortunately, we do not have much descriptive research on accommodation decisions, and we know of no research that has directly examined their reliability and validity.

However, a variety of decision frameworks have been proposed to help increase reliability and validity. For instance, L. S. Fuchs, Fuchs, Eaton, and Hamlett (2003) devised the Dynamic Assessment of Test Accommodations (DATA) for students in Grades 2 through 7. Briefly, a student takes a series of alternate forms of reading and mathematics tests under different conditions (e.g., different time allotments, regular print vs. large print) to determine if the student benefits more than most of the students in a norm group from each accommodation. This kind of performance-based decision tool is rare; more common are checklists and other procedures that make discussions about accommodations somewhat more standardized. For instance, Elliott, Kratochwill, and Schulte (1998) described the Assessment Accommodation Checklist, which helps multidisciplinary teams by providing a list of many (74) accommodations to consider using and asking teachers to "rate the helpfulness and fairness" of accommodations that are used. Similarly, the Council of Chief State School Officers developed an accommodations manual (S. J. Thompson, Morse, Sharpe, & Hall, 2005) that provides checklists and even a sample accommodations plan form for ready use.

Many other available decision frameworks are even less formal; Braden and Joyce (2008) provided a general flow chart for determining whether any accommodations are needed, and Hollenbeck (2002) provided specific questions to help determine if each of a variety of common accommodations is needed. In addition, many state offices of education have developed manuals designed to provide assistance to decision makers; New York State, for instance, has a manual that combines state policies on testing accommodations with practical advice for applying the policies to cases of individual students (Office of Vocational and Education Services for Individuals with Disabilities, 2006). In later chapters of this book, we provide our own guidance to be used to help determine the appropriateness of several common accommodations.

With the exception of the DATA (which is restricted to a small number of accommodations and grade levels), little research has been done on the reliability and validity of any of these decision frameworks. Indeed, there is not even descriptive research on whether most schools or testing agencies (or independent professional diagnosticians who recommend accommodations) use any of them, although it is our own experience (through consulting with school districts and testing agencies) that most do not use formal procedures for decision making. Phillips (1994) suggested that if the decision procedures lack either reliability or validity, accommodations are inappropriate. Although this position may be a bit extreme, given the difficulty of developing such procedures, more research evaluating these procedures is certainly needed.

TESTING ACCOMMODATIONS RESEARCH DESIGNS

As we noted in Chapter 1, there is a need for practice in accommodation decision making to become increasingly research based, and the present book is designed to provide guidelines that are informed by empirical research. We conclude this chapter by considering some of the more common types of research studies on testing accommodations. Like the rest of the chapter, this discussion is relatively nontechnical, but we believe that even nonresearchers (e.g., practicing psychologists, special education teachers) should understand how testing accommodations research is done. Our discussion is based on a prescient paper by Thurlow et al. (2000) that made recommendations for future research on accommodations; much of the research that has been done since then has used the designs that Thurlow et al. described.

Investigating Accommodation Effects

The simplest way to study accommodation effects is to treat them as environmental manipulations and to examine effects on individual students using single-participant designs, such as those common in applied behavior analysis. In classroom settings, where tests and quizzes are given fairly frequently, teachers can administer assessments under different conditions (perhaps under the guidance of a school psychologist) to determine if an accommodation is effective. Figure 3.1 shows hypothetical data from an ABAB reversal design, where a student's weekly spelling quiz was administered in either a group setting (with the rest of the class) or in a separate, distraction-reduced setting. After 5 weeks being quizzed under standard conditions (the baseline, or "A" phase), separate room administration occurred for 5 weeks (the intervention or "B" phase). Then, the separate room accommodation was withdrawn and reintroduced. These data would suggest that the setting accommodation was effective in raising scores.

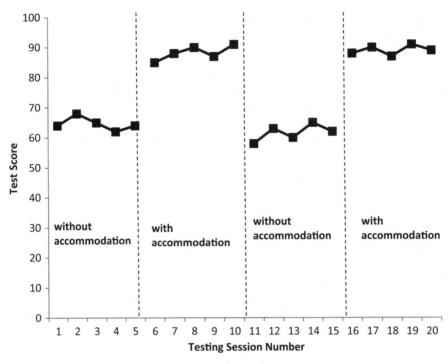

Figure 3.1. Evaluating the efficacy of accommodations using an ABAB reversal design.

If two or more accommodations are being investigated, we can use an alternating treatments design. Figure 3.2 shows hypothetical data from such a design being used to investigate whether breaks during exams are as effective as extended time for a student. After baseline data are collected, the teacher alternates between administering the exam with additional time and with break periods. These data would suggest that breaks were as effective as additional time; given that breaks are not thought to be as likely as additional time to compromise validity, these data could be used to support providing a student with breaks instead of additional time. Other single-participant designs can be used as well (see Cooper, Heron, & Heward, 2007, for more detailed discussion of these designs), and the simplicity of these designs (especially that they tend to be interpreted through visual inspection instead of statistical analysis) makes them especially likely to be useful in school settings.

Investigating Differential Benefits

As we mentioned earlier, much of the research on accommodation effects has involved investigating whether students with disabilities benefit

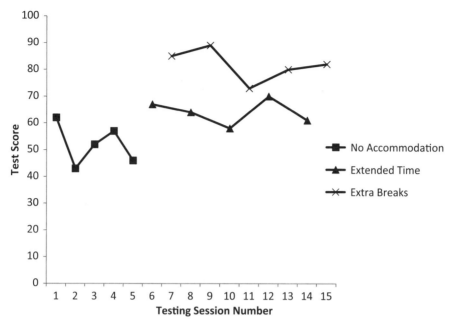

Figure 3.2. Evaluating the relative efficacy of two interventions using an alternating treatments design.

more than nondisabled students from an accommodation. These studies are typically done with four groups of students:

- students *with* disabilities who take a test under *standard* conditions,
- students *without* disabilities who take a test under *standard* conditions,
- students *with* disabilities who take a test under *accommodated* conditions, and
- students *without* disabilities who take a test under *accommodated* conditions.

At times, the students in Groups 1 and 3 and the students in Groups 2 and 4 are the same students; each student in the study, then, takes a test both with and without accommodations. (Two alternate forms of a test are sometimes used in this case, to reduce practice effects.)

To test the MPT (Zuriff, 2000), we would compare the two groups of nondisabled students' scores, and then we would compare the groups of disabled students' scores. If the MPT holds, the first comparison should not show a significant difference; that is, nondisabled students should not benefit appreciably from the accommodation. In addition, the latter comparison

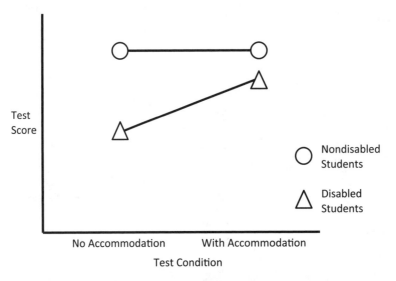

Test Score

No Accommodation   With Accommodation

Test Condition

○ Nondisabled Students

△ Disabled Students

Figure 3.3. Graph of results meeting the standards of the maximum potential thesis.

should show a significant difference such that students with disabilities benefit appreciably from the accommodation. Figure 3.3 shows a graph of hypothetical data supporting the MPT.

To test the weaker DBH (Sireci et al., 2005), we would determine if there is a statistical interaction between the effects of disability status and accommodation status on performance—that is, if the degree of benefit that the accommodation yields differs depending on the examinees' disability status. A factorial analysis of variance (ANOVA) is typically used to test this. If the DBH holds, inspection of the four group means should indicate that students with disabilities show a larger boost from the accommodation than nondisabled students do. Figure 3.4 shows a graph of hypothetical data supporting the DBH (in a case where the MPT would not be supported).

Investigating Score Comparability

Several techniques have been used to investigate whether scores obtained under accommodated testing conditions are comparable to scores obtained under standard testing conditions. Each technique tells us something different about comparability, and the best evaluations of comparability use multiple techniques.

Factor Analysis

Factor analysis is a set of statistical tools that can be used to discern the internal structure of a test (or some other set of variables). In a factor

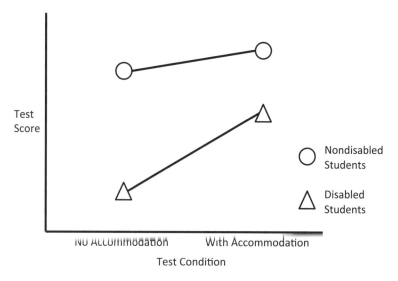

Figure 3.4. Graph of results meeting the standards of the differential boost hypothesis but not the maximum potential thesis.

analysis, the relationships between different parts of a test (subtests or individual items) are analyzed to determine "factors" that are thought of as the trait dimensions that underlie performance on the test, and the different test parts are differentially related to each factor. For instance, on a typical intelligence test, there are many subtests. If we correlate people's performance on each subtest with their performance on each other subtest, we might find that a number of subtests requiring vocabulary skills cluster together, and a number of subtests requiring quick perceptual speed cluster together; these two groups of subtests would be strongly related to the two different factors (vocabulary skills and perceptual speed), respectively.

Factor analysis is one tool used when collecting construct validity evidence for a test, because if a test is designed to measure a particular construct, and theoretical work on that construct suggests that it has a certain structure, a factor analysis of scores on the parts of that test should find the expected structure (Messick, 1995; B. Thompson & Daniel, 1996). If an accommodation does not alter the construct being measured, we should find that a test has the same factor structure whether it is taken with or without the accommodation. Sometimes, researchers use exploratory factor analysis (EFA), where no particular structure is being hypothesized, and researchers examine whether data from testing with and without accommodations happens to yield the same structure in an EFA—that is, are the same number of factors found, and do the different parts of the test show the same relationships to the factors across data from standard and accommodated conditions?

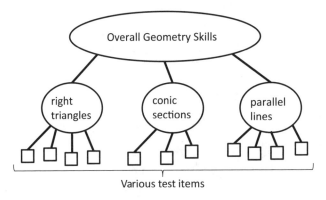

Figure 3.5. Hypothetical factor structure of a test.

At other times, researchers use confirmatory factor analysis, in which a particular structure is specified, and the data are compared with the hypothesized structure to determine how closely the two fit, for data from both standard and accommodated testing. Figure 3.5 shows a hypothetical internal structure for a test that might or might not be found to be different under accommodated conditions.

Criterion-Related Validity

Early in the chapter, we noted that one type of validity evidence for a test involves showing that the test predicts an important and relevant outcome (a criterion). If testing accommodations do not change the meaning of a test score, the accommodations should not change the relationship between a score and a criterion. There are two especially important ways that such a relationship might change. First, its strength could change; it could become stronger or weaker when accommodations are provided on the test. Researchers usually explore this by computing a correlation coefficient that indexes the relationship between test scores and performance on some criterion when the test scores were obtained under standard testing conditions, and then computing a second correlation coefficient where the test scores were obtained with accommodations. Figure 3.6 shows two scatterplots, one with a stronger test–criterion relationship and one with a weaker relationship.

A test–criterion relationship could also change in a different way; test scores could overpredict or underpredict the criterion for examinees in the (usually much smaller) accommodated group. For instance, we might use performance on a high-stakes mathematics test to predict mathematics grades in middle school students. Most students will take the test under standard

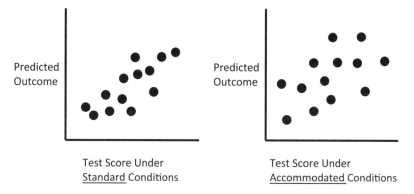

Predicted Outcome — Test Score Under Standard Conditions

Predicted Outcome — Test Score Under Accommodated Conditions

Figure 3.6. Scatterplots showing better prediction of an outcome using test scores obtained without accommodations.

conditions, whereas a small group of students (students with disabilities) will take the test with accommodations. If the test scores of students who receive accommodations overpredict their school grades, this may mean that the accommodations are providing an inappropriate boost to their test scores, leading us to make inaccurate interpretations about their mathematics skills and likely mathematics achievement in educational settings. In an admissions testing setting (e.g., using SAT quantitative scores to predict performance and determine placement in a first-year college mathematics course sequence), the consequences of overprediction could be costly.

Differential Item Functioning

A final method used to determine whether accommodations threaten score comparability occurs at the level of individual test items. *Differential item functioning* (DIF) occurs when there are "differences in the way that a test item functions across demographic groups that are matched on the attribute measured by the test or the test item" (Osterlind & Everson, 2009, p. 8). That is, DIF happens when different examinees respond differently to an item even though their levels of the trait measured by the test/item are the same. It is common for psychometricians to examine potential DIF across ethnic and gender groups, but DIF can also occur across examinees who receive standard and accommodated versions of a test. To illustrate this, Figure 3.7 shows the relationship between students' levels of reading comprehension skill and their chance of answering a particular item correctly on a reading comprehension test. As their skill levels increase, students are more likely to answer correctly. Figure 3.7 shows how the relationship between skill level and correct response likelihood might (hypothetically)

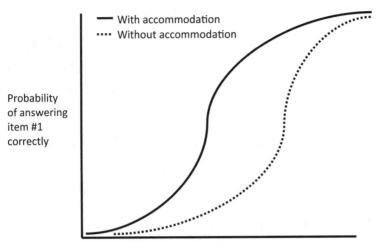

Figure 3.7. Graph showing differential item functioning dependent on whether a testing accommodation is provided.

differ depending on whether an accommodation is provided. DIF analyses are conducted using a variety of technically sophisticated procedures, and these methods are beyond the scope of our discussion; our intention here is just to provide a conceptual understanding of what DIF would mean, because certain DIF results are generally viewed as a threat to the validity of a testing procedure.

4

DISABILITY CONDITIONS AND FUNCTIONAL LIMITATIONS

In addition to the development of legal protections for persons with disabilities, there has also been an expansion in awareness and identification of persons with disabilities. A historical review of the *Diagnostic and Statistical Manual of Mental Disorders* (DSM) over the past 30 to 40 years will reveal the broadening of mental health diagnoses, as well as increasing prevalence rates of some disorders. For example, the prevalence of autism in 2000 was estimated to be 6.7 per 1,000 children, whereas in 2012 the estimate is one per 88 (see http://www.cdc.gov/ncbddd/autism/data.html). The sociological fact is that as a society, we now recognize more disabilities than ever, and each disabled person is entitled to considerations such as test accommodations under antidiscrimination laws.

What may have started as initiatives to make adjustments in public places to accommodate persons with obvious disabilities (e.g., blindness and

http://dx.doi.org/10.1037/14468-004
Testing Accommodations for Students With Disabilities: Research-Based Practice, by B. J. Lovett
and L. J. Lewandowski

physical impairments) has morphed into a large and diverse field that provides various accommodations to a wide range of individuals with myriad needs. Changes in laws and practices have broadened special services to those persons with less obvious disorders, such as various cognitive disabilities (e.g., traumatic brain injury [TBI]), learning disabilities [LD] and behavior disabilities (e.g., auditory processing disorder, attention-deficit/hyperactivity disorder [ADHD]) and mental/psychiatric disabilities (e.g., anxiety, Asperger syndrome). Even as recently as 2008, the ADA Amendments Act (ADAAA) served to broaden the types of impairment (e.g., writing, concentrating) by which a person may be considered to have a disability, and debates are ongoing as to whether things like test anxiety or processing speed weaknesses are actual disabilities covered by the law. Whereas there is little disagreement about allowing a blind person to use Braille or giving an amputee an adjustable desk chair, there has been controversy about allowing a person with anxiety more time on a high-stakes exam or providing a separate test room to someone with a diagnosis of ADHD. Some of the controversial issues stem from differences in philosophies about what constitutes a disability and whether all persons with a diagnosed disorder should be considered as disabled. How do we know if a person with a sleep disorder is truly disabled? Is a person who worries constantly more disabled than a person who worries only in certain situations? Is an LD a true disability even if the student has above-average academic and test performances?

What constitutes a disability is a complicated issue. Is a person disabled if he or she is diagnosed by a professional as having a medical condition or mental disorder? That puts a lot of weight on the diagnostic acumen of a clinician, given that a diagnosis could mean a lifetime of stigma, special services, and government support. The public school systems generally work on such a model. If a student receives a diagnosis (i.e., physical, sensory, intellectual, emotional, or LD) from school or private professionals, the school will provide that student appropriate services (via the individualized education program [IEP] or 504 plan). This service model is covered under special education law (Individuals With Disabilities Education Improvement Act of 2004 [IDEIA]) and applies as long as the student is in high school. Once the student enters college or the private world, she or he is covered by the ADAAA. The ADAAA definition of disability in some ways is more conservative than the IDEIA: a physical or mental impairment that substantially limits one or more major life activities of such individual.[1]

This law states that in addition to having a diagnosed disorder, the individual must also demonstrate a substantial limitation in a major life activity.

---

[1]We should note that in ADA, "impairment" does not indicate *functional impairment* (i.e., problems performing real-world activities). It instead refers to a clinical condition.

An individual is substantially limited in the ability to perform a major life activity if he or she "is unable to perform a major life activity that the average person in the general population can perform." This standard is slightly relaxed from the previous ADA standard of an impairment that "prevents or severely restricts" a major life activity (§504). However, even the amended law maintained the "average person" standard for determining a substantial limitation. Of note is that the requirement for an individual to demonstrate evidence of impairment in functioning is similar to the standard found among the classification criteria for most *DSM* diagnostic classifications.

The standard suggested by the ADAAA or the *Diagnostic and Statistical Manual of Mental Disorders* (4th ed., text rev.; *DSM–IV–TR*; American Psychiatric Association, 2000) and now the fifth edition (*DSM–5*; American Psychiatric Association, 2013) is not required under the IDEIA and not universally used by K–12 school systems.[2] As noted in Chapter 3 of this volume, accommodation decisions are often based on the affective concerns for students such as reducing their stress and frustration while preserving their self-esteem (Crawford & Ketterlin-Geller, 2013). If schools do not incorporate the impairment criterion in service delivery models, then, for example, a student with an ADHD diagnosis who performs above average academically might be receiving support services and accommodations. However, this same person when applying for extended time on the GRE may be denied this test accommodation, presumably because there is a lack of demonstrated impairment. The argument would be that if the person already performs better than most people in school and on tests, then there is no substantial limitation, and therefore the person is not considered disabled under the law. One could see how this change in interpretation of disability could be confusing as well as upsetting. This scenario is being played out every day as students make the transition from high school to college and beyond, applying for test accommodations under the ADAAA in postsecondary schools, on high-stakes graduate admissions tests, and for professional exams (see Chapter 9).

DISABILITIES, IMPAIRMENT, AND ACCOMMODATIONS

Functional impairment is the "800-pound gorilla in the room" when it comes to test accommodations. It bears repeating that having a diagnosis and demonstrating functional impairment (a substantial limitation) are related yet separate issues. A diagnosis is a necessary but not sufficient condition for

---

[2]In one sense, then, IDEIA is broader than the ADA because it requires things (e.g., special educational services) that the ADA does not. However, in a different sense, ADA is broader, because it covers both children and adults, whereas IDEIA only covers children up until the age of 21.

accommodation eligibility. Most test accommodation controversies do not emerge from disagreements over a professional diagnosis. If a student has repeated diagnoses of an LD across K–12 schooling, the question is not about the LD diagnosis but rather the extent of impairment in a major life activity that would restrict access to taking a test under standard conditions. For example, the *DSM–5* definition of specific learning disorders suggests that evidence of significant impairment on an achievement test is a standard score of below 78 (> 1.5 standard deviations below the age-based mean of 100). As Sparks and Lovett (2009b) indicated, most college students with LD diagnoses do not have achievement scores below 78, creating an issue about whether they are substantially limited and qualified to receive test accommodations.

The same issue would apply to a student with a long-standing diagnosis of ADHD or depression. Despite these diagnoses, the key question is: Can the individual demonstrate that she or he is functionally impaired or substantially limited such that the limitation restricts access to the exam? This requirement can put a burden on a student and/or clinician that was not present before. Hopefully, the student has a documented track record of poor grades or test scores, school records including IEPs or 504 plans, records of treatment (e.g., medication, therapy, tutoring), and previous professional evaluations showing individual test performances that are "impaired" or below average. Many if not most students with disabilities have such proof of impairment. Students with intellectual and sensory handicaps easily pass this test. Students with severe or multiple disabilities likewise have no issue. Students with cerebral palsy may not have intellectual deficits, but they are impaired in movement and require certain accommodations. Others with significant communication, learning, and mental disorders have little problem finding evidence of impairment. On the other hand, a student who is both gifted and has a disability and is performing at least average may have little proof of impairment. Similarly, a student with mild ADHD may struggle with relationships, behave impulsively, and get distracted quickly yet perform quite well academically and on high-stakes tests. The distinction here between diagnosis and significant functional impairment is critical in accommodation determinations.

These case examples raise the following question: Does a person with symptoms of a disorder necessarily demonstrate functional impairment in a major life activity that restricts his/her access to education or taking a test? Some authors have tried to disentangle the symptom–impairment connection, suggesting that although related, they certainly are not one and the same. For example, Barkley et al. (2006) posited that symptoms are the behavioral expressions associated with a disorder, whereas impairments are the consequences that ensue for the individuals as a result of these behaviors. A person with symptoms of restlessness, distractibility, and impulsivity may be considered for a diagnosis of ADHD because these are common symptoms of ADHD. But having these symptoms does not mean the person is necessarily impaired in functioning. Perhaps, despite the symptoms, an individual is highly energetic, productive, and able to manage daily functions at home and in school. Let's say that this individual has obtained very good grades and above-average standardized test scores. Is this person impaired enough to warrant a diagnosis? Does he or she need special services? Are test accommodations indicated? Then take another person with similar symptoms of ADHD. This individual has not performed well academically (despite average intelligence), has repeated second grade, does not finish work or tests in a timely manner, has used tutors for years, and seems to constantly underachieve. Given this apparent impairment, one can argue more readily for the diagnosis, special services, and test accommodations.

There is a body of research that shows that measures of symptoms and impairment are far from perfectly correlated. For example, Gordon et al. (2006) examined the relationship between ADHD symptoms and measures of impairment in four extant data sets and showed small to moderate correlations (most $rs < .50$) between the two sets of measures. They concluded that symptoms accounted for only about 10% of the variance in impairment for the ADHD sample. Further, they noted that in one data set, 77% of the children identified as having ADHD on the basis of symptom criteria would not have been diagnosed if the impairment criterion had been considered. Numerous other studies have demonstrated that the proportion of individuals identified with psychiatric diagnoses drops dramatically when impairment is included along with symptoms (Bird et al., 1988; Costello, Angold, & Keeler, 1999; Graetz, Sawyer, Hazell, Arney, & Baghurst, 2001). It should be apparent that the measurement of impairment and inclusion in diagnostic decisions is crucial. However, not all clinicians appear to interpret the law and the impairment criterion as described previously. For example, Gordon, Lewandowski, Murphy, and Dempsey (2002) surveyed 147 evaluators who prepared disability documentation for students seeking accommodations on the Law School Admissions Test (LSAT). Approximately one third of the clinicians indicated that the Americans With Disabilities Act of 1990 (ADA) was intended to increase students' test scores and academic performance, as well as help individuals with disabilities perform "at their best." Apparently, there are different interpretations of the law, what constitutes a substantial limitation, and even the purpose of test accommodations.

Documentation of functional impairment that substantially limits a person in a major life activity is the main criterion for determining eligibility for test accommodations. A person who applies for test accommodations on the SAT, in college, or on the bar exam should be able to demonstrate that she or he is negatively impacted by a disorder such that he or she cannot fully access a test under standard test conditions. The standard for making this determination has been a comparison to the "average person" or to "most persons." This standard, controversial in its own right, has been upheld in numerous court cases and amended legislation. It is the only standard that offers guidance to an interpretation of what constitutes a substantial limitation. There are ways to operationalize this standard when making accommodation determinations. For example, documentation from teachers should show that in comparison to other students, a particular student performs less well on specific academic tasks (e.g., writing, reading, language, problem solving). Documentation from psychologists should show that on reliable and valid tests that provide age-based standardized scores, the examinee performs below average compared with age peers. Even in these cases, one can argue about what constitutes "below average" performance. Is it a grade of F in a class or a score that is one or two standard deviations below the mean on a standardized test? Despite some ambiguity, what is clear from this standard is that average performance is not impairment relative to most people. If a student performs in the average range academically and on timed, standardized tests, and there is no other documentation of impaired performance, then that person would not qualify for test accommodations under the law even though the person carries a diagnosis from a professional. This is the major difference between clinical criteria for a disability versus the legal criteria.

Related to the documentation of functional impairment, although not a legal requirement per se, is the history or chronic nature of impairment. Certain disorders such as depression and anxiety may be late-occurring and/ or episodic. Such disabilities may impair functioning considerably yet may have a recent (adult) genesis. However, the most common disabilities seen in the testing accommodations field are LD and ADHD, and both are developmental disorders. Typically, these disorders are identified in childhood and accompanied by professional attention (i.e., assessment and treatment), special school services (i.e., IEPs or 504 plans), and records of learning and behavioral difficulties. It would not be surprising for students with such a history to demonstrate functional impairment and easily qualify for the legal definition of disability. By contrast, a high school student with a stellar academic record who complains of difficulty completing tests such as the ACT or SAT, and who does not have a documented history of impairment, will most likely not meet the legal definition of disability, even if a clinician liberally makes an LD or ADHD diagnosis. Although a history of functional impairment is not a necessary condition for test accommodation eligibility, it certainly helps make a compelling case for individuals with LD and ADHD diagnoses, especially when those diagnoses occur later in life.

Another controversial issue concerning functional impairment and test accommodations has to do with one's understanding of the purpose of the law. Many individuals applying for test accommodations, and also their evaluators, indicate in their accommodation applications that they could perform better on a test if given more time or a separate room (for example). They may view impairment as a gap between how they score on a test (average) and how they think they should perform (above average) or how they perform on other tasks (high grades). Again, the law has been fairly clear on this point. The law is not intended to maximize or guarantee a certain level of success (also known as *outcome neutral*), but, rather, it only ensures equal access to taking the test. Impairment must be based on comparison to the average person; it is not a comparison with one's other abilities, and it is not a comparison to a specialized group (e.g., other medical students). Like it or not, the average person standard is probably the most fair and objective comparison possible for determining one's level of functional impairment. As we progress through this chapter and highlight the various disability types that may require test accommodations, we examine the kinds of functional impairment that should be demonstrated for each disability type before accommodations are provided.

INTELLECTUAL AND DEVELOPMENTAL DISABILITIES

By definition, intellectual and developmental disabilities are chronic and impairing disabilities, typically causing limitations and restrictions in a variety of life domains (i.e., language, learning, self-care, employment, and independent living). Within this broad category of disability are listed genetic disorders (e.g., phenylketonuria, neurofibromatosis, Huntington's disease, fragile X syndrome), chromosomal anomalies (e.g., Down syndrome, Turner syndrome, Prader-Willi syndrome), environmental/toxic causes (e.g., fetal alcohol syndrome, crack-cocaine addiction, lead poisoning, birth trauma), acquired illness (e.g., meningitis, viruses, brain tumors, medical conditions), as well as unknown and psychosocial causes. Many of these individuals, although certainly not all, will have subnormal intelligence, defined as IQ and adaptive behavior scores more than two standard deviations below the mean (< 70).[3]

There is little question that individuals in this category qualify under the law as having a disability. On the basis of their age, they would be covered under the IDEIA or the ADAAA and would be afforded accommodations to access their education or employment. Test accommodations for these

---

[3]It is interesting that the special education field has come to accept these score cutoffs as reliable indicators of intellectual disability, yet many professionals reject the notion that students with LD should demonstrate achievement test scores below a certain cutoff (see Dombrowski, Kamphaus, & Reynolds, 2004).

individuals are probably the least of their concerns. Schools have become adaptive in their ability to accommodate severely and multiply handicapped students in the learning environment. For those with the intellectual capacity to take standardized and high-stakes tests, certainly the minority of this group, there is little controversy about making accommodations. For example, students may need readers, scribes, communication devices, assistive technology, extended time, enlarged print, response aids, and/or a separate proctor, as well as comfort measures such as breaks, water and medication, and pillows for posture support. Although these accommodations are routinely made in the classroom, the matter becomes more difficult on standardized tests. The question here becomes the degree to which the test administration is altered from standard conditions. It may be possible for a student with cerebral palsy who has an IQ of 85 and visual impairment to take a standardized test with a host of accommodations. However, then one has to ask how valid the test result will be.

Is there a point at which it makes sense to assess the student's skill levels in other ways, rather than to radically alter the conditions on a standardized test? If the test is needed to graduate or to gain admission to a community college, perhaps one should alter the admission policy rather than take a test that is not readily interpretable. Except in rare instances, there will be little controversy about test accommodations for this category of disabilities. Generally it will be a moot point because many of these students will not complete a regular education program or apply to postsecondary school. In certain cases, usually those with high enough intellectual capacity, accommodations will be provided and test results will be informative, and in other cases, even multiple test accommodations may not be the appropriate approach to evaluate student knowledge. Some students will have alternative assessments that are based on meeting standards that are different from those of their peers.

DEAFNESS AND HEARING DISABILITIES

This is a large and diverse disability category, although cochlear implants have made hearing possible for students who would not have been able to hear 10 or 20 years ago. According to the National Institute on Deafness and Other Communication Disorders (2010), hearing loss is present at birth in about two to three children of every 1,000. With age, the prevalence continues to increase, such that almost half of individuals who are 75 years and older have a hearing loss. These rates are quite high, but in many cases technology has normalized hearing. Just as eyeglasses can improve faulty vision, hearing aids, amplifier systems, and cochlear implants have restored near normal hearing to many people. Consequently, those who are most impaired are the deaf and hearing impaired for whom technology is ineffective. Audiologists have reliable methods for assessing and grading degree of hearing impairment, such that they can ascertain who has mild, moderate, severe, and profound hearing loss and in what sounds and frequencies. One estimate of the number of deaf or hearing impaired children who are receiving special education is about 80,000 (Gallaudet Research Institute, 2008), and 45% of these students have severe to profound hearing loss.

Approximately half of those with congenital deafness, including progressive hearing loss, are the result of genetic causes (e.g., Stickler syndrome, Usher syndrome, Pendred syndrome). The remainder of cases is usually a result of certain acquired viruses at or before, during, or after birth (e.g., measles, mumps, chicken pox, syphilis, AIDS, meningitis, cytomegalovirus). Approximately 40% of those who experience genetic or viral causes of hearing impairment also tend to have some combination of disabilities (e.g., cognitive, language, physical, neurological; Vernon & Andrews, 1990). These comorbid conditions can figure prominently into academic and test accommodation determinations.

If the deaf student has near average intellectual capacity, then regular education and standardized test taking are possible. Such students, particularly those who have delayed or unintelligible oral speech, are taught American Sign Language, as well as how to read and possibly lip reading. In this way they can understand speakers, signers, and television/movies (closed captions). Such adaptations, although not perfect solutions, have allowed the hard of hearing to thrive in all aspects of life. In a testing situation, such as a high-stakes standardized test, the main accommodation has to do with oral directions frequently given by a proctor. Hearing-impaired students need written directions and enough time to understand them. They also may need a proctor who can communicate (answer questions) by using sign language. Most standardized tests involve reading text, and this is usually not the core problem for the deaf, but hearing impairment can create delays in learning to read or reading efficiency. Research has shown that hearing-impaired children tend to have weaker vocabulary (e.g., Pittman, Lewis, Hoover, & Stelmachowicz, 2005) and lower levels of reading comprehension than peers (e.g., Traxler, 2000). In fact, Wauters, Van Bon, and Tellings (2006) found that only 4% of their hearing-impaired Dutch sample (ages 7–20) was reading at their age-appropriate level.

Given the widespread reading weaknesses in the hearing-impaired population, it makes sense to assess these students' reading to see if they need extended time or a dictionary for reading. For example, Wolf (2007) examined test accommodation use and performance on the SAT-9 in 105 high school students with hearing impairment. Extended time was the most frequently used accommodation, and the type and degree of hearing loss was significantly related to reading achievement. Similarly, Cawthon (2006) reported on a national survey of teachers and administrators on the most common accommodations used (in 2003–2004) by students with hearing impairment on a statewide math test and found that extended time was the most common, followed by an interpreter for directions and a separate room. In 2010, Cawthon reported on a survey of 290 teachers from 38 states who worked with students with hearing impairment. Again, extended time, private/semiprivate administration, and an interpreter for directions were the most commonly offered test accommodations. There often is not a great need for more specialized test accommodations because tests are rarely delivered in an oral format, but obviously that would not be a suitable test format for someone with significant hearing impairment. Therefore, the most challenging accommodation cases will arise for hearing-impaired students who have comorbid conditions (i.e., visual, physical, learning, or emotional disabilities).

In addition to deafness and hearing loss, some students may have more centralized auditory impairment that affects their ability to process auditory information efficiently. These children experience severe distractibility, trouble following directions given orally, and generally poor listening skills. They frequently need information to be repeated and suffer academic consequences. Although these are symptoms associated with disorders such as LD and ADHD, they are also among the symptoms most likely to lead to a diagnosis of auditory processing disorder (APD; also called central auditory processing disorder, or CAPD). Indeed, audiologists surveyed about various symptoms rated these as among the most likely to be seen in cases of APD (Chermak, Tucker, & Seikel, 2002).

APD has been defined as "the defective processing of auditory information in spite of normal auditory thresholds" (Jerger & Musiek, 2000, p. 467). APD has become an increasingly common diagnosis, both in the United States and abroad (Dawes & Bishop, 2009). Audiologists, speech-language pathologists, and psychologists all are involved in APD assessment and treatment. Children with APD are often described as showing difficulty paying attention or remembering orally presented information; poor listening skills; slow processing of auditory information; problems carrying out multistep instructions; receptive and/or expressive language difficulties; academic problems in verbal domains such as reading, spelling, and writing; as well as behavior problems such as not listening to commands. Clearly, these behaviors are all seen in children with ADHD as well.

There are a variety of management strategies for APD, but few have a strong evidence base. In terms of test taking, common sense suggests that instructors use preferred seating, make oral directions very clear, repeat important instructions, and ensure that noise is kept to a minimum. Test accommodations then might include a quiet room with no distractions, extended time for reading instructions and the test, and directions given in multiple modalities (e.g., oral and written). The main problem with APD is the validity of this controversial diagnosis and the proof that the student is indeed substantially limited in a major life activity (e.g., listening, reading, concentrating). In particular, it is difficult to distinguish APD from other developmental disorders, and many of the assessment instruments used to diagnose it are flawed. We would add here that we have seen extended-time testing accommodations given to students with APD, but without clear evidence of slow reading or related skill deficits, this use of extended time is not supportable.

BLINDNESS AND VISUAL DISABILITIES

Visual disabilities, just as hearing disabilities, are varied in type and severity. As with hearing difficulties, many visual difficulties are correctable, such as near- and farsightedness, cataracts, and certain oculomotor problems. Despite these corrections, some individuals have total blindness or low vision (moderate to severe impairment), and others have varying levels and causes of visual impairment (e.g., albinism, glaucoma, retinopathy, strabismus, color blindness, macular degeneration, visual field loss, Usher syndrome). According to the World Health Organization, most visual impairment (43%) is due to uncorrected refractive errors (myopia, hyperopia) or cataracts (33%) (see http://www.who.int/mediacentre/factsheets/fs282/en/index.html). Whatever the cause of the visual disability, the threshold for visual impairment is the best-corrected visual acuity < 20/40 in the better seeing eye (see http://www.nei.nih.gov/eyedata/vision_impaired.asp#3b). According to the National Institutes of Health, approximately 12 of 1,000 children under age 18 have a visual impairment, whereas less than one of 1,000 are legally or totally blind. According to the National Dissemination Center for Children with Disabilities (2012), as of 2011 there were

> 490,420 children with vision difficulty (the term "vision difficulty" refers only to children who had serious difficulty seeing even when wearing glasses and those who are blind); 42,000 children with a severe vision impairment (unable to see words and letters in ordinary newsprint); and 59,341 children who were legally blind. (p. 3)

As with hearing, vision experts such as optometrists and ophthalmologists have specialized technology to measure types and degrees of visual impairment, and they are able to fully or partially resolve many visual impairments. In the classroom setting, modifications can be made to mitigate visual impairment, including special seating, spectacles, proper lighting, large-print instructional materials, magnifiers, computer-assisted technologies, and Braille. These same measures can be used in a testing situation. Common test accommodations for blindness include Braille, extended time, and dictation or voice-recognition technology to record narrated responses. For those with partial vision yet some degree of impairment, test accommodations often involve enlarged print, magnification devices, extended time, a reader/scribe, and use of a computer. Sometimes audio versions of tests are most suitable and essay writing is conducted on a computer with a large visual display. As with all test accommodations, the task is to assess an examinee's skills using test conditions and procedures that are closest to standard.

LEARNING DISABILITIES

According to the Individuals With Disabilities Education Act (IDEA), *specific learning disabilities* (SLDs) refer to

> a disorder in one or more of the basic psychological processes involved in understanding or in using spoken or written language, which may manifest itself in an imperfect ability to listen, think, speak, read, write, spell or do mathematical calculations. (Sec. 602 (30)(a))

The American Psychiatric Association (2013) has proposed a new definition of SLD that appeared in the *DSM–5*. The new definition states that all learning disorders are specific and demonstrate impairment in reading, written expression, and or mathematics. There is only one diagnosis for all learning disorders, and it includes specifiers for the type of learning impairment experienced (e.g., reading fluency, math calculation). There is no longer a diagnosis of LD-Not Otherwise Specified. There are now four criteria that must be addressed for the diagnosis.

Criterion A of the SLD definition requires that at least one symptom of learning impairment (e.g., difficulty understanding what is read) be present for at least 6 months. Criterion B notes that "the affected academic skills are substantially and quantifiably below those expected for the individual's chronological age" (e.g., >1.5 standard deviations below the mean score for a person's age on a standardized achievement test). Criterion C stipulates that the learning difficulties begin during school-age years but may not become fully manifest until academic demands exceed one's limited capacities. Last, Criterion D delineates the rule-outs for the diagnosis. In other words, the learning difficulties are not better accounted for by intellectual sensory, emotional, or neurological disorders, as well as lack of instruction, language proficiency, or psychosocial adversity.

This new definition is clearly more in line with the "average person" standard used by the ADA and subsequent case law. This definition is based on a comparison of a person's measured skills with those in his or her same age cohort, but not with those at the same intelligence level. *DSM–5* goes on to suggest that impairment on a standardized achievement test would be a score less than 78 on a test with a mean of 100 and standard deviation of 15. Clearly, a person with an IQ score of 130 and achievement score of 100 would not come close to meeting this threshold. In fact, many college students with LD diagnoses might not meet the more stringent *DSM–5* diagnostic criteria (see Sparks & Lovett, 2009b).

What is not mentioned in either the IDEA or *DSM–5* definitions is exactly how one determines the presence of LD. There is no biological marker or gold standard test that can positively identify LD. For decades, professionals have relied on a numeric discrepancy between IQ and achievement test scores (i.e., 1.5 standard deviations or 22 points); however, this practice has been widely criticized. Some of the criticisms of the discrepancy analysis include that (a) young children have little chance of documenting a significant IQ-achievement discrepancy, thus setting up a "wait-to-fail" scenario (e.g., Lyon, Fletcher, Fuchs, & Chhabra, 2006); (b) it appears that many children identified by this model do not meet state or federal eligibility criteria, and conversely, students who met eligibility criteria did not meet discrepancy cutoffs (Gresham, MacMillan, & Bocian, 1996; MacMillan, Gresham, & Bocian, 1998); and (c) children with low average IQ scores ($80 < IQ < 90$) tend to have a difficult time reaching the cutoff even if their achievement scores are below average, prompting some critics to ask why IQ score should be part of any LD diagnosis (e.g., Siegel, 1992). Without question, any cutoff score system for identifying LD will be imperfect in the absence of biological marker.

In part because of discontent with the discrepancy model of LD diagnosis, there has been a paradigm shift to a new educational model called *response to intervention* (RTI; D. Fuchs & Fuchs, 2006). RTI is an educational reform that directs schools to provide universal, evidence-based core instruction to all students, referred to as Tier 1 intervention (see Figure 4.1). Students are provided this instruction while their academic progress is closely monitored to determine adequate growth in achievement. For the 10% to 15% of students who do not respond well to this level of instruction, a more specialized and targeted type of intervention (Tier 2) is applied, often in small groups or with the help of specialists. Again, frequent progress monitoring is used to determine academic growth. It is assumed that about 5% of all students will not be successful at Tier 1 and 2 levels and consequently will need more intensive and individualized intervention, typically from specialists (Tier 3). At this level, students are more likely to be referred for individualized evaluation. If

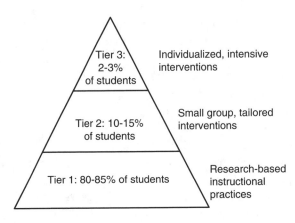

Figure 4.1. Three-tiered response-to-intervention model.

academic progress is insufficient and the student meets criteria for a disability designation (e.g., LD), then that student would qualify for special education services as determined by the school district Committee on Special Education.

Whichever model is used to determine LD, there are inherent problems of measurement error and bias, clinical interpretation and subjectivity, as well as politically influenced decisions. The *DSM–5* definition explicitly advocates for consideration of impairment in the diagnosis and requires that a clinician specifies all academic domains and subskills that are impaired, as well as the severity of the impairment. However, the definition seems open to method of diagnosis, whether using a psychoeducational testing approach such as an academic achievement test score below 78 (e.g., Dombrowski, Kamphaus, & Reynolds, 2004) or an RTI model that shows skill impairment despite best evidence-based academic interventions. Although some scholars and practitioners might feel that a gap between one's own IQ and an achievement score is significant enough to constitute impairment and qualify for a diagnosis and test accommodations, it appears that the *DSM–5* and RTI approaches have taken a very different direction. Clearly, how one defines impairment will largely determine conferral of the diagnosis, and this surely leads to inconsistency, confusion, and disagreements. Sadly, such confusion has plagued the LD field since 1963 when the term first came into use.

Considerable research has examined possible etiologies for LD. Biological underpinnings such as abnormal brain activity (e.g., Hoeft et al., 2010; Richlan, Kronbichler, & Wimmer, 2011; E. Temple et al., 2003) and brain dysfunction (Rourke, 1975) have been linked to LD. Other work has found evidence of a genetic link within families with LD (dyslexia in particular; see Petrill, 2013) and between identical twins (Pennington, 1995;

Wadsworth, Defries, Olson, & Willcutt, 2007). LD has also been found in greater proportions in certain biological conditions such as Turner syndrome (C. M. Temple & Marriot, 1998), fetal alcohol syndrome (Mattson & Riley, 1998), and Klinefelter syndrome (Rovet, Netley, Keenan, Bailey, & Stewart, 1996) and has been associated with illnesses such as meningitis and the late effects from cancer treatment. Despite the extensive biological and neurological connections to LD, most cases are idiopathic, and so the diagnoses are made purely on behavioral data rather than physiological correlates.

LD is estimated to be the largest disability group in the schools (U.S. Department of Education, National Center for Education Statistics, 2010), with prevalence rates typically ranging between 5% and 10%, with approximately 90% of these disabilities related to reading (Kavale & Reese, 1992). Most cases of LD are identified in elementary school because of problems acquiring basic academic skills and professionals in the schools being acutely aware of learning differences. Students are usually referred by teachers or parents for a multidisciplinary assessment. If a student is identified with LD, the school's multidisciplinary team will design an IEP for the student that typically specifies changes in learning environment, types of supplemental support and services, as well as any test accommodations deemed appropriate.

According to a recent National Center for Education Statistics report (Raue & Lewis, 2011), students with LD are the largest group receiving test accommodations in the schools. Although documented statistics are hard to find, test agencies such as the ACT, College Board, and the Law School Admission Council (LSAC) have indicated that they receive more accommodation requests from students with LD than any other clinical group (U.S. General Accounting Office, 2011). High-stakes tests tend to be heavily reading based and time constrained. Not surprisingly, students with LD generally report having problems because they read slowly, inaccurately, or must reread material to understand it. The vast majority of accommodation requests from these students are for extended time, usually time and one half or double time. Students used to request the use of a computer for writing with spell check, but a growing number of high-stakes tests allow or provide laptop computers for essay portions of their exams. (In K–12 schools, many students with LD still have special word processor accommodations for teacher-made tests and related assignments.) In cases of severe reading and writing disabilities, students may request a reader or a scribe to assist with the exam. If the student's problem is in the area of auditory processing, it might be wise to provide written rather than oral directions and make sure the student knows what is expected on the exam. If a student has visual processing difficulties, it might make sense to consider larger print, avoid bubble-response sheets, and go over test directions orally. Sometimes students will ask for a separate testing room, although there seems to be no clear rationale for this request, and there is no research showing that private room testing improves performance (see Chapter 7). In certain instances, students will have an LD in math and request the use of a calculator or access to certain formulas. This practice is more common in the classroom than on high-stakes tests. Students with more involved reading and writing disabilities may prefer to use assisted technology such as screen reading programs for a computer or voice-recognition programs that turn dictation into written text. It seems that as schools train students to use these technologies, they are being used more often as test accommodations on high-stakes exams.

ATTENTION-DEFICIT/HYPERACTIVITY DISORDER

ADHD, like LD, is considered a high-incidence disorder that occurs in 3% to 7% of children (American Psychiatric Association, 2013; Barkley, 2006b). It is a heterogeneous disorder with three subtypes, or in the *DSM–5*, "presentations": Predominantly Inattentive presentation, Predominantly Hyperactive/Impulsive presentation, and Combined presentation. Also, there are two special categories called Other Specified ADHD and Unspecified ADHD. The former refers to a case in which the individual does not meet full criteria for any of the subtypes yet experiences significant distress or impairment, and the clinician states the reason that the presentation does not meet criteria. The unspecified category is essentially the same case, but the clinician does not specify a reason why the criteria were not met.

ADHD is characterized by a number of enduring and frequently occurring symptoms (e.g., easily distracted, often on the go) that are present before the age of 12 in more than one setting and are causing significant impairment in school, work, or social domains. In addition to the defining criteria, ADHD has been associated with deficits in executive functioning (i.e., Barkley, 1997; Willcutt, Doyle, Nigg, Faraone, & Pennington, 2005) that may underlie problems such as disorganization, poor planning, lack of task persistence, careless errors, and erratic motivation. Theses deficits are thought to account for some of the school and behavior problems observed with ADHD students, such as not completing homework, losing assignments and work products, getting work in late, performing inconsistently, and peer conflicts (DuPaul, 2007).

It should be noted that ADHD is more common in boys (2–4 times more common; Sciutto, Nolfi, & Bluhm, 2004) and frequently coexists with other disorders such as LD, anxiety, oppositional defiant disorder, conduct disorder, and mood disorders (see *DSM–5*, pp. 63–65). The specific cause for ADHD is unknown, but it is believed to be highly heritable, with heritability estimates typically exceeding 0.7. Research also has shown a variety of anomalies in brain structure and activity that implicate the prefrontal lobes among other regions (i.e., cerebellum, cingulated cortex, caudate; Bush, Valera, & Seidman, 2005) and the neurotransmitter dopamine. Medication has been the treatment of choice in approximately 90% of diagnosed cases (Greenhill, Halperin, & Abikoff, 1999), and most (> 65%) have reported some positive response from the medication (Pliszka, 2007), although debate still exists over the reliance on stimulant and nonstimulant drugs and underuse of behavioral interventions (Pelham, Wheeler, & Chronis, 1998). Although medication has been shown to effectively mitigate some symptoms of ADHD, it does not mean that an affected person will be symptom free or functioning normally. Even treated individuals with improved self-control and better focus still can experience impairment in academic, vocational, and social domains, especially if they have a comorbid condition. That is why medication is often supplemented by special education services, therapy/coaching, behavioral interventions, and test accommodations.

There is not much formal research on ADHD and test accommodations. Generally, test accommodations have been apportioned with little empirical support or validity evidence, and accommodations for ADHD are no different. As noted in an earlier chapter, extended time is the most often requested and granted test accommodation regardless of the person's diagnosis. This is also true for ADHD. There is an assumption that people with ADHD are slower to process information, an assumption that has some empirical support, although not always consistent or robust. For example, Mayes and Calhoun (2007) found a difference between children with ADHD and controls on the Symbol Search subtest of the Wechsler Intelligence Scale for Children (WISC–III and WISC–IV; Wechsler, 2003), suggesting a difference in processing speed. Similarly, Lewandowski, Lovett, Parolin, Gordon, and Codding (2007) found significantly lower performance for middle school students with ADHD versus peers on the Processing Speed index of the WISC–IV and also on a timed math fluency task.

Alternatively, Piek, Dyck, Francis, and Conwell (2007) found no differences between children with and without ADHD in processing speed. Yet, Shanahan et al. (2006) found that both children with ADHD and Reading Disability demonstrated processing speed deficiency, and that this cognitive weakness might be a shared risk factor. There appears to be no definitive word on the processing speed characteristics of students with ADHD. Studies differ in how groups are defined and how to measure processing speed, probably leading to the inconsistency in findings. Despite the lack of confirmatory research, there is a belief among individuals with ADHD (as well as their clinicians) that they have difficulty getting things done in a timely manner, including exams. This may apply to some students with ADHD much more than to others; research has identified a subgroup of students with ADHD-Inattentive Type who present with a "sluggish cognitive tempo" (Carlson & Mann, 2002;

McBurnett, Pfiffner, & Frick, 2001), and these students may genuinely require additional time.

A common complaint of those applying for extended time is that symptoms such as distractibility and lack of concentration cause an individual with ADHD to "lose time" on a test and then fail to finish an exam or rush through it. Interestingly, research by Lewandowski and colleagues has shown that students with ADHD tend to access as many test items as their peers in a standard amount of time, although they may make more errors on certain tasks. For example, Lewandowski, Hendricks, and Gordon (2012) found that high school students with and without ADHD performed similarly on a test of reading speed and answered essentially the same number of questions on a time-constrained reading comprehension test. Lewandowski, Gathje, Lovett, and Gordon (2013) found the same results on the same reading measures in a sample of college students with and without ADHD. Miller, Lewandowski, and Antshel (in press) compared college students with and without ADHD on the Nelson-Denny Reading Comprehension Test (J. I. Brown, Fishco, & Hanna, 1993) and found no differences between groups in the number of items attempted or correct. Studies such as these suggest that even if there are small processing or motor speed (e.g., slower reaction time) weaknesses within the ADHD population, or brief lapses in concentration during a test, these subtle weaknesses may not result in significant slowing on timed academic tests. In other words, students with ADHD may not be significantly impaired in the speed with which they perform academic tasks. Again, it may be that a subgroup of these students has unusual extended time needs, underscoring the importance of individualized assessment when making accommodation decisions.

As noted previously, Miller et al. (in press) found that college students with an ADHD diagnosis who were receiving test accommodations at school performed just as accurately and fast as peers on the Nelson-Denny Reading Comprehension Test. They also were interested in what would happen when the ADHD students were given their usual accommodation of 50% more time. In this condition, students with ADHD performed much better than peers given no extra time; when given double time (100% extra) they answered 103% more items than peers given only standard time. So although it may seem that students with ADHD process some information more slowly on some tasks (e.g., reaction time tasks), they may not perform significantly slower on timed academic tests (e.g., reading comprehension) and may not need extended time, especially double time. In fact, these recent findings beg the question of whether extended time is even a valid test accommodation for college students with ADHD. Of course, as noted earlier, the accommodation decision should be made on an individual basis.

Another recent study of college students with and without ADHD examined the effects of extended time on a math test (Wadley & Liljequist, 2013).

The study design was different from the one in the Miller et al. (in press) study, in that students were told they were getting standard or extended time (double), but actually everyone received the same 45 minutes to complete the test. Results showed that in general students with ADHD attained lower scores than peers, took more time, and had lower self-esteem scores. However, there was no effect for "extended" time in either group. In fact, the ADHD group performed a bit worse in the extended time than standard condition. Apparently, neither actually getting nor believing oneself to be getting extended time may be a necessary or valid accommodation for college students with ADHD.

Other test accommodations that make sense for ADHD and have less impact on altering the actual test include a separate room and extra breaks. Admittedly, there is no research to suggest that either of these accommodations is helpful or valid, but a logical case can be made for each. Extra breaks make sense if a person has difficulty staying on task for long periods of time, certainly a characteristic associated with ADHD. There are numerous tests and an extensive literature in the ADHD field on continuous performance tests and their use in assessing ADHD. Tests like the Gordon Diagnostic System (Gordon, 1991) or the Conners Continuous Performance Test II (Conners & Multi-Health Systems Staff, 2000) examine functions such as sustained attention, vigilance, impulsivity, and inhibition. These tests have proven to be sensitive to ADHD, suggesting that various attention and executive functions are deficient. Because issues of attention, distractibility, and lack of concentration are so central to ADHD (see Barkley, Murphy, & Fischer, 2010), most clinicians and educators rather instinctively arrange testing situations to minimize distractions. A separate room has become a commonly recommended and requested accommodation for those with ADHD.

A separate room may make sense if it actually reduces distractions and allows the student to concentrate better. Unfortunately, no study has actually compared test settings for students with ADHD. In a recent study of typical college students taking tests in a group or private room, Wood, Lewandowski, and Lambert (2012) found better performance in the group-testing situation ($d = 0.53$). It seems plausible that there is a social facilitation effect on test performance in a group that is not present in a private test situation (Guerin & Innes, 2009). Whether this effect is the same or different for persons with ADHD is a question that awaits future research.

Another test accommodation that makes sense logically for ADHD test takers is extra breaks. On the basis of the behavioral and executive function characteristics of this group as noted earlier, one can imagine that sustained attention, vigilant concentration, and ongoing use of working memory will present challenges to individuals with ADHD. They describe sustained mental activities as very effortful and tiring. To break this cycle and allow someone with ADHD time to "recharge their batteries," extra breaks are sometimes requested and given during lengthy tests. There is no research that examines the validity and efficacy of extra breaks on the test-taking performance of students with and without ADHD, or any disability for that matter. There is some limited research on testing over multiple days that suggests no benefit for students with or without disabilities (Walz, Albus, Thompson, & Bolt, 2000). In fact, E. Burns (1998) cautioned that breaks within a test may distract and disrupt the natural problem-solving rhythm a student has developed. With regard to one's rhythm in taking a test, K. S. Lee, Osborne, Hayes, and Simoes (2008) studied the effects of self-pacing versus computer pacing on the test performance of 21 college students with ADHD. They tested all students on a computer, with half the students randomly assigned to a self-paced condition and half to a condition in which the computer presented items at a fixed pace. They found no difference between the conditions, but noted that the computer pacing made some students more anxious. In general, students liked the computer-testing environment, and they preferred an isolated and quiet setting. It should be noted that this is one small study, and the preference information was based on qualitative responses to open-ended questions.

In addition to the accommodations discussed previously, other accommodations that could apply to ADHD, especially in a classroom setting, are preferred seating, earplugs or headphones, and assistive technology. These accommodations presumably could help reduce distractions and improve task focus. No research exists on whether test performance is improved when such accommodations are used. Assistive technology for reading and writing can be useful if the students also have LD or their ADHD symptoms interfere significantly with reading or writing performance (see reviews by DuPaul, 2007; Frazier, Youngstrom, Glutting, & Watkins, 2007). Rather than offer students with ADHD a menu of accommodations they might prefer, it seems wise to assess their domains of impairment that substantially restrict access to an exam. Accommodations then can be targeted to mitigate any restrictions from specific impairment(s).

EMOTIONAL DISABILITIES

There are many emotional disorders listed in *DSM–5*, but only a handful of disorders seem to generate a significant number of accommodation requests. Of this category, anxiety disorders probably account for the greatest number of requests. Exams make some people anxious and worried about not achieving their academic and vocational goals. Many people view exams as obstacles in their path toward advancement. This can evoke the fear that a goal will be thwarted. Many people, even those without disorders, will report worry and nervousness before and during a high-stakes exam. Some individuals develop such bad performance anxiety that they avoid exams or become physically ill when forced to take one. This has been referred to as *test anxiety*, although there is currently no *DSM* disorder by this name.

Test anxiety can be defined as physiological, psychological, or behavioral outcomes resulting from concern over failure on an exam or evaluative situation (Zeidner, 1998). For years, researchers have considered two components of test anxiety: affective (*emotionality*) and cognitive (*worry*; Liebert & Morris, 1967). Essentially, an evaluative situation arouses physiological symptoms (e.g., heart racing, excessive sweating), referred to as the emotionality component. The physiological symptoms then activate worry cognitions stored in memory and interfere with the test-anxious individual's performance on an exam. The worry or cognitive component consists of negative self-talk and negative cognitions individuals experience when taking examinations (Sena, Lowe, & Lee, 2007). For example, the test-anxious student may not be afraid of the test or exam, or even poor grades, but what the test or the failure outcome may potentially represent for future threats and challenges (Hagtvet, Man, & Sharma, 2001). The worry–achievement component has been shown to have a larger negative effect on academic achievement (Sena et al., 2007; Sud & Prabha, 2003). Additionally, research has shown that small amounts of anxiety act as a motivator that can enhance performance by encouraging students to put forth more effort. On the other hand, too much anxiety can disrupt mental processes that are needed to perform well (Wachelka & Katz, 1999).

High test anxiety has been associated with low self-esteem, poor reading and math achievement, failing grades, disruptive classroom behavior, negative attitudes toward school, and unpleasant feelings of nervousness and dread that stem from an intense fear of failure (Swanson & Howell, 1996). Additionally, test-taking skills and GPAs of highly anxious students are often poor and suggest that test anxiety is synonymous or correlated with ineffective test taking (Swanson & Howell, 1996). In a meta-analysis, Hembree (1988) reviewed over 500 studies, finding that higher test anxiety was consistently associated with lower performance on tests, as well as with students' GPAs and standardized achievement test scores ($d = 0.52$). It is difficult to conclude whether anxious students perform worse because of their anxiety or if doing more poorly on tests heightens an individual's anxiety regarding performance.

Typically, individuals with anxiety disorders request extended time so as to relieve stress and worry, as well as to compensate for time lost while engaged in task-irrelevant cognitions. Again, proving that one needs more time to make up for lost time is not as straightforward as documenting a reading fluency deficit. In addition to extended time, those with anxiety disorders often ask for a separate test room. Not only might a separate room reduce anxiety, it also might prevent disruptions to other examinees, especially if the anxiety eventuates in a panic attack or unusual behaviors (e.g., compulsive movements, sounds) that might cause distractions. In some cases, giving such a person a separate room may be better for all examinees. Despite the inherent logic in these arguments, questions surface as to whether test anxiety is an actual disorder and also whether it should warrant test accommodations. The *DSM* has never recognized test anxiety as a distinct disorder, and among the various types of anxiety disorders listed in *DSM–5*, perhaps *specific phobia* comes the closest to explaining test anxiety. One could argue that a test takes on the properties of a phobic object and becomes a stimulus that engenders various anxiety symptoms, possibly leading to a panic attack. If a mental health professional can provide evidence of this scenario, the test anxious/phobic individual may have an argument to support a test accommodation request. Short of such documentation, just saying one gets quite anxious in an exam is not likely to sway decision makers.

Another psychiatric disorder that sometimes triggers test accommodation considerations is depression. Requests from those with diagnoses of major depression or chronic depression such as dysthymia also tend to specify a need for more time. The logic is that depression, and/or the medication used to treat it, could reduce processing speed. There is a very diverse literature that shows depression in old age, schizophrenia, and multiple sclerosis, for example, reduce processing speed (e.g., Salthouse, 1996). Another rationale for extended time is that it is difficult to maintain attention and concentration because of the effects of depression. In cases of bipolar depression, ADHD is often a comorbid condition, which strengthens the argument for extended time. It should be noted that accommodations for psychiatric disorders are not based on research showing their validity or effectiveness, but rather determined rationally as a matter of advocacy.

AUTISM SPECTRUM DISORDER

We will not go through the entire *DSM–5* list of disorders, but we do want to include autism spectrum disorder (ASD) in this discussion. Autism is considered to be a spectrum of disorders that consists of Asperger syndrome, high- to low-functioning autism, and pervasive developmental disorder. It has become recognized as a spectrum disorder with increasing prevalence, recently with a rate of one per 88 children (Centers for Disease Control and Prevention, 2012). This spectrum disorder is considered to be quite heterogeneous, yet generally characterized by impairment in social interaction, atypical and repetitive behavior patterns, and underdeveloped or unusual verbal and nonverbal communication. Because the function level and style of these students is so wide ranging, there is no simple treatment, educational modification, or test accommodation suitable for everyone.

Many students with autism cannot and will not be tested in a standard fashion, so a regular education curriculum, statewide tests, and college admission tests are out of the question. For those students with high-functioning autism, or what used to be termed Asperger syndrome, there is a potential role for test accommodations. Students with autism, by definition, lack certain communication and social skills. Occasionally, certain forms of tests may not be suited to their individual characteristics. In some cases students use adaptations like communication boards, screen reading devices, and pointing systems for responding, all part of new computer technologies that did not even exist when the Rehabilitation Act of 1973 was conceived. In addition to technological accommodations, many of these students may benefit from a one-on-one proctor to reliably conduct the assessment. For this reason and also the social difficulties of these students, important tests are best given in a private room with only the proctor/examiner present. Extra breaks may be necessary to avoid frustration and quitting. Even tangible positive reinforcement may be necessary to encourage a student to complete a test session.

A more difficult issue is raised by the "familiar examiner" or "familiar proctor" accommodation. Some students with ASD will perform significantly better on tests when they have prior experience with the person administering the test (e.g., Szarko, Brown, & Watkins, 2013). However, this accommodation can be difficult to implement because during high-stakes K–12 exams, students often take exams in many different rooms with whatever staff are available to serve as proctors. In postsecondary and admissions settings, the accommodation may be impossible to implement for obvious reasons, and so students with ASD who will be testing in such settings should receive psychological interventions that will help them to adjust to standard testing conditions.

The most comprehensive data on accommodation use in this population comes from the National Longitudinal Transition Study–2 (NLTS-2), Wave 1 student's school program survey, conducted in 2002. Table 4.1 is taken directly from the longitudinal study of secondary students with disabilities. As noted in these statistics, test accommodations are common for this group of students, and extended time once again is the most common.

A SPECIAL ISSUE: THE PROBLEM OF MALINGERING

In this chapter, we attempted to outline certain issues that must be considered in making test accommodation decisions, as well as address some of the different types of accommodation requests that have been linked with

TABLE 4.1

Accommodations and Modifications Provided to Students With Autism

Accommodation	Percent provided
Any type of accommodation or support	91
Additional time to complete assignments	52
More time in taking tests	52
Alternative tests or assessments	49
Slower paced instruction	41
Shorter or different assignments	38
Modified tests	33
Modified grading standards	30
Tests read to student	25
Modifications to physical aspects of the classroom	16

Note. Students may receive more than one kind of accommodation, support, or learning aid. Data from the U.S. Department of Education, Institute of Education Sciences, National Center for Special Education Research (2002).

certain disabilities. One issue that has not been addressed thus far is that of malingering. According to the *DSM–5*, *malingering* (V65.2) is defined as "the intentional production of false or grossly exaggerated physical or psychological symptoms, motivated by external incentives such as avoiding military duty, avoiding work, obtaining financial compensation, evading criminal prosecution, or obtaining drugs" (American Psychiatric Association, 2013, p. 726).[4] A surprising variety of situations will increase the chance of malingering. For example, professional athletes (e.g., football players) will even go as far as performing poorly on a baseline concussion test, so if tested after a concussion, there would be no difference in their test scores. So it appears that some people will fabricate, exaggerate, or deny symptoms depending on the outcome that they are seeking. Admittedly, this is generally more of an issue with adult clients, but a growing literature (currently small) shows malingering in pediatric cases as well (e.g., Kirkwood, Kirk, Blaha, & Wilson, 2010; Walker, 2011).

Whereas in most cases, disability status and type of impairment are well documented and accommodations are readily provided, there are cases of questionable diagnoses, marginal impairment, possible faking, and low effort. One such case study was the subject of a book by Gordon (2009), titled *ADHD on Trial: Courtroom Clashes Over the Meaning of Disability*. The case featured a college student requesting accommodations for the Law School Admission Test (LSAT), who along with his mother presented certain

---

[4]Of course, as this definition shows, *malingering* doesn't quite capture the more general phenomenon of putting forth suboptimal effort when being evaluated for eligibility for testing accommodations. Outright malingering is likely far less common than simply not trying one's best during diagnostic evaluations.

mistruths (e.g., claims of taking medication that never happened) and misdirection (e.g., a letter from an employer supporting symptoms of ADHD that turned out to be written by the student's mother) in his application. The book chronicles the discovery of facts by the LSAC lawyers and experts, including Dr. Michael Gordon, a psychologist, as well as the manner in which truth emerged during the trial. Needless to say, the judge ruled in favor of the LSAC. Part of the irony in this case was that the student already had taken the LSAT under standard conditions and performed reasonably well. In fact, he was admitted into law schools before the case went to trial. The waste of time and money, not to mention the ultimate embarrassment, were apparent casualties of an attempt to get a better LSAT score so as to get into a better law school. Having a powerful incentive, so it appears, can cause a person to deceive or "fake bad" to seem disabled and impaired.

No area is more accustomed to malingering than neuropsychological assessment, particularly applied to patients with suspected TBI. Mittenberg, Patton, Canyock, and Condit (2002) reported data on malingering as estimated by the American Board of Clinical Neuropsychologists: mild TBI 39%, disability cases 30%, and personal injury cases 29%. Larrabee (2000) also estimated that 30% to 40% of accident victims with mild TBI exaggerate neuropsychological deficits. For example, a person with a head injury from a car or work accident could be in line for a large sum of money if a professional evaluator can attest to brain injury and impairment in functioning. This scenario might influence the examinee to purposely perform poorly on a test battery or reduce effort in some way, perhaps even unconsciously. In response to the possibility of malingering during assessment, Green and colleagues (Green, 2007; Green, Flaro, & Courtney, 2009; Green, Iverson, & Allen, 1999; Green, Rohling, Lees-Haley, & Allen, 2001) have developed simple "effort" tests that can be passed by young children, as well as by individuals with significant brain injury and intellectual disability. Effort testing is becoming a standard component of neuropsychological assessment, and it seems that money is not the only incentive for faking.

Spenceley (2012) used an analog procedure and had college students simulate the characteristics of having a mild head injury. She then randomly assigned students to incentive conditions. One group was told to perform in such a way as to justify test accommodations for their brain injury (fake bad), another group was told to pretend that they were Division I athletes that wanted to return to play after sustaining a concussion (fake good), and the no-incentive group just simulated having a concussion. Only 3% of the fake-good group failed effort testing, whereas 64% of the fake-bad group (motivated by test accommodations) failed effort testing. Interestingly, even 45% of the no-incentive group, just simulating a concussion, failed effort testing. The data from these studies suggest that malingering is relatively common and easy to orchestrate. Consequently, even in this book on test accommodations, we need to bring up the possibility that people could be putting in suboptimal effort when they are evaluated for a disorder. If most accommodation requests are for extended time, and most reasons are due to slow reading, how hard would it be to read slowly on timed tests of reading and receive a poor test score?[5] Hence the concern for faking and the growing interest in effort testing in all diagnostic assessments (Harrison, Green, & Flaro, 2012).

It appears that neuropsychological settings are not the only place to find feigning and exaggeration during assessment. B. K. Sullivan, May, and Galbally (2007) found that 47.6% of college students evaluated for ADHD and 15.4% of those tested for LD failed the Word Memory Test (Green, 2003). Suhr, Hammers, Dobbins-Buckland, Zimak, and Hughes (2008) also examined effort failure in college students assessed for possible ADHD. They found that 31% of their sample gave noncredible responses (i.e., failed) on the Word Memory Test.

As noted earlier, the diagnosis of ADHD is sometimes based heavily on self-report of symptoms. Various studies have shown that it is easy to fake symptoms of ADHD in such a way that faking is undetectable. For example, Quinn (2003) found that college students could easily fake ADHD symptoms both currently and retrospectively. Further, Jachimowicz and Geiselman (2004) had college students complete various ADHD checklists after reading over the DSM–IV diagnostic criteria for ADHD. When asked to feign these symptoms, the majority of students (75%–90%, depending on the measure) reached criteria for the ADHD diagnosis. Similar success rates were found by Harrison, Edwards, and Parker (2008), who asked college students to perform as if they had a reading disorder. Most of the nondisabled feigning students (70%–90%) scored lower than students with actual reading disabilities on measures of reading and information processing.

The assessment landscape has been so rocked by such findings that effort testing is becoming recommended practice in clinical assessment, especially when a particular outcome is a goal of that assessment (e.g., test accommodations). Clearly, it makes sense for clinicians who evaluate applicants for test accommodations to administer symptom validity and effort tests. Because malingering is so common and feigning is easy to do, it seems like good practice to assess this possibility in every examinee.

---

[5]Indeed, research has shown that slow test taking is a common malingering strategy, and Lovett (2007) found that students asked to simulate having a learning disability obtained much lower scores on measures of processing speed and reading fluency.

5

TIMING AND SCHEDULING ACCOMMODATIONS

Testing heightens the experience of time in a variety of ways. Many readers will recall their teachers handing out an exam and admonishing, "Take your time; it's not a race!" Some readers will recall waiting on their classmates to finish an exam; other readers will remember being the one on whom classmates were waiting. And most of us can recall feeling time pressure when taking admissions tests such as the SAT and GRE and perhaps on some classroom exams in high school and college (the command "Pencils down!" may still inspire a conditioned response of fear in some readers). Students with disabilities may feel time-related frustrations during testing more keenly, and in this chapter we discuss alterations to the temporal aspects of tests: how much time is allotted, when testing is conducted, and related characteristics. These are among the most commonly proffered accommodations, and many postsecondary examinees only receive this kind of accommodation.

http://dx.doi.org/10.1037/14468-005
Testing Accommodations for Students With Disabilities: Research-Based Practice, by B. J. Lovett and L. J. Lewandowski

IMPLEMENTATION OF TIMING
AND SCHEDULING ACCOMMODATIONS

Extended Testing Time

By far the most common testing accommodation is giving students additional time to take a test (e.g., Lazarus, Thompson, & Thurlow, 2006). In part, this commonness is due to other accommodations (e.g., read-aloud, scribe) that require extended time to be properly implemented. The amount of additional time varies, although the two most common allotments are 50% and 100% additional time ("time and one half," and "double time"), so if the standard time allotment for an exam is one hour, an examinee with a disability might be given 90 minutes or 120 minutes, whereas other examinees are given 60 minutes.[1] Unlimited time ("untimed testing") is less common, and it is very rarely seen on standardized exams, if only because of the logistical difficulties of engaging proctors for unspecified amounts of time. On certain high-stakes exams, 25% additional time is seen (e.g., on the Medical College Admission Test), although this allotment appears to be rare in classroom settings.

Extended time does not usually require additional accommodations to be implemented, with the possible exception of a separate location (e.g., if students in a class are beginning other teacher-led activities immediately after the exam). Otherwise, the test administration conditions can and should be identical to those of other students, unless additional accommodations are determined to be appropriate and are deliberately provided.

Time-Management Aids

Time-management aids include a variety of accommodations that help students to use their time wisely when taking an exam (E. Burns, 1998). One management aid is *time cues*—a teacher or other proctor is present to remind the student how much time has passed and how much is remaining, or else an electronic timer is used for this purpose. A more intensive aid is *item pacing*, in which the total testing time is divided into discrete units of time and students are given a small amount of time to complete each test item before the item is removed and the next item is presented. Computer-aided test delivery makes item pacing easy to implement, and many computer-testing problems will also record the time that a student takes to answer each item.

---

[1]We should note that 50% and 100% extensions are common in the United States, but not necessarily elsewhere. In the United Kingdom, for instance, our experience is that extensions of 10% and 25% are common, a surprising difference from the United States. We have no reason to think that exams are less speeded in other countries, but the variability in time allotments suggests their arbitrary and culture-bound nature.

Time-management aids are more commonly given as accommodations on classroom exams than high-stakes exams. However, high-stakes exams that are delivered via computer (e.g., the GRE) often feature a timer counting down the remaining time in each test section; the timer is available to all examinees rather than just those with disabilities.

Scheduling Accommodations

Scheduling accommodations simply alter the time at which a test is administered; these accommodations might specify a time of the day or a day of the week for tests. A special form of scheduling accommodation involves giving breaks during test administration. In cases of lengthy exams, these breaks may involve multiday testing schedules; for instance on high-stakes licensure or certification exams, the standard test administration time may run from 4 to 8 hours, and so frequent or lengthy breaks would extend the total time well beyond a typical workday, unless multiday schedules were used. On the other hand, many state achievement tests require that tests be given in a single day, and so test administrators and proctors should check to ensure that multiday scheduling is allowed, if this kind of accommodation is being considered.

Note on Test Security

When administering timing and scheduling accommodations, it is important to consider potential breaches of test security. If an exam is being given across multiple days, or additional, unsupervised breaks are being given, the exam should generally be broken into sections to ensure that examinees cannot continue to work on items outside of the exam situation (especially when they will have access to materials that would allow them to cheat). Most lengthy exams (e.g., state achievement tests, college admissions tests) are already naturally in sections, and students should not be given unsupervised breaks (including ending the test for the day) while still working in a single section.

FACTORS AFFECTING ACCOMMODATION RELEVANCE

Test Characteristics

Test Speededness

Some tests have standard time limits that are generous, allowing most or all examinees to finish at a leisurely pace; other tests have severe time limits that force most examinees to work faster than they otherwise would.

These tests differ in their *speededness*, or the degree to which test-taking speed affects performance on the test. Psychometricians place tests on a spectrum ranging from pure speed tests, in which the items are easy to answer but too numerous to solve in the allotted time, and pure power tests, in which the time allotment is sufficiently generous that additional time will be of no help (Nunnally, 1978). In pure speed tests, variability in examinees' scores is attributable solely to differences in their speed; in pure power tests, score variability is solely due to differences in knowledge or skills apart from speed.

Pure speed tests are rare, except when cognitive speed is deliberately being measured or when a speeded skill is of importance (for instance, on a typing test). Interestingly, pure power tests are also quite rare; most tests have some kind of time limit. This is often an administrative necessity—in elementary school classrooms, tests are delivered between periods of instruction by the same teacher; in high school and college classrooms, an instructor has a relatively short period of time in which to deliver an assessment; and on standardized exams taken at testing centers or other special locations, proctors cannot be kept waiting indefinitely for examinees to finish a test.

Therefore, most tests are *timed power tests*, which are designed to measure knowledge or skills distinct from speed, but we also apply a time limit to the test administration. This allows at least some speededness to creep in to test scores, and psychometricians have characterized this speededness as potentially problematic (e.g., Lu & Sireci, 2007). Certainly, if speed is not a skill of interest, speededness can lead to construct-irrelevant variance in examinees' scores (see Chapter 3). Moreover, it is often assumed that tests are more highly speeded for students with disabilities—that is, the test scores of students with disabilities are more affected by time limits. Finally, extended-time accommodations are based on perceptions of speededness (at least for a particular examinee), and the degree of perceived speededness is often related to the amount of additional time being considered. We discuss research on these and other issues later in the chapter.

Test Length

Test speededness is intimately bound up with *test length*—the number and complexity of items on the test. Whereas speeded tests suggest that extended time may be beneficial, lengthy tests may make time-management aids and scheduling adjustments beneficial as well. Test length, and by extension test speededness, are mostly under the control of test developers, and decisions about time limits and number of test items can seem arbitrary. Indeed, many classroom teachers (including—perhaps especially—college professors) have little training in determining how long a test should be and how much time should be allotted for it, and instructors rarely pilot test assessment tools for length before using them in classroom settings. In contrast, high-stakes tests, which are designed with input from psychometric experts, usually have length and time limits that were carefully considered or even empirically examined. Even so, these standardized tests are not designed to ensure that a test is not speeded at all; instead, a common guideline is that a test is not substantially speeded if 80% of the examinees are able to complete the entire test and all of the examinees are able to complete 75% of the test (this is "Swineford's rule"; see, e.g., Rindler, 1979). Thus, at least some speededness is to be expected on almost all tests, even professionally designed high-stakes tests. A further implication is that a student's inability to complete a high-stakes test within the standard time allotment is not, by itself, proof of a disability condition; it is not even unexpected.

The appropriateness of timing and scheduling accommodations hinges in large part on the appropriateness of test speededness and (long) test length. Later in this chapter, we discuss research on the effects of altering speededness and length for all examinees. For now, we merely note that if speededness and (long) length are important elements of a test's interpretation (e.g., if a large number of items are needed to sample the content domain or if the examinee's speed of responding to items is relevant), timing and scheduling accommodations must be provided with great caution; if, on the other hand, speededness and length are accidental features of the test's design, timing and scheduling accommodations may be of little threat to validity and may increase validity for certain examinees.

Examinee Characteristics

Processing Speed

Like electronic computers, the human mind processes information, and mental tests require efficient and appropriate information processing. Also like electronic computers, minds vary in their processing speed. Schneider and McGrew (2012) defined *processing speed* as "the ability to perform simple, repetitive cognitive tasks quickly and fluently" (p. 119; see Schneider & McGrew for more on the complexity of classifying speed-related abilities). At the operational level, cognitive ability tests measure processing speed intentionally through simple visual–motor tasks; for instance, on the Wechsler intelligence tests, the Symbol Search subtest asks examinees to determine if either of two target symbols is present in a row of symbols and to indicate this by marking "yes" or "no."

At least in theory, examinees' processing speed will affect their speed of completing a test and thus the chance that they will need additional time beyond some time limit to complete a test. Indeed, one of the narrower abilities under processing speed, found in factor analyses of cognitive tasks, has been named *rate of test-taking* (Carroll, 1993; Schneider & McGrew, 2012). However, in practice, the usefulness of clinical tests of processing speed in predicting completion of a particular achievement test is limited by several factors. First, abilities other than processing speed affect performance on clinical measures that are designated "processing speed" tests. Second, one's speed of information processing changes according to the type of information being processed, and achievement tests vary widely in the tasks required of examinees (and thus the type of information to be processed). Finally, achievement tests may be more likely or less likely to motivate or engage students than the processing speed tests did. Therefore, we should not be surprised by the modest relationships found empirically between processing speed tests and the chance of completing a test under standard time limits (e.g., Ofiesh, Mather, & Russell, 2005). Given these modest relationships, deficits in processing speed are insufficient evidence to warrant extended-time accommodations in the presence of average or above average academic fluency.

Academic Skill Fluency

More closely related to achievement test completion than processing speed is fluency in basic academic skills. For instance, reading fluency has been defined as involving "*accurate* and *automatic* word recognition, with appropriate *prosody* or inflection" (McKenna & Stahl, 2003, p. 72, emphasis in original). As the mention of prosody suggests, reading fluency is often measured through oral reading. As school psychologists and special educators know well, fluency is a major focus in measures that are used in many response-to-intervention (RTI) models of monitoring academic skill development. Students complete brief, timed probes measuring skills that they have been exposed to during instruction and often the exact materials are derived from school curricula (curriculum-based assessment; Shapiro, 2010). In addition to measuring students' oral reading fluency, there are curriculum-based assessment probes measuring fluency in mathematical calculation, spelling dictated words, and even composing brief stories in response to standardized prompts. Increasingly, standardized diagnostic achievement tests—for example, the Wechsler Individual Achievement Test III (Pearson, 2009) and the Woodcock-Johnson III Tests of Achievement (WJ-III; Woodcock, McGrew, & Mather, 2001)—have incorporated fluency tasks that measure speed as well as accuracy of performing academic skills.

Studies that measure both processing speed and academic skill fluency (Lovett, 2007; Ofiesh, Mather, & Russell, 2005) have found that the latter is more related to scores on timed academic tests. This is to be expected because at least some of the time devoted to taking a test involves performing the same academic skills (especially reading) that are represented on academic fluency tasks. Many students are provided extended-time accommodations because of deficits in reading fluency and related skills. However, this provision not only assumes that fluency deficits will affect test completion, but that examinees' test scores should not reflect their task fluency. This latter assumption is problematic, especially because in the past decade, fluency has become a primary outcome measure in academic interventions and a sign of early trouble in academic skill development. In addition to voluminous research showing that early oral reading fluency predicts later general reading achievement (e.g., Y. S. Kim, Petscher, Schatschneider, & Foorman, 2010; Schilling, Carlisle, Scott, & Zeng, 2007), research has also supported the idea that speed in work is often accompanied by qualitative differences in performance. Kubina and Morrison (2000) distinguished between fluent and merely accurate performance by comparing two hypothetical students:

> Student one reads 40 words per minute with no errors. Student two reads 120 words per minute also without error. Both achieve 100% accuracy, but the first reader's performance may sound hesitant, slow and labored while the second reader sounds quick, flowing and automatic. Applying frequency [i.e., fluency] measures to a wide variety of behaviors and skills facilitates the congruence of subjective descriptions of poor, good, and excellent performances with the quantitative precision afforded by a standard unit. (p. 87)

Martens and Witt (2004) argued that fluency is a stepping stone toward even more important instructional outcomes, such as retention of skills over time; the ability to apply academic skills to new situations; and the development, as needed, of related academic skills that are not directly taught (e.g., high-level reading comprehension skills; Yovanoff, Duesbery, Alonzo, & Tindal, 2005). In sum, then, academic skill fluency is related to the ability to complete tests under timed conditions, but its reach is far broader with regard to academic success, and so especially in younger students, it may be important to measure as part of academic competence.

Attention and Motivation

Examinees' speed at completing tests—or anything else—is influenced heavily by attentional and motivational factors. Examinees who are distracted will be slower in completing even simple tasks (Lustig, Hasher, & Tonev, 2006), and those who are not motivated to do well on an exam may not put forth much effort to work as quickly as possible through test items. Test instructions and other situational factors under the control of test administrators can affect motivation, and to some degree attention as well, but these charac-teristics will still vary across examinees, contributing to variance in scores and perhaps especially so on speeded tests. Motivation in particular is an important factor to consider, given that in many K–12 settings, high-stakes tests do not actually have high stakes for individual examinees. For instance, the state assessments used as part of accountability systems may have large consequences for schools (and more recently, for individual teachers), but scores on these tests often do not affect students' grades, and so students' motivation to perform well on these tests is largely based on their general personality traits, such as compliance, conscientiousness, and agreeableness.

Problems deploying attentional and motivational resources may also lead to a student using time-management aids. For instance, students with attention-deficit/hyperactivity disorder (ADHD) may not be slow in their task speed itself, but they may benefit from reminders emphasizing how much time is left, or other cues to stay on task.[2] Similarly, students who are generally unmotivated (perhaps because of an emotional or behavioral concern) may benefit from a pacing accommodation in which only a single item is presented at a time, rather than having to face a lengthy set of items.

As always, the question is raised of whether attention and/or motiva-tion is part of the construct to be measured by a test. Generally the answer is no, although in certain postsecondary settings, it may be assumed that examinees have sufficient attention and motivation to perform tasks that are like those on examinations, and in these settings, it is difficult to separate attention and motivation from the skills that the test is designed to mea-sure. For instance, on Step 3 (the final part) of the United States Medical Licensure Examination, examinees respond to standardized medical patients' cases through a computer program, ordering diagnostic tests and treatments, etc. Although this test is not explicitly described as measuring attention and motivation, it may be inappropriate to provide pacing accommodations (or even extended time) if the test scores are to be interpreted as indexing how the examinee will perform in a real-life setting where those accommoda-tions will not be present.

Stamina

Finally, students who have emotional or health-related conditions may lack the stamina to take a test without scheduling or other accommoda-tions. For instance, a high school student whose health condition causes her to become substantially more fatigued throughout the day may receive an

---

[2]This is another potential focus for interventions, of course; students with attention problems can benefit from self-monitoring interventions that make them aware of their deficits in attention and work productivity (e.g., K. R. Harris, Friedlander, Saddler, Frizzelle, & Graham, 2005).

accommodation allowing her to take exams in the morning, during the first or second period of her high school's class schedule. Similarly, a prospective graduate student whose health condition causes intense discomfort while sitting for lengthy periods of time may be permitted to take breaks during an exam to walk around. We offer only one caution with regard to stamina-based accommodation rationales: Empirical research has found that the mental experience of fatigue during tests is more strongly related to personality traits than to objective indices of stamina, and subjective mental fatigue alone does not appear to result in significant decrements in test performance (Ackerman & Kanfer, 2009). Therefore, although accommodations given when an examinee reports fatigue may decrease the examinee's discomfort, a score obtained under standard testing conditions may not actually result in inappropriate inferences about the examinee's skills.

RESEARCH ON TIMING AND SCHEDULING ACCOMMODATIONS

Extended time is perhaps the most researched accommodation, whereas very little research has been done on any other timing and scheduling accommodations. Therefore, our discussion of research in this chapter focuses on extended-time accommodations. However, we review research on other accommodations where it is available,[3] and we apply research from extended time to other accommodation situations where it is possible.

Efficacy of Accommodations

With any accommodation, we might begin by asking whether it has any effect on scores of students who are eligible for the accommodation. With regard to timing and scheduling accommodations, we can summarize the literature thus:

- We have a large literature showing that students with learning disabilities and related high-incidence disabilities tend to benefit from extended time, as do nondisabled students (Lovett, 2010; Sireci, Scarpati, & Li, 2005).
- We do not have sufficient research literature available to conclude whether students benefit from extended time on typical classroom exams in K–12 or higher education.

---

[3]We discuss most of the research on time-management accommodations in more detail in Chapter 7 because many of these accommodations are really more presentation accommodations, and they are often included with other alterations to the presentation of exams (e.g., oral administration).

- We have essentially no research on the efficacy of extra/extended breaks during an exam, despite the common nature of this accommodation, and its strong theoretical rationale.
- We have limited research on multiple-day scheduling accommodations and time-management aids, but the limited research has not shown them to generally improve scores of students with disabilities (Walz, Albus, Thompson, & Thurlow, 2000).

Score Comparability

As we discussed in Chapter 3, there are three primary methods for investigating the effects of accommodations on the statistical interpretation of test scores. The first such method involves testing the predictive validity of test scores obtained with and without accommodations. Many tests are either designed to predict some outcome or else their validity can at least be indexed by their ability to predict some outcome; if test accommodations lead to more accurate test scores, then the scores of students with disabilities who receive accommodations should predict outcomes better than the scores obtained by these students without accommodations.

Research studies have examined this issue somewhat indirectly by comparing the predictive validity of scores of students with disabilities obtained under accommodations to the predictive validity of scores of nondisabled students obtained without accommodations. For instance, Cahalan, Mandinach, and Camara (2002) examined the predictive validity of SAT scores of students with learning disabilities who received extended time on the test. The correlation between SAT scores and freshman-year college GPA in this group was lower ($r = .35$) than the correlation for nondisabled students (who took the test under standard conditions; $r = .48$). This is a substantial difference, suggesting that the SAT scores obtained with extended time showed a significantly weaker relationship with freshman-year GPA.

In a similar study, Thornton, Reese, Pashley, and Dalessandro (2001) examined the predictive validity of scores from the Law School Admissions Test (LSAT) that were obtained with extended-time accommodations. Here, the outcome was first-year law school grades, and just as with the SAT study, LSAT scores obtained with extended time had a lower correlation with first-year law school GPA ($r = .34$) than did LSAT scores obtained under standard timing conditions ($r = .40$). Here the difference was not as large as in the SAT study, but given the large sample size of this study (over 100,000 examinees), the difference was statistically significant.

In these two studies, the investigators noted another phenomenon in addition to the lowered predictive validity; scores obtained with extended-time accommodations tended to overpredict examinees' later GPA. In the SAT study, Cahalan et al. (2002) found that scores from accommodated testing overpredicted GPA by .21 points for male students (no overprediction was found for female students), and in the LSAT study, Thornton et al. (2001) found that scores from accommodated testing overpredicted law school GPA by 5.7 percentage points. Therefore, in addition to showing weaker relationships with outcomes, admissions test scores obtained with accommodations led to systematic overprediction of outcomes; students who took tests with extended time did not do as well in college or law school as they were expected to do based on their admissions test scores. All this suggests that time extensions can threaten the validity of predictions based on admissions test scores.[4]

A second way to examine whether the meaning of test scores changes with accommodations involves investigating the relationships between items or sets of items within a test through factor analytic techniques. In the case of timing and scheduling accommodations, this type of research is somewhat less relevant than predictive validity research because it is unclear why timing or scheduling accommodations would be expected to affect these relationships. Even so, an important study of this kind was conducted by Huesman and Frisbie (2000), who gave a group achievement test (the reading comprehension test from the Iowa Tests of Basic Skills [Hoover, Dunbar, & Frisbie, 2001]) to sixth-grade students with and without learning disabilities. These investigators gave all students the opportunity for extended time if it was needed; if students had not finished the test at the end of the standard time limit, they circled the last item solved and were given additional time to finish. Huesman and Frisbie conducted a principal components analysis (similar to a factor analysis) on each set of test scores and found that when the students with learning disabilities were given additional time, the factor structure of their test scores was more similar to the structure of nondisabled students' scores, suggesting that the extended time enhanced the interpretation of their scores. Lindstrom and Gregg (2007) used a related technique, confirmatory factor analysis, to compare the factor structures of SAT scores of students with disabilities who were given extended time and nondisabled students who took the test under standard conditions. These investigators found no differences in structures, suggesting again that when students with disabilities are given extended time, their test scores have the same meaning as those of nondisabled students.

---

[4]Admittedly, in these studies, disability status and accommodation status confound each other; it is possible that admissions test scores are simply less valid for students with disabilities, regardless of whether they receive accommodations. We are skeptical of this possibility because it suggests a basic, essential difference between students with and without high-incidence disabilities, and research on identification of high-incidence disabilities would cast doubt on there being such a difference.

A third method for investigating the effects of accommodations on test score meaning is differential item functioning (DIF), which examines the relationship between students' ability levels and their chance of correctly answering individual items with and without accommodations. Bolt (2004) found that extended time led to significant DIF for between 16% and 44% of test items, depending on the sample, and she found less DIF when students with disabilities did not use extended time. A. S. Cohen, Gregg, and Deng (2005) found that even more items (over 75%) in their study exhibited DIF between standard and extended time, but these investigators used more complex statistical models to conclude that students' unique profiles of mathematics skills contributed to the DIF (rather than it being caused solely by the accommodation itself). Most recently, Finch, Barton, and Meyer (2009) found very little DIF based on different time allotments in their study; only three of 343 test items (across various tests) exhibited significant DIF.

Examining the body of predictive validity, factor analysis, and DIF research, we can conclude that extended-time accommodations do not generally lead to changes in the factor structure of tests, but they can lead to substantial amounts of DIF in certain samples, and they can affect the relationship between test scores and outcomes, weakening that relationship and leading to overestimation of students' likely future performance. Although more research is clearly needed, especially predictive validity work with K–12 samples, the extant research raises sufficient concerns to not provide extended time indiscriminately; it is not a psychometrically "free" accommodation to be given without worrying about the consequences and should only be used when necessary.

Differential Benefits to Students With and Without Disabilities

Do timing and scheduling accommodations benefit all students or only students with disabilities? Five studies examined this question with regard to extended-time accommodations in the 1980s and 1990s (Halla, 1988; Hill, 1984; Runyan, 1991a, 1991b; Weaver, 1993), and these investigators generally concluded that extended time's benefits were specific to students with learning disabilities. This conclusion continues to be widely reported (e.g., Shaywitz, 2003). However, more recent work has not supported this conclusion, and instead the opposite appears to be true.

The first suggestion that extended time's benefits may not be specific came from a critical analysis of the five early studies published by Zuriff (2000). First, Zuriff noted that fully half of the analyses across the studies actually showed that nondisabled students' test scores rose when extended time was provided. Second, he pointed out that even in analyses in which the average score for nondisabled students did not rise, certain individual nondisabled students (who are denied accommodations in the real world) experience score gains (see Runyan, 1991a). Finally, he argued that some of the studies had methodological flaws.[5] On the basis of these issues, Zuriff concluded that these studies in no way established that extended time's benefits are unique to students with learning disabilities.

The next blow to the specificity hypothesis came with a wider review of the literature by Sireci et al. (2005), who examined studies across various grade levels and disability types; in all, these scholars reviewed 14 studies on extended time. They concluded that "it is clear that extra time appears to improve the performance of all student groups, not just those with disabilities" (p. 483). However, Sireci et al. also hastened to note that "the gains for SWD [students with disabilities] were significantly greater," and suggested that "extending the time limits for all examinees" is often a good solution (p. 483).

Sireci et al. (2005) emphasized that students with disabilities did benefit more from extended-time accommodations than nondisabled students did, but even this has been called into question since their review. Indeed, whether this is the case seems to depend on the speededness of the test. Lewandowski, Lovett, Parolin, Gordon, and Codding (2007) administered a highly speeded mathematics computation test (consisting of 540 three-digit by three-digit addition problems) to middle school students with and without ADHD, at standard time (12 minutes) and extended time (18 minutes); students with ADHD improved their score with extended time, but the nondisabled students benefited even more, solving more problems during the 6-minute extension. In a related study, Lewandowski, Lovett, and Rogers (2008) found the same interaction when administering a somewhat speeded reading comprehension test to high school students with and without reading disabilities; again, the nondisabled students showed significantly greater gain from a time extension. In a third study, Lewandowski, Cohen, and Lovett (2013) found, similarly, that nondisabled college students benefited just as much from extended time as college students with learning disabilities. All three of these studies used tests that may be more speeded than is typical, but the findings nonetheless contradict Sireci et al.'s conclusion.

It seems safest to conclude, then, that more often than not, students both with and without disabilities benefit from extended time. The degree of benefit and the difference in how much each group benefits will depend on the characteristics of the students and the tests under study, but clearly, extended time's benefits are not specific to students with disabilities.

---

[5]Specifically, some of the early studies suffered from "ceiling effects" in which the "standard" (nonaccommodated) time limits for the tests were so generous that students could not improve with additional time. As we noted earlier, actual high-stakes tests, at least in postsecondary settings, often have at least some time pressure.

We should also mention one experimental study (the only one we could find) that looked specifically at multiple-day testing accommodations, administered without any other accommodations. Walz, Albus, Thompson, and Thurlow (2000) administered three reading passages during either one lengthy period or three brief periods (one passage each day) to students with and without disabilities. (The students with disabilities were a mixed-diagnostic group, but they had much lower oral reading fluency, on average, than the nondisabled students.) These investigators found that students with disabilities did not receive any benefit from the multiple-day accommodation, although this was nonetheless a kind of differential boost, because surprisingly, the nondisabled students actually had appreciably lower scores on the test administered over multiple days. Because the passages used in the two administrations were not identical, it is possible that test content accounted for these effects (although passages were equated for difficulty), but in any case, the study did not support the use of multiple-day accommodations.

Ability to Adapt to Standard Conditions

Can students with disabilities adapt to typical timing and scheduling of exams? Uncritical advocates of extended time are skeptical; for instance, Shaywitz (2003) equated extended-time accommodations for students with dyslexia to insulin for individuals with diabetes. On the other hand, Ofiesh and Hughes (2002) worried that students with disabilities "might take more time than needed . . . simply because they were given more time" (p. 10).

The study that bears most directly on this issue suggests that at least some students who are eligible for extended-time accommodations can adapt to standard time limits. Pariseau, Fabiano, Massetti, Hart, and Pelham (2010) administered language arts and mathematics worksheets to children with ADHD under two time conditions: 30 minutes and 45 minutes (i.e., 50% extended time). During the more liberal time limit, the children completed an average of 2.15 correct problems per minute, but in the time-pressured condition, this increased to 2.74 correct problems per minute (an effect size of $d = 0.64$). Note that this was the rate of *correct* solutions; the children were not merely guessing at answers to finish up. As would be expected, the total number of problems solved was higher in the 45-minute conditions, and there was a slight decrease in accuracy when more time pressure was present (88% accuracy in the 45-minute conditions; 85% accuracy in the 30-minute conditions), but it is clear that the rate of (accurate) work was quite malleable and responsive to changes in time constraints.

In a similar study, Colón and Kranzler (2006) administered curriculum-based measurement (CBM) oral reading probes to fifth-grade students with either no special instructions, targeted instructions to "read as fast as you can," or targeted instructions to "do your best reading." Each set of instructions led to an oral reading rate of correct words per minute that was significantly different from each of the other two sets of instructions; as might be predicted, the speed instructions led to the highest rate of correct words read, whereas the best-reading instructions led to the lowest rate. Although the measures were CBM probes rather than a typical "test," the results reinforce the point that students modulate their pace to situational demands.

In some ways, an even simpler approach to the question of adaptability involves seeing whether students who receive timing and scheduling accommodations even use them. The rationale behind an accommodation is that, without the accommodation, the student cannot access a test; if the student does not even use the accommodation, this suggests that it may not be necessary. In theory, data should be easy to collect on this point, but few research studies are available. Indeed, although many standardized testing agencies do monitor actual accommodations usage, we are only aware of one study publishing such data. In that study, Cahalan-Laitusis, King, Cline, and Bridgeman (2006) observed the test-taking behavior of nondisabled students, as well as students with ADHD or learning disabilities who had been deemed eligible to take the SAT with extended-time accommodations. The students were given 45 minutes to complete each of two sets of items, where the standard time limit would be 30 minutes (students were informed that they were receiving 50% extended time). Surprisingly, students with disabilities only used 4% to 14% additional time, on average, per section. At least some students with disabilities who receive extended time appear not to use it. In the case of younger students, this lack of use might signal the need for instruction or counseling regarding the accommodations, but with older students (this study involved high school juniors and seniors), it is possible that the lack of use signals a lack of need.

Less direct evidence on adaptability was provided in an earlier study by Huesman and Frisbie (2000). These investigators examined the score gains from standard to extended time on the Iowa Tests of Basic Skills (Hoover et al., 2001) reading comprehension scores for *nondisabled* students who were either instructed to work "at a slow and careful pace" or "at a normal rate." The students in the latter condition did not show significant gains, whereas students in the former condition did. Although these were nondisabled students, the results—when combined with those of Pariseau et al. (2010)—reinforce the notion that students' rate of work is malleable, and when given additional time (or asked to slow down), the students will work at a slower rate (which would lead to more benefit from extended time). The implication is, again, that students are able to work faster, making extended time of less benefit (and therefore less necessary).

A different way of addressing the question of adaptability involves finding whether the primary determinants of test-taking speed are easy or difficult to modify. Anecdotal evidence suggests that many students request or prefer extended-time limits because it reduces test anxiety or other kinds of discomfort with testing. To investigate this empirically, Lovett (2007) examined predictors of college students' perceptions of their time needs, measured with a standardized questionnaire with items such as "I could do better on my exams if I had additional time." Predictors included, among other things, reading fluency and self-reported test anxiety. Not only was test anxiety a significant predictor of perceptions of time needs, but also the correlation remained significant when actual reading fluency was statistically controlled; anxiety appears to be a distinct influence on these perceptions. Understanding the role of anxiety is important, because it suggests a potential alternative to accommodations (i.e., interventions).

In sum, the studies examined in this section all suggest that students' test-taking paces (and therefore their timing needs) are more malleable than we sometimes give them credit for. In Chapter 8, we discuss interventions in more detail, but the studies reviewed here make us quite optimistic about students' ability to adapt to standard time allotments.

Technical Adequacy of Decision Procedures

Extended time is given to students with a wide variety of disability conditions, and when students with high-incidence disabilities only receive a single accommodation, it is usually extended time. Therefore, the issues regarding diagnosis discussed in Chapter 4 must be considered carefully when making decisions about this accommodation; this is especially true when students have diagnoses thought to be relevant (e.g., ADHD), but where there is no evidence of a particular need for extended time.

One decision point of particular interest is the *amount* of extended time to provide to students. Ofiesh and Hughes (2002) were the first to consider this question in detail, noting that "too little time will not accommodate the disability. Too much time may accommodate the disability, as well as nondisability-related factors such as motivation or anxiety, and therefore provide an unfair advantage to students" (p. 3). These scholars reviewed the existing literature on extended-time accommodations for college students with learning disabilities, endorsing the current typical practice of granting either 50% or 100% additional time: "The range of time and a half to double time . . . is a good place to start and provides enough time for most students" (p. 10). However, none of the studies reviewed by Ofiesh and Hughes had directly tested the appropriateness of different amounts of extended time. Moreover, the *Standards for Educational and Psychological Testing* state the following:

> If a test developer recommends specific time limits for people with disabilities, empirical procedures should be used, whenever possible, to

establish time limits for modified forms of timed tests rather than simply allowing test takers with disabilities a multiple of the standard time. (American Educational Research Association, American Psychological Association, & National Council on Measurement in Education, 1999, p. 107)

Clearly, then, such empirical research is needed.

The only published study we are aware of that directly examined this issue empirically is our own (Lewandowski, Cohen, & Lovett, 2013). We gave a reading comprehension test to college students with and without learning disabilities, examining their performance at standard time (15 minutes), and then at 50% and 100% extended time. In addition to calculating their overall cumulative performance at each time interval, we examined the number of questions that they had answered (regardless of the correctness of their answers); because accommodations are designed to grant access to exams, this is an important indicator of whether students were able to reach test items. As in prior work, we found that students both with and without disabilities benefited from extended time. However, we also found that the average access score (items answered) of students with learning disabilities at 50% extended time was substantially greater than the access score of nondisabled students at standard time (37 items vs. 30 items). On the other hand, when both groups were only given the standard time limit, students with learning disabilities were not able to access as many items as nondisabled students (23 items vs. 30 items). Interpolating from our data, it appears that giving 25% extended time only to students with learning disabilities would have granted equal access. Certainly, more studies like this one must be conducted with different kinds of samples and tests, but we believe that it at least provides a tentative answer and a model for future research. The tentative answer it suggests is that even 50% extended time may give students with disabilities an unfair advantage.

RESEARCH-BASED DECISION MAKING

All research-based decisions about testing accommodations begin with a clear conceptualization of the test's desired constructs, then a consideration of the student's characteristics, and finally a consideration of whether the accommodation is necessary.

Test Constructs

Timing and scheduling accommodations are inappropriate when tests are intended to measure certain constructs. Extended-time accommodations change the meaning of scores from tasks that are designed to measure speed, fluency, automaticity, and related constructs. In addition, less frequently a test (perhaps in occupational settings) might be designed to measure endurance or persistence; breaks or multiple-day administrations would then be inappropriate. But in most classroom exams and many high-stakes exams, there is no deliberate attempt to measure any of these different constructs, making timing and scheduling accommodations potentially appropriate. Still, when this determination is made, all relevant personnel should be consulted. For classroom exams, classroom teachers should be consulted and asked to carefully consider whether fluency is a target of measurement. For high-stakes exams, test developers' intentions must be considered (typically by reviewing test manuals and other documentation), but test users' potential interpretations of scores are also important to consider. Accommodation decision makers must ensure that an exam is not designed to measure, and will not be interpreted as showing, constructs such as task fluency.

It may be helpful to distinguish between different types of fluency. As Lovett (2013) noted, on some tests, especially in postsecondary professional settings, it is important to be able to retrieve and use knowledge in a timely manner, but it is not important to be a fast reader. Reading fluency would be an ancillary skill only measured unintentionally, whereas *fluency of knowledge retrieval and use* would be a target skill designed to be measured. This would mean that extended-time accommodations are appropriate for examinees with poor reading fluency when taking a written test, but time limits should otherwise be kept strictly.

We would also caution that scheduling accommodations (including breaks) may create unintended and unfair advantages for examinees, especially when combined with extended time. For instance, if students are given access to the entire set of items for a lengthy exam and are then given a break that other students are not given, the student can use the break time to work (if only mentally) on the exam items, giving them additional time as well. This may or may not be problematic, but if it is, test administrators should consider breaking up exams into multiple parts, so that only a portion of items are given before the break. If this is not possible, examinees taking high-stakes tests may be able to arrange for "on the clock" break time, allowing them to allocate some of their exam time to breaks.[6]

---

[6]It may seem odd that students receiving "on-the-clock" break time would not simply take a mental break for a few moments, turning away from the test or computer screen. Students with certain kinds of disabilities may need to stand, walk around, or do other things that would be difficult to do without a formal break. Obviously, on-the-clock breaks also raise certain security issues; test administrators must ensure that examinees do not use the break to access information.

Student Functional Limitations

Because most tests are presented in text format, reading problems, especially problems with reading speed, are centrally relevant deficits. Students' reading fluency should be measured, as should their reading comprehension under timed conditions. Useful tests include typical norm-referenced reading tests, such as the WJ-III reading fluency task and the timed comprehension section of the Nelson-Denny Reading Test (NDRT; J. I. Brown, Fishco, & Hanna, 1993). The Scholastic Abilities Test for Adults (SATA, not to be confused with the SAT; Bryant, Patton, & Dunn, 1991) also has a reading comprehension subtest that can be given with a standard or nonstandard time allotment. The Gray Oral Reading Tests (GORT; Wiederholt & Bryant, 2012) are a popular measure that generates rate and fluency scores, although the format is very unlike a high-stakes test (i.e., on the GORT, the examinee must read passages aloud and cannot refer to the passage when answering comprehension questions). At times, other sorts of fluency tasks (mathematics fluency, writing fluency) will also be relevant when the test to be altered requires these skills. As with reading, it is best to have students answer typical test items under timed conditions, rather than only using diagnostic tasks that officially measure fluency. Classroom teachers' observations of prior test behavior, as well as the student's rate of completion of other academic work, can be invaluable in showing genuine deficits. We caution decision makers that slow rates of work completion (including the completion of test items) can be due to low effort, noncompliance, or even past experiences with liberal time limits (see Pariseau et al., 2010); these possibilities should be considered and ruled out, because otherwise testing accommodations are unlikely to be effective. Moreover, we note that performance on measures of fluency or timed skills should be below average in an absolute sense; as we have discussed, scores that are merely lower than the student's other test scores (especially his or her IQ score) say nothing about the appropriateness of accommodations.[7]

We have discussed fluency and task completion speed, but we have not mentioned processing speed. This is because even though, as we discussed at the beginning of the chapter, processing speed is theoretically related quite strongly to a need for extended time, the diagnostic tasks used to measure processing speed are typically devoid of realistic academic content. Consider,

---

[7]Diagnosticians and documentation reviewers should be on particular alert for score profiles that show low scores on all speeded tasks. Although these profiles may represent genuine problems (especially in the case of neurological insult), they may also represent deliberately reduced effort or even malingering, which may be present because of examinees seeking testing accommodations. Deliberately slow performance is a common strategy used by examinees who malinger neurocognitive deficits (e.g., Harrison, Edwards, & Parker, 2008). See Chapter 4 for more information on malingering and its detection.

for instance, the Digit-Symbol Coding and Symbol Search tasks on the Wechsler series of intelligence tests; these tasks require rapid visual-motor processing but no skills that are specifically academic. If students' slow processing speed leads them to require additional time on educational tests, the slow processing speed exerts its effects *through* low academic skill fluency and slow performance on timed academic tasks; measuring these latter skills is therefore more relevant. We would say the same thing about measures of attention and concentration; it is certainly possible for a student with ADHD who is unusually distractible to need additional time to make up for periods of distraction, but if this is the case, deficits should appear on tests of fluency and timed-task performance. Such deficits are sometimes found, but inconsistently and only rarely, in high-achieving individuals with ADHD (e.g., Lewandowski, Gathje, Lovett, & Gordon, 2012; Lewandowski, Hendricks, & Gordon, 2012). Finally, we should note, as we did in Chapter 4, that low-processing speed is not itself a disorder, and so some other disorder diagnosis or disability classification should be present.

With regard to additional/extended breaks and multiple-day accommodations, we have far less research to guide us. Here, we would suggest examining students' levels of relevant skills, gauged by diagnostic test scores but also though parent/teacher reports and observations. Students with low levels of stamina, who easily become fatigued, appear to be candidates for these accommodations. However, as with slow workers, again not every student who seems to be fatigued during exams should receive accommodations. Indeed, many nondisabled students find exams to be unpleasant experiences, not only stressful but cumulatively taxing ones; many typical examinees feel mentally "drained" of energy during and after a test, and so there is nothing diagnostic about reports of such experiences. A more promising approach is to document decrements in actual performance that occur over time during the course of a diagnostic test battery (even during engaging tasks) or to look at documentation of health-related disorders that have been linked to objective indices of fatigue and stamina.

We often see accommodations of additional/extended breaks for students with ADHD, and they are sometimes proposed as an alternative to extended-time accommodations for these students. Frankly, the rationale for these accommodation requests is unclear. If students are unusually distractible or impulsive, they are likely to benefit from redirection and increased supervision during tests—that is, they seem likely to benefit more from *presentation* accommodations (e.g., pacing accommodations that help with time management, redirection accommodations in which a proctor ensures that they are focused on test items) than from scheduling accommodations. Extra break time is best used with students who do have the capacity to manage time well but whose stamina keeps them from working continuously for lengthy periods.

The Need for Timing/Scheduling Accommodations

With regard to extended-time accommodations, several assessment strategies can be used to assess need. First, because benefit is a necessary but not a sufficient condition for need, it is helpful to have data comparing the student's performance on timed and untimed tests. This is most commonly done in the domain of reading. For younger children, comparing scores that are timed and untimed from the GORT, or (more relevantly) the Gray Silent Reading Tests (Wiederholt & Blalock, 2000), gives valuable information. For adolescents and adults, tests that come in alternate forms can be helpful; for instance, the NDRT comprehension task comes in two parallel forms, and one can be given under the standard time limit, with the other given with extended time. Although the NDRT has norms for extended-time administration of the comprehension task, they are not especially useful; we recommend that examiners administer the comprehension task with a time extension such as 25% or 50% and score the task using standard time norms. We stress that it is not enough for the student to improve with extended time (as we have noted previously, many nondisabled students will show such improvement); the student should have a below-average score (using normative comparisons) under timed conditions, and the extended time should improve this score.[8]

We are often asked, "How much time?" and here we can offer several rules of thumb. First, with younger children, it can be especially dangerous to overaccommodate, because these younger students lack good time management skills. Instead, it is better to give a standard time allotment, with warnings of when the allotment is running out, and then add additional small time increments (25%) as needed if speed is not a desired object of measurement. Second, with older students, it may be helpful to inquire (of the student or teachers) about how much additional time the student has actually used in the past; this can guard against overaccommodation. Third, reading fluency and timed reading comprehension scores can be of some use in determining the magnitude of extended-time allotments; scores that are just below the average range (between the 15th and 25th percentiles) should not require more than 25% additional time to have equal access to test content, whereas 50% or 100% additional time might be considered for those students with extremely slow reading skills or who require additional,

---

[8]The current version of the Nelson-Denny Reading Test (Forms G & H; J. I. Brown, Fishco, & Hanna, 1993) only has grade-based norms, and so once someone is in college, it is possible for their reading skills to be average or above average for the general population but below average for college seniors (for instance). Diagnosticians sometimes use first-year college students as a general population proxy group, and this is generally a reasonable practice.

more intensive accommodations as well and need more time to use these accommodations.

With regard to breaks during exams, so little research is available that we can only offer recommendations based on the logic behind the accommodation. As we did earlier in our discussion of student functional limitations, we hasten to distinguish between students who would feel more comfortable with breaks and those students who genuinely need them to access tests. Many students (both with and without disability conditions) would prefer breaks, even if their performance does not benefit from breaks—taking a test can be an aversive experience even for good students, and breaks can help to lessen any discomfort, but this does not make them an appropriate accommodation. Most students who need breaks either have some kind of physical or health-related disability. They may have a motor problem such that they can only work on a composition task for 10 to 15 minutes at a time, or they may show mental fatigue more quickly than other students do. There should be some evidence that their fatigue is related to poor performance on objective measures. In addition, older students with valid diagnoses of moderate or severe ADHD may be unable to sit for long exams but would benefit from additional breaks. In younger children, when breaks are not warranted, they can provide undue interruptions that may be pleasant but that still actually impede test performance by distracting the student and preventing continuous work.

Other scheduling accommodations (scheduling exams during a certain time of the day or across multiple days) are very similar to additional breaks, in that a clear need for the accommodations should be demonstrated. Students with health-related disorders are most likely to qualify for such accommodations on the basis of information from a physician about the student's medical condition backed up by a classroom teacher's observations of how the student is able to function in the classroom environment. These scheduling accommodations are among the most logistically problematic accommodations to implement in K–12 settings (it is difficult to administer exams with these accommodations without removing the child from other class activities), which is another reason to ensure that they are only used when necessary.

Finally, determining a student's need for time-management aids depends on which aid one is considering. Some time-management aids raise issues of universal design; for instance, examinees should generally have access to a clock or watch so that they can check the time at any moment. Reminders about the amount of time left are also generally permissible for all examinees, unless they are thought to be too disruptive. When reminders are being considered for students who are able to stay on task but who manage their time poorly, we recommend that these students (even fairly young students) be encouraged to rely on the timing devices that all examinees have access to. However, if a student has trouble staying on task, prompts to stay on task that include reminders of remaining time may be needed. In these cases, evidence of need should include actual poor performance on tests taken without any prompts.

CASE STUDIES[9]

Jessica

Jessica is a 10-year-old girl in fourth grade who has just been identified as having a learning disability in reading. During the comprehensive evaluation, the following relevant data emerged:

1. On the Wechsler Intelligence Scale for Children (4th ed., WISC–IV; Wechsler, 2003), she obtained a full-scale IQ of 108 (70th percentile).
2. On the WJ-III, she obtained the following scores on reading subtests (all scores are based on age norms):
   Letter–Word Identification = 84 (14th percentile)
   Reading Fluency = 80 (9th percentile)
   Reading Comprehension = 85 (16th percentile)
   Broad Reading Composite = 80 (9th percentile)
3. Jessica's teacher reported that Jessica's grades range from B to F and that poor reading skills seem to be impacting her grades in multiple subject areas. Moreover, Jessica often leaves parts of tests and quizzes undone because she takes longer than other students to finish. On several occasions, for the more important unit tests, the teacher has allowed Jessica additional time to continue the tests elsewhere, and Jessica has obtained higher scores than she has on other exams.
4. The school psychologist completed three brief classroom observations during exams and noted that Jessica appeared to work diligently during exams. In addition, her teacher reported no problem behaviors.

Jessica is a "textbook case" of a student who would typically merit an extended-time testing accommodation. She has below-average reading skills generally (part of the evidence needed to substantiate a learning disability

---

[9]Our analysis of the case studies does not address the restrictions on accommodations that may be in place for certain high-stakes exams (e.g., that certain states do not permit certain accommodations for any students on statewide achievement tests). Readers should always consult local regulations.

diagnosis in the area of reading), and her reading fluency skills are particularly weak, placing her in the bottom 10% of students her age. In addition, she is academically impaired in the classroom, and informal evidence suggests that she takes longer than other students to finish exams and benefits from having additional time.

On the basis of this evidence, we would generally recommend extended-time accommodations for Jessica on exams where information is presented in written form (not, say, on spelling tests where oral dictation is used) and where speed is not a construct of interest. This would apply to many class-room tests and most high-stakes (e.g., statewide) exams. We would recommend that 25% additional time be given initially and that this be monitored to see if this amount of time is sufficient. Moreover, we would recommend that Jessica's individualized education program (IEP) include reading-related goals that include fluency and that her specialized instruction specifically include strategies for building reading fluency. The amount of extended time may be modified as needed on classroom tests, and the need for continued extended-time accommodation as a whole should be reviewed in 12 months or after significant progress toward IEP goals is noted.

Matthew

Matthew is a 20-year-old student in his second year of college. He was diagnosed last month with a learning disability in reading after he failed a course and earned a grade of D in another, and a counselor at the student services office suggested that he be evaluated for possible subtle learning problems. He is now requesting extended-time accommodations on exams in his classes. To document his need for accommodations, he has sub-mitted the report from his recent evaluation. The evaluation concluded with a diagnosis of a learning disability in reading and recommended 50% extended-time testing accommodations. The evaluation data included the following:

1. On the Wechsler Adult Intelligence Scale (4th ed., WAIS–IV; Wechsler, 2008), Matthew obtained a full-scale IQ of 120 (91st percentile).
2. On the Nelson-Denny Reading Test (NDRT; Form G), Matthew received the following scores (standard scores have a mean of 200 and a standard deviation of 25 for the entire Nelson-Denny norm group; all percentiles are based on grade norms):
   Vocabulary = 222 (54th percentile)
   Comprehension (under standard time limits) = 210 (39th percentile)

Comprehension (when given unlimited time)[10] = 231
(72nd percentile)

3. On the SAT, which Matthew took without accommodations, he obtained scores of 550 (Verbal) and 580 (Quantitative). In addition, he graduated high school with a cumulative GPA of 3.40.
4. Matthew reports that he does not always have time to finish his exams and often wishes that his exams did not have time limits.

Matthew's case is similar to many that we see in our postsecondary consulting work; he has recently begun to do poorly in school, at least relative to his past performance, and he has obtained a learning disability diagnosis for the first time in adulthood. He reports needing more time to finish certain tests in his classes, and his score on the NDRT comprehension task improved when he was given additional time. Moreover, his reading scores were all at least somewhat below his IQ in terms of percentile scores.

However, despite these points, we would not recommend extended-time testing accommodations in this case. First, there is not sufficient evidence that Matthew has any disabilities at all, and certainly not a learning disability in reading. All of his reading scores are in the average range, we have no evidence of early problems acquiring reading skills as a child, and his high school performance (both on the SAT and in classes) suggests a lack of academic impairment. The discrepancy between the IQ and the reading scores is not relevant in making a diagnosis of a learning disability (see Chapter 4). Second, even if there were evidence of a learning disability, Matthew's performance on the NDRT comprehension task under standard time conditions was in the average range, suggesting that he does not need accommodations to be able to access tests (the legal standard under the Americans With Disabilities Act of 1990). His improved score on the task when given additional time is irrelevant because (a) the task is not designed to be finished under standard time limits, and (b) most students benefit at least somewhat from additional time.

However, despite our recommendation against accommodations, we would still recommend that Matthew speak with his course instructors regarding his request for additional time on exams. If his instructors are not trying to measure fluency or automaticity of skills, they may wish to reduce the time pressure on the exams, either by reducing the number of items or lengthening the time allotments. His instructors may even wish to make special

---

[10]In this case study, we are assuming that Matthew's "unlimited time" NDRT reading comprehension score was obtained by using the norms for standard-time administration, not extended-time administration.

arrangements for Matthew in particular, but this would happen outside of any formal accommodations requirements.

Luis

Luis is a 13-year-old boy in sixth grade who has recently been diagnosed with ADHD by a local child clinical psychologist. The psychologist recommended certain educational accommodations, including testing accommodations, but did not specify which accommodations she thought to be appropriate. His parents forwarded the psychologist's report to the school, which is developing a Section 504 plan to meet Luis's needs. During the 504 plan meeting, the following relevant information was noted, much of which was from the psychologist's report:

1. Standardized behavior rating scales, completed by both of Luis's parents as well as two of his teachers, showed wide consensus that Luis's ADHD symptom levels were abnormally high. Broadband rating scales suggested that outside of hyperactivity and inattention, Luis does not exhibit significant psychiatric symptoms.
2. On a computerized attention test, Luis showed abnormally high numbers of errors that suggested both unusual impulsiveness and inattention.
3. Luis's primary teacher (who teaches both his math and science classes and who is also his homeroom teacher) notes that he often skips items on exams and rarely finishes every item; items that are later in the exam are, on average, less likely to have been answered. His teacher reports that during exams, as during many class activities, Luis seems restless and gets bored frequently, appearing to have trouble staying engaged with low-energy tasks like test taking.
4. Luis's grades vary greatly from report card to report card and from subject to subject; his average would be in approximately a C range, but his teachers all report that his inconsistency in completing and turning in assignments partially accounts for this grade average, and they stress that "at his best," Luis has academic skills that are higher.
5. A special education teacher at the school completed a brief screening of Luis's academic skills on diagnostic achievement tests, finding his skills to be in the average range, even on timed CBM tasks of academic skill fluency.

It is common for schools to give testing accommodations to students with ADHD, and the practice makes common sense, but determining the precise accommodations that are appropriate is a difficult matter, as Luis's case shows. Although extended-time accommodations are commonly given to students with ADHD, we have no evidence that they would be beneficial, let alone appropriate. Taking tests seems to be an activity that Luis dislikes, and making him spend even longer in this activity would appear to be counter-productive. It is possible that giving breaks during an exam would be a help-ful accommodation, but we do not have any evidence to suggest that Luis would uniquely benefit—he does not show unusual levels of fatigue, and it is also possible that he would have trouble returning to take the exam after each break. And of course, giving extended time or additional breaks when the accommodations are not warranted could get Luis used to these things, further decreasing his test-taking skills.

Therefore, in this case, we would be unlikely to recommend any timing or scheduling accommodations. However, we would likely recommend a set of classroom accommodations that would encompass both instructional and testing situations. These may include, for instance, a reinforcement-based, self-monitoring system in which Luis would assess at random intervals whether he was on task, and he would receive reinforcement for increasing his on-task time, including during exams. We might also recommend that his teachers provide prompts and reminders during tests to help Luis stay on task in these important situations. If the self-monitoring system does not work, a daily behavior report card (along with reinforcement contingencies for good reports) may help to increase time on task. As with any prompting or reinforcement-based techniques, we would recommend gradual fading, so that Luis does not become too dependent on the external contingencies.

6

RESPONSE FORMAT ACCOMMODATIONS

Many students with disabilities have at least average levels of intelligence and learn as well as most of their peers, yet they cannot always readily express or display that knowledge on a particular test. Sometimes there is a poor match between a student's skills and the response demands of a test. Clearly, an oral exam makes little sense for a student with an expressive language disorder or someone who stutters. Standard paper-and-pencil exams that involve reading are similarly inappropriate for blind students. In addition, students with motor difficulties—such as those with cerebral palsy, dysgraphia, and fine motor impairment—are at a disadvantage on tests that involve handwriting or typing. These are just a few quick examples that highlight the need for response format test accommodations. In this chapter, we discuss some of the ways in which schools and test agencies can better allow students to respond to test questions.

http://dx.doi.org/10.1037/14468-006
Testing Accommodations for Students With Disabilities: Research-Based Practice, by B. J. Lovett and L. J. Lewandowski

TEST FEATURES

Exams vary in terms of response format. The most common formats tend to be multiple-choice tests that use "bubble sheets" or Scantron sheets, handwritten responses for essays or mathematical calculations, and computer-assisted responses that use a keyboard or mouse to select a particular response or type a written response. Less often, students may be asked to make an oral response, and in rare cases they are asked to demonstrate a certain complex skill, such as when medical students conduct a medical examination of a simulated patient. The common denominator of test responses is a motor act of some type (e.g., writing or typing, bubbling, key press). Even spoken responses or skill demonstrations involve motor activity. Thus, students with any type of motor disturbance (e.g., cerebral palsy, tics, tremors, hemiplegia, amputation) may need a response accommodation. In other words, if the standard response format (i.e., handwriting) is impeded by the student's disability (e.g., dysgraphia), and the skill of interest cannot be fairly assessed in a standard manner, then a more suitable response format must be sought (e.g., scribe).[1] The accommodation analysis depends on the features or demands of the test as contrasted with the impairment of the student with a disability. Just because a student has a disability (e.g., attention-deficit/hyperactivity disorder [ADHD]) as well as sloppy handwriting does not necessarily mean that he or she is entitled to the use of a scribe or word processor. On the other hand, a student with spasticity in his upper extremities will likely require a scribe to write for him. An understanding of the demands of a test is crucial to making appropriate accommodation decisions.

The crux of all test accommodation decisions focuses on equal access to an exam. As noted previously, there may be a variety of ways to accomplish this goal for those who demonstrate limitations that restrict their exam access. In some cases, this might even include an alternative assessment. Recent changes in federal policy allow schools to alter a test (e.g., make it shorter, modify test items) for as many as 2% of students with disabilities. Presumably, this is done in such a way that the assessment is still a valid assessment of grade-level academic content. Kettler and colleagues have provided some guidance on considerations for modifying assessments (Kettler, Elliott, & Beddow, 2009) and have shown that assessments can be modified and still maintain comparable reliability to a standard exam (Kettler, Rodriquez, et al., 2011). As noted in earlier chapters, it is important to maintain the reliability

---

[1]We should note that taking a test often requires motor responses beyond those required to respond to individual items. For instance, someone may need to get to the room where a high-stakes exam is being administered, and a wheelchair prevents the individual from accessing the room. Accommodations to address these kinds of deficits rarely involve difficult decisions and should be implemented on a common-sense basis.

and validity of exams, whether one alters the test content or provides accommodations that alter standard test procedures.

STUDENT CHARACTERISTICS

Another important variable in the test accommodation equation is the student, particularly his or her specific disability, type of impairment, and special needs. Although there are only so many ways one can express knowledge on a test, there are many different types of disabilities and great variation in type and severity of functional impairments. A number of impairments (not just motor impairments) can affect the way in which a student with a disability might respond on a particular test and therefore require different and specific-test accommodations.

Physical Limitations

This broad category encompasses students with cerebral palsy, amputations, developmental coordination disorder, broken limbs, and various musculoskeletal problems. These conditions could cause limitations in posture, body positioning, motor movements, and other activities that may affect grasping and using a pencil, typing, turning pages, using a bubble sheet, or interacting with a standard computer. It also is possible that certain tests, although manageable by the student, become a source of fatigue, which may require a different type of accommodation. Clearly, to fully access an exam, a student with physical limitations must be allowed to respond in a manner most conducive to his or her abilities rather than limitations. This may mean that writing is replaced by dictation or a scribe, bubble sheets are replaced by a scribe or marking in a test booklet, computer keyboarding is substituted for handwriting, and so on. Because motor problems often involve reduced speed, there may be a need for extended time. Issues of motor fatigue are often offset by extra breaks, which generally raise fewer score comparability concerns than extended time does. For severely limited individuals, such as students with quadriplegia, specialized assistive technology may be needed, including communication boards and engineered response formats (e.g., use of response buttons; switches; or technologies activated by eye movement, breath, pointing).

Visual Limitations

Obviously, visual impairments affect input of information and would require various presentation accommodations (see Chapters 4 and 7). With regard to response-format accommodations, students with visual disabilities often need to use a scribe or an audiotape for oral responses. Multiple-choice responses are made rather easily, whether the student is taking a test in Braille or having questions read and then responding orally. With regard to essay tests, dictation to a scribe, tape recorder, or voice recognition system can be used; however, severely visually impaired or blind students would not be able to perform computer editing of their dictation. Generally, oral responses are made more quickly than written ones, so there may be no need for extended time on such tests. Instructors may need to be flexible with regard to certain technical issues of writing such as spelling, grammar, and punctuation because oral responses cannot be graded as easily on every such detail. Response-format accommodations become more challenging in cases of multiple disabilities (e.g., deaf–blind, visually and physically impaired).

Speech and Language Limitations

Speech and language disabilities form the second largest disability category of children serviced in special education. Approximately 1.4 million of these students (3–21 years of age) receive special education services each year in the United States (U.S. Department of Education, National Center for Education Statistics, 2012). Of course, many of these cases apply to young children with speech articulation and fluency impairments. These do not tend to require test accommodations unless oral exams are necessary (unusual in K–12 education). Students with receptive, expressive, or mixed-language disorders are more likely to need test accommodations. Children with these language disorders also may have comorbid conditions such as learning disabilities (LD) that are language based (Bishop & Snowling, 2004), autism, or hearing disabilities. Depending on the nature and severity of the language impairment, students with language impairments may need a wide variety of test accommodations. Because most tests are verbal in nature, these students may be at a disadvantage in understanding the meaning of words and text or may be slower to read and process verbal information. In some cases, students may need test directions in written, spoken, and/or demonstration formats. For those with serious communication disorders, there may be a need to use augmentative and alternative communication systems. Just like students with severe cerebral palsy who have dysarthria or those with autism who may not use functional language, students who do not have expressive language (including selective mutism) may require manual signs, picture-exchange communication, communication boards or devices, and language-generating technology (Loncke, 2011). A comprehensive assessment of language and learning (e.g., reading and writing) abilities will inform the choice of test accommodations for specific test demands.

Behavioral Limitations

More often than not, the literature on test accommodations has not addressed testing of students with behavioral problems. Yet, a sizable number of students present with a variety of behavioral challenges in a test situation. In addition to students with ADHD, who may be easily distracted, fidgety, and unable to concentrate or focus, examiners may encounter students who are oppositional, disruptive, distracting, and even deceitful. Students with emotional and behavior disorders (e.g., ADHD, oppositional defiant disorder, conduct disorder, bipolar disorder) may have great difficulty taking a test in a classroom and maintaining standard test conditions. The key issue for these students is getting them to respond and do so continuously with adequate effort. For such students, accommodations may involve a proctor to keep them on task, and this might require a separate location. It is sometimes in everyone's best interest to test such students in a separate location and use a proctor to instruct, prompt, and motivate the student to complete the exam as required. Other children may not have a behavior disorder per se but display unusual behaviors that might distract from a typically quiet testing condition. For example, behavioral distractions may arise from the student with Tourette's syndrome who barks utterances randomly, or the student with autism who repetitively taps his pencil on the desk, or the student with panic attacks who commands everyone's attention during an attack. In a sense, these adjustments are setting and presentation accommodations; however, they alter response conditions as well.

TEST-RESPONSE ACCOMMODATIONS

Word Processor

In the past decade, use of computers in schools has increased dramatically along with the use of computers as tools for assessment. According to the National Center for Education Statistics (2010), the majority of all universities (public, private, 2 year, and 4 year) permit the use of assistive technology (including word processors) as testing accommodations for college students with LD and other disorders. Bolt, Decker, Lloyd, and Morlock (2011) found that college students considered a word processor with spell check to be a more helpful accommodation than did high school students. As computers in elementary, middle, and high school become more widely used, accepted, and required, we likely will see more word processors used on tests in K–12. Therefore, it is important that we evaluate the relative benefits of computerized writing as either a test accommodation for some or an applied technology for everyone.

Word processors serve as tools for writing and learning as well as accommodations for students with impairments in writing. A word processor can accommodate students with difficulties in spelling, grammar, organization, and penmanship. Of course, it may be desirable (e.g., in a language arts class) to measure a student's spelling or grammar skills, making word processing a hazardous accommodation. One way to address this issue is to use special word-processing programs that lack spell-check features, etc.

There are a variety of studies on the effect of word processing on composition, but very few studies have described word processing as a test accommodation per se. In general, research comparing word processing on a computer versus handwritten essays has yielded mixed results. Some studies have shown a scoring bias in favor of handwritten work (Arnold et al., 1990; MacCann, Eastment, & Pickering, 2002). However, studies that type (transcribe) handwritten essays and then compare them with word-processed essays have found little difference in essay quality (MacCann et al., 2002). In two recent studies (Berger & Lewandowski, 2013; Lovett, Lewandowski, Berger, & Gathje, 2010) comparing word-processed and handwritten essays in college students, the word-processed essays were significantly longer but of comparable quality. They also found that students preferred typing over handwriting and found spelling and editing easier on a computer. It appears that computers afford various technical and efficiency benefits for writing without adding (or losing) much in overall quality (e.g., idea generation, thematic coherence, vocabulary).

Most of the research on word processing and disabilities has focused on students with LD and the instructional value of computerized writing (MacArthur, 1996). For example, Graham and MacArthur (1988) found that students with LD benefited from use of a word processor and using self-instructional strategies. They had fifth- and sixth-grade students with LD take essays they had written and revise them on a computer. Students were able to produce longer and better quality essays with this method, and they had more confidence in their ability to write and revise essays. Outhred (1989) compared handwritten and word-processed creative essays in a small group of children with LD. She found that the word processor helped students in different ways; some improved in spelling and others wrote longer stories. In another format comparison, Hetzroni and Shrieber (2004) examined handwritten and word-processed written assignments of three junior high school students with writing disabilities. They found word-processed essays to have fewer spelling and reading errors, as well as better structure and organization. More recently, Gregg, Coleman, Davis, and Chalk (2007) compared 65 college students with dyslexia with 65 students without dyslexia on the quality of essays composed in handwritten, typed, and typed/edited formats. Students had 30 minutes to compose an essay on an expository topic. For both groups of participants, quality scores were not significantly different between the handwritten and typed essays. Quality scores were significantly lower for students with dyslexia on all three formats. Additionally, there was a high correlation between verbosity (quantity of writing) and quality. Finally, out of the students with dyslexia, only 71% completed their handwritten essays in the allotted time, whereas 91% of their peers completed their essays. In general, the consensus seems to be that the use of a word processor in writing intervention studies has been beneficial for students with LD (Graham, Harris, & McKeown, 2013; Li & Hamel, 2003).

Comparatively few studies have examined exclusively the effects of a word processor as a test accommodation. Recently, Berger and Lewandowski (2013) examined the usefulness of a word processor for essay writing in college students with and without LD. They found no differences between the groups in essay quality, but they did find that word processing produced longer essays and length was predictive of quality for all students. They also noted curiously that 72% of students with LD (averaged across handwritten and computer formats) used the allotted time, whereas 91% of peers used all of the time. Berger and Lewandowski concluded that a word processor lacked "specificity" as a test accommodation because it helped both groups equally. In fact, there appears to be no research that has shown word processing to only help students with disabilities. Whatever advantages it offers (e.g., word length, spell checking, editing and revising) seem to be a benefit to all students, not just those with disabilities. Perhaps that is why we are seeing some testing agencies now offering word processing as an option on writing tests rather than an accommodation (law bar exams in many states offer this option). In the future, as computerized writing becomes the more common format for writing, we expect it to become a universal design feature in testing and not a test accommodation.

Consistent with this universal design suggestion, Lovett et al. (2010) found that use of a word processor had generally beneficial effects on college students' essay writing. They randomly assigned 140 college students to conditions of handwritten or word-processed essays under standard time conditions (10 minutes) or 50% extra time (15 minutes). Students wrote longer essays when they used a word processor, and this advantage was increased under extended time. Students averaged 215 words handwritten when given 10 minutes to write, and 365 words on a word processor when given 15 minutes. The researchers did not find differences in quality across conditions, but they concluded that word processing certainly can increase output, save time for the writer, and produce an essay that is easier to read and grade. Whether it is viewed as an accommodation or not, word processing seems to have merit as a test-taking tool.

In making decisions about the use of a word processor as a test accommodation, one first must determine whether or not a word processor is a standard option on a test. Some instructors and test administrators allow students to take exams on a computer or via paper and pencil. Given some of the research findings reviewed previously, this is probably not an ideal situation. It is probably better to use one format or the other to make essay grading equitable. Another consideration regarding the use of word processing has to do with the underlying construct(s) being assessed by an exam. If a teacher is assessing spelling or grammar, then a word processor with spell and grammar correction is inappropriate. Similarly, if one is assessing writing fluency or writing quantity (productivity), a word-processor accommodation may not be appropriate (a word processor saves time when compared with handwritten work; Berger & Lewandowski, 2013). Therefore, decision makers may want to be careful in providing multiple accommodations such as extended time and the use of a word processor for a written exam. Paired together, these accommodations give students a double boost of time.

Determining who should receive a word-processor accommodation should involve careful assessment. Certainly, students with a writing disability that involves handwriting might qualify for a word-processor accommodation. In some cases, their handwriting is illegible and a teacher might opt to grant the use of a word processor. In less obvious situations, a student may be tested for handwriting skill on a measure such as the Handwriting subtest on the Woodcock-Johnson III Tests of Achievement (WJ-III; Woodcock, McGrew, & Mather, 2001). In addition to assessing student handwriting concerns, it is a good idea to examine a student's facility with a word processor. Has the student used this accommodation before, is the student capable of typing at a reasonable rate, and does the student have the motor coordination to type efficiently? If the need is present and the typing skill adequate, then a word-processing accommodation makes sense. If a teacher or psychologist is unsure about the need for a word processor or whether a student will benefit, then the teacher can conduct a brief experimental analysis. An evaluator can complete the essay portion of both forms of the Test of Written Language (TOWL; Hamill & Larsen, 2009), one in handwritten format and one on a word processor. This comparison should help determine whether a word processor is a beneficial accommodation for a student with writing problems. Of course, mere benefit does not indicate appropriateness; the student should show below-average writing skills under standard-response conditions, and even then accommodations would only be appropriate on exams not designed to measure writing skills per se.

Dictated-Response Recording

If a student cannot legibly or adequately write or type a response to a test question, the obvious replacement is to record the student responding orally, also known as dictation. There are several ways to record spoken responses, and these are all considered accommodations because they are alterations of standard test procedures. The most common recording options are a scribe (amanuensis), a tape recorder, and voice-recognition software on a computer. In K–12 settings, the scribe is likely the most common recording option. A student with a writing impairment can be tested individually by a teacher or learning specialist who records his or her responses. A concern raised in such cases is that teachers may not just record verbatim, but record what they think is the intent or a more understandable version of the response. They may even provide cues to a student (knowingly or unknowingly) or answer student questions in a way that assists the student. This could open the door to possible examiner bias, especially if the teacher is being evaluated on the basis of the performance of the student.

Tape-recorded responses provide for a low-tech, cost-efficient recording accommodation. The problem here is that someone has to transcribe (or directly score) the responses, which can be challenging when children are rambling, speaking softly, or have articulation problems or if there is background noise. In addition, there could be mechanical problems associated with starting, stopping, and rewinding the tape. The use of tape recorders in testing is long-standing and noted as an approved test accommodation by most schools and test agencies, yet there appears to be little research as to its usefulness or validity. One early study by Lane and Lewandowski (1994) compared seventh- and eighth-grade students with and without LD on essays that were either written or oral (into a tape recorder). The performance of students with LD was inferior to that of peers on the written essay, but similarly to peers on the dictated essay, suggesting that dictation may help level the playing field for LD students on writing tasks. Most notably the writing fluency of the LD group increased by 44.3 words on average in the Oral (dictated) condition, whereas the normal achievers (NA) only gained an average of 10.79 words. These results suggest that there is a differential boost for the LD group when given a dictation accommodation. This boost was also noted for thematic maturity, in that dictation provided a significant gain for students in the LD group and actually lowered performance for the NA group. Although this study supports the use of dictation for students with LD, it should be noted that it did not take into account potential problems raised by dictation, such as one's ability to spell, punctuate, or revise work. Certainly, a careful analysis must be made of the test constructs an instructor wants to assess before implementing dictation as a test accommodation.

The most sophisticated recording system is voice recognition (speech-to-text conversion software). A student can speak a response to a computer that turns the dictation into text. The text can then be read and edited on the computer display if the student so chooses. This combines the benefits of a recording device and word processing. If a school or test agency has the technology, as more and more agencies do, it can be an easy and efficient way for students to write. Content is recorded, and the student has the option of editing, spell checking, and revising. Because the finished product is an electronic or printed text, there is no manual transcription and no examiner bias involved. A potential problem, especially in early versions of voice recognition, is unfamiliarity with the student's voice that then leads to unintended dictation errors (e.g., I say "decode" and the computer writes "the coat"). The writer, especially one with LD, is unlikely to catch all such errors and may be wrongly penalized for them.

Despite the potential problems of voice recognition, Higgins and Raskind (1995) found that college students with LD achieved higher holistic essay scores using voice recognition compared with writing with no assistance. They had 29 college students with LD write essays in three conditions: (a) speech recognition, (b) dictated to a scribe, and (c) handwritten. The investigators argued that speech recognition allowed students to more effectively use their vocabularies, resulting in better vocabulary usage (more words of seven or more letters). It should be noted that the positive effects in this study were quite modest, and they did not examine whether nondisabled students also would perform better in the voice-recognition versus no-assistance condition.

Not only did voice recognition seem to have benefits for the writing of LD students, but Raskind and Higgins (1999) found that it also improved word identification, spelling, and reading comprehension. They compared 19 LD students (ages 9–18) using speech recognition 50 minutes a week for 16 weeks with 20 LD students receiving general computer instruction. They also found that the students using voice recognition improved significantly in phonological processing, which is related to reading. It appears that voice recognition not only can be an effective accommodation for writing, but also can be an important instructional technology.

Any of these accommodations may work well for recording dictated responses, depending on the resources available. It is unclear whether one type of dictation is better for certain tasks or certain students or should be determined based merely on user preference. There seems to be little empirical guidance as to whether these accommodations are valid, let alone helpful. One study (MacArthur & Cavalier, 1999) compared writing performances of eighth and 10th graders with and without LD across three writing conditions: handwriting, scribe, and voice recognition. They found that students with LD performed better on both dictation conditions than handwriting and best when using a scribe. Normally achieving students performed similarly across all three conditions. In a similar study, MacArthur and Cavalier (2004) found that high school students with LD could dictate to a scribe or a voice recognition system accurately and that both of these conditions produced better essays than a handwriting condition. These studies suggest that dictation methods are valid accommodations for students with LD and that a scribe might be superior for producing the most accurate results and best performances.

If a written exam is used to evaluate one's knowledge, and technical aspects of writing and penmanship are not constructs under investigation, then dictated responding should be a valid accommodation. However, if teachers are evaluating handwriting, spelling, punctuation, or grammar skills, then dictation is probably not a valid test accommodation. Even if teachers ask students with LD to review and revise their dictated work, these students often have poor transcription skills. They often miss words that are misspelled or inappropriate, and they ignore or make errors of capitalization and punctuation (MacArthur & Graham, 1987). Decisions about dictation as an accommodation must first consider the construct(s) under examination so that skills being assessed are actually being performed by the student and accurately reflect the student's skill level.

Another consideration before implementing dictation as an accommodation is a careful assessment of a student's language skills. Students that dictate responses must have adequate expressive language ability, otherwise their responses may reflect a language weakness rather than a knowledge deficit. We do not want to use an accommodation that will underestimate a student's true abilities. One must also consider that oral language varies from written language. Oral communication involves various inflections, emphases, and expressions that may not come across in a transcription. On the other hand, test graders might tend to make inferences on the basis of what they believed the student was trying to say. It may be helpful at times to have a second person grade an exam or give an interpretation of what a student is saying in a particular response. Sometimes listening to a tape and reading the transcription will yield a better picture of the student's responses. A particular problem can exist with regard to voice recognition responding. Depending on the quality of the system being used and the familiarity between dictator and computer software, errors in transcription can be made and can be difficult to detect when proofreading (e.g., *here* for *hear; the maid owes* for *tomatoes*). What is most important in using any of these dictation systems is that the student is comfortable and capable of using the method effectively. Young students are not likely to use a voice-recognition system. Practice with these systems before exams is a necessity.

It does appear that dictation can be a useful and valid accommodation, especially for students with LD. Research has suggested that dictation tends to help these students mitigate their slow fluency, reduced written output, and technical writing errors. It appears that a scribe is the safest of the dictation methods, reducing the ambiguity that can come from transcribing an audiotape or the sound-word errors found with voice recognition. Instructors need to carefully assess students' various writing skills using tests such as the TOWL or WJ-III and determine what impairment the student has and whether the specific skill deficit (e.g., handwriting, fluency, thematic maturity) of the student is relevant or irrelevant to the construct(s) being assessed. If a student has a deficient handwriting score and handwriting is not relevant on the classroom test, then a dictation method would seem to be appropriate. However, if spelling and punctuation are targets of an assessment, then dictation would defeat the purpose of the test. Obviously, accommodation decisions must be made on an individual basis after careful considerations of a student's specific writing impairment juxtaposed against the skills being measured by a given exam.

Calculators

Thus far, we have focused most attention on writing accommodations that are due to various physical, visual, or learning impairments. Mathematics tests offer a different kind of challenge when it comes to accommodating functional impairments. A student who cannot perform calculations manually, or who has a math disability or makes careless calculation errors, may be best served by using a calculator on certain exams. Such an accommodation would obviously not be appropriate for an exam specifically designed to test math calculation skills (e.g., how well a student can multiply or divide). However, a calculator may make perfect sense on a math problem-solving test in which the proper steps and methods are more important than mere calculations. The same could be true on chemistry, physics, or engineering tests that contain math calculations that are not part of the constructs being assessed by the exam.

Research on the use of calculators as a test accommodation is relatively sparse. This may in part be due to teacher decisions to allow calculators for certain exams rather than treat them as an accommodation. For years teachers have allowed students to use calculators on various exams in which calculations are not the essential construct of the test. Much like the use of computers for writing, calculators are becoming a more standard part of the classroom and less of an accommodation. It remains the case that for some high-stakes exams (e.g., Graduate Management Admission Test, Medical College Admission Test) the use of a calculator is typically provided only as a test accommodation. However, when given the chance, virtually all students choose to use a calculator on such exams. For example, Scheuneman, Camara, Cascallar, Wendler, and Lawrence (2002) found that 95% of students taking the SAT I reasoning test in mathematics used a calculator on the test, and 65% used it on a third or more of the test items. Certainly, students find calculators helpful and prefer to use them when given the opportunity. Such widespread use is consistent with a universal design feature rather than a test accommodation.

There are only a handful of studies that have examined calculators as a test accommodation, and most of these pertain to students with LD. Bouck and Bouck (2008) studied the math performance of sixth-grade students with and without disabilities (LD, ADHD, emotional impairment) on assessments that excluded or included calculator use. They found that all students benefited from access to a calculator, calling into question the specificity of a calculator as an accommodation. Bouck (2009) conducted a similar study to assess the effects of a graphing calculator on a math assessment for seventh-grade students with and without disabilities. Results indicated a benefit for students with disabilities, although students without disabilities improved even more. This study once again demonstrated the lack of specificity of a calculator as an accommodation and suggests that calculators should be a component of standard test conditions whenever they do not keep target skills from being measured.

Parks (2009) added a twist to the evaluation of calculator use on a math test. This study of middle school students with disabilities (LD and ADHD) and without disabilities also examined students' math anxiety. Parks found that students without disabilities performed better in general and that students with disabilities did not differ in performance whether they used a calculator or not. Approximately half of the LD and ADHD students reported increased anxiety when using a calculator. Parks argued that teachers should be careful when assigning this accommodation to certain students, particularly if students have not been taught to use a calculator effectively and feel uncomfortable using it. Here is where preassessment can be helpful. Teachers not only need to assess a student's computation accuracy and fluency, they also need to assess a student's competency with and without a calculator. A teacher can do this informally by administering math problems to a student under two conditions: paper and pencil versus calculator. If calculation by hand is a clear deficit and is not a target skill of an exam, and calculator facility is good, then the use of a calculator could then be considered.

Engelhard, Fincher, and Domaleski (2010) recently examined various accommodations on a statewide assessment in Grades 3 and 6 for children without and with disabilities (various types). They reported that the use of calculators as a test accommodation was "somewhat mixed with both small positive and negative effect sizes varying by grade" (p. 22). Clearly, this is not resounding support for the use of calculators as a test accommodation. It appears that, if anything, calculators tend to help all students and may even help nondisabled students more. Perhaps then, calculators should be treated as a universal resource for exams that do not intend to assess calculation skills. The use of calculators as an accommodation then would be relegated to specific instances in which a student has impaired calculation skills and a clear need for a calculator whereas other students do not. In such instances, the accommodation decision would be individualized and relatively rare.

When making decisions about the use of calculators, instructors must decide what skills are to be assessed and what skills are unimportant. The easiest decision seems to be one in which calculation is not a skill of interest (i.e., answering math word problems) and the instructor permits calculators for all examinees. In other exam situations, calculation and calculation fluency may be skills of interest, and in such cases a calculator would not be a valid accommodation. It is important to avoid situations in which test scores are not comparable. To determine need for a calculator, it is important to first assess a student's calculation skills. Subtests from the WJ-III or the Wechsler Individual Achievement Test III (Pearson, 2009) could be used to assess calculation skill and math fluency. Students with clear impairment in these areas can benefit from a calculator accommodation on tests that do not measure calculation as a central construct.

An instructor should keep in mind that use of a calculator is likely to save students time. The more calculations required, the more time saved compared with hand calculations. If students also request extended time, the instructor must carefully weigh the time saved with the use of a calculator coupled with an amount of extended time. Extended time may not be necessary if, for example, the student has a math fluency deficit and the calculator completely mitigates the speed problem. In this case, one or the other accommodation might suffice rather than combining two accommodations.

Marking Answers in a Test Booklet

Most standardized tests, such as national and statewide achievement tests as well as education admission tests like the ACT and SAT, have historically favored multiple-choice formats that use Scantron or bubble sheets. Many colleges with large lecture classes ($n > 50$) also regularly use this testing system. Students tolerate such tests, but many do not particularly like bubble sheets. There is always the worry that a skipped item will throw off all subsequent responses, or an erased item may not be registered correctly. Another concern is the extra time it takes to scan the bubble sheet for the correct item and then fill in the correct bubble. If a student has visual impairment, spatial or perceptual difficulties, scanning problems, fine motor impairment, or attention limitations, he or she might be better served by answering questions in the test booklet (i.e., circling A, B, C, or D) directly. This accommodation is a slight alteration of standard conditions and should help students with various disabilities make more accurate choice selections.

This particular accommodation may have been originally developed for students with mobility or eye–hand coordination problems, making the transfer of answers from a test booklet to a bubble answer form difficult (E. Burns, 1998). The ability to fill in bubbles on an answer form requires adequate attention to ensure that the intended answer is being marked on the intended item. Despite the fact that circumventing bubble sheets is an approved accommodation in most states, there is very little research showing that it is effective and applicable for certain types of disabilities.

Rogers (1983) conducted a study of 156 students with hearing impairments between the ages of 8 and 10 years. The assessment focused on a multiple-choice spelling test, with students randomly assigned to respond on the test or on a bubble sheet. There were no significant differences in spelling test performance for those using the accommodation and for those who did not.

Tolfa-Veit and Scruggs (1986) tested a sample of 101 fourth-grade students with and without LD on subtests from the Comprehensive Test of Basic Skills (McGraw-Hill, 1990). They found that students with LD answered fewer items than peers in a given time period, although there was no difference in response accuracy. They also found that the groups were similar in percentage of items accurately copied onto answer sheets (both groups approximately 97%), with 3% of the items marked outside the necessary area. They did not find that this response format, marking on an answer sheet, helped or hindered either group of students; however, this study did not systematically compare performances on two identical tests given in two response formats (booklet vs. bubble sheet).

Tindal, Heath, Hollenbeck, Almond, and Harniss (1998) also used a sample of fourth graders in both special ($n = 78$) and regular education ($n = 403$) programs. The authors used statewide reading and math multiple-choice tests, and all students responded on the test booklet for half the test (accommodated condition) and a bubble sheet for the other half (standard condition). They found that performance was not influenced by the condition under which the students were responding, and both groups' answers were comparable whether they were using the bubble sheet or answering directly in the test booklet.

Mick (1989) examined the effects of multiple test accommodations, including "marking answers in the test booklet" on the Virginia minimum competency test. Participants included samples of 36 students with LD and 40 students classified as "educable mentally handicapped" (ages 15–18). The results suggested that students performed better on the unmodified version of the test, suggesting that marking in the booklet, large print, and other test modifications did not improve test performance for students with disabilities. Because the study used multiple accommodations, it was unable to evaluate the effects of any one accommodation.

Using the results from these four empirical studies, Thurlow and Bolt (2001) concluded the following: "Overall, there is no empirical support for this accommodation if the criterion is increased test scores. Test scores for students taking the test with and without this accommodation are similar; only one study suggested otherwise" (p. 25). However, they also concluded that because of the relative lack of research regarding this accommodation, especially with specific populations of students (i.e., those with motor impairments, attention problems), the accommodation still might be warranted.

Recently, Potter, Lewandowski, and Spenceley (2013) completed a response-format study of college students with (LD and ADHD) and without disabilities. They administered the vocabulary subtest from the Nelson Denny Reading Test (Forms G & H; Brown, Fischo, & Hanna, 1993) in two conditions. Each student took one form of the test using a bubble sheet (standard condition) and another form by responding in the test booklet (accommodated condition). The test forms and conditions were counterbalanced and controlled for order. They found that, in general, students with disabilities answered fewer test items and got fewer correct answers than nondisabled students. This was no surprise and not the point of the study. More important, they found that both groups answered approximately 50% more items in the accommodated condition. In essence, booklet responding was a more time-efficient response method, allowing students to access more of the test in a given amount of time. Clearly, booklet responding was an effective accommodation, although it was not specific to students with a disability. All students were able to benefit. Such a finding actually suggests that, if at all possible, instructors would be wise to stay away from bubble sheets. They make grading easier but test taking more difficult.

If bubble sheets are the test method of choice, then examiners will need to assess students' ability to visually track and manually mark the correct test item in an efficient manner. Students with visual, motor, spatial, and even attention problems may be at a disadvantage on a test with bubble sheets. Because no test has bubble filling as a construct of interest, we do not have to worry about interfering with what is being assessed by a test. What needs to be considered is whether a student's access to a test is impeded by a disability, because the disability causes impairment that is incompatible with bubble responding. If the student is significantly slowed or makes more mistakes, then an accommodation may make sense. Typically, responding right on the test booklet solves the problem. If booklet responding is not possible for some students (i.e., blindness, severe cerebral palsy), a scribe may be used to mark answers. Once again, a careful assessment of the student's visual, motor, and attention skills could inform the need for an accommodation. Examiners should be aware that this accommodation could also be a time saver for the examinee, and therefore this accommodation should be given only on tests that are not significantly speeded (otherwise the accommodation would be unfair to other examinees).

Dictionary/Thesaurus Access

The use of a dictionary during a test is not always a response-format accommodation, although it could be one. Students usually ask for dictionary access to better understand words in a question or in a reading passage. On occasion, a dictionary may be used during an essay exam if a student needs to check on a word meaning or find a particular spelling. A thesaurus is helpful in finding a word's synonyms, and this can serve to augment and diversify a student's diction. Such an accommodation should be considered with caution in that a student's actual vocabulary may be inflated by the use of a thesaurus, whereas other students are deprived of this writing resource. Obviously, one would not use such an accommodation if the central construct of a test was vocabulary knowledge. Students with language disabilities and LD are particularly vulnerable when it comes to reading and writing skills. Ample research has suggested that these students are lacking in vocabulary skills (Hock et al. 2009; Ransby & Swanson, 2003), and this weakness has effects on the quality of one's comprehension and writing. As Mark Twain (1888) once noted, "The difference between the right word and the almost right word is really a large matter. It's the difference between lightning and a lightning bug." Students with language-based disabilities are more likely to use the "almost right word." It may be that a vocabulary resource for such students could serve to "level the vocabulary playing field" and not create an unfair advantage.[2]

Simulations

Another recent and rare development on the student assessment scene is the use of simulations. Perhaps the most sophisticated example is the medical board exam that requires interviewing and diagnosing of confederate medical patients. An examinee enters a room with a patient/actor, receives a brief chart, conducts a live interview, and then makes decisions about what condition the patient may have, what tests to order, and/or what treatment to prescribe. Other professional board exams sometimes involve interviews in which experts present case scenarios to examinees, who then have to "solve" the case and make recommendations for treatment or action.

In the case of a medical student who is blind or deaf, has language impairment, or suffers from a psychiatric disorder such as social anxiety, an accommodation may be needed to complete the patient exam. One could envision the possibility that an examinee would need to have extended time, have the chart read aloud, or even have a coexaminer/reporter in the room to make observations and conduct parts of the exam as directed by the examinee with a disability (e.g., blindness). Clearly, these are rare instances, but they do show that for every assessment devised, there could be a need to alter the

---

[2]Another group that might benefit from dictionary access is English language learners (ELLs). Two comprehensive meta-analyses (Abedi, Hofstetter, & Lord, 2004; Kieffer, Lesaux, Rivera, & Francis, 2009) have examined research on the effectiveness and validity of ELL testing accommodations. Abedi et al. (2004) found the use of customized English dictionaries was both valid and effective for ELLs in the public schools. Consistent with Abedi et al. (2004), Kieffer et al. (2009) found that English language dictionaries and glossaries were an effective accommodation for English as a second language (ESL) students.

testing conditions and response methods for a person with a disability. As yet, this type of assessment is too new and little used; thus, there is no research on the validity of test accommodations for simulated assessments.

Computerized Assessment and the Future of Response Accommodations

Even the most casual survey of the assessment landscape over the past decade shows a significant increase in the number and types of tests being converted to a digital format. Clinical tests used for psychological assessment, classroom tests in schools and universities, and even high-stakes tests such as the GRE have become computerized. The advantages of this change are obvious, including efficiency of test delivery, scoring, data storage, and adaptability. Computerized testing means that multiple-choice questions can be answered with a key press; essays can be typed, edited, and spell checked with word processing software; and dictionaries, calculators, and graphing programs are built-in resources. The computer also is the best tool for making test accommodations, such as screen reading or voice-recognition technologies, modifying test questions, controlling and extending time, etc. Students are becoming increasingly used to learning and working on computers, so why shouldn't they be tested on them (Chappuis & Chappuis, 2008; Tomlinson, 2008)?

Computers, in conjunction with infrared and satellite technologies, have made other forms of question responding possible. College classrooms have been using active responding systems ("clickers") that allow an instructor to ask a question and students to click a handheld device with their responses to the question (Bruff, 2007). This gives the instructor immediate information on student learning or opinions, and the students get immediate feedback regarding the accuracy of responses. These systems also are being used for testing purposes, either by loading the test right on the device or just using the device for making response choices. One of the newest developments is to take tests and make responses right on one's smartphone or iPad. Students are very familiar with this technology, and it is relatively easy to access and read questions as well as make multiple-choice responses. The problem with using one's own phone is security, because phones these days are computers and can access any information on the Internet. Although this technology does not appear to be heavily incorporated into test accommodation practice, it could be on the horizon as tests become increasingly digital. An iPad may offer better visual characteristics to a student with visual impairment, and a touch screen may be easier to use for a person with motor difficulties. If anything, these new technologies allow for creativity in circumventing functional impairments when testing. Of course, we have no research on their effectiveness or validity as test accommodations, but then again, this field has always been lead more by technological developments than scientific ones.

CASE STUDIES

Teddy

Teddy is a 14-year-old eighth grader with a diagnosis of an LD in writing, first made in second grade. He has just undergone a planned triennial reevaluation, and during that evaluation, the following facts emerged:

1. His history indicates that he was born premature (at approximately 32 weeks gestation) and struggled with fine and gross motor skills throughout his development.

2. He still has below-average motor skills, which show when he performs in physical education classes and on writing, drawing, and typing tasks. He has above average intelligence (his full-scale IQ on the Wechsler Intelligence Scale for Children (4th ed., WISC–IV; Wechsler, 2003) was 116), average achievement scores in reading, and above average scores in math. His scores on various tests of writing—from the WJ-III and the Wechsler Individual Achievement Test II (WIAT–II; Psychological Corporation, 2001)—were between 75 and 85 on spelling, grammar, handwriting, and overall quality. On the WJ-III, his Writing Fluency score was 79 and his score on Dictation (i.e., spelling) was 75. His composite writing score on the WIAT–II was 85.

3. Teddy has a history of occupational and physical therapy services and currently receives resource assistance from an LD specialist twice a week. When Teddy was younger, he used a scribe for written exams, including spelling tests. During sixth grade, he began writing on a computer. Although the various features on the computer were helpful to him (i.e., spell check, revising), Teddy was still a very slow typist. The school tried voice recognition as an alternative to typing because he had good oral language skills. He quickly learned how to use this software, and his writing output improved dramatically, as did the quality of his work.

Teddy is a student with a long-standing LD in written expression. He qualifies for and has used accommodations for writing assignments and written exams. Teachers have typically given him extra time on essay tests because his writing is slow and laborious. Also, his written assignments are proofread and sometimes edited by a learning disability specialist. As Teddy transitions into high school, it will be important that academic supports and accommodations remain in place. Writing demands will increase, and he will need to rely on a computer for most of his writing needs, whether he types or dictates his responses. This summer, Teddy will be taking a special keyboarding class at the high school to improve his typing skills. He also has been given a copy of the voice-recognition software used by the school district so he can use the same system at home and school. On Teddy's high school individualized education program (IEP), these writing accommodations will be specified, along with 50% extended time for written exams to be taken in a resource room. The resource specialist will assist with appropriate punctuation, a difficult thing to insert during dictation. The specialist will also help correct voice recognition errors (e.g., *hear* for *here*). Teddy will receive extended time and a dictation accommodation of his choice (scribe or voice recognition) on all written tests, including statewide assessments. The extended time will be needed to proofread, edit, and revise, all of which come slowly to Teddy. He (his parents) will have to apply for test accommodations on the ACT and SAT exams. Although Teddy qualifies for accommodations on writing tests, he will not need accommodations for multiple-choice exams. Further, he should not need accommodations for certain subjects such as math and foreign language. It is important to note that qualification for test accommodations does not permit a carte blanche to a wide array of accommodations. Test accommodations must be specific to the demonstrated functional limitation that restricts exam access. In Teddy's case, that is writing and spelling. Given Teddy's intelligence and other academic skills, appropriate test accommodations should allow him to succeed academically and attend college. Postsecondary planning should start well before high school graduation and involve a search for a school with a proven track record in assisting students with disabilities.

Jackie

Jackie is a 22-year-old who recently completed college and is applying to graduate school. Her GRE performance was below what she expected, especially her Quantitative score (480). Her verbal score was better (550), but still not enough to meet the minimum requirements of many programs in her desired area of graduate study (sociology). Math has always given Jackie more trouble than most subjects, and math tests definitely stress her. Jackie has a friend who received test accommodations on the basis of a diagnosis of ADHD. She thought she might have a learning problem because she struggles with math, so Jackie sought a comprehensive psychoeducational evaluation from a clinical psychologist in private practice.

Results of the evaluation revealed a Wechsler Adult Intelligence Scale (4th ed., WAIS–IV; Wechsler, 2008) full-scale IQ score of 120, including a Verbal Comprehension score of 131 and a Perceptual Reasoning score of 108, with a Working Memory score of 125 and a Processing Speed score of 102. Her WIAT-II Reading composite score was a robust 123, whereas her Math composite score was 94. Neuropsychological testing was generally within normal limits, including above-average scores on tests of memory, language processing, and motor coordination. She did perform in the borderline range on the recall portions of the Rey Complex Figure Test (Corwin & Bylsma, 1993).

Despite the generally strong cognitive and achievement scores, all of which were at least average, the evaluator concluded with a diagnosis of nonverbal learning disability (NVLD), largely because of the discrepancies between different index scores on the IQ test. It should be noted that Jackie had no history of an LD and no school records indicating learning problems. She graduated high school in the top half of her class and achieved a college GPA of 3.25 without special help or test accommodations. Yet the evaluator said that even though her scores were within normal limits, she was experiencing visual processing deficits. The evaluator recommended large print for exams, marking responses in the test booklet, and extended time.

This is a real case that was sent to one of the authors for review and consultation (we have changed certain details, including the applicant's name). In this case, the requests for test accommodations were denied. Despite the evaluator's efforts to advocate for Jackie, there was not sufficient documentation of a learning disability. Jackie had no history of educational impairment, previous testing and diagnosis, special education services, or test accommodations. She performed above average in school and on the individualized psychoeducational test battery. Although math may be a relative weakness, and something that causes her uncertainty and worry, it is not a substantial limitation, relative to the general population.

Moreover, NVLD is not a *Diagnostic and Statistical Manual of Mental Disorders* (5th ed.; American Psychiatric Association, 2013) diagnosis and only has modest support in the literature. On the basis of research descriptions of NVLD, Jackie does not even appear to fit this profile well. Furthermore, there is no evidence that Jackie really has visual deficits of any kind. Perhaps a referral to an ophthalmologist would clarify this issue, but if she has any visual deficits, they did not lead to substantially below-average performance on cognitive testing.

Lauren

Lauren (age 13) was born with cerebral palsy that resulted in significant spasticity in all her limbs and affected her speech as well. She has been receiving special services since infancy, including occupational therapy, physical therapy, and speech therapy, as well as an instructional specialist. Lauren has needed a host of adaptations and modifications to her curriculum, as well as accommodations on tests (e.g., scribe, extended time, separate location). Despite her limitations, Lauren has normal intelligence and is on grade level (eighth grade). She can see and hear reasonably well, so input of information is unimpaired. Her verbal intelligence measured by the WISC–IV Verbal Comprehension index is 110. Her nonverbal abilities are lowered by her motor difficulties and slow fine-motor speed, thus a nonverbal IQ estimate is not a valid indication of her general intelligence. Her receptive language ability is a clear strength as noted on the Peabody Picture Vocabulary Test (PPVT–4; Dunn & Dunn, 2007a; score of 122). Additional testing on other measures indicated that learning and memory abilities were within average limits, thus allowing her to acquire and retain content. Lauren's major impediment is output. She does not have the motor coordination to write or type and does not have the oral motor ability to speak in lengthy sentences that are easily intelligible. Testing with Lauren takes time, creativity, and special technology.

Multiple-choice tests are the easiest type of test for Lauren. She can either read the question in large print or listen to a reader speak the question and then press a response keypad for A, B, C, or D. Teachers try to give most tests in this format. Lauren can take standardized tests this way as long as she is given double time. A bigger problem occurs on essay exams in which a narrative response is required or on a written report or term paper. Such tasks are arduous for Lauren and need to be kept to a minimum; however, she is willing to work exceedingly hard to compose an essay.

What seems to work best for Lauren is a scribe who is familiar with her speech patterns (i.e., her mother or resource teacher). A one-page essay may take an hour, which includes dictation, sometimes pointing to pictures or symbols on her communication board, and some clarification questions between Lauren and her scribe. Her essays are not lengthy or sophisticated, but they generally get her ideas across.

Key issues in this case are the extent to which one has to alter tests for Lauren to access them, and the subsequent meaning of a test score aided by many accommodations. For example, on a statewide writing test, Lauren received extended time, a separate room, a scribe, extra breaks, and testing over multiple days. The scribe was very familiar with Lauren and very much an advocate who may have added words here or there to promote clarity. Given these multiple accommodations, is the assessment of Lauren valid? Is it a comparable evaluation to the standard exam taken by other students? Might this test score overestimate Lauren's true abilities in writing? We have no research that answers these questions, and in a single case such as this there is no easy way to determine the validity of these test accommodations.

7

SETTING AND PRESENTATION ACCOMMODATIONS

Many students with disabilities require accommodations because they cannot understand what test items are asking them to do. These students may be unable to see or hear the test directions or item content, or they may simply be too readily distracted by extraneous noises during the testing session. *Setting and presentation accommodations* pertain to alterations in the exam itself or exam conditions prior to the examinee beginning to take the test. These "front-end" alterations include changes to the test location, the test directions, and/or the test format. In this chapter, we describe most such accommodations and discuss some of them in more detail, particularly those that are more common and have been researched.

http://dx.doi.org/10.1037/14468-007
Testing Accommodations for Students With Disabilities: Research-Based Practice, by B. J. Lovett and L. J. Lewandowski

SETTING ACCOMMODATIONS

Exam Location

The most common setting accommodation involves changing the test location. The accommodation goes by a variety of names: separate room, private room, quiet room, small group testing, distraction-free room, etc. It is often proffered or requested so that the examinee has fewer distractions. In other cases, a separate room is needed in order to implement other test accommodations. Most often, it is students with a diagnosis of attention-deficit/hyperactivity disorder (ADHD) who request this accommodation. However, it is not unusual for students with other diagnoses to also ask for a private or semiprivate room.[1] In a minority of cases, a private room is requested because the individual has a medical problem that might require rest breaks, medication access, food and water access, frequent bathroom use, or even (typically in postsecondary settings) breast pumping. In a small percentage of cases, examinees with psychiatric conditions request a private room. For example, a person prone to panic attacks may be less likely to have an attack in a private room and would not disturb other examinees should an attack occur. It is easier for a proctor to manage this situation in a private room than a room with 500 examinees. Another condition that might warrant a separate room is Tourette syndrome, in which a person has motor and vocal tics that would be disruptive to those around him. Similarly, a person with obsessive–compulsive behaviors (e.g., hair twirling, pencil tapping), or a person with autism spectrum disorder who makes odd repetitive behaviors (e.g., hand flapping), would probably be best served in a separate location.

Private and semiprivate test locations that reduce noise distractions are by far the most common setting accommodations. Other setting accommodations are relatively rare. For example, a situation may arise in which a student is bedridden and cannot go to a public location. In a sense, the test has to come to the student. Although this is unusual, some students have been tested at home or even in a hospital setting. In schools, it is not uncommon for students in special education to take tests in a resource room, sometimes in small groups. In certain situations, adaptations need to be made to a test setting. For example, a room with increased or reduced lighting may be necessary for students with certain visual problems or with certain acoustic properties for students with auditory problems. Students with physical disabilities may need certain furniture or equipment to get them properly and comfortably

---

[1]Over the last 500 accommodation request cases (dealing with LD, ADHD, and traumatic brain injury) reviewed by the authors, 98% requested extended time and 45% also requested a special location.

seated. These kinds of accommodations are not usually controversial. Often, they are based on the availability of space and personnel. Thus, most schools and colleges do whatever they can to accommodate students in this way. For high-stakes exams administered by private testing agencies (e.g., when students take the SAT), location accommodations are sometimes scrutinized more closely because agencies must pay additional proctors to administer the exam in additional locations and want to ensure that the accommodations are actually needed by examinees and are not merely a preference or a product of the examinees having received the accommodations in the past.

Although there are multiple reasons for using a private test location, including medical comfort, reduced distractions, and avoiding disruptive behavior, there seems to be very little specific research on the potential effectiveness or validity of private versus group testing. Most instructors and test providers probably see no threat to the constructs being assessed if an examinee takes a test in a private room, and indeed, it is difficult to think of a circumstance in which a test developer would want to measure an examinee's ability to perform in the presence of others. Perhaps professional licensure or certification exams, or occasionally music performance assessments, might require this, but these situations are quite rare.

Apparently, most schools and test agencies do not feel that a private room is an unfair advantage, but in fact little research is available to show if it helps or hurts. One could argue that a private room should improve a student's performance because it removes distractions and may even quell test anxiety levels. On the other hand, a private room might work against the examinee who will not benefit from an instructor's comments and clarifications during an exam.[2] It is even possible that tests given in a group format may have a social facilitation function that keeps students motivated and focused on the test. At this point we do not have sufficient research to answer these questions confidently. Chances are that benefits from a private room are person specific and possibly disability specific as well.

To begin to address this accommodation, Wood, Lewandowski, and Lambert (2012) examined performances of nondisabled college students on a reading comprehension test taken in a private setting and a group setting. They administered both Comprehension Forms G and H of the Nelson-Denny Reading Test (J. I. Brown, Fishco, & Hanna, 1993) to students who either took a form in a private setting first ($n = 35$) or a group setting first

---

[2]Indeed, in the context of college/university classroom exams, this can be a significant problem. College students who receive testing accommodations often take their exams at an administrative location, such as an office for disability services, or a study skills center. The exams are administered by proctors rather than the class instructors, and so students do not have the opportunity to ask questions about items, even if there are apparent errors in the items. This is especially problematic when one considers that students with certain disabilities may be more likely to need clarification.

($n = 27$). The private setting was a small (6' × 8') room with a desk and no windows. The group-testing room was a classroom that seated a maximum of 50 students at tables on either side of a center aisle. There was approximately a 2-week period between each student's test sessions. The results indicated no significant effect for test setting, with a mean score of 25.45 correct when taking the test in a private room versus a mean score of 27.02 in a group setting. Wood et al. concluded that testing in a private room did not have any positive effect on students' scores, and if anything, there was a trend to perform better in a group setting, perhaps because of social facilitation. At the very least, then, private testing accommodations do not appear to be unfair to nondisabled students who do not receive them. As Wood et al. noted, it is possible that a private setting might be beneficial to students with disabilities, and such an effect would then be specific only to those students. To our knowledge, no study has been conducted comparing disability and control groups across private and group-testing conditions.

So in the absence of research evidence, what might guide a decision about the use of a separate test location? One approach would be to conduct a brief experiment in which the target student is given comparable tests in a group or private setting. If there is a clear difference in performance favoring a separate room, and this accommodation mitigates impairment that interferes with test access and performance, then the accommodation should be used. Unfortunately, test agencies that administer standardized exams do not have this luxury. They must infer that certain types of impairment interfere with a person's test-taking performance. Students with significant distractibility or unusual medical needs are good candidates for such an accommodation. In other cases, an examinee who may be disruptive in a group setting (e.g., tic disorder) may warrant a separate test location. The potential downside of a separate location, at least for classroom tests, is that the isolated examinee may miss opportunities to ask or hear questions about the test that are raised in the group setting. This possibility, coupled with the data from the Wood et al. (2012) study, might make an individual think twice about requesting a separate testing room.

Changes in Seating

One setting accommodation that has been around for many years is preferential seating. Often, teachers have used this procedure without considering it an accommodation. It is natural for teachers to place a child with mild visual or hearing problems closer to the teacher, usually in the front of the class. It is no surprise that teachers also might place some of the more rambunctious and disruptive students in the front as well, if for no other reason than to keep an eye on them and quickly quell any undesired behavior. This practice has been extended to the test setting as well. In a standardized or high-stakes setting, there may be no teacher with prior knowledge of a given student. Instead, there is a proctor who has been trained to follow specific procedures.

If students have visual or hearing impairment that could make hearing directions or seeing writing on a blackboard a challenge, a reasonable accommodation is preferential seating. The same would apply to a student seated by the door who may need frequent bathroom breaks. In more extreme cases, a student may be placed in the testing room, yet in a study carrel or behind a partition so as to reduce visual and auditory distractions. Preferential seating has not been a controversial accommodation because it takes little effort to implement and is not likely to provide any test advantage. This is not an accommodation that is likely to affect the skills or constructs being assessed, so it should be available to students who can demonstrate a relevant deficit in sensory functioning or attention.

ACCOMMODATIONS FOR TEST DIRECTIONS

Often, test directions are written on the test itself. For students with dyslexia or visual impairments, as well as some with ADHD and other disabilities, written directions can be challenging or confusing. Sometimes students ask that directions be read to them, or they may be given extra time to reread the directions. This is seldom a problem for instructors giving classroom tests, especially because all students can benefit from hearing the directions. In rare cases, students may be given permission to ask questions about the directions or have them paraphrased. The goal here is to assure that the student understands what he or she is being asked to do on the exam. Of course, to make some of these accommodations means the student will probably need to be tested in a private or semiprivate setting.

For some tests, including standardized tests, the written directions are accompanied by instructions from a proctor. These oral instructions are intended to help students understand the test directions as well as the procedures, timing, and rules of the exam process. In some cases, instructions need to be simplified or paraphrased, and these subtle changes are considered accommodations. Students who have a hearing impairment may need to have test instructions conveyed via sign language. If there are only written test directions, and it is unnecessary to read the directions to all examinees, then students with dyslexia, blindness, and visual impairment may be given an audiotape version of the test directions or given the directions in a manner consistent with presentation accommodations (e.g., large print). More than likely, however, a classroom teacher would have the opportunity to read directions aloud to an entire class.

There seems to be no systematic research that compares different ways in which students receive test directions. It is assumed in any type of assessment that examinees must have a clear understanding of what is demanded by a test. If the goal of assessment is to get the best estimate of a student's target skill, then it is essential that all students have a common understanding of the test directions and procedures. Sound test development extends to the quality and clarity of the test's directions. All test examiners should do whatever they can to accommodate students in this regard, whether it means written, oral, or signed directions, including a combination of these modes. The issue of clarifying/simplifying instructions is more difficult; it is easy for teachers to inadvertently provide additional information that makes items easier when clarifications are offered. In the case of teacher-made exams, clarifications should generally be made to the class as a whole (to prevent unfairness; students' willingness to ask for clarification should not affect their scores). In the case of high-stakes exams, clarifications should only be done very rarely and very carefully, and the exact nature of the clarifications should be documented in writing for potential review by test users.

PRESENTATION ACCOMMODATIONS

Format Alterations

Among the earliest and most straightforward test accommodations are those that involve changes in the format of presentation. Typically, tests have been delivered on paper, and students have responded via a pen or pencil. Before computers and assistive technology, most tests were presented via paper and pencil, and most classroom tests are still presented this way. The most obvious examples of a presentation alteration are a Braille version of a test given to a blind student and a large-print test for someone with visual impairment.

Vision-Based Accommodations

No one would need to submit a Braille accommodation for a blind student to a specificity analysis per Phillips (1994), because it is obvious that a test in Braille would not help a sighted person, only a blind person. In general, Braille is considered to be an equivalent alternative to print reading, although the characters being read are raised dot configurations that are felt by one's fingertips. With regard to Braille reading speed, it would appear that Braille reading is generally slower than sight reading. Legge, Madison, and Mansfield (1999) found that the median reading speed of a group of

44 experienced Braille readers (adults) was only 124 words per minute. This is slower than the average oral reading speed (approximately 190 words per minute) of most nondisabled adults (Lewandowski, Codding, Kleinmann, & Tucker, 2003). Thus, it is likely that Braille readers will need extra time (e.g., 50%) to complete exams with heavy reading loads.

With regard to mathematics, there are additional problems of nonvisual accessibility. Braille is essentially a linear and sequential process like sighted text reading. Mathematics leans heavily on two- and three-dimensional representations, and many test items include graphs, shapes, length measurements, spatial estimation, and various other visual diagrams. These are not easy to convey in Braille and require familiarity with additional Braille codes. This may prompt test examiners to interpret math-testing results with caution and find ways to better assess certain math skills. For example, Landau, Russell, Gourgey, Erin, and Cowan (2003) evaluated the Talking Tactile Tablet (Touch Graphics, New York, NY) as a math-testing tool for students with visual impairment. This device could read test items as well as display tactile representations of shapes and graphs. Although such technologies are still under development, they are making advances in creating math tests that are more accessible to the visually impaired.

The remaining question about Braille as an accommodation is whether the school or test agency is obligated to produce a Braille version of a test. It may be less expensive and more efficient for a blind student to take an audiotape version of the test and make responses into a tape recorder or use a reader/scribe. If one of these alternative test methods is agreeable to both parties, and the method is a valid way of assessing the student's target skill (i.e., no pictorial information in the test), then such an accommodation can be substituted for Braille.

Under the ADA Amendments Act of 2008 (ADAAA), the test entity must administer exams in such a way as to "best ensure" that the exam measures underlying skills rather than examinees' disabilities. The best ensure goal is weighed in the context of another ADAAA concept, "undue hardship." Depending on the test entity's size, structure, and resources, it may not always be able to supply the most ideal accommodation, but it may be able to provide a reasonable alternative. In our previous example, let's say the student will be at a charter school for one year and the school does not have a Braille machine to make tests. Is it absolutely essential that the school buy this machine? Or could the school and student work out an alternative method of testing that both assures fair and equal access while not creating an undue hardship on the school budget? Questions such as these are not clearly addressed by legislation and therefore must either be handled in a sensitive and collaborative manner or by the court system. As we have said before, an important aspect of test accommodations is a match between the student's individual characteristics and needs and an accommodation method that mitigates the student's impairment while arriving at the best possible assessment of the student. If we do a good job of objectively identifying students' impairments, then we should be able to find ways to mitigate them in most test situations.

Students with learning disabilities (LD), particularly in reading, may have almost as much trouble accessing a written exam as a blind student, yet they have not learned to read in Braille. In such cases, the student may opt for an audio version of the test. Recordings for the Blind makes audio textbooks available for such students, so why not do the same for exams? For students who read yet tend to make numerous decoding errors, they may be best served by both visual and audio input when presented the test. There are now a number of assistive technologies that will allow students to both see words on a page and hear each word spoken, thus assuring accurately read test information.

Colored Overlays. Before turning to assistive technologies, we should mention a few more minor format alterations. Some students report becoming easily overwhelmed by too much information on a page. One accommodation used for this situation is limiting the amount of text or number of math problems on a page. In a sense it means spreading the exam out over more pages. In a similar vein, students who are distracted by extraneous information may benefit from underlining, visual cues (e.g., direction arrows), and increased space between items. On occasion, examinees request covered overlays to place over the text in a test. They have been told by a clinician that they have scotopic sensitivity syndrome (SSS; also known as Irlen syndrome), a controversial disorder regarding possible problems in the visual system that could contribute to reading disorders. The antidote for this syndrome, according to believers in SSS, is to change from the harsh black on white reading to a color (e.g., yellow, pink) that may ease eyestrain and presumably improve reading input. Research has suggested that some people do have visual symptoms that are exacerbated by reading (Hoyt, 1990). Colored overlays, as well as other vision therapies, have been known to reduce these symptoms. However, research has not found that colored overlays significantly improve reading performance or "cure" dyslexia (Blaskey et al., 1990; Wilkins, 2003). Because the theory and technique has not been empirically validated, schools and test agencies may be hesitant to approve such an accommodation. At the K–12 level, it would be helpful for teachers or school psychologists to use small-N design methods (particularly reversal designs) to determine whether the lenses are even helpful. However, at the postsecondary level, if an examinee wishes to bring a sheet of yellow acetate to place over a test page, there probably is no harm done or no unfair advantage conferred.

Large Print. Large-print accommodations have been defined in a variety of ways, including 14-point Helvetica font (Mick, 1989) and twice the size of standard print (Burk, 1999). The point sizes most often used are 10 and 12 point for documents to be read by people with good vision reading in good light (Gaster & Clark, 1995). Although the optimum font size will vary for each individual depending on acuity loss and related factors, print that is too large will reduce reading efficiency (Lovie-Kitchen, Oliver, Bruce, Leighton, & Leighton, 1994) and may even be confusing.

Fourteen-point type has been found to increase readability and can increase test scores for both students with and without disabilities, compared with 12-point type (L. S. Fuchs, Fuchs, Eaton, Hamlett, Binkley, et al., 2000). It appears that larger font sizes are most effective for young students who are learning to read and for students with visual difficulties (Hoener, Salend, & Kay, 1997), and they also serve to reduce eye fatigue (Arditi, 1999). It appears that 12- or 14-point type is used for ease of reading for most people, and larger print may be required for those with visual impairments, depending on the type and degree of impairment. Of course the relationship between readability and point size is also dependent on the typeface used (Gaster & Clark, 1995). Furthermore, letters that are too close together are difficult for partially sighted readers. Spacing needs to be wide between both letters and words (Gaster & Clark, 1995). Justified text is more difficult to read than unjustified text—especially for poor readers (M. Gregory & Poulton, 1970; Zachrisson, 1965). Staggered right margins are easier to see and scan than uniform or block-style, right-side margins (Arditi, 1999; Grise, Beattie, & Algozzine, 1982; Menlove & Hammond, 1998). Obviously, there are a number of visual features to keep in mind when designing a test, let alone developing accommodations for students with visual disabilities.

A small body of research has shown that large print helps students with LD (Burk, 1999; Grise, Beattie, & Algozzine, 1982; Mick, 1989) and visual impairments. For example, Bennett, Rock, and Jirele (1987) found that students with visual impairments performed similarly to nondisabled peers when they alone used a large-print version of the GRE. Bennett et al. also supported the validity of a large-print accommodation for students with visual impairments taking the SAT. Although large print seems to be an effective accommodation for students with visual impairments, Wright and Wendler (1994) found that large-print and Braille exams take longer and require extended time. It appears that the larger the font type, the greater the need for extended time, so this combination of test accommodations should be a consideration. Typically, students with visual needs will have experience with various font sizes and know what size works best for them. Most such requests are honored by test examiners because once print is going to be modified, the size does not really matter and there is little worry about this accommodation providing an unwarranted advantage. In fact, in an accommodation preference survey study, Lewandowski, Lambert, Lovett, Panahon, and Sytsma (in press) found that large print was rated by nondisabled college students as the least likely accommodation to improve their test performance.

Audio Accommodations

Students who are deaf or hearing impaired typically need test presentation accommodations. They usually have no problem responding on multiple-choice, written, or computerized exams and also have no difficulty reading stimulus materials. Their main difficulties concern test directions and orally delivered test information. In most cases, directions can be thoroughly produced in text form, yet instructors often verbalize special instructions to students, alert them to time remaining, answer student questions, and clarify ambiguous words on a test. These verbalizations during a test need to be conveyed to the student with hearing impairment. Some examinees will access this information with hearing aids or a sound amplification system in the room, and less frequently, others will use a sign language interpreter. Certainly for oral exams, such as a childhood spelling test or an oral defense of a master's thesis project, an interpreter would need to be on hand. There is little research on signed directions, but what little there is seems to suggest a benefit for students with hearing impairment without inappropriately inflating performance (Benderson, 1988; P. M. Sullivan, 1982). In other words, signing directions seems to be a valid accommodation for the deaf and hearing impaired.

In a school or classroom, audio accommodations are typically quite individualized. Depending on a student's hearing ability, the instructor can use amplification, elaborated text, or sign language to deliver test directions and content. In such cases, the audio accommodation attempts to circumvent hearing limitations. Other audio-based accommodations are used to actually take advantage of good hearing when limitations occur in visual or reading abilities. For example, a blind student may take an auditory version of a test, or a student with dyslexia may use a screen reader to pronounce the words on an exam. In a sense, these are also considered audio accommodations.

Live Read-Aloud Accommodation. One of the more common presentation accommodations, and one that has been studied more than most, is the use of a read-aloud protocol. In this accommodation, students are read test questions by a teacher or examiner. Typically, this is a one-on-one procedure, but it is possible to do such testing in a group. In a one-on-one interaction, the student may be more likely to ask questions of the reader or ask for parts to be reread. Students with severe reading disabilities in particular say that they need to hear the words to enhance their comprehension of text. Older students, including those taking professional exams, may be so used to the read-aloud system that they ask to be in a separate room so they can read the exam aloud themselves. Despite the common use of this accommodation, particularly in K–12 grades, the research findings on its effectiveness are somewhat mixed (S. J. Thompson, Blount, & Thurlow, 2002).

Although a number of studies have shown positive effects of read-aloud accommodations (e.g., Fletcher at al., 2006; Huynh & Barton, 2006), including differential boost effects (i.e., that the accommodations help students with disabilities more than nondisabled students; Crawford & Tindal, 2004; L. S. Fuchs, 2000; Randall & Engelhard, 2010; Tindal, Heath, Hollenbeck, Almond, & Harniss, 1998), other studies are not supportive and/or raise controversial issues with this accommodation. In their review of research, Royer and Randall (2012) indicated that 19 studies showed positive results of oral presentation for students with disabilities, 10 studies showed no effect on the scores of students with disabilities, and five studies found evidence that the accommodation alters the constructs of the test. An alteration of the construct may have been evidence that students with and without disabilities both improved in test performance, or there was a statistical change in the construct being measured that was due to the accommodation.

Results from various studies seem to depend on the type of test (e.g., reading, math), age, and disability of the students, and complexity of the reading material. For example, some investigators have shown that read-aloud effects on mathematics tests may be contingent on the item difficulty as well as the readability level of the text (L. S. Fuchs, Fuchs, Eaton, Hamlett, & Karns, 2000; Helwig, Rozek-Tedesco, Tindal, Heath, & Almond, 1999). L. S. Fuchs, Fuchs, Eaton, Hamlett, and Karns (2000) found that students with poor oral reading skills and good math proficiency benefited from a read-aloud accommodation, whereas students with high reading skills did not. Weston (2003) also noted that students with LD who were poor readers gained the most from a read-aloud accommodation on a math test. In a somewhat related finding, Elbaum (2007) demonstrated that students with and without LD benefitted slightly from oral administration of a math test, but only elementary students with LD showed greater gains than their nondisabled peers—among secondary students, read-aloud gains were actually greater for students without LD.

To confuse matters further, some authors have found that the read-aloud condition had no positive effect on the performance of students with disabilities (Elbaum, Arquelles, Campbell, & Saleh, 2004; McKevitt & Elliott, 2003). For example, Helwig and Tindal (2003) studied the effect of the read-aloud condition on math performance of students with and without disabilities in Grades 4 through 8. They expected the read-aloud accommodation to work best for students with low reading skills and adequate math skills.

Contrary to their expectations, they found that these students performed better in the standard, nonaccommodated condition. Similarly, McKevitt and Elliott (2003) examined the effects of read aloud (by teacher) in junior high school students with and without disabilities. They found that neither group improved test performance in the read-aloud condition, even though students preferred the accommodation and thought they did better with it.

In a related yet different study, Elbaum, Arquelles, Campbell, and Saleh (2004) examined the effect of students themselves reading a test aloud as a test accommodation. The study included 456 students (283 with LD) in Grades 6 through 10. Students took a reading comprehension test constructed of third- to fifth-grade-level reading passages and accompanying questions. All students took the assessment first in the standard condition and second with instructions to read the passages aloud at their own pace. The researchers found that test performance did not differ between the two conditions for either group of students (i.e., with or without LD). The researchers noticed, however, that the scores of students with LD were more variable in the accommodated condition than were the scores of students without disabilities, raising the possibility that certain students may benefit more from this accommodation than others, thereby underscoring the need for individualized assessment.

In addition to the mixed results on read-aloud presentations, some researchers have suggested that this accommodation may under certain conditions alter the construct being tested, thereby adding a source of construct-irrelevant variance. For example, Bielinski, Thurlow, Ysseldyke, Freidebach, and Freidebach (2001) examined differential item functioning (DIF) across large groups of students with and without disabilities who had taken math and reading tests with and without accommodations (read aloud). They found that approximately 50% of the reading items and 20% of the math items were identified as having DIF when read aloud. Cahalan-Laitusis, Cook, and Aicher (2004) examined DIF on third- and seventh-grade assessments of English language arts by comparing students with LD who received a read-aloud accommodation with students with and without LD who received no accommodation. Their results showed that 7% to 12% of the test items functioned differently for the students with LD who received read-aloud accommodations compared with either of the comparison groups. A similar study by Bolt (2004) compared smaller samples of students on three state assessments of reading or English language arts. In all three states, the read-aloud accommodation resulted in significantly more items with DIF than other accommodations. These studies, to varying degrees, provide evidence that a read-aloud accommodation may change the construct being assessed. However, it should be noted that several studies reported that the read-aloud accommodation did not alter the construct of the test or meaning of the test scores (Barton, 2001; Barton & Huynh, 2003; Huynh, Meyer, & Gallant, 2004; D. Kim, Schneider, & Siskind, 2009).

Several issues may affect the validity of read aloud as a test accommodation. First, it may not work; even the studies that show some positive results tend to produce small effect sizes, and a number of studies find no positive results. Second, it may be helpful on items that have high reading complexity but interfere with performance on less complex items (Bolt & Thurlow, 2007; Elbaum 2007; Weston, 2003). Finally, reading the test aloud may add a source of construct-irrelevant variance. Indeed, read-aloud accommodations change a task from reading comprehension to listening comprehension. Test examiners have to consider whether listening comprehension is a skill that is relevant to their assessment and/or is an acceptable proxy for reading comprehension. In summary, it does not appear that read aloud is for everyone or every situation. Examiners will need to be careful when and how they use it. It appears that it is most suited for poor readers on tests that require good reading skills. Read aloud may not be well suited for students with good reading skills and or items that are designed to measure reading skills. Students may find that this accommodation is paced too slowly and may interfere with processing the information.

Because read-aloud or oral-administration accommodations are so varied in use and effectiveness, we thought it might be instructive to illustrate how an agency might implement this accommodation. Following is an example of instructions to proctors for oral administration of statewide exams in Texas from the *2011–2012 Accommodations Manual* (Texas Student Assessment Program, 2012).

> An oral/signed administration is an accommodation for eligible students taking TAKS, TAKS (Accommodated), or TAKS–M mathematics, science, and/or social studies tests. For students who are deaf or hard of hearing and are eligible for this administration, specific guidelines for signing test content for a state assessment are included in Appendix C. Student eligibility is described on the following page.
>
> Oral administration can encompass different levels of reading support for each student on any part of the test (including the state-supplied mathematics and science charts) or on allowable supplemental aids. The test administrator may provide the following levels of support:
>
> Reading only a few words or phrases at student request
> Reading multiple sentences throughout the test at student request
> Reading the test in its entirety
>
> It is the responsibility of the ARD committee, the Section 504 committee, or the committee of knowledgeable persons to appropriately document the level of reading support the student needs. A student may

request a change in the level of reading support provided during testing only if this option is documented.

It is important to remember that for all students in grade 3, reading assistance is part of test administration procedures on the mathematics test and is not considered an accommodation. Documentation of reading assistance in this case is not required. However, if a grade 3 student needs the entire test read aloud, the eligibility criteria for an oral administration must be met and documentation is required. (pp. 77–78)

Obviously, students' needs for a read-aloud accommodation can vary greatly and may require the reading of certain words, phrases, or complete text. Clearly, students with reading or visual difficulties who cannot fluently access written material will need to be assessed for reading ability as well as adequate hearing. Similar considerations must be given to a student who needs a test signed because he or she has both hearing and reading impairments. Note that the Texas state guidelines prohibit read aloud on a reading test because reading is the target skill being assessed.

CD Test Versions. Many high-stakes test agencies offer their exams on a CD for students with various disabilities (i.e., visual and reading impairments). Because some agencies conduct thousands of exams each year and have hundreds of examinees with disabilities requesting accommodations, they invariably have a need to convert their exams from print to audio. Exams on a CD require the use of a CD player that can be stopped, rewound, and replayed. Examinees also typically use headphones with this accommodation or take the test in a separate room. Often this accommodation is accompanied by extended time because of the time taken to stop, start, and replay sections of the CD. Another consideration, as noted earlier, is that a CD version of a test does not require reading, but rather requires listening comprehension. The test agencies must understand that this is a fundamental change in the test procedure and may affect the construct being examined. For example, if the test purpose is to measure reading comprehension, then an audio version of the test makes little sense. However, if the purpose of the test is to assess knowledge of American history, an audio version should be comparable to a text version and not threaten the validity of the exam. CD versions of an exam can be costly to make and may alter what is being assessed. Test agencies are urged to consider these accommodations requests carefully.

Presentation Accommodations Using Technology

Increasingly, presentation accommodations are provided using high-tech solutions. We explore several of the more common solutions next.

Read-Aloud Technology

We have already discussed read-aloud variations that do not involve technology. These accommodations can be varied with the assistance of technology. One large-scale study compared the effects of teacher read aloud with the effects of a computer that read the oral script from a CD. L. W. S. Harris (2008) examined the performance of over 5,000 students with disabilities in Grades 6 through 8 on English language arts tests. The results showed no significant difference in performance between the two read-aloud conditions, as well as similar factor structures. These results suggest that these read-aloud variations are essentially equivalent. Calhoon, Fuchs, and Hamlett (2000) reported a similar finding. They administered math tests to high school students under standard conditions, teacher read, computer read, and computer read with video. They found better performance in all three accommodated conditions, yet no difference among these three conditions. This again suggests that read-aloud accommodations are generally equivalent to one another and can be somewhat helpful to students with disabilities.

The read-aloud accommodations have been found to be effective under some circumstances. Tindal (2002) showed that read-aloud effects are not universal. He examined 2,000 students in fourth through eighth grades with and without disabilities on state mathematics tests. The tests were given in a standard condition as well as read aloud using a videotaped administration. The results showed a benefit for the videotaped condition, but only for fourth- and fifth-grade students with and without disabilities. This study suggests that the performance outcomes may be more dependent on age than on disability status. Laitusis (2010) similarly found that fourth-grade students tended to benefit more from an audio version (vs. standard administration) of a reading comprehension test, but she also found that the gains were larger for students with disabilities than for those without disabilities. Again, the findings across these studies reveal a trend in support of read-aloud accommodations, even using technology, particularly for certain types of tests, age groups, and students with reading disabilities. However, the results are not always consistent across task, age of student, presence of disability, and technology used.

Reading Pen. One type of read-aloud technology is a reading pen. There are different versions of this easy-to-use, handheld technology (e.g., ReadingPen TS by Wizcom; Text Reader by TopScan; see Figure 7.1).

Essentially, these devices act as scanners that use an optical character recognition system. As a student moves the pen across a word or words, the text is scanned into the pen and/or into a computer. These pens have text-to-speech capabilities and can readily sound out the scanned word(s). Therefore,

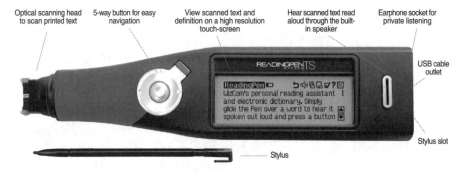

Optical scanning head to scan printed text

5-way button for easy navigation

View scanned text and definition on a high resolution touch-screen

Hear scanned text read aloud through the built-in speaker

Earphone socket for private listening

USB cable outlet

Stylus slot

Stylus

Figure 7.1. ReadingPen TS by Wizcom. From Wizcom Tech Ltd. promotional materials. Adapted with permission.

the student gets an accurate reading of any word. Some of the reading pens also have a dictionary capability, allowing a student to immediately retrieve the definition and synonyms for a scanned word. Obviously, this technology is handy and easy to use. Reading pens have extensive scanning capabilities that can be helpful in school or work, but it is the text reading capability that can serve as a test accommodation. Students with dyslexia as well as English language learners certainly benefit from this learning tool, and some request to use this technology for exams.

One of the only studies on the efficacy of reading pens was conducted by Higgins and Raskind (2005). They administered the passage comprehension subtest from the Woodcock Reading Mastery Test (Woodcock, 1987) to 30 students with LD (ages 10–18) in both standard conditions and with Reading Pen II assistance (counterbalanced order). Students had 2 weeks to practice with the reading pen. Students were able to use the text to speech and dictionary capabilities of the pen. These researchers' results showed a clear advantage for use of the reading pen ($d = 0.69$), with students averaging seven more correct comprehension items (with reading pen, $M = 23.38$ items; without reading pen, $M = 15.8$ items). Unfortunately, there is no way of knowing how much benefit accrued from the word reading versus the dictionary use.

A more recent study by Thurlow, Moen, Lekwa, and Scullin (2010) examined the effectiveness of the Reading Pen II on reading comprehension performance (Gray Silent Reading Test; Wiederholt & Blalock, 2000) of sixth- and eighth-grade students with ($n = 32$) and without ($n = 44$) disabilities. Unlike the findings of Higgins and Raskind (2005), their results showed no significant gains from the use of the reading pen for either group. In fact, only 11 of 76 students had a better comprehension score in the pen-assisted condition. The characteristics of these 11 students were not reported. The authors concluded that the reading pen was not particularly useful, even for students receiving special education reading services. It is possible that the difference in findings between the two studies is that Higgins and Raskind (2005) allowed students to use the dictionary features for word definitions and synonyms. This assistance with vocabulary, a well-documented predictor of comprehension, may help explain the positive effects noted by Higgins and Raskind.

Text-to-Speech (TTS) Screen Readers. Because reading pens require manual control to scan text and essentially read one word at a time, they are less desirable for reading text passages, particularly when the examinee is a poor reader needing to hear every word read aloud. In these cases, computerized screen readers using text-to-speech (TTS) software are most often requested. This TTS software is so advanced that most new computers as well as smart phones have a version built into the operating systems. In addition to these TTS applications, there are stand-alone systems that may offer additional learning features. Some examples of these include the following: Jobs Access With Speech (JAWS) from Freedom Scientific; the Kurzweil 3000; Dolphin Supernova; and ZoomText Magnifier/Reader from Ai Squared. The Kurzweil systems have been widely used as assisted learning/testing tools for persons with disabilities. The latest version, Kurzweil 3000 with Firefly from Kurzweil Educational Systems (2013), has the following features:

- read text by word, line, sentence, or paragraph;
- customize reading to continuous, word by word, or self-paced;
- increase or decrease size of display;
- look up definitions of words;
- translate text;
- customize reading speed;
- choose from four different high quality voices;
- choose location of toolbar;
- cloud storage for digital files; and
- flexible user management system.

There are many different software versions of TTS, and these can be applied to a wide variety of devices, including desktop and laptop computers, pads and tablets, and even phones. Typically, students are looking at a visual display that presents text. The student can scroll through text and determine how much and how fast the material is presented. Most TTS systems allow for simultaneous highlighting of the visual word and the spoken word. A user can manually highlight words or have the entire text read aloud and highlighted as it goes. In most cases, the reading speed can be set by the user. Some computers have TTS capabilities built into their operating systems, and in addition, there are a number of TTS software products that are commercially available (e.g., JAWS, ZoomText, WordRead, Dragon).

A number of investigators (P. B. Brown & Augustine, 2000; Burk, 1999; Calhoon, Fuchs, & Hamlett, 2000; Dolan, Hall, Banerjee, Chun, & Strangman, 2005; Elkind, Black & Murray, 1996; Higgins & Raskind, 1997; Hollenbeck, Rozek-Tedesco, Tindal, & Glasgow, 2000; Torgesen & Barker, 1995) have examined the effectiveness of TTS systems for presenting test material to students with LD. Most of these studies have found support for the benefits of computerized read-aloud systems. As early as 1993, Elkind, Cohen, and Murray found that a TTS format improved the reading comprehension of middle school students with dyslexia. This finding was corroborated by Leong (1995), as well as by Montali and Lewandowski (1996). Higgins and Raskind (1997) found reading comprehension benefits from TTS for post-secondary students with severe reading disabilities. Dolan et al. (2005) found that high school students with LD had better reading comprehension on the TTS format versus paper and pencil when passages were more than 100 words in length, and they also noted that students generally preferred the TTS presentation. Other research showed that students could read faster and had better reading endurance when using TTS on a computer (Elkind, Black, & Murray, 1996). Secondary and postsecondary students who have problems with decoding and have slow (< 150 words per minute) reading speeds appear to benefit most from TTS (see Elkind, 1998). Because most studies have focused on students with disabilities, we do not know whether the benefits of TTS are specific to only students with disabilities.

Computer-Assisted Testing

We have already discussed some of the technologies used for reading tests and making responses on tests, most of which involve computers. Computer-assisted testing (CAT) allows for a wide variety of alterations in the way exams can be presented. At a very general level, there is research to suggest that students perform better on CAT than paper-and-pencil testing (PPT) and that students prefer CAT to PPT (Dolan et al., 2005). However, the use of technology is far more complicated and varied than just CAT versus PPT. Computer technology allows tests to be given under varied luminance, background, and contrast, as well as variation in font size and type. CAT is much more versatile than PPT and can serve a wide variety of visual accommodations. CAT is also a more refined technology for timing. Exams can be started, stopped, or extended very precisely and without human error. The use of computers as presentation devices also adds the feature of dual modality inputs. We have already described voice recognition technology that allows students to dictate what they want to write as well as text-to-speech systems that convert written text on the computer display to oral speech as words are highlighted on the computer screen (screen reading). Other technologies that have become standard features on computers are sometimes used as accommodations, such as spell check, grammar check, thesaurus, dictionaries, and language translation. Clearly, a test presented via computer opens up many other possibilities for test accommodations.

A number of studies have been conducted on the comparability of CAT and PPT presentation formats, including several reviews of the many studies. For example, Mazzeo and Harvey (1988) reviewed 30 comparability studies across a variety of test types (i.e., intelligence, aptitude, personality, and achievement tests). They found mixed results concerning the comparability of CAT and PPT formats. In particular, they suggested that test mode seemed to have no effect on power tests, but there was a significant effect on speeded tests in favor of CAT (see also the meta-analysis by Mead & Drasgow, 1993). In a later meta-analysis by J. Kim (1999), CATs and PPTs were found to yield comparable scores on a variety of ability measures. A more recent meta-analysis similarly found no differential effect of these formats on reading assessments for K–12 students (Wang, Jiao, Young, Brooks, & Olson, 2008). Some studies found CATs to yield lower scores than PPTs (e.g., Bennett et al., 2008, Choi & Tinkler, 2002), and a few researchers suggested that perhaps lack of computer familiarity could be a moderating factor (e.g., Goldberg & Pedulla, 2002; Pomplun & Custer, 2005).

Although it is difficult to easily summarize the number and variety of comparability studies, it appears that the majority tend to find little difference in performance on CAT versus PPT formats or favor CAT because of its speed, efficiency, and adaptability (Poggio, Glasnapp, Yang, & Poggio, 2005; Wang, Jiao, Young, Brooks, & Olson, 2008). In fact, Paek (2005) concluded that "in general, computer and paper versions of traditional multiple-choice tests are comparable across grades and academic content" (p. 17). The results across studies tend to indicate that administration mode has no statistically significant effect on student math or reading achievement scores (Kingston, 2008). Similarly, it appears that administration mode (CAT vs. PPT) does not interact with either gender or ethnicity subgroups (e.g., Bennett et al., 2008; Clariana & Wallace, 2002). Also, in a large-scale assessment study, D. H. Kim and Huynh (2010) found that both students with disabilities and those without disabilities performed comparably on a statewide English test regardless of presentation mode (CAT or PPT). It appears that CAT is definitely preferred by students and may afford some benefit on speeded tests.

The use of a computer for test presentation also allows for manipulation of the visual display (e.g., font size or magnification, brightness, color). McKee and Levinson (1990) said that these variables could change the nature of a task so dramatically that items administered in CATs and PPTs no longer measure the same construct. Kamei-Hannan (2008) provided reading and language tests to 75 students with disabilities. Results indicated that magnification actually increased the time students required on a test. Bridgeman, Lennon, and Jackenthal (2003) used a computer-presented math test to examine the effects of screen size, resolution, and presentation delay on the test scores of high school students. They found that screen display conditions and presentation rate had no effect on math performance, but that the highest resolution display resulted in somewhat higher scores. So it appears that making changes in the visual features of computer presentations may change performance only slightly and could, depending on the alteration, make performance a little better or worse.

In general, CAT seems to be preferred by students even though it does not significantly improve performance when the computer is used only as a visual display device. When other features are added, such as text-to-speech capabilities, students with disabilities—such as poor readers—seem to benefit. CAT also can offer other features, such as spell and grammar check or a dictionary/thesaurus, that may be helpful to some students on some tests. What is most interesting is that all the various technology-assisted accommodations tend to help students perform slightly better if at all, and none of these accommodations have the impact that an extended-time accommodation appears to have (see Chapter 5).

Accommodations for Hearing Limitations

As with vision, hearing impairment poses more of a problem with the presentation of information (e.g., class lectures, exam instructions) than responses. A variety of presentation accommodations can be useful here. Certainly sound amplification systems help in this regard. Most of these students have intact visual and motor systems that allow them to read and write like typical peers, and these skills generalize to most test situations. It should be noted that students with hearing impairment are at greater risk for literacy problems (Pittman, Lewis, Hoover, & Stelmachowicz, 2005; Traxler, 2000), so examiners might need to assess the student's skills carefully to determine the best means of testing. If a hearing-impaired student is taking a common paper and pencil test, one should not assume that reading fluency, vocabulary, or language skills are comparable to other students, and therefore extended time or the use of a dictionary may be reasonable accommodations if deficits in relevant skills are documented. In addition, some students may need test instructions signed to them as well as written on the test, and they may need access to a clock to help with time management on a test. For the most part, test accommodations for hearing-impaired students do not require much in the way of technology or test altering, as long as the students do not have multiple disabilities.

CASE STUDIES

Jonathan

Jonathan is a 15-year-old boy in ninth grade who was first identified as having an LD in reading in second grade. Since then, he has been receiving special education services that include testing accommodations. His parents have requested that his accommodations be reevaluated at an annual review meeting to ensure that he is able to access all tests. At the meeting, the following information is revealed:

1. As of his last triennial reevaluation, his reading scores remain severely below what would be expected for his age and grade. On the Woodcock-Johnson III Tests of Achievement (Woodcock, McGrew, & Mather, 2001), his Broad Reading composite score is a 53, with a grade-equivalent score of 3–5. This score is also quite discrepant from his general intellectual ability (his Wechsler Intelligence Scale for Children [WISC–IV; Wechsler, 2003] full-scale IQ is 105, at the 63rd percentile).

2. Jonathan's reading problems developed early, and at different points in his childhood he has struggled with mastering his alphabet, phonics, decoding, reading fluency, and comprehension. His father and one of his brothers have also been diagnosed with dyslexia, suggesting a genetic trend.

3. Since fourth grade, Jonathan has been using a screen reader on his laptop computer for almost all of his reading. The school district obtained electronic books and scanned relevant text materials into his computer. The computer software would highlight words and read them to Jonathan, who listened through a headphone set. By sixth grade, Jonathan was taking most of his tests on the computer except statewide, standardized tests that were read to him. Jonathan also uses a computer for writing, including essay exams. He is allowed to use spell check as well as grammar and thesaurus features of the word processor. Jonathan has tried voice recognition for writing, and he is getting better at using it, although he did not like it at first. When using these test accommodations, Jonathan is in a room with his learning specialist and has 50% additional time on all tests.

Now that he is in high school, Jonathan will likely rely heavily on computer-assisted test accommodations. Teachers agree that without these technologies, Jonathan would be at a great disadvantage as a learner and a test performer. He uses screen reading software on a computer to read most materials including tests, and he uses voice-recognition software to dictate most writing assignments. Because he uses these technologies and exams generally take him longer to complete, he is given 50% extended time for all exams. He usually takes large exams in the resource room with a learning specialist on hand should he need help. There are some exams, usually certain math and science exams, that contain combinations of text, formulas, and graphs. In these instances, Jonathan relies on the learning specialist as a reader. He usually asks the specialist to read instructions and certain parts of questions. With these accommodations he has been able to stay on grade level and perform in the average range.

It should be noted that a case like Jonathan's is quite involved and fairly unique. A careful assessment of academic strengths and weaknesses is vital, as with many accommodation cases. So is an assessment of Jonathan's ability to use the various accommodations efficiently. Instructors should expect there to be a learning curve for the student when using computer-assisted testing, and they may have to adjust and augment the accommodations with training sessions, practice, and extended time.

Michael

Michael is a 10-year-old, fifth-grade student who has just received a diagnosis of ADHD, combined type, from his pediatrician. Certainly, he is very active and fidgety, easily distracted, and quite impulsive. Although Michael presents as bright (his WISC–IV full-scale IQ is 116), his work is characterized by stops and starts, off-task behavior, and careless mistakes. Thus, he tends to perform well below his apparently high intellectual ability, and in a classroom where grades are heavily determined by classwork and homework (as well as exams), his grades range from B to D. Michael also serves as a distraction to other students because he blurts out verbal remarks, often at the very worst times. In the classroom, his teachers tend to seat Michael in the first row so their presence can dampen his tendency to go off task and disturb others. But even preferential seating has limited success in a test situation. On lengthy tests, teachers note that Michael tends to lose interest and focus, sometimes just hurrying to complete the test without putting in consistent effort. He often is the first to finish an exam, but usually that is because he hurries and guesses. On some tests, he fails to process or follow the instructions and has had some tests invalidated. Teachers also report that a Scantron sheet may come back looking like a complete mess, with some answers crossed out and others skipped. Consequently, Michael's teachers and parents were all eager to discuss the possibility of a formal 504 plan to address Michael's needs and specify appropriate testing accommodations.

Although Michael is a capable young man, his behavioral tendencies interfere with his ability to perform on tests in an efficient and timely manner. To avoid excess distractions and minimize his tendency to disrupt others, the school decided to have him take tests in the resource room with a teaching assistant. The teaching assistant also serves as a proctor who is allowed to read and paraphrase directions for Michael to be sure he knows what is expected. The proctor, who is familiar with Michael and the instruction going on in his classes, is able to answer clarifying questions similar to what a classroom teacher would do during an exam. Michael has been granted 50% extended time, but he tries to finish tests as fast as he can and tends not to use the additional time. Instead, Michael and the school have found that extra breaks help him to refocus his attention on the test. He is allowed a 3- to 5-minute break every 10 to 15 minutes of testing. Therefore, a 50-minute exam could take 75 minutes to complete (50 minutes of testing and five 5-minute breaks). He usually takes one to two breaks per exam, however. Another role played by the proctor is to prompt Michael to work on the test if it appears that he is daydreaming or engaging in irrelevant behaviors (e.g., playing with his pencil or watch). One additional accommodation is used for multiple-choice tests that use bubble (Scantron) sheets. Michael is allowed to circle answers on his test booklet. This simple adjustment has helped both Michael and the teachers who grade his work. Circling also seems to minimize errors and keep Michael on task. Such accommodations, along with structure, guidance, extra breaks, and no distractions, allow Michael to perform considerably better than when left to his own devices. An added benefit is that the other students in his class can take the test in peace and quiet, lest we think that all accommodations are only for the students with disabilities!

Juan

Juan is a 13-year-old student in seventh grade with a rare inherited condition called retinitis pigmentosa. This is a progressive visual disease that initially presents as degeneration of the rods in the retina. Juan's first symptoms surfaced several years ago as difficulty seeing in dim lighting. His night vision has become progressively worse, and he is now developing tunnel vision as well. His visual condition will continue to deteriorate and likely result in blindness. Yet, Juan is a bright young man with an outgoing personality and a good sense of humor. He is well liked by teachers and fellow students. Unfortunately, his first love, baseball, is getting too difficult to play at a competitive level.

Because of Juan's visual impairments, certain environmental considerations are necessary for him to see adequately. What matters most to Juan is that visual materials are presented under adequate lighting. Natural light seems to work best. Because of his gradual loss of peripheral vision, Juan needs to have visual stimuli presented in the center of his visual field. It also helps if visual stimuli such as text are presented with adequate contrast (e.g., black print on a white background), and the font size of the letters is 14 point or larger.

Juan is examined twice a year by his ophthalmologist, who consults with the school that Juan attends. Juan is also tested annually by the school psychologist to assess visual skills and their impact on psychoeducational functioning. The school uses this information to determine what academic modifications and test accommodations are needed. Juan has been provided a computer with a special visual display that provides symbols with high acuity, sharp contrast, and excellent color definition. This also allows materials to be enlarged and still presented centrally. Most of Juan's important exams are scanned and presented via this computer setup. Print materials and brief paper-and-pencil exams are modified for regular classroom use. The text and math symbols are enlarged to 14-point font, and all stimuli are placed on paper that is 6 inches wide and bordered by thick black lines so as to frame the visual stimuli. Teachers have been instructed to assist with clarifying instructions and ensuring that the test materials are presented clearly.

Juan has taken standardized, statewide tests thus far using enlarged print. This year, the school asked the state to allow the test to be scanned and presented on a computer. Eventually, Juan will have to ask for certain visual accommodations for the PSAT and then SAT and/or ACT exams. By the time he takes these exams, his condition could be worse and the necessary visual parameters would need to be changed (e.g., type of display, font size, lighting). Given Juan's degenerative visual condition, his visual impairments will need to be regularly assessed and adjustments to his accommodations will need to be made. These adjustments will continue into college, depending on the field of study chosen and type of exams required.

8

ACCOMMODATIONS AND INTERVENTIONS

This chapter may seem out of place to some readers who are familiar with the accommodations literature; we are not aware of any coverage of interventions in other books on accommodations. However, we believe that accommodations and interventions are often closely related, especially in K–12 settings, and that schools that make accommodation decisions without linking accommodations to intervention plans are often not doing a complete job. Even in postsecondary settings there is a place for interventions, as we will show. Indeed, we are surprised that accommodations and interventions are so rarely discussed together. Oddly, during the same time that testing accommodations have become so prevalent, the field of school psychology has become far more focused on the design and evaluation of interventions (Merrell, Ervin, & Peacock, 2012), but the two parallel trends have not led to much interaction.

One area of overlap that has been explored is the connection between testing accommodations and instructional accommodations. For instance,

http://dx.doi.org/10.1037/14468-008
Testing Accommodations for Students With Disabilities: Research-Based Practice, by B. J. Lovett and L. J. Lewandowski

just as a student with visual impairment may take tests printed in a large-print format, the same student's instructional materials would generally be presented in that format. Similarly, students with disabilities might be permitted to participate in classroom activities (e.g., seatwork, small-group discussions) by recording their responses on a word processor. As Ketterlin-Geller and Jamgochian (2011) noted, "to support the educational needs of students with disabilities, accessible instruction is inseparable from accessible assessments" (p. 137). Therefore, it is generally thought that instructional accommodations should match testing accommodations, although this match has not always been found in practice (e.g., DeStefano, Shriner, & Lloyd, 2001).

A different approach to the intervention–accommodation connection explores whether interventions may obviate the need for some accommodations, at least in certain students. In Chapter 3, we considered Phillips's (1994) five questions that should be asked in determining whether a testing accommodation is appropriate; her fourth question concerns the capacity of students to adapt to standard testing conditions. Because accommodations necessarily raise difficult questions of score comparability, they should only be used when an examinee is unable to access a test under standard administration conditions. Interventions, like accommodations, can promote test access, and they do so without raising any comparability concerns. Therefore, in this chapter, we describe how interventions can address the same skill deficits that accommodations address. We begin by discussing a conceptual model of skill development that can be used to guide interventions. We then provide brief, selective reviews of the literature on interventions in three areas: general test-taking skills (test-wiseness), reading skills, and test anxiety.

A CONCEPTUAL MODEL FOR INTERVENTION: THE INSTRUCTIONAL HIERARCHY

Interventions often target skills, and the development of most academic skills can be considered within the framework of the instructional hierarchy (IH). The IH proposes that skills develop through five stages: acquisition, fluency, maintenance, generalization, and adaptation (Martens & Witt, 2004). A review of these stages will also show the relevance of the IH to testing accommodations.

Acquisition

In the *acquisition* stage, the goal is for students to make a response accurately (e.g., to say "Albany" when asked "What is the capital city of New York?"). Given the massive curricular content that teachers are expected to cover, it is tempting to believe that a skill has been mastered when a student responds accurately. But just as musicians do not stop rehearsing once they have played a song accurately, and athletes do not stop practicing because a particular sequence of athletic moves has been executed flawlessly, students should understand that their accurate performance of academic responses is only the first step in a hierarchy. Similarly, as many students with disabilities know, although they may be able to perform responses accurately (i.e., they have certain knowledge and skills), accuracy may not be sufficient to perform well on a test.

Fluency

In the second step of the IH, *fluency*, a higher level of proficiency is demanded, and this is measured using the rate at which skills can be performed. Colloquially, to do something "fluently" implies automaticity, expertise, and general deftness (Binder, 1996), and rate is simply a handy index for these qualities. As Binder (2003) noted, measures of accuracy often fail to discriminate between skill levels because they have a ceiling: 100% correct. Fluency has no such ceiling because it is always possible (at least in theory) to become faster at something; such fluency requires practice beyond 100% accuracy. Fluency in academic skills is increasingly recognized as important; the current edition of the Woodcock-Johnson III Tests of Achievement (WJ-III; Woodcock, McGrew, & Mather, 2001) includes tests of fluency in reading, mathematics, and writing, and many reading curricula emphasize oral reading fluency as an index of early reading skill. The distinction between accuracy and fluency has obvious implications for the most common testing accommodation: extended time. As we discussed in Chapter 5, students are often given additional testing time because the skills that they need to access the test (reading test items, performing mathematical calculations, composing text) are not fluent. We discuss reading fluency interventions later in this chapter; here we merely note that increasing skill fluency can decrease examinees' need for extended-time accommodations.

Maintenance

The IH's third stage, *maintenance*, is actually an extension of fluency (Martens & Witt, 2004); at this stage, students are able to respond accurately at a fast rate after a period without practice or over lengthier intervals of fatiguing work. Students have achieved the maintenance stage when they maintain their skills without practice and can persist for long periods of time. Skills reach this stage through practice that continues past the point of apparent fluency, optimally conducted in spaced practice sessions (Alberto & Troutman, 2009). Some psychologists and educators will be familiar with the concept of overlearning, in which retention of material is enhanced by continuing to study the material even after the subject can reliably recall it (Driskell, Willis, & Copper, 1992); maintenance of skills is simply the behavioral equivalent of this phenomenon.

Maintenance—and its absence—intersect primarily with accommodations that allow students breaks during tests, alternative scheduling of tests, or other remedies for fatigue. Interventions that bring students' skills to the maintenance stage can improve their endurance over time, obviating the need for these kinds of accommodations. The athletic analogy is again helpful; jogging and solving mathematics word problems are both experienced initially as quite draining by many learners, but with practice, the learners can persist on these tasks for far longer. More generally, maintenance is key to test access when it is not possible to study test information immediately prior to the exam, as happens when students have multiple exams in a short interval or when exams (e.g., high-stakes exams) cover too much material to allow this. Thus, learning to space out study sessions rather than cramming leads to skill maintenance and higher exam performance in important settings.

Generalization

The fourth stage of the IH, *generalization*, has the most implications for testing accommodations. When this stage has been reached, students can apply a skill to new situations. Formally, through the process of *stimulus generalization*, students learn to perform the same response to similar stimuli (Powell, Honey, & Symbaluk, 2013). Young children learn to say /bee/ when they see the symbol "B" or the symbol "b," even though the two stimuli look different. Older children learn to respond by multiplying two numbers not only when they see a traditional X-like multiplication sign between them, but also when they see a central dot or when they see numbers separated by parentheses. Even older students learn that *garrulous*, *loquacious*, and *voluble* all have very similar meanings, and good students come to respond similarly to all three words (either through explicit instruction or implicit context cues).

So far we have given instances of generalization on a small scale; on a larger scale, students have reached the generalization stage when they can perform responses fluently in a variety of novel settings and in the presence of novel stimuli. Students whose skills are not yet at this stage have "hit-or-miss" skills; sometimes they can perform, and at other times they cannot. Consider a student who can answer questions fluently when the teacher poses them orally, but not on a written exam. Or consider a student taking a public speaking class; the student can deliver a speech fluently when practicing at home, but not in front of an audience. Finally, consider a student learning to drive; the student can drive fluently on a sunny day in an area with little traffic, but not in heavy rain in a congested city. As these examples suggest, testing situations often involve novel settings and stimuli. For instance, a student taking the SAT may never have seen the testing room, the proctor, or other examinees before, and the exact items will not have been available; moreover, the student will be under significant stress. Even on a class-room exam, students will typically encounter questions that have never been phrased in quite that way before. Therefore, when students insist that they "don't test well," they are often reporting (unknowingly) that their skills are not at the generalization level.

Testing accommodations are often present to address deficiencies in skill generalization. Students may be permitted to take their exam in a sepa-rate, quieter setting (free from novel stimuli that can be distracting), or in certain K 12 settings, they may even be permitted an accommodation where a familiar person administers the test. With other accommodations, a stu-dent may always be tested orally or may be permitted to respond orally. Even extended-time accommodations can be viewed as altering the testing situ-ation (from one with time pressure to one without), essentially minimizing the need to generalize skills.

Raising skills to the generalization level can therefore reduce the need for a variety of accommodations. Interventions that are designed to promote generalization require that learners be given experience with diverse stimuli in diverse settings delivered in diverse modes. Cooper, Heron, and Heward (2007) gave several specific strategies for promoting generalization (most of them derived from the seminal article on generalization by Stokes & Baer, 1977). For instance, skills can be taught "loosely," such that incidental aspects of the setting are changed. If students learn to perform responses in noisy set-tings as well as in quiet ones, where light and heat conditions vary and stimuli are presented in a variety of formats, students will adapt to this variability (Baer, 1999). Therefore, students should practice responding under different conditions so that they can properly perform in the test setting. Moreover, as we mentioned in Chapter 2, we should be careful that we are not impeding generalization by permitting unnecessary accommodations that restrict the conditions under which students need to perform.

Adaptation

In the final stage of the IH, *adaptation*, learners have complete command of a skill, to the point that they learn novel responses (which are essentially new skill variants) as needed. A foreign-language learner at this stage might successfully use a word that he has never been taught, inferring it from his wide knowledge of patterns of that language. A surgeon at this stage might successfully execute an operative procedure that she has never seen before, when it is unexpectedly called for in the middle of surgery; her considerable experience with various surgical situations guides her hands to fluent performance of this novel response. Although there are no testing accommodations particularly designed to address deficiencies in adaptation, this stage of skill development is important in certain very high-level testing situations, such as board certification exams.

Implications of the Instructional Hierarchy

The five stages of the IH are relevant to testing accommodations, as we have shown. The essential point is that raising students' levels of certain academic skills (i.e., raising those levels beyond accuracy) may make certain accommodations unnecessary, at least for some students. Obviously, students with certain low-incidence disabilities often have certain functional impairments that cannot be remediated; we would never suggest that a blind student with no functional vision could be trained to take typical written tests in the same format as other students, without accommodations. However, when a student with a learning disability is given a reader for her test, or a student with an anxiety disorder is permitted to take his tests in a separate room, interventions should certainly be considered. Moreover, even in the case of more severe, low-incidence disabilities, students may receive several accommodations when only a subset of these would be needed after appropriate interventions are used.

We now turn to different targets for intervention. We first examine instruction in general test-taking skills, and then we examine interventions for specific problems that can interfere with test taking: poor reading skills and test anxiety. Each of these intervention targets can be viewed through the lens of the IH, as we show.

INCREASING GENERAL TEST-TAKING SKILLS

In Chapter 3, we discussed how test scores vary because of variation in examinees' levels of target skills (e.g., variation in knowledge of history on a history test) as well as variation in other factors. One such other factor is general test-taking skills, or *test-wiseness* (Ferrier, Lovett, & Jordan, 2011). By increasing test-wiseness, students' academic skills are raised toward generalization because students can demonstrate those skills on a variety of tests.

Elements of Test-Wiseness

In their seminal paper on the concept, Millman, Bishop, and Ebel (1965) defined *test-wiseness* as "a subject's capacity to utilize the characteristics and formats of the test and/or test-taking situation to receive a high score" (p. 707). These scholars classified test-wiseness skills into six categories:

1. time-using strategies, such as not taking unnecessary mental breaks from the test and using any extra time to recheck one's work;
2. error-avoidance strategies, such as carefully attending to test directions and individual item prompts, and asking for clarification if it is needed;
3. guessing strategies, such as determining whether it is sensible to guess on multiple-choice tests when wrong answers are penalized with a guessing correction formula;
4. deductive reasoning strategies, such as first ruling out implausible answer options and then choosing from the remaining options, when answering multiple-choice or similar selected-response test items;
5. strategies based on considerations of the item developer's intentions, based on previous experiences with items written by the same developer or similar features; and
6. strategies based on unintended answer cues, such as noticing when certain response options are grammatically inconsistent with the way that the question is phrased.

Since Millman et al.'s treatment of the topic, many measures of test-wiseness have been developed by various investigators, with each measure testing some of the strategies outlined in the original article (for a review, see Rogers & Yang, 1996).

Training in Test-Wiseness

Entire books are now available to train students in test-taking strategies (e.g., Durham, 2007), and some of these books are specifically targeted to teachers of students with disabilities (e.g., Scruggs & Mastropieri, 1992). These books typically offer instruction in certain problem-solving techniques, but they focus on test-wiseness skills. For instance, Durham's (2007) book has chapters on how to eliminate answer options in multiple-choice items until only two options are left; how to pace oneself so as to use time effectively; and how to ensure attention to the details of test and item directions. In these kinds of books, students are typically given explicit training in strategies for handling various types of test items. For example, Mangrum, Charles, Iannuzzi, and Strichart (1998) provided a list of rules for answering true/false items, including "if a statement has two negatives in it, get rid of both negatives" (p. 94). At times, rules for test taking are even captured in catchy mnemonics, such as PACER (Preview the test, Arrange work to manage time well, look for Clues, answer Easiest questions first, and Review all test answers; Shaffer, as cited in Conderman & Pedersen, 2010).

Perhaps the best-known comprehensive test-taking skills intervention is called simply the Test-Taking Strategy (TTS). Hughes and Schumaker (1991) reported having developed the TTS on the basis of prior research on core test-taking skills, the test-taking behaviors of students with high-incidence disabilities, and the types of items used in actual classroom exams. The TTS consists of seven elements, which can be remembered with the aid of the acronym PIRATES:

1. **Prepare to succeed:** Students get mentally prepared for the test and devise a plan for going through this particular test form.
2. **Inspect the instructions:** Students carefully read the instructions, noting and underlining any especially important elements of the instructions.
3. **Read, remember, reduce:** Students read each test item in its entirety, recall answers from memory as needed, and reduce the number of answer choices to choose a response by elimination.
4. **Answer or abandon:** Students either mark an answer to the test item or abandon it for the time being.
5. **Turn back:** Students return to the beginning of the test form.
6. **Estimate:** Students use guessing strategies for items that had been abandoned earlier.
7. **Survey:** Students review the test to ensure that they have answered all items, and if appropriate, an answer is changed.

These elements are taught in a formalized intervention consisting of a pretest, modeling, and several opportunities to practice the elements.

A strong case can be made for teaching test-taking skills. Tests are increasingly common in educational settings (Koretz, 2009), so much so that in a recent comprehensive analysis of the major factors affecting K–12 academic performance, J. Lee and Shute (2010) concluded that test-taking skills are one of these factors. Moreover, substantial research exists to show that training in test-taking skills is effective at increasing actual performance on achievement tests. In a meta-analysis of early studies, Samson (1985) estimated the average effect size to be approximately $d = 0.33$; although this would typically be interpreted as a small-to-moderate effect size (e.g., J. Cohen, 1988), we would note that longer and more intensive training programs had higher average effect sizes (approximately $d = 0.50$) and that even a smaller effect size is impressive, considering that test-taking skills are only a relatively small factor in test performance (compared with the major factor of the target knowledge/skills being tested). Scruggs and Mastropieri

(1992) reported that training in test-taking skills is likely to be more effective for students with disabilities, and that "on standardized tests, we have found that gains of 10–15 percentile points, or six months of school achievement, are common" (p. 7).

Several recent studies have examined the effects of training programs (generally the TTS) with various disability groups. Songlee, Miller, Tincani, Sileo, and Perkins (2008) taught the TTS to four high-functioning students with autism spectrum disorders in middle and high school; the students all had full-scale IQ scores at or above the average range and spent most or all of the school day in general education classes. The TTS was delivered during an intensive after-school program, and at baseline, all four students showed relatively low levels of strategic test-taking behavior (on baseline probes, students averaged between 41% and 53% of the possible strategic responses). After the intervention, all four students had increased their strategic responding dramatically, making at least 90% of the possible strategic responses on a postintervention probe, and the students generally showed excellent generalization of the responses to actual classroom tests. Moreover, a questionnaire showed that students were generally satisfied with the intervention, and all four students reported that they would use it in the future.

Two studies have shown that the TTS can also be effective when delivered through an electronic medium. Lancaster, Lancaster, Schumaker, and Deshler (2006) used the TTS CD with 12 students who had been identified as having learning disabilities. These investigators found that all 12 students had stable baseline scores showing relatively low levels of strategic responses (no student ever made 60% or more of the possible strategic responses); these scores rose substantially during the TTS intervention and remained high (90% or higher for all students) after the TTS. In a second study, Lancaster, Schumaker, Lancaster, and Deshler (2009) replicated the success of the electronic TTS in two larger samples of middle school ($n = 52$) and high school ($n = 60$) students with learning disability diagnoses. These two studies also found the same positive results as Songlee et al. (2008) with regard to student satisfaction.

The TTS has also been shown to be effective for college students. Holzer, Madaus, Bray, and Kehle (2009) taught the TTS to five college students who were accessing support services for students with learning disabilities (all five were receiving extended-time testing accommodations, among other services). The extension to postsecondary settings is important because students in these settings often have higher academic skills, but they may still benefit from such interventions. The TTS program was modified in various ways because of the setting (students were taught the TTS in one-on-one sessions, and actual classroom exams were not available for practice), but the results were similar to those from other studies; at baseline, students showed low levels of strategic responding that improved dramatically during and after TTS training. Moreover, four of the five students showed moderate-to-large increases in actual test performance, something not measured in previous studies.

Finally, Kretlow, Lo, White, and Jordan (2008) investigated a downward extension of the TTS to younger students (fourth and fifth graders) with "mild mental disabilities" (students' full-scale IQ scores ranged from 61 to 71) in a self-contained classroom. The students were also receiving a variety of testing accommodations, including extended time, separate setting, read aloud, and tests scheduled over multiple sessions. Just as in other studies, students' strategic responding increased substantially from baseline to postintervention measures. Even more important, students' performance (in percentage correct) on achievement probes went from baseline scores in the F range (45–55) to the B/C range (77–84).

We have discussed these studies in some detail to show that a common test-taking skills intervention (the TTS) has shown efficacy across different populations, suggesting that many students with disabilities who are receiving testing accommodations may benefit from instruction in general test-taking skills. However, such instruction must be designed and undertaken with care. Indeed, Kettler, Braden, and Beddow (2011) raised concerns about such instruction that are worth addressing. First, they noted that "students with more or better strategies may benefit more from training than students with fewer or poorer strategies" (p. 149), meaning that, rather than helping to narrow performance gaps, instruction in test-taking skills would widen them. Although this may occur, we do not view this as problematic. Increases in absolute, not relative skills are what should be valued; if students with disabilities exhibit moderate increases in test scores and nondisabled students exhibit large increases, students with disabilities have still clearly benefited. If this concern were valid, any intervention applied universally could be dangerous because many interventions tend to widen rather than narrow gaps in outcomes (Ceci & Papierno, 2005). If this is perceived to be a serious problem, test-taking instruction could be selectively directed at students with disabilities.

Kettler, Braden, and Beddow (2011) were also concerned that time spent on test-taking skills might be better spent teaching actual content-area skills that will be tested. We are in sympathy with this concern; certainly, devoting large amounts of instructional time to teaching test-taking skills is poor practice. Therefore, test-taking skills should occupy only a very small fraction of class time, compared with the time spent in teaching actual academic skills. This does not pose a problem; the most basic test-taking skills that elementary school students need to know can be taught quickly (as part of how to follow test instructions), and as students grow older, they should themselves become motivated to become strategic test takers, practicing on their own time if they are concerned about test outcomes. More important, educators of students with disabilities can target test-taking skill instruction to particular students who seem to show a gap between their test scores and their actual academic skills. In sum, we believe that there is a strong, evidence-based case for spending time (a small fraction of class time, again) on test-taking skills.

BUILDING READING FLUENCY AND COMPREHENSION

We can divide the skills needed to succeed on a test into two types: the skills that the test is designed to measure, and the skills that are needed to access the test (Kettlerlin-Geller, Jamgochian, Nelson-Walker, & Geller, 2012). These latter skills, called *access skills*, may be deficient in certain students with disabilities. One way to address these deficiencies is through accommodations that administer a test through a format without the same access skill requirements; a different way is through interventions to increase the access skills. Because most tests, both classroom tests and high-stakes tests, are presented in written form, reading comprehension is usually among the skills needed to access a test. In addition to reading comprehension, reading fluency is often an access skill, given the timed nature of many tests. A detailed discussion of reading skills and interventions is beyond the scope of this chapter, but we hope to provide readers with an entry point into this literature.[1]

Reading Fluency Interventions

Although reading fluency is almost universally acknowledged as valuable, it is defined in somewhat different ways by different scholars. McKenna and Stahl (2003) are typical in arguing that "there are three components to fluency: Fluent reading should involve *accurate* and *automatic* word recognition, with appropriate *prosody* or inflection" (p. 72, emphasis in original). This tripartite distinction has been criticized for not explicitly mentioning comprehension (e.g., Hiebert, Samuels, & Rasinski, 2012), but its advocates argue that each of the three components is required for comprehension, the theory being that as word decoding becomes automatic, cognitive resources are freed up to be used for comprehension of meaning.

In practice, reading fluency is assessed using several different methods, and the methods do not always show strong statistical relationships with each other (e.g., Lewandowski, Codding, Kleinmann, & Tucker, 2003). Any timed

---

[1]Certainly, students with very low reading skills (including adult examinees with low literacy levels) will benefit from basic reading skill interventions (e.g., interventions that target decoding). We focus on reading *fluency* because of its connection to the most common accommodation (extended time), and we cover reading *comprehension* because it is the ultimate goal of most reading instruction.

reading task has the potential to measure fluency, at least its rate aspect. The reading rate task on the Nelson-Denny Reading Test (NDRT; J. I. Brown, Fishco, & Hanna, 1993) asks students to indicate how far they have read in a passage after 1 minute; this task is problematic in its ignoring accuracy and comprehension, but the NDRT timed reading comprehension task is (for high school students and adults) better, requiring reading of multiparagraph passages and correct answers to questions about each passage, all under a time limit. The WJ-III reading fluency task asks students to indicate whether each of a list of statements (e.g., "A chair has two legs") is true or false, and students are given 3 minutes to evaluate as many sentences as they can under that time limit. Increasingly, especially in younger students, reading fluency is measured through oral methods; students are given standardized reading passages and asked to read them aloud, with examiners recording how many correct words are read in a minute. Sometimes comprehension questions follow the passages as well. We should note that none of these measures directly assess the prosody aspect of fluency; as McKenna and Stahl (2003) reported, prosody is thought to be a key indicator of automatic, confident reading, but it is difficult for judges to agree on scoring readers' prosody.

Regardless of how it is measured, there are several standard guidelines and methods used to increase reading fluency. Kuhn (2011) provided four general principles of instruction for fluency; these form the basis for many specific interventions. First, teachers should model expressive reading with appropriate prosody, so that students understand how fluent reading should sound and can apply this when reading to themselves (both aloud and silently). Second, students should spend substantial time reading connected text (rather than isolated words) at a variety of levels of difficulty; that is, teachers should not read aloud to the exclusion of opportunities for students to read themselves. Third, students (especially those with relevant disability conditions) should have the opportunity for supported reading, receiving assistance as necessary. Finally, teachers should discuss appropriate phrasing with students, considering how best to parse sentences into meaningful elements, so that students can identify these elements and adjust their prosody accordingly.

Subsets of these four instructional principles can be found in the most common interventions for reading fluency (see Kuhn, 2011; Kuhn & Stahl, 2003; Rathvon, 1999; Wendling & Mather, 2009, for more details on the interventions that follow). In *repeated readings*, students read a single passage repeatedly until their fluency in reading that passage reaches a preset standard. Sometimes feedback is given in between readings, at which time students may practice especially difficult words in the passage. In a variant of repeated readings, *previewing*, students browse text ahead of reading, or hear the teacher read the passage before they attempt it themselves (*listening previewing*). In *assisted readings*, students are provided various kinds of support while reading; they may be asked to read a passage aloud along with a skilled reader (or a recording of a skilled reader). Sometimes a class is divided up into pairs to allow for classwide peer tutoring using assisted readings.

Three meta-analyses have considered the efficacy of these interventions on reading fluency in students of different ages. Chard, Vaughn, and Tyler (2002) reviewed the literature on fluency interventions for elementary school students with learning disabilities. These investigators found 24 relevant studies and concluded that repeated reading interventions without a model had moderate to large effects on fluency (average $d = 0.68$); adding a model seemed to make repeated reading at least somewhat more effective. More recently, Wexler, Vaughn, Edmonds, and Reutebuch (2008) reviewed the fluency intervention literature for older struggling readers (Grades 6–12). In general, the effects on fluency were not as strong as those shown in elementary school students, but consistent effects on reading rate were still found. It is interesting that in secondary students, there was little support for repeated reading as being preferable to reading the same amount of total text in a non-repetitive fashion (i.e., it appears to be just as helpful to read one 1,000-word passage as to read a 100-word passage 10 times).

Finally, Morgan and Sideridis (2006) performed a statistically sophisticated meta-analysis of 30 single-subject design studies (total $N = 107$) that delivered fluency interventions to students with learning disabilities (or deemed at risk for learning disabilities). All of the included studies reported gains in reading rate in terms of correct words read per minute, allowing the investigators to estimate the magnitude of each intervention in this unit of measurement. Surprisingly, the interventions that we have discussed so far (e.g., repeated readings) were inferior to what the investigators termed *motivation-focused interventions*: goal setting, feedback, and reinforcement. The highest estimate of efficacy was goal setting plus feedback (average effect of 94 words per minute). These findings remind us that rate of reading is in part determined by effort and motivation, a fact that we return to at the end of the chapter.

Together the three meta-analyses of reading fluency interventions suggest that these interventions are worth using when students' ability to complete tests in allotted time limits is hampered by slow reading. Certainly, extended-time accommodations may be appropriate for these students (indeed, this is a primary reason for providing additional time), but these interventions should generally be attempted as well.

Reading Comprehension Interventions

Just as reading fluency deficits often lead to extended-time accommodations, reading comprehension deficits often lead to reader (or read-aloud) accommodations, where someone else reads some or all of the test stimuli to examinees. Reading comprehension, then, is a test access skill that is worth considering as a potential target of intervention. Although it is easy enough to define as the process by which a reader understands (creates meaning out of) what he or she reads, reading comprehension is an exceedingly complex set of processes, and deficits in comprehension can be due to a wide variety of factors, including low general ability, working memory deficits, low fluency, vocabulary/general knowledge deficits, and a passive approach to reading (Pressley et al., 2009). Assessment of reading comprehension is similarly complex (Fletcher, 2006); different measures of comprehension vary greatly in task requirements (e.g., Morsy, Kieffer, & Snow, 2010) and consequently measure very different skills (Cutting & Scarborough, 2006). The three most popular methods of assessment are asking the reader questions about a passage, asking the reader to fill in missing words from the passage (*cloze assessment*), and asking the reader to retell everything that he or she can remember from the passage (McKenna & Stahl, 2003). Most common diagnostic tests of academic achievement and high-stakes tests of reading comprehension rely on some or all of these three assessment methods.

Some students with reading comprehension deficits benefit from fluency interventions, consistent with the theory that increasing fluency will free up cognitive resources for comprehension. A second approach to increasing comprehension is instruction in vocabulary, because knowledge of individual word meanings enables comprehension of larger text passages. However, there are additional interventions specific to comprehension deficits. Most of these involve instruction in comprehension *strategies*—techniques that students can use to alter their approach to reading (Klingner, Vaughn, & Boardman, 2007; Wendling & Mather, 2009). One such strategy is *questioning*—at various points in a reading assignment (e.g., after a title, after a section heading, after the first sentence, at the end of the passage), readers—or teachers—pose questions, either questions that have been answered by the passage (to see just what information the reading has provided) or questions that may be answered ahead. A second strategy is *summarizing*—readers are asked to reformulate a passage in a concise manner, or state its main idea, or even diagram the relationship between the main idea and supporting evidence. Other strategies include *visualizing* (making a passage's referents more concrete by visualizing the objects that it mentions) and *comprehension monitoring* (in which the reader notes whether various parts of a passage make sense, as well as other reactions, such as disagreement).

Edmonds et al. (2009) reviewed the literature on various reading interventions for secondary students (Grades 6–12) classified as struggling readers, looking specifically at the effects of these interventions on students' reading comprehension skills. Thirteen of the studies were similar enough to allow for a meta-analysis, and the average effect size was large ($d = .89$). A more recent article reviewed the literature on reading comprehension interventions for middle school students with learning disabilities (Solis et al., 2012) and generally found encouraging results. Fourteen relevant studies were examined, and the comprehension strategies studies included questioning, summarizing, and others. The majority of the effect sizes were large ($d > 0.80$), although somewhat larger effects were generally observed for comprehension of researcher-developed passages than the effects seen on standardized reading comprehension tests.

Our survey of the reading comprehension intervention literature has been relatively brief, but nonetheless it seems sufficient to note that effective reading comprehension interventions are available. As with reading fluency and extended time, it is sometimes appropriate to provide readers to students with reading comprehension deficits, but especially at the K–12 level, educational professionals should also be using appropriate reading comprehension interventions, considering the possibility that a reader may not be always needed in the future.

DECREASING TEST ANXIETY

Although interventions that directly increase access skills can be helpful to many students, other students already have access skills but are hampered by *test anxiety*, defined by Zeidner (1998) as "the set of phenomenological, physiological, and behavioral responses that accompany concern about possible negative consequences or failure on an exam or similar evaluative situation" (p. 17). Interventions that decrease test anxiety may allow these students to demonstrate their target skills, indirectly increasing their test access. This is especially relevant in cases of students with disabilities who receive accommodations (commonly including extended time) but choose not to use them, noting that just having the option to use the accommodations makes them less anxious during tests. Decreases in test anxiety can also be viewed as increasing students' generalization of academic skills, because students are able to demonstrate their skills in high-pressure situations (i.e., tests) rather than just in low-pressure situations (e.g., classwork, homework).

The Nature of Test Anxiety

Beidel, Turner, and Taylor-Ferreira (1999) cited research demonstrating that test anxiety is quite prevalent, with recent estimates suggesting that more than one third of children experience substantial test anxiety. Some scholars (e.g., Casbarro, 2003) have attributed this prevalence to the recent increased emphasis on testing in the schools, although this is a controversial inference, and Cizek and Burg (2006) argued that "test anxiety has existed as long as there have been tests" (p. 7). Regardless of any historical trends, test anxiety appears to be common at this time, meaning that teachers should expect that at least a small number of their students have test anxiety. Moreover, test anxiety is associated with other affective problems, such as low self-esteem, dependency, and clinical anxiety disorders.

It is unclear whether students with disabilities have higher levels of test anxiety. Although such a relationship is often reported (e.g., Salend, 2011), the empirical literature is small and inconsistent. A large-sample study (Sena, Lowe, & Lee, 2007) found essentially no effect of learning disability status on test anxiety, and an earlier study (Fulk, Brigham, & Lohman, 1998) found that only students with emotional and behavioral disorders (not learning disabilities) had higher levels of test anxiety than nondisabled students. However, given the high general prevalence of test anxiety, the problem should still be expected in many students with disabilities, and empirical research has suggested that test anxiety has the same effects on these students as on nondisabled students (Swanson & Howell, 1996).

In addition to being common, test anxiety tends to have an impairing effect on test performance. Admittedly, there are certainly individual times when anxiety has a motivating effect on performance, but this appears to be the exception rather than the rule. In a meta-analysis of all of the test anxiety literature from 1950 on, Hembree (1988) found moderately sized negative effects of test anxiety on performance on standardized tests ($k = 73$ studies; $d = -0.48$) as well as on GPA ($k = 4$; $d = -0.46$). Hembree also found that test anxiety was especially impairing for lower ability students and on tests that were perceived by students as difficult. Finally, test anxiety was associated with taking more time on the test ($k = 13$, $d = 0.30$), a finding with possible implications for extended-time testing accommodations.

Test anxiety appears to affect performance through a cognitive route, disrupting processing of test information by generating intrusive thoughts ("cognitive interference") about one's likely poor performance on the test and the negative consequences of this performance. Consistent with this theory, Putwain, Connors, and Symes (2010) found that cognitive distortions fully mediated the effects of test anxiety on performance (see also Owens, Stevenson, Hadwin, & Norgate, 2012). Converging evidence is provided by the work of Calvo (e.g., Calvo & Carreiras, 1993; Calvo & Eysenck, 1996), who has found that test anxiety slows reading and that reading aloud can compensate for anxiety's effects (presumably by blocking the intrusive thoughts concerning failure). Sadly, test anxiety often involves a vicious cycle in which anxiety causes poor performance that vindicates the negative intrusive thoughts about failure, and those thoughts are then more likely to occur the next time that a student is tested.

Interventions for Test Anxiety

There are a variety of interventions for test anxiety, some of which focus on testing (addressing test-taking skills), and some of which focus on anxiety (trying to reduce worries or physiological fear). We have already discussed test-taking skills in a previous section of this chapter, but the anxiety-focused interventions merit more discussion. These interventions are based on treatments for other anxiety problems. One group incorporates behavioral treatments, such as progressive muscle relaxation (tensing and releasing tension in different muscle groups to increase awareness and control over anxiety) and systematic desensitization (exposure to increasingly anxiety-provoking aspects of test situations until they no longer lead to anxiety). A second group incorporates cognitive therapy techniques, such as testing students' negative beliefs about themselves and retraining attributions for poor test performance. Increasingly, test anxiety interventions include both behavioral and cognitive elements, as in cognitive behavior therapy for other disorders.

Hembree's (1988) landmark meta-analysis found that behavioral, cognitive behavioral, and test-wiseness interventions all had significant effects on test anxiety reduction, whereas cognitive interventions (without behavioral components) and study skills training did not. The effect sizes for the three groups of effective interventions were all above $d = 0.5$, and one group (a certain type of systematic desensitization used with college students) was over $d = 1.0$. In a more recent meta-analysis, Ergene (2003) reviewed 56 intervention studies and largely confirmed Hembree's earlier conclusions. Ergene found that the average overall effect of interventions was in the moderate-to-large range ($d = 0.65$), with behavioral interventions showing the largest effects of single-focus interventions (average $d = 0.80$), and multiple-focus interventions (that incorporated skill training as well as anxiety-reduction techniques) showing even larger effects ($ds > 1.0$). Together, these two meta-analyses suggest that test anxiety interventions are generally quite effective.

Recently, von der Embse, Barterian, and Segool (2013) surveyed the test anxiety intervention literature, focusing only on child and adolescent studies published between 2000 and 2010. Although these scholars could only locate 10 studies, nine of these studies reported positive effects of their intervention procedures. The effect sizes in these studies varied greatly, and often varied across different subsamples and outcome variables, but were often quite large ($d > 0.50$ and sometimes $d > 1.0$).

To help illustrate the nature and efficacy of interventions, we give a more detailed discussion of two empirical studies that were both quite successful, but with very different methods and samples. In the first study, Wachelka and Katz (1999) administered a comprehensive but brief intervention to 11 students in high school and college who had clinically significant test anxiety and learning disability diagnoses. The intervention was administered in eight 1-hour, one-on-one sessions, one session per week; the sessions included training in progressive muscle relaxation, ways of responding to irrational beliefs, systematic desensitization with imagery, and test-taking/study skills. At the beginning and end of the intervention, students completed the Test Anxiety Inventory (TAI; Spielberger et al., 1980), a widely used measure. On this scale, students' scores reduced dramatically ($d = 2.37$) and far more than a control group of 16 students who were given the TAI at the beginning and end of 8 weeks without any intervention.

In a second study, Beidel et al. (1999) administered an 11-week, group-based intervention to eight nondisabled students in Grades 4 through 6 who had clinically significant test anxiety. Interestingly, this intervention did not explicitly address anxiety; all of the intervention's elements addressed study skills and test-taking skills. Students were taught appropriate study behavior (e.g., not studying while watching TV), specialized study techniques (the widely used SQ3R technique for reading assignments), general test-preparation hints (e.g., getting enough sleep the night before an exam), and test-wiseness hints (e.g., eliminating wrong answer choices before guessing). Before and after the intervention, the students completed the Test Anxiety Scale for Children (TASC; Sarason, Davidson, Lighthall, Waite, & Ruebush, 1960), and the intervention was associated with a statistically significant reduction in TASC scores; the effect size was $d = 2.37$ (coincidentally, the same as for the Wachelka & Katz, 1999, study), and students' postintervention scores were no longer in the clinical range. As these two studies show, a variety of types of interventions can lead to real reductions in test anxiety.

Other Responses to Test Anxiety

Before leaving the topic of test anxiety, we note that in addition to specific interventions, schools and test agencies may consider other responses as well. First, it has often been noted (e.g., Casbarro, 2003; Salend, 2011) that testing accommodations may themselves reduce test anxiety. Indeed, a sizeable literature has shown that accommodations are associated with increases in comfort and decreases in anxiety during testing (for a review, see Lovett & Leja, 2013). However, as we discussed in Chapter 4, test anxiety itself is not considered a disability condition that would make accommodations appropriate. If appropriate accommodations are given to students with disability conditions, a reduction in test anxiety can often be expected and celebrated, but this should not be the cause of the accommodation.

A more promising response to test anxiety involves certain test administration policies that can be applied to all examinees and will reduce anxiety among some of those who experience test anxiety. Zeidner (2007) gave several suggestions in this vein, including providing students with information about the test ahead of time, moving easier items to the beginning of the test to relax and motivate examinees, allowing examinees a degree of choices in which items to answer, and relaxing time limits. Of course, some of these strategies may not be appropriate, depending on the test's target constructs, and test policies that are the most effective at reducing anxiety may have psychometric disadvantages (e.g., on the topic of letting examinees choose which items to answer, see Wainer & Thissen, 1994). However, where these strategies are appropriate, they are valuable, and they fall under the concept of universal design that we discuss in greater detail in Chapter 10; briefly, assessment tools should be designed to allow as many examinees as possible to access the assessment as fully as possible, and reasonable methods of reducing examinee anxiety are a step toward this goal.

CONCLUSION: THE CASE FOR INTERVENTION

We have discussed the general process of intervention and skill development (through the instructional hierarchy), as well as making the case for interventions in general test-taking skills, reading skills, and test anxiety reduction. Unfortunately, even though our clinical experience has involved working with many students with disabilities who would like to overcome deficits, making their accommodations unnecessary, we see little attention to intervention in the accommodations literature. At the postsecondary level, this is at least partially understandable because it is unclear who would be responsible for implementing the interventions, and it might be thought to be too late to remedy deficits in, for instance, reading fluency. However, at the K–12 level, where skill development is the explicit focus of special education, the lack of attention to interventions when designing accommodation plans is odd. Specifically, a presumed lack of intervention efficacy is not a valid excuse for ignoring interventions, because at times a large research base exists showing intervention efficacy.

We conclude the chapter on a broad philosophical note. As we have pointed out earlier in the book, too often the model for thinking about accommodations derives from a sensory/physical disability model in which examinees' disabilities are relatively permanent and their inability to access tests in standard form is clear and unlikely to change. For high-incidence disabilities, this model is inappropriate, and the problems that keep students from accessing tests in standard form—low reading fluency or high test anxiety—are sometimes quite amenable to intervention. Accommodations may take pressure off of school staff who no longer need to intervene (because the student can now access the test, with an accommodation), but the student is left with problems that could be addressed.

Even students express concerns over accommodations that could be dealt with by a preference for interventions. Taylor and Houghton (2008) interviewed 15 students with attention-deficit/hyperactivity disorder (ADHD) about extended-time testing accommodations; most of the students were at best ambivalent toward the practice, and their concerns included unfairness to peers, as well as a worry that they might be held to higher standards after receiving the accommodation. If given the choice, these students might well prefer an intervention that would allow them to take tests under the same conditions. Of course, the intervention option requires a change in perspective, such that disability-based deficits are viewed as modifiable.

Viewing deficits in test access skills as permanent can become a self-fulfilling prophecy—a belief that becomes true through believing it. We are reminded of Dweck's (2006) work showing that students who have an *entity* theory of ability (believing that their skill levels are set and cannot change) are less likely to try hard and especially less likely to try again after failing, when compared with students who have an *incremental* theory of ability (believing that their skill levels will improve with practice and feedback). There are, of course, times when entity theories are correct (often in cases of physical or sensory disabilities), and there are certainly limits to what practice and environmental pressures can do, but too often schools appear to foster entity theories of ability inappropriately, when they should instead be actively encouraging incremental theories (see also Jordan & Lovett, 2008). A focus on interventions provides just this encouragement.

9

ISSUES IN THE TRANSITION TO POSTSECONDARY SETTINGS

Transition planning refers to preparing students to leave high school and enter postsecondary education programs or the workplace. Transition planning for students with disabilities has been a legal requirement for decades, and this charge has only been strengthened by reauthorizations of the Individuals With Disabilities Education Act (IDEA).[1] The law requires that transition planning be initiated no later than a student's 16th birthday. This transition process continues between the ages of 16 and 21 years, a time by which the student will graduate or leave secondary school.

Although transition planning is not part of decision making for test accommodations, often the same individuals are responsible for both tasks. Thus, this chapter offers important information and guidance to the book's

---

[1]When the 1997 Individuals With Disabilities Education Act (IDEA) was reauthorized in 2004, it was renamed the Individuals With Disabilities Education Improvement Act (IDEIA). Throughout this chapter, IDEA refers to the earlier 1997 law, and IDEIA refers to the reauthorized 2004 law.

http://dx.doi.org/10.1037/14468-009
Testing Accommodations for Students With Disabilities: Research-Based Practice, by B. J. Lovett and L. J. Lewandowski

target audience, who must help students with disabilities transition to college or employment. We begin by highlighting the general difference in procedures and laws for seeking accommodations in K–12 school versus postsecondary school and the workplace. Next, we discuss the trends and prevalence of accommodations in postsecondary settings, as well as possible future prevalence trends. Finally, we provide recommendations for planning a disabled student's transition to postsecondary school or employment.

DIFFERENT ACCOMMODATION PROCEDURES FOR K–12 SCHOOL, POSTSECONDARY SCHOOL, AND THE WORKPLACE

Students leaving high school for college will embark on a new and somewhat different accommodations journey. No longer will students have school psychologists and special education staff determining and implementing test accommodations, but rather they will need to request accommodations on their own, either from disability services staff and professors (if they are in college) or from human resources professionals and supervisors (if they enter the workforce directly).

Actively requesting test accommodations will be a new experience for most students, and they may have to obtain an independent or private evaluation before they even apply. Also, postsecondary education is less uniform than high school, including both public and private, 2- and 4-year programs in technical schools, community or residential colleges, and universities. In a sense, the accommodation procedures, decision making, and implementation are more varied and less predictable than in high school, although every bit as important and meaningful. Students, evaluators, disability services staff, and teachers at all levels need to educate themselves about the various test accommodation processes, each prepared to perform his or her role throughout the process.

DIFFERENT ACCOMMODATION LAWS FOR K–12 SCHOOL, POSTSECONDARY SCHOOL, AND THE WORKPLACE

IDEIA and the ADA Amendments Act of 2008: Which Laws Cover Which Settings?

A major difference between high school and college involves the legal mandates that govern accommodations and the practices spawned by these mandates in both postsecondary school and work settings. As mandated by the Individuals With Disabilities Education Improvement Act (IDEIA) of 2004, the local education agencies (LEAs) must "facilitate students' movement from school to post-school activities." The LEA is responsible for working with the student and parents to develop a Summary of Performance (SOP), meaning the LEA "must provide the child with a summary of the child's academic achievement and functional performance, which shall include recommendations on how to assist the child in meeting the child's postsecondary goals" (§300.305(e)(3)). There is no mention that test accommodations must be part of the SOP, but they often are included. Also, there is no obligation for the LEA to conduct a psychoeducational assessment before a student transitions to postschool activities. In a sense, the SOP represents the last legal obligation of the LEA under the IDEIA to students with disabilities. From that point on, secondary school "leavers" are protected under Section 504 of the Rehabilitation Act of 1973 and the ADA Amendments Act of 2008 (ADAAA).

There is a caveat with regard to legal protection during the K–12 years. There are several situations in which the IDEA does not apply but Section 504 does. One involves situations in which a student has a disability but it is not one of the 13 categories listed in the IDEIA, and another pertains to a student who may or may not have a disability, does not qualify for special education services, yet struggles in an academic area (Madaus, Shaw, & Zhao, 2005). In both of these circumstances, students would qualify for some services under Section 504. It should be noted that even under these special circumstances, any awarded accommodations should be matched to a student's specific functional impairment(s), and each impairment should represent a substantial limitation relative to same-age peers.

Another case in which non-IDEIA laws apply during the K–12 years involves standardized or high-stakes testing. In high school, students begin taking college admission exams such as the ACT and SAT. Whether students are in special education and have an individualized education program (IEP) or have a disability that does not require special education, any such student may apply for test accommodations under the ADAAA. Test agencies are then obligated to consider the accommodation application and make a decision as to the appropriateness of the accommodation request. In other words, testing agencies need to decide whether the applicant meets the legal definition of disability, whether the accommodation request is reasonable and appropriate given the applicant's impairment, and whether the accommodation can be implemented without significantly altering the test (does not compromise reliability and validity). ADAAA protections instead of IDEIA cover these special circumstances, and after secondary school, Section 504 and ADAAA become the only laws that address test accommodations.

Those of us in clinical practice, particularly working in schools, have seen that a diagnosis is usually tantamount to eligibility for test accommodations.

But as students transition to college and the workplace, the focus shifts somewhat from their diagnosis to the extent to which they are substantially limited in a major life activity, an activity that is essential to their ability to access education and/or a job. Generally, individuals in college, graduate study, or employment seeking accommodations are going to have a diagnosis. Diagnoses are plentiful (see the *Diagnostic and Statistical Manual of Mental Disorders* [5th ed., *DSM–5*; American Psychiatric Association, 2013]) and fairly easy to come by. What disability offices and test agencies tend to focus on is the nature and extent of one's functional limitations. Whether a person has been diagnosed with learning disabilities (LD), attention-deficit/hyperactivity disorder (ADHD), autism spectrum disorder (ASD), or some other disorder is not as determinate as whether that person reads well below average, and reading is an essential activity to access a class, exam, or job. Consequently, most accommodation decisions after high school are based on whether an applicant demonstrates a substantial limitation.

Differences Between IDEIA and ADAAA

One of the main distinctions between the IDEIA and the ADAAA is that the ADAAA is a civil rights law forbidding discrimination, whereas the IDEIA is an education law that guarantees free and appropriate public education to all in the least restrictive environment. Colleges and universities are not obligated to provide free education nor are they mandated to provide special services (i.e., note taking, tutoring) to students with disabilities, although many postsecondary schools do offer these services. Postsecondary schools and employers are required to provide individuals with disabilities equal access to educational and occupational opportunities. In that regard, they are responsible for providing *reasonable accommodations* to individuals who meet disability criteria under the law.

More specifically, *an individual with a disability* is one who has a physical or mental impairment that substantially limits one or more of his or her major life activities. *Major life activities* were most recently delineated by the ADAAA to include walking, seeing, hearing, speaking, breathing, reading, learning, thinking, concentration, and working (and that list is not intended to be exhaustive). A substantial limitation in any major life activities because of a disability condition qualifies an individual for accommodations. With regard to test accommodations, often the impairment involves reading, learning, thinking, or concentration, but impairments in sensory abilities and physical skills would also lead to accommodations (see Chapter 4). The recent amended act also established that disability status must be determined apart from the ameliorative effects of mitigating measures. In other words, a diabetic who controls metabolism with medication is still a diabetic and may warrant certain school or work accommodations (e.g., extra breaks to consume food or juice). Further, the law ensures that episodic impairments (e.g., seizures), if they are substantially limiting, are covered by the ADAAA.

Not only are the applicable laws different for postsecondary versus secondary students, but so are the responsibilities of the individual with a disability. Under the IDEIA, schools assumed the responsibility to evaluate students, identify disabilities, recommend reasonable and appropriate services, and then provide any approved test accommodations. Under the ADAAA, individuals who believe they have disabilities must disclose the disability to a school, testing agency, or employer and essentially *apply* for test/work accommodations. Also, it is the individual's responsibility to provide documentation of the disability and a substantial limitation to the entity. This is done in accordance with the entity's posted guidelines, which the Department of Justice has ruled should not place undue burden on the applicant. Nonetheless, the person with a disability typically must generally provide a recent professional evaluation that would attest to the disability and limitation(s) in major life activities. Clearly, all the initiative in procuring an accommodation shifts from the school under the IDEIA to the individual under the ADAAA. This is one reason why the proportion of accommodated individuals drops dramatically during this post-high school transition.

Additional differences between the IDEIA and the ADAAA involve their philosophy and documentation requirements, which are discussed next.

Philosophical Differences Between the Laws

It should be obvious that the IDEIA and the ADAAA are quite different laws even though both offer protections such as accommodations to individuals with disabilities. The differences in these laws also serve to create different views among the persons that must uphold them. For example, the IDEIA casts a wide net to any student with an identified disability who requires special education, and schools react by providing special education services, instructional modifications, assistive technology, special transportation, adaptive physical education, tutoring, test accommodations, and academic interventions aimed at facilitating a student's learning outcomes. Some educators may even perceive their responsibility is to "optimize" student achievement (e.g., test scores). This broad-based involvement engenders a philosophy of advocacy for the child and a focus on whatever can be done by well-meaning professionals to enhance learning success. By contrast, the ADAAA does not seek a certain outcome or guarantee success. This law is "outcome neutral." It is a law that bans discrimination in education, government, and employment settings, including places of public accommodation (e.g., hotel, theater). The ADAAA is a civil rights law that guarantees access not outcomes. It entitles persons with disabilities to have the same access as those without disabilities to educational, recreational, and occupational opportunities. A man in a wheelchair can get to a sales job if his office building has a ramp and an elevator; a deaf woman can attend a training program if information is provided in print and via sign language; a student with a writing disorder can take a college admission exam if allowed to use a word processor. The ADAAA entitles these individuals to reasonable accommodations to mitigate their impairments and access an opportunity. It does not guarantee that they will pass a test, succeed in a class, or achieve employment success. Therefore, in postsecondary settings, it should not be assumed that accommodations are needed (or that current accommodations are insufficient) just because an individual does poorly on a test.

The change in purpose and philosophy from the IDEIA to the ADAAA is not trivial. Not only is there more of a burden placed on postsecondary students to apply for accommodations, but also the students quickly learn that test accommodations are not necessarily automatic. Many of these students face challenges from postsecondary schools' office of disability services as well as from test agencies administering high-stakes tests (e.g., Graduate Management Admission Test [GMAT], GRE, Law School Admission Test [LSAT], Medical College Admission Test). Students may not understand that the ADAAA is not the same as the IDEIA, that college is not the same as high school with regard to services for disabilities, and access to educational opportunities is not the same as a free and appropriate education.

A pivotal and contentious issue regarding the difference between the IDEIA and the ADAAA, which has been discussed in previous chapters, is that of a substantial limitation. In the K–12 setting a formal diagnosis of LD, for example, would routinely initiate a cascade of services for a student. The student would have an IEP or 504 plan that delineated support services as well as test accommodations. Not much attention may have been paid to what we call the *impairment criterion*. In some cases, the diagnosis may have been substantiated by a discrepancy between a student's highest cognitive score and lowest achievement score, and that difference may have been as small as 15 points. Another example again involving LD is the case of a so-called gifted/LD student. This is a student with a very high IQ score (e.g., 135) and merely an average achievement score (e.g., reading test score of 105). In both of these cases, there has been controversy about whether the criteria for LD were met (see Lovett & Lewandowski, 2006; Lovett & Sparks, 2010). When such students come to college where the ADAAA law is primary, disability is determined and accommodations granted based on whether the student can or cannot demonstrate a substantial limitation compared with most people. The previous case examples, and others like them (e.g., a student with a diagnosis of ADHD but high test scores and achievement), are likely to be contested at the postsecondary level and/or by testing bodies for law, business, and medical schools.

As noted in other parts of this book, there is evidence that students with disability diagnoses in college may not meet official *DSM* criteria for a diagnosis or may not demonstrate a substantial limitation relative to the average person. Sparks and Lovett (2009b) examined LD classification rates in 378 college students already identified as having an LD. They found that only 6.9% of this sample met *DSM* Criteria A and B for a Learning Disorder, whereas only 6.3% of the students met an educational impairment criterion (achievement test score < 85). Mean achievement test scores across a number of measures ranged from 96.3 (*n* = 6) to 120.5 (*n* = 24), indicating essentially average achievement for the majority of LD students. Sparks and Lovett (2009a) confirmed this last point in another archival study. They examined test scores (IQ and achievement) reported in 120 empirical studies of LD. They again found average achievement among the LD groups, although their scores tended to be somewhat lower than their peers. In other words, it appears that most LD college students no longer meet criteria for the diagnosis and do not demonstrate a substantial limitation in achievement. Although these students likely were provided services and accommodations in K–12 under IDEA, one could argue that they do not qualify for accommodations under the ADAAA.

Although most students who apply for accommodations are granted them, postsecondary students are more likely than before to be denied accommodations by a college or a test agency. In some of these situations students are shocked at being denied for the first time or being asked to supply more or updated documentation. They may become upset or angry, feeling that their honesty about the disability is being questioned or that their rights are being challenged. Although the ADAAA has become less restrictive since amended in 2008, it still is a law about access and still boils down to whether or not a person has a documented substantial limitation in a major life activity. At the postsecondary level, we tend to see many students who may seem impaired relative to an elite group of people (e.g., biochemistry majors, law school applicants) but are certainly not impaired when compared with the general population (see Sparks & Lovett, 2009a, 2009b). We also see students who may show some relative intrapersonal weakness (i.e., their skill in math calculation is not nearly as good as say reading comprehension, yet it is well within the average range). In both of these cases, it would appear that the student does not meet ADAAA guidelines for having a disability, and therefore test accommodations do not seem to be warranted.

Another philosophical difference between accommodation practices under the IDEIA and the ADAAA involves the perspective of the professionals making accommodation decisions. We have already noted that there is an advocacy perspective that permeates K–12 education. Professionals want to see young children succeed academically, and in many cases, student success reflects directly on the school and its staff. In a sense, teachers and administrators have a vested interest in the performance outcomes of their students. Given this, school professionals would tend to be generous with granting test accommodations. An accommodation such as extended time, by far the most often used accommodation, requires very little in the way of effort or resources and is relatively easy to implement. Additionally, providing an accommodation to a student just feels like the right thing to do. A teacher feels that he or she is reducing the students' stress or frustration and is helping students achieve their true potential.

To this point, recall Rickey's (2005) study (first mentioned in Chapter 1) of accommodation decision making in three middle schools. She observed multidisciplinary team meetings and interviewed stakeholders in the accommodations process. She found that the primary reason for justifying accommodations was to reduce students' frustration and anxiety with testing and improve their ability to emotionally handle the testing experience. In some cases, validity of test results was occasionally considered, but most often the staff recommended accommodations to make students more comfortable.

This perspective of educators toward granting accommodations so as to reduce stress and promote self-esteem seems to be validated by students themselves. Elliott and colleagues examined students' perceptions of accommodations and found that students with disabilities perceived tests as easier, experienced less test anxiety and greater self-efficacy, and more generally preferred testing when accommodations were provided (e.g., Elliott & Marquart, 2004; Feldman, Kim, & Elliott, 2011; Lang, Elliott, Bolt, & Kratochwill, 2008). Interestingly, these studies have also found that, on average, nondisabled students have an improved testing experience as well when they receive accommodations (see Lovett & Leja, 2013, for a more detailed review of relevant research).

If educators at the K–12 level are granting test accommodations largely for affective reasons, and students with LD classifications are transitioning to college with average achievement and no demonstrable impairment, then one can begin to understand the conundrum facing disability service officers in postsecondary schools or high-stakes test agencies. This is one reason why K–12 diagnoses need to be data driven, scientifically accurate, and informing accommodations that are necessary and appropriate. If a student receives a diagnosis in elementary school, however liberal the diagnostic procedures may be, and school officials automatically check a box on the IEP or 504 plan to allow test accommodations, that sets in motion a cascade of services that could go unchallenged for the next 20 years. School personnel typically do not see the use of test accommodations as one student getting an advantage over other students. As Rickey (2005) and others have shown, accommodations are viewed as a way to help a struggling student, particularly at an emotional level.

By contrast, consider what happens when the same student serviced under the IDEIA by a helpful, generous, advocacy-oriented group of professionals is applying for test accommodations on a college admissions test. The context for this accommodation review is now the ADAAA. Rather than a team of educators who have known the student since kindergarten, the paper review is conducted in an impersonal and dispassionate manner by one or more hired professionals whose job is to review disability documentation and make accommodation recommendations based on their agency's guidelines and ADAAA regulations. This review is not about advocacy or trying to optimize a student's potential. It is about an evidence-based demonstration of a disability, both historical and current, that ultimately produces a verifiable substantial limitation in a major life activity. It is not about providing emotional support, but only about the facts of the case as set forth in the documentation as supplied by the student.

Students as well as their parents and evaluators often are not prepared for this paradigm shift in accommodation practices. In making a decision, the agents of the postsecondary testing body are interested in doing what is fair and just. In other words, any examinee who meets the requirements of the law, including the rather steep hurdle of a substantial limitation relative to the average person (e.g., cannot see or hear efficiently, cannot read or write as well as most people, has restrictions in movement) should be granted reasonable accommodations. Anyone who fails to document a disability involving a substantial limitation should be denied (e.g., performs well despite claims of inattention, anxiety, distractibility, slow reading). In addition, the accommodation decision makers take the notion of reasonable accommodation more seriously. Just because a student was allowed to take tests in a private room with double time does not mean that such extensive accommodations are necessary or will be granted on the college admissions test. The greater the alteration of standard test conditions, the less likely the test is measuring the skills intended and more likely validity is compromised.

Hence, test agencies tend to be more conservative than schools in apportioning test accommodations. By being more conservative, the test agency not only protects the integrity of its test, it also protects all examinees from discrimination. Because high-stakes tests are competitive by nature, in that some students get into a school or get a scholarship whereas others do not, test agencies feel the responsibility to arrange a test that is fair to all examinees. Therefore, persons with disabilities and limited access to an exam should have the necessary accommodations, whereas persons without substantial limitations are not entitled to accommodations. For an accommodation decision maker, an error can be made in two directions: either denying a person with a disability a needed accommodation or granting an accommodation to a person who is not limited and already performs comparably to most other examinees. Decision makers try to avoid either of these errors. Similarly, they try to avoid excessive accommodations. For example, there is no research to suggest that most examinees with high-incidence disabilities need double time to access a test, but there is recent research that indicates double time overaccommodates students with LD and ADHD. Our own research group recently showed in studies of LD and ADHD college students that time and one half allowed these students to perform at higher levels than their peers without disabilities, and double time conferred a large advantage to the students with disabilities (Lewandowski, Cohen, & Lovett, 2013; Miller, Lewandowski, & Antshel, in press). These are not the only studies showing that students either do not need or do not use the time they have been allotted to complete tests (Cahalan-Laitusis, King, Cline, & Bridgeman, 2006). Thus, accommodation decision makers, especially with regard to high-stakes tests, have a much different approach to accommodation decisions than K–12 staffs.

Documentation Requirement Differences Between the Laws:
The Documentation Disconnect

The differences highlighted previously between the IDEIA and the ADAAA are nowhere more apparent than with regard to the types of documentation required for test accommodations. This has been seen as such a widespread problem that Gartland and Strosnider (2007) labeled it as a "documentation disconnect." What this refers to is the difference between disability eligibility documentation at the secondary and postsecondary levels and the fact that the former often does not suffice for the latter. In this section, we discuss, in broad terms, the differences between documentation requirements at the two levels of education; for more practical details about requirements, including our recommendations for documentation policies and for those helping applicants to document disabilities, see Appendix A.

At the secondary level, a student may have an IEP or 504 plan, a multidisciplinary psychoeducational report, and (on graduation) an SOP. Of this documentation, the psychoeducational report is most likely to provide comprehensive test data on cognitive and achievement functioning. In many cases, however, this report is more than 3 years old by the time the student enters postsecondary school. Most schools require a diagnostic report completed within 3 years. In fact, Hatzes, Reiff, and Bramel (2002) surveyed 73 disability service providers at the college level about documentation guidelines for students with LD. The service providers indicated that the main reason accommodation requests are denied is because documentation is outdated or fails to meet other institutional guidelines. Gormley, Hughes, Block, and Lendmann (2005) examined the accommodation eligibility requirements of 104 colleges and universities in 36 states for students with LD.

They found that the majority of schools followed the Americans With Disabilities Act of 1990 (ADA) or Section 504 guidelines, required recent assessments with test scores (i.e., aptitude and achievement), relied heavily on the recommendations of a professional evaluator, and strongly considered the reasonableness of the accommodation request. The emphases on recent assessment data, discrepancy analysis, *DSM–IV* diagnosis, and demonstration of clinical impairment may not all be reflected in documentation collected in high school. Also, the focus on norm-referenced testing is not compatible with the response-to-intervention (RTI) models increasingly used by schools that rely on curriculum-based assessment and reduce access to formal psycho-educational testing (Keenan & Shaw, 2011; Lindstrom & Lindstrom, 2011). As the generation of RTI students begins to enter postsecondary schools, we are likely to see more, not less, documentation disconnect unless college disability providers change their guidelines with the times.

As indicated in Section 504 and the ADAAA, a person seeking test accommodations at a postsecondary school must first disclose his or her disability to the school. Then the student must meet the school's documentation requirements, which typically include a recent professional report detailing the basis for a diagnosed disability and attendant functional limitations. Typically, schools require that the evaluator is appropriately licensed or credentialed and has the appropriate education to provide the clinical judgment. Many postsecondary schools specify that the evaluator should provide a clinical history as well as test data, a formal diagnosis, and explicit recommendations (Gormley et al., 2005). It is helpful if the professional evaluator has had ADA and test accommodation experience, but as Gordon, Lewandowski, Murphy, and Dempsey (2002) have shown, a significant percentage of clinicians are not fully aware of the requirements of the law or the documentation needs of those applying for accommodations. In a survey of clinicians that perform assessments for accommodation requests, they found that many clinicians were not aware of the requirement for a recent evaluation report, and the clinicians varied considerably in what they thought was needed in such reports. A substantial proportion of clinicians did not consider a substantial limitation as necessary for diagnosis or qualification for accommodations. Because postsecondary schools are looking for recent, comprehensive evaluations of a student's history and current functional status including evidence-based diagnoses and a data-based rationale for reasonable test accommodations, many students are faced with the expensive prospect of seeking a private evaluation. The documentation from school districts often serves the purpose of providing a track record of the student's disability designations and specialized services, but it typically fails to provide a recent comprehensive evaluation. If high schools cannot provide the necessary documentation, and private evaluators fail to deliver appropriate reports, then students may have difficulty obtaining their requested accommodations. There is no substitute for a recent, comprehensive, data-driven evaluation that makes an evidence-based argument for the presence of a disability and need for specific test accommodations.

We should note that in addition to the disconnect between secondary school and postsecondary documentation requirements, there is also frequently an absence of any prior school record of a disability. Many students seeking accommodations in college or on postgraduate exams such as the GMAT or LSAT never had a disability diagnosis or special education services during their K–12 education. In some cases, parents opted for private schools with highly individualized instruction or private tutoring to remediate learning weaknesses. In other cases, parents indicated that the child was bright enough to overcome learning weaknesses in K–12 classes through hard work, but the demands of college began to overwhelm the student. Still others come to college and for the first time realize that they may have LD or ADHD or finally admit to a psychiatric problem. For any of these cases, and there are many like them, the postsecondary disability service office is faced with little or no documentation and must refer the student for a comprehensive evaluation. Of course, these cases beg the question of how impaired or limited the student could be if he or she never had an evaluation, a diagnosis, special education services, or test accommodations, yet is in college and on the doorstep of the disability office. If there is no early diagnosis, in some ways this makes early documentation even more important. Although a student was never officially diagnosed with a disability by a clinician or identified by a special education team, accommodations may be granted if she or he can provide clear, objective evidence documenting impairment as a child (impairment that, for whatever reason, did not lead to special education identification). K–12 teachers and administrators should keep this in mind when determining procedures for record keeping.

It should be noted that reviewers of accommodation documentation, whether at a college or test agency, approve the majority of accommodation requests. Despite the difference in philosophy and procedures (when compared with those of K–12 schools), there are many cases in which stated documentation requirements may not be fully met, and yet accommodations are approved, especially in college settings (employment settings tend to be somewhat more stringent, and independent testing agencies can be the most stringent). In many cases, then, the documentation review process is not as burdensome as it could be. For example, a student with significant visual impairment or blindness need not prove a history of disability designation and special education. Whether the visual impairment occurred at birth or last week, the student should need only a written report from a qualified vision professional that details the type and extent of visual disability, what the student can and cannot do, and what the accommodation needs might be in a classroom or for various types of exams. Cases like this one, where there is a clear physical, sensory, or mental impairment that is easily documented, should provide little angst to the applicant or the reviewer.

The cases that create the most tension in accommodation decisions seem to involve high incidence disorders such as LD, ADHD, and anxiety, all of which have no clear biological marker, have no consensus definition or singular diagnostic formula, and whose symptoms occur to varying degrees in everyone. In these cases, a developmental history documenting the disorder is helpful, as is a record from the school system regarding disability designation and special services, as well as previous professional diagnostic evaluations. It also is useful for the accommodation applicant to provide evidence of impairment in learning and test taking, including grade reports, standardized test scores, and teacher comments. And last but not least, there is a need for that recent, comprehensive, clinical evaluation that affirms the presence of a disability, delineates the areas of functional limitation, and provides a rationale for reasonable test accommodations (in college and/or for high-stakes exams).

POSTSECONDARY OUTCOMES FOR INDIVIDUALS WITH DISABILITIES

Whereas the previous section discussed the legal requirements of the IDEIA and the ADAAA, this section discusses what might be considered the results of the IDEIA and the ADAAA (among other factors): the outcomes of students with disabilities who have graduated from high school. Specifically, this section covers the prevalence of college enrollment for students with disabilities, as well as the prevalence or trends in accommodations in postsecondary education, admissions and licensing exams, and employment.

Prevalence of Students With Disabilities in College

Students with disabilities historically have fared less well than peers when it comes to college attendance, graduation, employment opportunities, and salaries (Barkley, 2006a; Blackorby & Wagner, 19996; Will, 1986). However, over the past decade there has been a dramatic upswing in college enrollment for students with disabilities. Data from the National Longitudinal Transition Study-2 (NLTS-2; Newman et al., 2011) indicate that 60% of young adults with disabilities have continued to postsecondary education within 8 years of leaving high school. This figure is up from only 14% in 1996. NLTS-2 indicates that of those students with various disabilities in postsecondary schools, the percentage by disability category is as follows: 31% LD, 18% ADHD, 15% psychiatric, 14% sensory or motor, 11% health impaired, and 11% assorted other disabilities. The bulk of these students fall into the category of "mild" high-incidence disabilities, and about half of postsecondary students with disabilities are impaired in some aspect of learning.

Other reports note that 10% of college freshmen are students with disabilities (Berkner & Choy, 2008), whereas this figure was 3% in 1978 (Henderson, 2001). Clearly, more students with disabilities than ever before have made the transition from high school to postsecondary school (44% community colleges, 32% vocational or technical schools, and 19% 4-year colleges or universities; NLTS-2; Newman et al., 2011).

Prevalence of Accommodations in Postsecondary School, Admissions and Licensing Exams, and Employment

Community College and Undergraduate College Programs

According to the NLTS-2 report by Newman et al. (2011), 63% of students identified in high school as having a disability did not consider themselves to have a disability by the time they transitioned to postsecondary school. Although 87% of these students received test accommodations in high school, only 19% received accommodations from their postsecondary schools. This information shows a large gap between secondary and postsecondary schools for both disability identification/disclosure and accommodation use. There may be a variety of reasons for this gap. At the postsecondary level, students must self-disclose their disability, provide the documentation of their disability that often includes a private evaluation at their expense, and demonstrate that they are substantially limited in a major life function. This combination of potential obstacles could play a role in reducing students' access to test accommodations in postsecondary school. Another possibility is that students make a jump in independence from high school to college, so they want to prove that they can manage college without a disability classification or special assistance. Right or wrong, many students want to manage college on their own. It should also be noted that students with disabilities in colleges and universities may be among the more successful students of their cohort. They may have made significant academic gains over the course of their education or developed compensatory strategies, thereby showing little or no academic impairment that would qualify them for test accommodations. Whatever the reason(s), many students with disabilities in high school are not being identified as college students with disabilities.

Graduate and Professional Programs

The higher one advances academically and professionally, the more difficult the accommodation request becomes. Accommodation requests at the K–12 level are quite common, should require little effort from the student, and usually are met with little resistance from school staff. At the college level, accommodations are increasingly common, require some effort on the part of students, and may conjure some resistance from a conservative disabilities official or reluctant faculty member. Graduate and professional schools tend to have small numbers of students with disabilities, may require even more work on the part of a student to apply for accommodations, and provide various forms of resistance to accommodations. For example, faculty at a medical or law school contend that students will need to adapt to a professional world rather than the other way around. They argue that a doctor is not given extended time in the emergency room, nor is a lawyer with a disability given more time to think of a proper response to an objection in the courtroom.

In a sense, there seems to be less advocacy and more "tough love" in graduate and professional schools. This attitude causes some students with disabilities to not even disclose their disabilities, which is the first step necessary to obtain test accommodations. Students feel that they may be stigmatized by professors or other students and that such disclosure may even hurt their chances for recognition, internships, and jobs. It is unfortunate that this attitude may exist in professional schools, but it is a scenario expressed by many graduate students we have worked with over the years.

It is impossible and naive to paint every professional school with one brush. It turns out that policies and attitudes toward students with disabilities and test accommodations vary significantly. For example, there are professional schools that screen all students for disabilities, refer them to diagnosticians to procure appropriate documentation, and then routinely provide the students with test accommodations and other services. On the other hand, there are schools that claim very rigorous admission standards, have very low numbers of students with disabilities, and have a small number of students who use test accommodations. The message here seems to be that students with disabilities must do their homework before applying to a professional school so they can find programs that will be more likely to meet their needs. A blind student will certainly receive appropriate services no matter what school is selected (but schools may differ in whether they feel that a blind student is "otherwise qualified" for some professions), whereas someone with a mild form of ADHD or LD could be in for an accommodation tussle at some schools, especially if the student has a record of academic success and high test scores that were obtained without accommodations.

In cases in which a disability or need for accommodations is being questioned, there is nothing like having the data on one's side. Typically, the quality of one's documentation is the force behind any argument for test accommodations. We cannot stress enough that the accommodation applicant needs to document, document, and document impairment over the course of his or her educational experience.

Admissions and Licensing Exams

The award for most rigorous accommodation processes has to go to professional credentialing examination agencies. This would include state Boards of Law Examiners, the National Board of Medical Examiners, and various other professional licensing agencies that require exams. One only has to look at ADA litigation cases over the past decade to see that these testing agencies have been the ones to actually test the boundaries of the law with regard to test accommodations. Licensing bodies have gotten a reputation for taking a somewhat conservative position on the use of test accommodations, not because they want to burden individuals with disabilities but because they feel a responsibility to be fair to all examinees and protect the integrity of their exams (see, e.g., Melnick, 2011; Sireci & Hambleton, 2009). Licensing exams often become the last gateway to professional practice, and exam developers want to create a test that ensures that only qualified and highly skilled practitioners enter the profession. They also know that test performance may be used to place people in internships, residencies, or jobs, and so getting an accurate ranking of a professional's abilities is extremely important.

These test agencies are exceptionally concerned about the validity of their tests and the decisions made from them. They are faced with the knowledge that some students and instructors cheat on high-stakes tests (Amrein & Berliner, 2002; Haladyna & Downing, 2004), and they are aware that some people malinger on clinical evaluations so as to get a disability diagnosis and receive test accommodations (see Harrison, 2006; Sollman, Ranseen, & Berry, 2010). They also see research literature that shows accommodations such as extended time tend to raise a person's test score regardless of disability status (see the research reviewed in Chapter 5, this volume). Putting this all together, these test agencies are concerned about the ability of accommodations to threaten their tests' security, fairness, and validity. Even so, it should be noted that according to the U.S. Government Accountability Office (2011) survey of large test agencies, the agencies reported "granting between 72 and 100 percent of accommodations that were requested in the most recent testing year for 6 of the 10 tests for which we received data" (p. 17). It is a small minority of cases that get denied test accommodations, and an even smaller minority that have drawn most attention because of litigation (e.g., Gordon, 2009).

Let us make one last point on the dilemma faced by licensing agencies regarding test accommodation decisions. Unlike high school and college, where an accommodation given to one student has no significant impact on other students, accommodations on licensing exams could affect the relative ranking of all students taking the exam. Certainly, one's score and test standing could have implications for occupational opportunities. In a sense, these tests are competitions, and there are always winners and losers. And so any accommodations decision has the real possibility of being discriminatory, either against the student with a claimed disability or against the rest of the examinees. There is a remedy that partially addresses this issue: designing tests that are more accessible, fairer to everyone, less time constrained, and more flexible in presentation and response formats. In other words, testing agencies need to incorporate universal design principles into their assessments (see Chapter 10).

Employment

As reluctant as many postsecondary school students may be to self-disclose a disability, this reluctance is even greater in employment settings. Madaus (2008) surveyed 500 college graduates with LD about their employment outcomes and experiences. Only 55% self-disclosed their disability, and a mere 12% reported requesting accommodations. Price, Gerber, and Mulligan (2007) reviewed literature on adults with LD and concluded that there is an underuse of the Americans With Disabilities Act (ADA) of 1990 in the workplace by these individuals. They characterize this as a missed opportunity and suggest that transition planning and preparation for adulthood involve training about the ADA. On a more positive note, data from the NLTS-2 indicate that 91% of young adults with disabilities out of high school up to 8 years reported having been employed, and 67% of them worked full time. However, only 26% of them disclosed their disability to employers, and 7% reported receiving some kind of accommodation on the job. It may be that many of the jobs did not require skills affected by their disability, but it is unlikely that this would account for all of the "nondisclosers." Although test accommodations are provided in K–12 grades to the vast majority of students with disabilities, we see a dramatic drop in accommodation use in postsecondary school (19%) and employment (7%).

To some extent, it is more difficult to write about accommodations in the workplace than accommodations on a high-stakes exam. An exam is narrowly focused and tightly controlled. In the workplace, where job types and tasks vary greatly, the number of accommodation possibilities seems endless. Further, the types of disabilities and limitations in major life activities are more varied. Employers are more likely to deal with situations such as cancer treatment, heart conditions, alcoholism, depression, eating disorders, and a host of disabilities that may not affect a test situation yet have significant impact on work life. In addition, many employers, especially small businesses, do not have an office of disability services as found in a university or a large testing company (e.g., Educational Testing Service). Human resources professionals vary in their level of knowledge and sensitivity toward disability issues as well.

In addition to workplace adjustments, some employers have occasion to test employees (e.g., a financial analyst, an air traffic controller), either as a precursor to employment, during employment, or prior to a possible promotion. Employees with disabilities may warrant some of the same accommodations students receive in school, including extended time, additional breaks, a room free of distractions, a computer to assist with reading or writing, or a calculator. However, job assessments can involve much more than reading, writing, and arithmetic. Tests for automobile technicians, for example, involve diagnostic and repair work on cars; assessments for airplane pilots involve activities in a flight simulator; and firefighters have a variety of paper-and-pencil tests combined with in vivo evaluations of numerous job skills. The military is in a class by itself when it comes to various job skill assessments—consider the skills needed by sonar operators, paratroopers, and those in special forces. Whatever the specific skill or task involved, any of these employers are obligated to create fair and accessible test conditions for persons with disabilities, and obviously, this may involve far more creativity and engineering than choosing from the typical school accommodations menu. As long as an employee or prospective employee is "otherwise qualified" to carry out the requirements of the job, an employer should attempt to arrange reasonable accommodations for any testing situation. So whether individuals with disabilities are taking tests in a classroom, for admission to a school program, or for a new job, they are entitled to reasonable test accommodations under the law.

Possible Future Prevalence of Accommodations: Implications of the Response-to-Intervention Model

Since the 1970s, students with LD have typically been identified on the basis of a gap or discrepancy between their aptitude or measured intelligence and their actual level of academic achievement (Kavale, 2002). Initially, the diagnostic convention was to identify a student who was performing two or more grade levels behind his or her current or expected grade level. A student in sixth grade reading at a fourth-grade level was considered to have LD, provided there was good instruction in place and no other reason for the delay. Over time the discrepancy calculations became based on standard scores from IQ and achievement tests, such that a difference of at least 15 points, but usually more than 22 points, was used to make the diagnosis. The dependency on test scores and the arbitrariness of some discrepancy calculations brought much criticism to the discrepancy practice (see Gresham, 2002; Reynolds, 1984; Stanovich, 1999).

The harsh criticisms and scientific repudiation have brought the discrepancy notion into disrepute, at least with regard to K–12 diagnoses of LD. The most recent amendments to the IDEIA have allowed for a limited use of discrepancy analyses in LD determination but also allow schools to use a RTI model for identification of students with learning issues. As we discussed in more detail in Chapter 4, this educational reform paradigm passes all students through several educational filters before concluding that a student might warrant a psychoeducational evaluation (see Figure 4.1).

For purposes of our discussion on the documentation disconnect, let us consider what RTI might mean for students who apply for test accommodations in college and beyond. On the basis of the RTI model, far fewer K–12 students should be referred for psychoeducational evaluations and identified for special education. That is a stated goal of RTI, and thus far it seems to be the trend (e.g., VanDerHeyden, Witt & Gilbertson, 2007). This means that in the next decade a smaller proportion of students will have school-based disability designations, IEPs, and documentation of a disability. Already we are seeing declining numbers of students classified with LD (Cortiella, 2011). Those students served by an RTI system who want to apply to postsecondary schools or testing agencies for accommodations may have little or no formal documentation of a disability or a substantial limitation. Take, for example, the gifted/LD student mentioned earlier in this chapter. Such a student is not likely to require Tier 2 or 3 interventions, let alone receive a diagnostic evaluation and a disability designation. Most gifted/LD students achieve at an average level, and so they would not "fail to respond" and not come to the attention of specialists.

In a sense, then, RTI could effectively remove an entire cohort of students who would have been active accommodation seekers in college and on high-stakes exams. The alternative for such individuals will be to seek private evaluations outside of the school system. It will be interesting to see what disability service officials do when they are faced with private evaluations that claim a disability and school records that show nothing. It would not appear that this scenario favors students seeking test accommodations. Essentially, most of what we suggested to students with disabilities and their parents would be moot under the current RTI paradigm. It is unlikely that this outcome was one of the intents of this reform, but a reduction in students with disabilities and fewer applications for accommodations will likely be outcomes of the RTI process. If RTI works as intended, the vast majority of these students will respond to interventions (at some level of intensity) and will not need accommodations.

RECOMMENDATIONS FOR TRANSITION PLANNING

Now that we know the difference between the accommodation laws and procedures for K–12 and postsecondary settings, as well as the current and possible future trends in accommodation prevalence, we are able to make recommendations that improve a disabled student's transition to postsecondary school and also minimize the documentation disconnect. A number of authors have developed suggestions to bridge these gaps (Gartland & Strosnider, 2007;

EXHIBIT 9.1
Transition Planning

Advice: Encourage the student and parent(s) to . . .
- Document the presence of a disability as early as possible. This includes professional evaluations, treatment services, and all school-related evidence of disability and special education.
- Document functional limitations in learning, reading, test taking, etc., throughout K–12 schooling.
- Provide accommodation decision makers with every piece of school and clinical documentation available, as well as evidence of how the client actually performs in real-world situations (e.g., grades, standardized test scores, response to treatment).
- Request and use necessary and reasonable accommodations—that is, accommodations that provide equal access to exams, rather than merely increase comfort or confidence.
- Try to improve the student's skills to potentially discontinue the need for accommodations. For example, a slow reader can learn to read more fluently. This may be more beneficial than reading slowly and relying on extended time. The student can try taking tests with and without accommodations, so as to either wean from the accommodations or prove the need for them.
- Work with school counselors, teachers, and school psychologists to assist with transition to college.

Education: Teach the student and parent(s) . . .
- How to advocate for the student.
- The student's basic legal rights, including the differences between IDEIA and ADAAA.
- The documentation requirements of postsecondary schools and high-stakes testing agencies.

Advocacy: On the student's behalf . . .
- Prepare a detailed history that comprehensively reviews the diagnostic and accommodation history, including explanations of functional limitations and how they impair major life activities.
- Recommend reasonable accommodations—ideally, the least alteration of the test that still will allow equal access. It looks suspicious to an accommodation reviewer when a clinician requests a private room, double time, extra breaks, etc., for a person with a mild impairment, while a request from someone with a more severe impairment asks only for 50% extended time.

Kochhar-Bryant & Izzo, 2006; Lindstrom & Lindstrom, 2011; Shaw, Madaus, & Banerjee, 2009). We have attempted to distill a number of these ideas into a list of suggestions that could inform the accommodation application experience (see Exhibit 9.1), in the hope that these suggestions might mitigate the documentation disconnect associated with transition from high school to college and beyond. Clinicians and educators can assist students in preparing an accommodation request. Following these suggestions will not guarantee that an accommodation request will be granted by a college or testing agency, but it certainly will increase one's odds significantly.

10

UNIVERSAL DESIGN FOR ASSESSMENT

Universal design (UD) is a broad concept that incorporates ideas about making environments, buildings, vehicles, products, and opportunities (e.g., education, employment, recreation) fully accessible to individuals with and without recognized disabilities. UD embraces an inclusive philosophy that assumes all individuals should have equal rights and opportunities to study, work, engage in leisure activities, and otherwise take part in all aspects of society regardless of any physical, mental, or other constraints. Such an approach requires a deep regard for human diversity and a commitment to meeting the unique individual needs of all persons. Whether this involves barrier-free buildings, wheelchair-accessible public transportation, closed-captioned television, or computerized communication systems, the goal of UD is a more inclusive society in all respects.

UD is not a legal mandate, although various laws and policies have language that promotes the implementation of universal design principles

http://dx.doi.org/10.1037/14468-010
Testing Accommodations for Students With Disabilities: Research-Based Practice, by B. J. Lovett and L. J. Lewandowski

(e.g., Individuals With Disabilities Education Improvement Act of 2004, No Child Left Behind Act of 2001, Assistive Technology Act of 2004). Unlike accommodations, which are based on laws that protect the rights of individuals and require equal access be provided to persons with disabilities, UD is based on principles that support the use of accommodations while also making accommodations less necessary. For the purposes of this book, we apply UD to assessment situations, and by extension, to the practice of test accommodations. We have noted throughout this book that test accommodation practices, in some circumstances, are flawed and likely invalid, in large part because they are only offered to selected examinees. UD offers an alternative to test accommodations that avoids this problem. In this chapter, we discuss the history of UD, its basic tenets and principles, and its application to assessment.

AN ARGUMENT FOR UNIVERSAL DESIGN

In our current society, we know that we need to break our dependency on gas and oil. We know that the use of gas engines negatively affects our environment, and we know that we have the capability to develop other sources of energy and rid ourselves of oil dependency. Yet, for some reason, we just cannot bring ourselves to make the investment, to break from our old habits, and to try something different that might be a bit uncomfortable initially. This is analogous to the apparent conflict between test accommodations and universal test design. We know that some test accommodations are invalid, we know they are often applied arbitrarily, we know they apply only to persons with disabilities rather than everyone, and we know that the research support for many of them is either nonexistent or weak. Most important, we know that UD approaches would attempt to make assessments fair and accessible to everyone. Yet, we have done very little to promote the use of UD for classroom or high-stakes tests.

We are not arguing to do away with all test accommodations. Certainly, they can be appropriate and helpful. Our position is that some test accommodations, as currently practiced, lack scientific rigor, are potentially discriminatory, serve as an incentive system for some test takers, and fail to adequately meet the testing needs of many people with disabilities and other differences. We believe that it is in everyone's best interest to find more equitable, inclusive, and well-designed assessments so as to minimize the need for test accommodations. We do not expect accommodations to go away entirely, or that UD procedures will solve every testing problem. But we do think that UD is worth pursuing as the first choice, with test accommodations as a fallback.

There may always be a need for some test accommodations. For example, blind persons will not read printed or computer-displayed exams without a conversion to sound or Braille, and deaf individuals will need printed or signed test instructions. There is little problem with accommodations for those with clear sensory, physical, or intellectual disabilities. In fact, we should continue to improve technologies that advance the best engineered test accommodations possible. The problems with test accommodations seem to center on high-incidence disabilities (i.e., attention-deficit/hyperactivity disorder [ADHD], learning disabilities, anxiety) for which there are no biological markers and whose symptoms are experienced by everyone to a degree; some individuals with these disorders even perform on tests as well or better than peers without disabilities (Lewandowski, Gathje, Lovett, & Gordon, 2012; Sparks & Lovett, 2009a). Another problem in this arena involves the most highly sought accommodation, extended time. This is a test accommodation that is not specific to individuals with disabilities and cannot be accurately titrated to the actual needs of the person requesting it (see Lovett, 2010). This last point, concerning the inaccuracy of extended-time allotments (e.g., Lewandowski, Cohen, & Lovett, 2013), has been argued in this book as discriminatory. In the absence of any empirical guidance, any assigned amount of extended time has a good chance of either under- or overestimating the needs of the person with disabilities. Thus, the amount of time will lead to either an advantage or disadvantage for the examinee or the rest of the pool of examinees. The smaller the amount of time allotted, the more likely the person with a disability is disadvantaged, whereas the larger the amount of extended time granted, the more likely it becomes that that person will have an advantage over other examinees (Lewandowski, Cohen, & Lovett, 2013; Miller, Lewandowski, & Antshel, in press).

There are other reasons why we feel that some test accommodation practices could be augmented by universal test design. The practice of applying for and granting or denying test accommodations has become a big business, often contentious, and sometimes losing a focus on universal justice. Some test entities want to hold the line on accommodations such as extended time, ensuring that people get what they need without creating a disadvantage to other examinees. They interpret the ADA Amendments Act of 2008 (ADAAA) literally with regard to an impairment that substantially limits a person and make decisions based on evidence of a substantial limitation. On the other hand, advocates for individuals with disabilities are more inclined to want test accommodations for any person with a diagnosis and history of test accommodations, regardless of the evidence of a substantial limitation. After all, the determination of a limitation is subjective and arguably known best by the person with the disability. Thus, there is an inherent friction between these two positions on test accommodation decisions. The friction has led to court cases, not to mention strained feelings among professionals who should be working together. UD has the potential to mitigate these conflicts and put the focus back on nondiscriminatory, accessible assessment for all.

Another potential benefit of UD is that it could essentially eliminate the inherent problem of test accommodations being considered an incentive or advantage. Some have argued that test accommodations are desirable, and in fact, a recent study showed that college students with disabilities (88%) and without disabilities (87%) would like to have extended time for timed exams (Lewandowski, Lambert, Lovett, Panahon, & Sytsma, in press). Others have noted that some individuals will malinger, or "fake bad" on an evaluation to qualify for an incentive (see Green, 2007). As noted in Chapter 4, malingering in diagnostic testing situations has become a growing concern. UD could minimize the likelihood of malingering. Under UD test administrations, ideally there would be no need for test accommodations like extended time that serve as an incentive. If time was no longer a critical part of exams, and most people had adequate time to access an exam, then this would remove the need to request extended time, which would reduce the need for test accommodation evaluations and therefore reduce the need to malinger on such evaluations. In fact, clinical assessment could be used to better design an examination for the individual, not just provide a nonspecific accommodation (extended time) that has nothing to do with the individual's impairment (i.e., a person with ADHD who rushes through tasks, or someone with obsessive–compulsive disorder who counts all the periods in a reading passage). Clinical evaluations could match a person's abilities and impairments to the demands of an exam to see whether that individual could access the exam. If a person cannot fully access the exam, then it is not sufficiently universally designed or cannot be, and therefore a test accommodation would come into play. Why not put energy into designing better tests, rather than retrofitting poorly designed test formats with accommodations that are controversial and potentially discriminatory? UD for assessment could change the way clinicians evaluate individuals with disabilities, reduce the need for such evaluations, eliminate malingering, and lessen the arguments over who warrants certain test accommodations. We strongly advocate for this shift from a test accommodation to more of a UD approach.

HISTORY OF UNIVERSAL DESIGN

Credit for the term *universal design* is usually given to Ronald Mace, a wheelchair user himself, who founded the Center for Universal Design at North Carolina State University. Mace and colleagues articulated a system for conceptualizing and implementing architectural and other designs with the least amount of restrictions, barriers, or specialized provisions in order to make environments accessible to people with special needs. Although there were already efforts to make buildings barrier free, the new UD philosophy sought to develop optimal designs that could suit a wide range of individual users with efficient systems rather than cumbersome and costly retrofits (Mace, Hardie, & Place, 1991). This proactive approach requires sensitivity to human diversity and anticipation of human needs in order to design inclusive environments (Covington & Hannah, 1997).

The UD movement may have started in the fields of architecture and environmental engineering, but it did not take long for other fields to embrace this general philosophy. A number of educators incorporated this new paradigm as an approach to classroom instruction, now known as Universal Design for Instruction (UDI; Chickering & Gamson, 1987; Silver, Bourke, & Strehorn, 1998). These authors identified instructional strategies that were appropriate for students with and without disabilities. For example, a UD approach promotes instruction delivered in multiple formats so it can be accessed by students of varying abilities and needs. Also, instruction is developed in a way that meets students at their skill levels and pace of learning, and in an environment that is best suited to various sensory and physical needs (e.g., space, reach, mobility). UDI is an approach to curriculum development and course designs that creates improved instruction and instructional environments for all students, ensuring maximum accessibility to course material. The application of UDI in schools will not totally replace the use of accommodations for some students with disabilities, but it certainly can reduce the need for accommodations if instruction is designed to be inclusive from the outset (McGuire, Scott, & Shaw, 2006).

PRINCIPLES OF UNIVERSAL DESIGN

Stemming from the early work of Mace and colleagues, the Center for Universal Design at North Carolina State University developed a set of principles to guide thinking about UD across environments, including education. Chickering and Gamson (1987) were among the first to adapt UD principles to instructional practices in postsecondary education, though many of these principles are considered best practices at all levels of education. In their seminal paper, they provided seven principles to guide effective instruction for all students at the college level, as follows.

Universally designed instruction:

1. encourages contacts between students and faculty,
2. develops reciprocity and cooperation among students,
3. uses active learning techniques,
4. gives prompt feedback,
5. emphasizes time on task,
6. communicates high expectations, and
7. respects diverse talents and ways of learning. (Chickering & Gamson, 1987, p. 2)

This work provided a structure on which others could build, and principles of good UD instruction continue to be elaborated (see Kameenui & Carnine, 1998; Scott, McGuire, & Foley, 2003).

Although most of the UD applications in education have involved instruction and learning, there have been efforts to apply UD to assessment and adapt UD principles to the testing environment. Four papers are particularly informative and should be given consideration by anyone interested in developing UD assessments. The narrowest of the four focuses on methods based on UD considerations for test items, such as those used on statewide assessments (Johnstone, Thompson, Bottsford-Miller, & Thurlow, 2008). These authors provide a detailed analysis of item review conducted by experts, statistical analysis, and think-aloud techniques. These methods allow one to remove problem items and develop a test that is accessible to more students.

Alternative assessments, created specifically for students with disabilities, have been the source of one research program applying UD to actual exams. Kettler et al. (2012) administered items from high school science tests with and without alterations to the items, and the items were administered to students with and without disabilities. The alterations included such things as modifying or eliminating graphics accompanying the item text, simplifying vocabulary used in the item, and adding white space around the item to reduce distractions. The alterations had inconsistent effects on total test score reliability but consistent effects on difficulty; students both with and without disabilities received higher scores on the test with altered items.

Ketterlin-Geller (2005) is one of a few investigators who developed a universally designed assessment from scratch and evaluated its characteristics. She developed a math test for third-grade students based on UD principles. She chose a computer-assisted platform to deliver the test and a multiple-choice (selection) format for test responding. The hardware and software design allowed for easy navigation, practice items, careful organization of items on the visual display, and the use of color and luminance changes to signify that a choice was made. Each test item had five possible choices in order to reduce error from guessing. Items were presented in 18-point black sans serif font, and one item was displayed on the computer screen without a need to scroll. Students could use a mouse or keyboard to make a selection by tabbing or clicking anywhere in the answer box. Item selection was based on a computer algorithm in which an estimate of student's ability was calculated after each response. That information was used to select the next item. Time was not a sensitive feature in the exam, and students could change answers before submitting their response. Both auditory and written text were provided for students with low reading skills. Care was taken to write the directions and test items in the most simple and understandable manner. The test items were piloted, evaluated, and modified until adequate reliability and validity estimates were achieved. Obviously, this test-development process was quite involved, and certainly not what the average teacher would do to develop a test. However, the process serves as a wonderful example of how UD considerations can be used to create a more flexible, applicable, and universal test.

Recently, Shinn and Ofiesh (2012) provided an overview of the cognitive demands involved in various types of assessments of individuals with individual differences (e.g., disabilities, age, language, poverty, culture) and the types of test accommodations that could mitigate the effects of these differences. In essence, they applied UD principles to the testing environment. For example, they urged test providers to design multiple ways of presenting test information both visually (e.g., adjustable font size, spacing, highlighting, Braille) and aurally (e.g., readers, text-to-speech software, amplification systems). They also suggested ways to make test content more accessible (e.g., clear and simple language, avoid irrelevant pictures/graphs, clear directions) and test responding most appropriate for individuals with a variety of needs (e.g., answering in a test booklet, using a computer for writing, or speech-to-text software).

The articles reviewed previously illustrate the ways in which test developers can adapt and redesign tests for the greater good. In this spirit, we thought it would be helpful to more closely review the key UD principles as applied to the area of assessment, and we briefly discuss how each principle might apply to a broad variety of exams and examinees. The principles that follow are adapted from Story, Mueller, and Mace, 1998, and Braden and Joyce (2008).

Principle 1: Equitable Use. The design is useful and marketable to people with diverse abilities. This principle encourages the design of assessments that are fair, identical wherever possible, and accessible to all persons. This means that to the extent possible the test and test environment should be as similar as possible across examinees, nonstigmatizing, and essentially equivalent for the assessment of target skills. This should be done with minimal alteration of the test and in a way that ensures privacy, security, and safety. Those examinees receiving test accommodations should not receive a "make-up" exam that has similar but different questions, nor should they be placed in a room with sound distractions or poor lighting just because it was the only testing room available for a person receiving extended time. Students receiving accommodations should have no worse test access or environment than the majority of examinees.

Principle 2: Flexibility in Use. The design accommodates a wide range of individual preferences and abilities. This principle encourages creativity in the way test materials are presented and responses collected. This principle seems to cover most of our commonly used test accommodations (e.g., enhanced visuals, read aloud, use of calculator, voice recognition, audio versions of tests). Such flexibility could apply to enlarging the print of a test, allowing an examinee to type a response rather than hand write it, using a screen reader that provides words by sight and sound, and allowing someone extra time to complete a test. In addition, test items should be chosen in part on the basis of their ability to be adapted. For instance, a picture stimulus may be difficult to describe to a student with visual impairments, even through an accommodation, so unless the picture stimulus is crucial to the skill being measured, it should be removed from the exam. (If interpreting pictures is the target skill, as in some art classes, than accommodations would not be appropriate.)

Principle 3: Simple and Intuitive Use. Use of the design is easy to understand, regardless of the user's experience, knowledge, language skills, or current concentration level. This principle encourages test designs that are elegant in their simplicity. Test designs should not be burdensome, punitive, or excessively long. They should strive to be user friendly, easy to understand, and uncomplicated in language and directions, and they should avoid the possibility of confusing or fooling examinees. Ideally, the layout of an exam should be clear, concise, predictable, simple, and intuitive for examinees.

For instance, the style of the language of exam items should be engaging but neutral. Sometimes instructors create exams using their own voice or language without considering the language comprehension and vocabulary of the examinees. Students with learning disabilities, language disorders, and English as a second language may have trouble understanding test directions and questions. Instead of testing student content knowledge, the instructor might be assessing language abilities, at least for some students. This adds construct-irrelevant variance to the assessment and is antithetical to a UD approach.

Principle 4: Perceptible Information. The design communicates necessary information effectively to the user, regardless of ambient conditions or the user's sensory abilities. This principle encourages test designs to maximize legibility and comprehensibility. Students have a right to know what they are being tested on and what instructions must be followed. There should be no gaps in this information and no ambiguity. If need be, information must be communicated in multiple modes (i.e., visual, auditory, pictorial, tactile, or in combination). No examinee with the requisite content knowledge should be penalized by not understanding the requirements or content of the test. This is particularly important for students with sensory limitations, but it also applies to students whose first language is not that used on the test. It is up to the test developers, test agencies, and course instructors to ensure that examinees fully understand what is expected of them and have complete access to every bit of information on the test. That is the only way to get the most accurate measurement of one's skills. Students must have complete access to test directions and content.

In accordance with this principle, a UD approach would ensure that instructions are written and spoken as well as unambiguous. The last thing an instructor should do is provide additional information to one examinee and not make that available to all examinees. This can be a problem when a student takes an exam in a private setting. That student might have peace and quiet, but he or she might not be privy to directions, explanations, or clarifications made by an instructor during an exam. A UD approach ensures that even if a student is in a different location or has a sensory impairment (e.g., hearing loss), he or she will receive complete access and understanding of the exam, its procedures, and any exam clarifications.

Principle 5: Tolerance of Error. The design minimizes hazards and the adverse consequences of accidental or unintended actions. This principle encourages tests that can still be administered properly when something goes wrong. A test that can tolerate error can accommodate a restroom break without costing the examinee, handle a liquid spill on the work area without affecting the validity of the assessment, or overcome an unexpected public address announcement or fire alarm. An experienced test giver knows how to design a test and environment to deal with a variety of unintended actions (e.g., what to do when a student has a panic attack during the exam). The key is to use test designs that are flexible, multiple, clear, and are able to anticipate variations in human abilities. This may involve building in alternatives (e.g., extra time, break time, extra seating, extra test materials). When technologies are used to deliver tests, there should be backup plans built into the technology as well as the administration protocols in case something goes wrong.

Principle 6: Low Physical Effort. The design can be used efficiently and comfortably and with a minimum of fatigue. The intent of this principle is to foster test designs that minimize nonessential physical effort in order to allow maximum energy and attention to the cognitive aspects of the test. Obviously, this does not apply to tests of physical strength and endurance such as a physical education exam in high school. Concerns about effort and fatigue are significant for individuals with chronic health problems (e.g., asthma, diabetes, pulmonary disease, cardiovascular disease, obesity), traumatic conditions such as broken limbs and head injuries, and stress-related conditions, as well as persons on certain medications or treatment regimens. Tests such as a 3-day law bar examination may be too taxing for some individuals.

Ideally, exams would be designed to be a short as possible while still accomplishing their job (i.e., assess target skills), but this is an ideal that is rarely lived up to. In an interesting study using the SAT I Reasoning Test, Bridgeman, Trapani, and Curley (2006) examined the effects of reducing the number of items per section, thus allowing students more time to answer to complete the test. They found very little difference between scores on the full test versus the shortened test, calling into question the need for long exams.

Under a UD approach, test makers would use as few test items as necessary to accomplish their assessment goals. In the case of long exams that are necessary, some examinees may need extra breaks, shorter test days, or even more days to take a test. If this is the case, test developers might consider making those options standard (universal). For instance, on certain medical licensure exams that take many hours, all examinees have the option of multiple breaks that they can choose to take (or else go on with the computer-administered exam). In addition, examiners should give thought to the physical demands of a test. How long might someone have to sit in a certain position, or stare at a computer display, or work without food and water? Not all individuals have the same tolerance for these various test conditions, and so accommodations, adaptations, and comfort measures may need to be provided. A UD approach would develop tests that minimize physical effort and obviate the need for accommodations.

Principle 7: Size and Space for Approach and Use. Appropriate size and space is provided for approach, reach, manipulations, and use regardless of user's body size, posture, or mobility. This principle serves to remind us that examinees vary in body size, hand size, reach, visual acuity, mobility, and posture. According to this UD principle, a test environment should be designed to accommodate all shapes, sizes, strengths, and speeds. This means the environment should be equally accessible and comfortable for all examinees. Flexibility in configuration would allow for optimal seating comfort, adjustable positioning of self and test materials, comfortable platforms for writing or typing, adequate space to move and work, and appropriate viewing distances. If assistive devices are needed, adequate space should be provided without taxing the examinee to reach or maneuver test materials more than other examinees. In a testing situation, flexibility to move tables and chairs, adjust heights, and position test materials including computers and assistive devices will better serve a wide range of examinees with various physical requirements. We embarrassingly confess that one of the authors once administered an exam to 420 students in an auditorium that seated 410 people. Students were cramped to say the least, and some chose to sit in the aisles or on the stage. Although this design may have ended up being universal in a convoluted sense, it certainly was not comfortable, safe, secure, or in line with UD principles. That is how not to arrange a test environment.

It should be obvious to all those who have taken classroom and standardized tests that many exams fail to live up to the UD principles previously described. To create UD assessments, test developers and examiners have to be committed to these principles and practice them beginning with the initial plan of developing a test. Just as an examiner considers the skills or constructs to be measured, as well as the content and method he or she will use, the examiner should be thinking of how to apply the seven UD principles in test development. UD requires that examiners anticipate the needs of various examinees, whether these include visual or hearing impairments, health conditions, psychiatric disorders, or English as a second language. UD means developing assessments that are equipped to test virtually everyone in an equivalent manner.

APPLICATIONS OF UNIVERSAL DESIGN PRINCIPLES

As we noted earlier, the universal design of assessments, creating a test that can be equally accessed by any person, is an ideal to strive for rather than a current legal mandate. Admittedly, no test will be ideal for all people at all times. Some individuals will prefer a room that is warm and others cooler, some like fluorescent lighting and others incandescent, and some like paper-and-pencil tests rather than computerized tests. UD is not about appealing to all personal preferences. In practice, it strives to find ways to attain equal access for the greatest number of examinees without compromising the test. Therefore, UD will not likely replace the use of test accommodations. In fact, UD should make the implementation of accommodations easier and more valid. If a test is developed according to UD principles, then the use of assistive technology for example should fit seamlessly into the test administration. Another aspect of UD that bears mentioning is that it in no way lowers standards. There is never a goal to make a test easier (i.e., such that less of the target skills would be needed to succeed on the test), only to make accessing the test easier.

Once a test developer (i.e., Educational Testing Service, National Board of Medical Examiners, teacher, or professor) embraces the UD philosophy, a cascade of considerations and decisions naturally will follow. The following is a natural progression of some of these considerations:

1. Carefully determine the constructs/skills that need to be measured.
2. Consider the purpose(s) of the assessment, whether it is intended to assist in grading students in a course, predict students' success in college, or determine eligibility for a professional license.
3. Determine a format (or multiple formats) of the test that best assesses the target skills while taking into account accessibility to the greatest number of examinees.
4. Develop test items that reliably and validly measure the target skills while having maximum readability, legibility, and clarity.
5. Ensure that test items are not biased in any way (e.g., cultural or language bias).
6. Design the test to be as brief and efficient as possible so that desired outcomes are achieved and possibilities of error, fatigue, and excessive physical effort are minimized. In other words, make every attempt to remove construct-irrelevant variance.

7. Design tests to be flexible and adaptable such that accessibility is maximized without compromising the validity of the test.
8. Design tests and testing environments in such a way that test accommodations can be implemented easily.
9. Work individually with examinees that have special needs to arrange the most accessible yet fair-testing procedures.
10. Monitor and evaluate the effectiveness of assessment procedures and results, including feedback from students about the testing experience. Make changes as appropriate.

A test developer that adheres to UD principles and follows these 10 steps when developing a test will likely meet the testing needs of a wide variety of examinees, coming ever closer to the goal of universal accessibility and fairness in assessment.

Fortunately, there is a literature that can serve to guide the UD-conscious test developer, even to the point of listing considerations for designing test items. Much of this work has been summarized in reports by the National Center on Educational Outcomes. In particular, reports by S. J. Thompson, Johnstone, and Thurlow (2002) and Johnstone (2003) are instructive. Next, we provide some of their guidance with regard to a UD approach to test development. (Much of the list in Exhibit 10.1 was drawn from a variety of sources, including Arditi, 1999; P. J. Brown, 1999; Gaster & Clark, 1995; Haladyna, Downing, & Rodriquez, 2002; Johnstone, 2003; Popham, 2001; Popham & Lindheim, 1980; Rakow & Gee, 1987; Shinn & Ofiesh, 2012.) The list of UD-friendly suggestions is surely a tall order for someone giving an examination. It all starts with a UD attitude and a willingness to do what is possible to make tests well developed, fair, and accessible for all. Although it may be impossible to consider every test design element mentioned here, it is always possible to improve one's ability to develop a more universally designed test.

EXHIBIT 10.1
Considerations for a Universally Designed Test

Adopting a universal-design attitude:
- Plan tests to be fair, adaptable, and accessible to all.
- Consider disability and limitations, age, language, culture, abilities, health, etc.
- Minimize skills required beyond those being measured.
- Avoid content that might unfairly advantage or disadvantage any student subgroup.
- Anticipate potential problems for students with special needs.

Preparing the environment:
- Give exams at a site that is most accessible by all examinees.
- Arrange seating with desired spacing and placement of students with special needs (i.e., front row to visualize the board, near door for restroom breaks).
- Ensure that lighting and sound conditions are optimal.
- Try to adjust seat and desk size as well as reach to the examinee.

EXHIBIT 10.1
Considerations for a Universally Designed Test   *(Continued)*

Test presentation:
- Provide multiple presentation options (paper and pencil, computer, audio version).
- Provide for technological flexibility (use of computer or assistive devices).
- Allow for the use of Braille or other tactile format.
- Allow for signing to a student.
- Allow for large print and/or less material on a page.
- Allow for the use of oral presentation to a student.
- Allow for the use of assistive technology (sound amplification, magnifier).
- Allow for translation into another language.
- Adjustable volume on audiotapes, videos, or computers.
- Test is compatible with current screenreader software.
- Twelve (12) point minimum for all print; font size adjustable.
- Wide spacing between letters, words, and lines.
- High contrast between color of text and background.
- Appropriate use of highlighting.
- Sufficient blank space (leading) between lines of text.
- Pictures have clearly defined features.
- All copies of the test have the same type darkness (no faded text).
- Sufficient contrast between colors.
- Color is not relied on to convey important information or distinctions.

Test content:
- Use simple and clear language; eliminate unnecessary words.
- Keep vocabulary appropriate for grade level.
- Keep sentences and item stems short.
- Avoid technical terms that are not the target of the evaluation or provide definitions.
- Avoid idioms unless idiomatic speech is being measured.
- Make the directions clear and unambiguous.
- Make all questions and response options clear and unambiguous.
- Allow the use of a dictionary or calculator if they do not invalidate the construct being assessed.
- Items must be free of content that may unfairly benefit or penalize students from diverse ethnic, socioeconomic, or linguistic backgrounds, or students with disabilities.
- Use just enough test items to accomplish the assessment goals; avoid long tests; consider multiple tests rather than one long one.
- Avoid errors in spelling and grammar and make noun–pronoun relationships clear.

Test output:
- Allow for multiple modes of responding (writing or typing, circling or bubbling, touch screen or key press).
- Ensure that students can easily navigate the test, whether turning pages or using a computer.
- Allow access to a computer for writing.
- Allow spell and grammar checking if not a target of the assessment.
- Allow speech recognition (speech to text software) for dictated responses.
- Allow a scribe for recording responses.
- Allow assistive technology; some examinees may only have isolated finger movement, a head movement, an eye blink response, or a breath response; there are technologies to record such responses and exams need to be tailored to these simple responses.

UNIVERSALLY DESIGNED TEST ENVIRONMENTS

Our focus, to this point, has largely been on the development of assessments, including considerations of actual test items. In addition, test developers should pay considerable attention to the testing environment. Here again, the UD principles readily apply. Unfortunately, many examiners have little control over the environments used for testing. In school situations, a teacher usually has an assigned classroom for testing, a classroom where instruction has also been delivered. That may or may not be ideal for testing, especially if lighting, sound, space, and other factors are fixed, inflexible, and less than ideal. In college settings, some exam rooms (e.g., final exams) are assigned and may be foreign to the instructor and students alike. Some advance scouting by the instructor may be beneficial in making adjustments for certain students with certain needs (e.g., opportunity to arrange desks, tables, and chairs; seating with fewest distractions or closer to a restroom; knowledge of resources such as a clock, blackboard, computer projector).

In most high-stakes test situations, the room is predetermined by the test agency. This could be a school classroom again (as in the case of the SAT), a large room in a hotel, or a workstation in a testing center, and everything in between. In such cases, the testing agency has considerable latitude in arranging the test environment. It is ideal when climate can be controlled, noise can be dampened, lighting optimally adjusted, seating position and comfort maximized, oral instructions easy to hear, mobility unimpeded, personal space adequate, and resources available to handle the unexpected. Some test agencies are pros at administering tests, and this includes the implementation of test accommodations, whereas others would benefit from reading a chapter on UD. A few test agencies contract test administration to professional test centers. Typically, these are computerized exams that can be given individually at a workstation in a quiet cubicle or booth. In some cases, the examinee can choose when to schedule the exam and also receives the test results before leaving the center. Such testing environments seem conducive to UD principles, and hopefully their use will increase.

CASE STUDIES

Michael

Michael is a 15-year-old high school sophomore who has spastic quadriplegia cerebral palsy. This means he has limited control of all his limbs, as well as slow, distorted speech. However, Michael presents as quite intelligent and a very diligent student. Fortunately, he can hear and see reasonably well, so he learns material taught in his classes with little problem. The issue is determining what Michel has learned and how he can apply this knowledge. Because of Michael's motor limitations, writing, typing and even oral dictation are not the best means of assessing his learning. He has the ability to make crude movements with his right hand and index finger. Consequently, his most accurate method of responding is by pointing or touching an area at least a square inch in size. Michael has been equipped with a large touchscreen computer tablet for almost all of his exams. Math, science, as well as English and social studies exams, are presented to Michael on his computer. Most of his tests need to be of a multiple-choice variety. Print has been enlarged, and one item is presented on the screen at a time. Next to each possible answer is a 1-inch square box, and the four choice boxes are separated by one inch in distance. When Michael taps his box of choice, a check appears. Should he want to change his response, he taps on another box, and a check appears there while eliminating the previous selection. The school has found a useful accommodation for Michael. He also needs extended time for most of his tests and sometimes, though not always, a separate location. Michael likes to see whether he can perform the test in class with his peers whenever possible.

Although this system works well for most classroom tests, it does not address tests involving essays or writing. Here Michael has learned to work with a scribe, who over time has become familiar with decoding Michael's speech. Of course, Michael needs extended time on such tests because his speech is quite slow. Any test will fatigue him, so it is preferable that he has extra breaks as well as a study period or lunch after an exam. We can see that the school has done a nice job of accommodating to Michael's special needs. Various learning modifications and testing accommodations have allowed Michael to flourish in regular education classes. So far, this case study sounds like a standard narrative about accommodations. But what makes this a UD case study is that Michael's teachers allow all students to use alternative response formats, regardless of disability status. Of course, on any college entrance exams, he would need true *accommodations*. At the very least he will need a scribe, a separate location, and extended time for the writing section; he also will need permission to convert multiple-choice questions, including figures and graphs, to his computer tablet. It may be that such testing is too great an alteration of standard conditions and would be considered as not valid. Michael may need to be assessed for college entry by other means. A closer look at Michael and his accomplishments would certainly carry the day over a (not so) standardized test score. Michael will surely need a college that will accommodate his needs as well as his high school did.

Michael has significant and multiple limitations. His greatest limitations revolve around test responding rather than test presentation. Viewed another way, his ability to acquire information (Input) is relatively intact, and his ability to understand what he takes in (Processing) is quite good. His impairments restrict his ability to respond to what he is asked (Output). Thankfully, his school district has been thoughtful and creative in finding ways to circumvent the output difficulties. Yet, even with their commitment to UD principles, questions about valid assessment of Michael's skills remain. Are his test scores comparable with those of other students? Are the test alterations so dramatic as to change the nature of the assessment? Should certain tests just be totally eliminated (e.g., keyboarding, oral foreign language tests)? Michael just may be one of those rare students for whom the assessment of knowledge and skills has to be very individualized and not always directly comparable with peers. More than likely, he will need this individualized approach in college, professional school, and the workplace. Hopefully, he and others will be able to advocate for the types of accommodations that will allow Michael to have a productive and successful education followed by a fulfilling career.

Monique

Monique is 11 years old and in fifth-grade at a public middle school. She has a Wechsler Intelligence Scale for Children (WISC–IV; Wechsler, 2003) IQ score of 111, including an average processing speed score of 97. On the Wechsler Individual Achievement Test III (WIAT–III; Pearson, 2009) achievement battery, she obtained a Math composite score of 114 and Oral Language score of 100, but she also had a Reading composite score of 83 and Written Language composite score of 89 (lowered largely by a poor spelling score of 79). Because most tests involve reading and/or writing, Monique has never done particularly well on tests, and frankly she detests them. Her school realizes her frustrations and, as noted on her individualized education program (IEP), has provided a variety of test accommodations. This school has done something very clever. Knowing that its school population included many students with disabilities and English as a second language, they set up a test center in a room next to reading and learning specialists. The room is equipped with computers that have screen reading and voice-recognition software. Each of the four stations has a computer with a large visual display, equipped with mouse, keyboard, microphone, and headphones. The room itself is well lit, away from most school traffic, and relatively quiet (for a school). Monique takes most of her exams in this room at the same time her class is in session. During the exam her teacher wears a headset with ear buds and small microphone. Everything she says to the class is played into Monique's headphones in her separate location. If she has a question for the teacher, she can press a button on a "walkie-talkie" device and ask the teacher her question.

The test itself has been uploaded to the computer through special presentation software. Monique has been trained to use this screen reading system, and she navigates it well. As the test is displayed on the screen, she uses a cursor to highlight each line, and the computer reads the material at a pace predetermined to be ideal for Monique. She can go back and forth and highlight words or phrases as much as she needs. She is allowed to double click on any word to get its definition. This works well for multiple-choice and fill-in exams. For written essay exams, Monique uses the voice-recognition software on the computer. Because her spelling is atrocious and her oral language reasonably good, voice recognition is an effective accommodation. Of course, Monique is granted 50% extended time for her tests. However, because she is facile with these computerized test administrations, she seldom uses much of her extra time.

Again, as with Michael's case above, what makes Monique's case study one about UD is that her school provides the same test-taking options to students with and without disabilities. What the school has achieved is somewhat unique for a middle school. It has designed a test center that is specially equipped to handle most any accommodation need. The center was designed by a school committee that included input from students and adults with disabilities. A small corporate grant made it possible to purchase special furniture, computer technology, sound dampening material, wireless communication systems, large print displays, special lighting, scanners, printers, headphones, etc. Monique obviously benefits greatly from the test center, and so do more than 50 other students who are able to receive various test accommodations all coordinated by the school's department of special education. Schools like this one that are proactive in meeting the needs of students with disabilities certainly have given thought to UD principles. In fact, the committee that designed the test center is now working on initiatives to make classroom tests more universal. A disability consultant has been meeting with the instructional staff to computerize all exams, eliminate bubble sheets, include oral and written directions, provide ample time for all exams, and incorporate both screen reading and voice recognition features as needed.

11

CONCLUSIONS

After surveying the literature on testing accommodations, we feel a mix of apparently contradictory reactions, best summed up in epigrams from the great 20th century philosopher of science Karl Popper. In an essay on the social sciences, Popper (1976) proposed two theses that are both reasonable despite pointing in opposite directions. His first thesis noted the triumph of scientific inquiry:

> We know a great deal. And we know not only many details of doubtful intellectual interest but also things which are of considerable practical significance and, what is even more important, which provide us with deep theoretical insight, and with surprising understanding of the world. (p. 87)

His second thesis, instead, noted the incompleteness of this triumph:

> Our ignorance is sobering and boundless . . . With each step forward, with each problem we solve, we not only discover new and unsolved

http://dx.doi.org/10.1037/14468-011
Testing Accommodations for Students With Disabilities: Research-Based Practice, by B. J. Lovett and L. J. Lewandowski

problems, but we also discover that where we believed that we were standing on firm and safe ground, all things are, in truth, insecure and in a state of flux. (p. 87)

The state of research on testing accommodations fits these two theses exactly. On the one hand, we know a great deal about testing accommodations, enough to use our knowledge to consult productively on individual accommodations decisions, suggest professional development programs, and even propose modifications to laws and regulations concerning accommodations. On the other hand, there are also a variety of important accommodations issues that have so far generated little or no empirical research, or where the available research has suggested that generalizations are not possible.

Our readers have likely felt the tension between these two points throughout the book: our growing knowledge, and our growing realization of our own ignorance. We have been eager to point out what we *do* know, and how this should influence practice. At the same time, we have been open in admitting that we lack relevant research findings on many points, some of them central to accommodations practice. In this final chapter, we summarize the most important findings from research and also note the most crucial research challenges. We also discuss several recent trends that suggest where testing accommodations research and practice may be going.

WHAT DO WE KNOW?

Perhaps the most researched topic in accommodations has been that of differential boost, investigating whether the benefits of accommodations are limited to students with disabilities. In general, research has suggested that (a) students with disabilities tend to benefit more from accommodations than nondisabled students, but (b) nondisabled students tend to show some benefit from accommodations, and (c) under certain circumstances nondisabled students benefit as much or more than students with disabilities do.

Another general point is that students with disabilities can learn test-taking skills that increase their confidence as well as their actual test performance. Although these skills are not usually thought of when writing individualized education programs (IEPs) and other intervention plans, the extant research base supports using interventions to develop these skills. Indeed, more generally there is support for considering a variety of kinds of interventions at the same time as accommodations, or even as stand-ins for accommodations in certain cases.

Still another point concerns the initial diagnoses of disability conditions that often lead to testing accommodations. Although learning, cognitive, and psychiatric disabilities often involve impairments that suggest reasonable, needed accommodations, current diagnostic practice has many flaws, keeping diagnostic labels from being useful, on their own, in making accommodations decisions. Moreover, recent research has suggested that in postsecondary settings, a substantial minority of students being evaluated for learning and attention problems (the highest incidence disability conditions) may exaggerate or feign symptoms, or otherwise display poor effort on cognitive tests, so as to be diagnosed and access resources that include accommodations.

When we turn specifically to extended-time accommodations (the most common type of accommodation), two other facts emerge. First, many students appear to receive extended time because of traits or skill levels that are modifiable. Test anxiety and reading fluency are both amenable to interventions that should be provided in conjunction with extended time, an accommodation that may only need to be provided temporarily. Second, the most common extended-time allotments (50% and 100% additional time) have no evidence to support them as optimal. If anything, they appear to "overaccommodate" students with high-incidence disabilities, leading them to have an unfair advantage on high-stakes tests. There is some support for 25% extended time in postsecondary populations as being the amount that allows students with high-incidence disabilities to access the same number of items as nondisabled students do under standard time conditions.

Research on other specific accommodations shows a mix of common-sense and counterintuitive findings. Students with vision impairment benefit from Braille, whereas other students do not, and deaf students benefit from sign language, whereas other students do not. Certain setting accommodations, such as a separate room or preferential seating, have little evidence to show that they benefit anyone. Read-aloud accommodations show some specificity in their effects (in terms of helping students with significant reading problems), although they are likely overused, being given to students who do not actually benefit from them. Finally, some response accommodations seem to show modest benefits for all students: word processor access and voice recognition may be helpful for any examinee.

WHAT DO WE STILL NEED TO KNOW?

One area with insufficient research concerns the effects of accommodations on the predictive validity of test scores. Although we have studies of postsecondary admissions tests (the SAT and Law School Admission Test, for instance), we lack K–12 research showing whether test scores obtained with accommodations show the same relationship with later outcomes that scores obtained under standard conditions do. We do not know if, for instance, scores from teacher-made classroom tests show different relationships with end-of-year state exam scores, depending on whether accommodations were provided on either or both types of exam.

More generally, we need better quality research on the comparability of test scores obtained with and without accommodations. Most of the research in this area suffers from a major flaw: All of the scores obtained with accommodations were obtained by examinees with disabilities, whereas all of the scores obtained without accommodations were obtained by nondisabled examinees. (In most studies, any examinees whose disabilities were known had been provided with accommodations, whereas nondisabled students generally did not receive accommodations in naturalistic settings.) When this confound is present, and we find an apparent lack of comparability in test scores, we cannot be sure whether it is the accommodations per se that are disrupting comparability, or if it is instead the examinees' different disability statuses. Optimally, then, studies on score comparability would include four groups, where the groups varied both by disability status and accommodation status.

We also need more real-world studies that separate out different accommodations in determining their effects. Many large-scale naturalistic studies on accommodations group all students receiving accommodations together, comparing them with students who receive no accommodations. When there is a group difference (finding, for instance, differential item functioning across groups), we do not know which accommodations are responsible for the difference. In laboratory experimental studies, we typically study one accommodation at a time, but the artificial setting and situation can lead examinees to behave differently than they would during a real examination whose results they are concerned about.

There are also certain specific accommodations that have not been sufficiently researched. Multiple-day accommodations are one of these, and research is truly needed here given that many K–12 state exams prohibit this accommodation. Separate room accommodations are frequently recommended or requested by students with a high-incidence disability (attention-deficit/hyperactivity disorder [ADHD]), but we have very little research exploring the efficacy or other consequences of separating one examinee from others. Similarly, Scantron accommodations, in which the examinee may mark his or her answers directly in the test book, are often provided to students with high-incidence learning and attention problems, but without much research to guide decisions about this particular accommodation.

Finally, we need far more research on the relationship between accommodations and interventions. Although we have an evidence base showing positive effects of test-taking skills training, reading fluency interventions, and similar treatments, investigators have not generally examined accommodations needs (or even students' benefit from accommodations) as explicit dependent variables in these studies. If studies can show, directly, that interventions can decrease students' needs for accommodations—sometimes to the point that they no longer benefit from them—we will have far stronger support for recommending interventions in lieu of accommodations.

When considering these various research needs, it sometimes saddens us that in school psychology, accommodations issues are not "hot," compared with certain other topics (e.g., mental health promotion). We see a growing divergence between the real world, where testing accommodations are increasingly controversial and talked about, and the research community, where accommodations issues continue to be a relatively ignored area. This is a pity, given that accommodations research demands the field's top minds. The real-world controversies actually make doing objective, independent research more difficult; as Malouf (2005) observed, "Research on assessment accommodations is not occurring in a vacuum. In fact, quite the opposite—it is occurring in a pressure cooker" (pp. 81–82).

Many of the thorniest accommodation issues do depend on findings from a related area of research: disability diagnosis. Good accommodations research is so challenging, in part, because students with disabilities form such a heterogeneous category; even within a single diagnostic category (e.g., learning disability), marked variability exists. As we have noted, many practitioners and scholars have an implicit model of accommodations in which the students receiving them have considerable impairment, and indeed, the logic of accommodations is clearest in the case of low-incidence, severe sensory and physical disabilities. But of course, in practice, most students who receive accommodations have high-incidence disability diagnoses (learning disabilities, ADHD, psychiatric disorders), where the level of impairment is variable (often quite mild), the criteria for diagnosis are debated, and the need for accommodations is far less clear. The close connection between diagnostic issues and accommodations decisions also shows the need for school psychology scholars and practitioners to become involved in accommodations research, rather than leaving such research to educational measurement researchers who often have little background (and sometimes seem to take little interest) in diagnostic issues, even when their findings are obviously attributable to the way that disability diagnoses are made.

PREDICTIONS: WHAT IS COMING?

It is also fitting in our final chapter to comment, albeit with some speculation, about coming changes that will affect testing accommodations. We see three changes that we can discuss with considerable confidence. First, there is a trend toward an increasing number of exams being administered through computers. This is already the case in many postsecondary exams, but the trend is slowly infiltrating K–12 education as well (Quellmalz & Pellegrino, 2009). In general, this trend will make accommodations easier to implement. For instance, when computers administer exams to students individually, in a 1:1 fashion, certain accommodations (e.g., extended time) can be more easily implemented. In addition, with supplemental software, certain accommodations (e.g., read aloud, dictation to scribe) can be provided by a computer rather than a human proctor/amanuensis. Still other accommodations (word processor access) are no longer needed, because they are a natural part of computer-based testing. However, occasionally students will need accommodations that they would not have needed on a paper-and-pencil test (e.g., to reduce glare on a computer screen), and it is not unusual for students with certain disabilities to request that they be permitted to take a computer-based test in paper-and-pencil format. Moreover, certain computer-based tests use technology to deliver very complex types of test content, leading to test items that require more access skills and are more likely to be problematic for students with disabilities.[1]

A second trend affecting accommodations is the Universal Design for Assessment (UDA) movement, which we reviewed in detail in Chapter 10. As the UDA movement has matured, resources have been developed for the routine consideration of universal design issues when creating test items and determining administration procedures. This trend will generally have positive effects on accommodations in two ways. First, it should make accommodations easier to implement; when tests are designed with diverse examinees in mind, administration procedures allow for accommodations to fit in seamlessly. Second, UDA should reduce the need for certain accommodations, by making test items maximally accessible from the start. The trend toward computer-based testing, noted previously, goes hand in hand with the UDA movement.

Finally, accommodations providers should be alert to legal developments that would change what and when accommodations are permitted or required. For instance, we suspect that the Americans With Disabilities Act of 1990, in its recently amended form (ADA Amendments Act of 2008 [ADAAA]) may be successfully challenged by testing agencies, given that its regulations (promulgated by the Department of Justice) appear to force testing agencies to provide accommodations even when an applicant's disability status or accommodation needs are in doubt (Lovett, in press). The ADAAA is generally invoked in postsecondary settings, but it also covers K–12 students, and scholars have observed that it may be even broader than the Individuals With Disabilities Education Act (IDEA) in some ways, so it will be exciting to watch as ADAAA issues get litigated.

---

[1]We should also note that an increasing number of high-stakes tests are computerized *adaptive* tests, in which the items presented to an examinee differ depending on whether he or she answered earlier questions correctly or incorrectly. These tests generally cannot be presented in paper-and-pencil form, even to students who need accommodations.

THE IRREDUCIBLE COMPLEXITY OF ACCOMMODATIONS

We conclude with a discussion of two topics that sum up points that we have tried to make throughout the book: the irreducible complexity of testing accommodations and the importance of evidence-based practice in accommodations decision making. With regard to the first topic, McKevitt, Elliott, and Kettler (2013) recently succinctly summarized the main point: "The use of testing accommodations may seem, at first, a simple and effective way to help students with disabilities demonstrate their true knowledge on a test. However, the use of accommodations is anything but simple" (p. 732). We frequently encounter practitioners, administrators, and even many trainers, researchers, and scholars who view the provision of accommodations as a simple issue, and these people always seem to us to be saying, "Why *not* just provide the accommodations?" But providing accommodations is complex in two ways.

First, accommodations are complicated in that individual decisions to provide accommodations should be made with care and circumspection. As we have stressed, the same accommodation is not necessarily appropriate for the same student on different exams. Moreover, just because one accommodation is appropriate, other accommodations may still not be. Finally, just because a student has a particular disability diagnosis (even if the diagnosis is valid), a given accommodation may or may not be necessary or appropriate for that student, given his or her particular ability and skill levels.

Second, accommodations are complicated in that a student's inability to fully access a test under standard administration conditions may have a variety of implications in addition to or instead of providing accommodations to that student. The implications may involve providing the student with skill-based interventions, counseling, or other management strategies. The implications may include altering the test (especially if it is a teacher-made classroom exam) so that all students can access the test fully. These kinds of implications are ignored by those who want to quickly and simply provide accommodations and be done with the matter. We hope that this book has gone some way toward raising awareness of the need for a broader, comprehensive responsive to suboptimal test access.

THE IMPORTANCE OF EVIDENCE-BASED PRACTICE

The second topic that we conclude with takes the book full circle to issues that we raised in our first chapter. As we have observed, too often accommodations decisions are guided by intuition, lore, and warm-hearted intentions rather than by evidence and careful reasoning. Admittedly, this problem extends far beyond accommodations practice; special education is replete with practices that have no data behind them (M. Burns & Ysseldyke, 2009), and it has been noted that school psychology has much pseudoscience as well as proper science (Lilienfeld, Ammirati, & David, 2012). Even so, just as other areas of psychology and education must continually strive to base their practices on a solid foundation of evidence, we in the field of accommodations must do the same.

Unfortunately, specific evidence-based movements have not touched on testing accommodations issues. The push over the past decade to move toward evidence-based practice (EBP) in school psychology (e.g., Hoagwood & Johnson, 2003) has emphasized interventions rather than assessment practices. Even the more recent development of evidence-based assessment (EBA) in clinical psychology (e.g., Hunsley & Mash, 2011) has been focused on the process of diagnostic assessment rather than on assessing skills in individuals who have already been diagnosed. Even so, we find inspiration and information in more general calls for evidence in practice. Before the EBP and EBA movements became popular, McFall (1991) composed a bracing polemic opening with his "cardinal principle": "Scientific clinical psychology is the only legitimate and acceptable form of clinical psychology" (p. 76). Consulting on testing accommodation decisions is an area of clinical service delivery, and we would hold, following McFall, that accommodations consultation that is not based on science is neither legitimate nor acceptable.

Unfortunately, McFall's (1991) call for a proud, scientific clinical psychology has sometimes been misinterpreted to put research before the goal of helping people, and similarly, our insistence on following research when making testing accommodations decisions might be misinterpreted as being insensitive to the needs of people with disabilities. These misinterpretations fail to acknowledge that the best way to help people is to help by using techniques that research has validated. So it is with accommodations; unless our accommodations decisions are based on scientific research, they are unlikely to help those who need it, and may even do harm. Excessive or improper accommodations can encourage self-fulfilling prophecies about skill levels, lead to unnecessary dependence, and ultimately impede the goals of developing autonomy among students with disabilities.

However, there is a larger point with which we wish to conclude. Even though we believe that evidence-based accommodations practices are the best way to help all students, the ultimate purpose of accommodations is not to help students obtain higher test scores, but to increase the validity of inferences about students' skills. In a world in which most stakeholders (students, parents, teachers, school administrators) wish to simply increase test scores, it is tempting to wield accommodations as a tool toward this goal and to view any increase in scores as a goal in itself, while not worrying about any negative side effects of unnecessary or inappropriate accommodations. But those charged with participating in accommodations decisions—and school psychologists in particular—should be more concerned with validity and interested in using accommodations as a tool to increase validity, rather than to increase scores per se. *Validity* should be the key word in both accommodations research and accommodations practice: Researchers should examine and practitioners should encourage validity in initial disability diagnoses, validity in accommodations decisions, and validity in score interpretation. Decision makers should be aware of the potential power of accommodations to increase validity, while also staying aware of the dangers of accommodations when they are used incautiously. It is these dangers that make the practice of providing accommodations so irreducibly complex, necessitating an entire book on them—a book that we hope has given the reader some first principles for making better decisions, or at least avoiding worse ones.

APPENDIX A
DOCUMENTATION REVIEW IN
POSTSECONDARY SETTINGS

The purpose of this appendix is to give educators, administrators, clinicians, and accommodation applicants an overview of the processes and procedures that govern test accommodation applications, reviews, and decisions. This section focuses on test accommodations in postsecondary school as well as on standardized and high-stakes exams.

K–12 ACCOMMODATION PROCESSES

The K–12 test accommodation process is considerably different from postsecondary accommodation processes. Essentially, there are three ways in which students receive test accommodations prior to high school graduation: Teachers arrange informal accommodations, accommodations are written into a Section 504 plan, or accommodations are stipulated by a student's individualized education program (IEP). The informal accommodation route typically involves a teacher–student arrangement that need not be based on the presence of a disability or specific documentation. Sometimes teachers notice that certain students repeatedly have trouble completing exams even though they are known to have mastered the content. These teachers find creative ways to allow such students a little extra time, preferred seating, or use of a dictionary or calculator, as long as the students do not get an unfair advantage. In other instances the students initiate the requests by telling teachers that they read slowly, must reread material to understand it, or need some aid (e.g., scratch paper, dictionary) to process the information on the test. The sympathetic teachers often try to meet these students' needs, again as long as the accommodations do not disrupt the school schedule or create an unfair advantage. Although students may get certain needs met in the short term, the lack of a formal accommodation process means that their diagnostic conditions and accommodations have not been documented. Should they apply for test accommodations on a high-stakes exam, such documentation is typically requested and carries considerable weight in the decision process. Therefore, students in K–12 who are believed to have a disability that warrants accommodations are best served by going through a more formal documentation process.

One of the formal processes followed by public school systems is a Section 504 plan. As noted in earlier chapters, this law gives individuals with temporary or chronic disabilities the right to access educational, social, and vocational opportunities. Under Section 504 of the Rehabilitation Act, a student can qualify for test accommodations so as to fully and fairly access an exam. A student does not have to be educationally impaired, but merely restricted in access. For example, a student who broke his arm in a skiing accident might use a scribe to write an exam. More commonly, a 504 plan might be used by a student with attention-deficit/hyperactivity disorder (ADHD) who, although bright and capable, is easily distracted and impulsive to the point of bothering other students. Hence, a 504 plan might be developed that allows the student to take exams in a separate location. A 504 plan can stipulate other accommodations, such as more frequent bathroom breaks, allowance of certain food or drinks for health reasons, precautions against certain allergens, and so on. Typically, these plans are used to cover accommodation needs that are not part of a special education plan.

The third vehicle through which to obtain test accommodations at the K–12 level is the IEP. The IEP is governed by the Individuals With Disabilities Education Act (IDEA) and applies to students who qualify for special education under state and federal guidelines. An IEP describes a student's present levels of performance as well as all special educational needs, including class type and size, educational supports, therapeutic interventions, academic modifications, and test accommodations. Once test accommodations are formally documented and agreed to by a committee of educators, parents, and school administrators, the accommodations become a mandatory part of the student's educational program. Thus, teachers are no longer doing the student a favor, but rather are obligated to follow the accommodation plan. Both 504 plans and IEPs officially document the use of test accommodations and are mandatory in their implementation. This documentation will be helpful when and if the student seeks test accommodations at postsecondary schools and for high-stakes exams.

DOCUMENTATION GUIDELINES FOR ACCOMMODATION DECISIONS IN POSTSECONDARY SETTINGS

When students request accommodations on a high-stakes exam such as the SAT, or when they apply for accommodations in a postsecondary setting, such as college, their request or application will be processed and a decision will be made in large part on the basis of the supportive documentation that they submit. School psychologists and other professionals should be aware of the appropriate documentation. Following is a list of documents that applicants and evaluators should consider before applying for accommodations (see also Gordon & Keiser, 1998):

- a well-documented history (developmental, medical, educational, and psychological);
- a personal statement outlining one's disability, impairment, areas of limitation, effects on test taking, accommodation needs, and ability to adapt to standard test conditions;
- any pertinent school records, including evaluation reports, teacher notes, school grades, standardized test scores, IEPs, 504 plans, and evidence of interventions and the individual's response to those interventions;
- all professional reports, including any test results (preferably standardized, norm-referenced scores) as well as formal diagnoses (e.g., *Diagnostic and Statistical Manual of Mental Disorders* [*DSM–IV–TR* and *DSM–5*] diagnoses for learning/cognitive/psychiatric problems);
- evidence of functional impairment in major life activities that could restrict access to test taking; and
- evidence of previous test accommodations used (i.e., when, where, what?).

It should be noted that generally more documentation is better than less; documented evidence is better than anecdotal; objective, multisource documentation is better than subjective, self-report information; and evidence of actual impairment is more important than the presence of symptoms. In addition, applicants should be aware that reporting being "the last person to finish an exam" or claiming to "work twice as hard as other students" are impossible to verify and relatively meaningless. Such statements are not helpful in the review process and do not provide a strong rationale for test accommodations. Similarly, the notion offered by applicants and evaluators that the examinee could perform "optimally" with test accommodations is not particularly relevant. Even if this were measureable, there is no provision in the law to help examinees perform optimally. Rather than making philosophical pleas, it is always better if applicants provide objective evidence to demonstrate a diagnosis, a substantial limitation, and a clear need for test accommodations. This is what blind, deaf, brain injured, and physically impaired individuals do in their applications, but those with learning or psychiatric conditions sometimes have more trouble in theirs.

POSTSECONDARY ACCOMMODATION PROCESSES

Most 2- and 4-year colleges and universities have an Office of Disability Services (ODS) that serves the various needs of students with disabilities. One service provided by such offices, in addition to providing tutors, note takers, assistive technology, and consultation, is the coordination of test accommodations on campus. As noted in an earlier chapter, test accommodations are no longer governed by IDEA at this educational level, but rather by Section 504 and/or the Americans With Disabilities Act of 1990 (ADA, as amended in 2008). These laws entitle all students to fully access educational opportunities. So, students with mobility issues must be given reasonable access to all classrooms, offices, and living units. Students with hearing impairments may receive sound amplification, sign language, or other ameliorative measures. And of course, many students will require a variety of test accommodations, as mandated by federal legislation.

Depending on the size of the college, the ODS may take on a variety of roles. Some institutions conduct diagnostic assessments of their own students, complete with professional diagnoses and recommendations. Other schools, probably the vast majority, rely on documentation from outside professionals to establish a person's diagnosis and needs. This could include a physician for physical and health conditions, a psychiatrist for psychiatric and mental health concerns, a psychologist for psychoeducational issues, and other experts as needed (e.g., ophthalmologist, audiologist). In most schools there is a review process that is conducted by the ODS. This could be undertaken by one person, or a small team that reviews all documentation, meets with the student, and then makes decisions as to accommodations and other provisions supplied by the ODS and school in general.

Another variation from school to school is the way in which the ODS interfaces with the college, administratively, academically, and economically. Some offices have good support and authority to carry out their missions, whereas others are poorly staffed and funded and not very influential on campus. (At some smaller schools, the only person in the "office" has other administrative duties having nothing to do with disability issues.) Similarly, some offices will make it easy for students to access services and become strong advocates for them, whereas other offices tend to meet the letter of the law and little more. Obviously, students need to be good consumers when looking for a school that will meet their needs. It always pays for students to be strong self-advocates, regardless of the ODS structure they find on campus. Ultimately, accommodation arrangements are made between the students and a wide range of professors and instructors, most of whom have not received teaching degrees or received formal training in special education, let alone the field of test accommodations. Self-advocacy becomes a must in these situations, with the student often educating the professor as to specific needs and accommodation possibilities.

Most 4-year colleges and universities have a formal process for applying for test accommodations. As noted earlier in this book, a big difference between high school and the IDEA versus college and the ADA[1] is that the student must self-disclose his or her disability to the school. In other words, students must go to the ODS office and apply for services because of their presumed disability. The ODS office then has students complete paperwork disclosing their condition, learning needs, and accommodation requests. The ODS reviews this information, and depending on the nature of the requests, asks the students to provide historical and professional documentation, essentially evidence of their disability and past interventions. There is no uniform application procedure found across colleges (see Madaus, Banerjee, & Hamblet, 2010); however, most schools follow similar guidelines and procedures, either through shared communications or based on the influence of external sources (e.g., Association on Higher Education and Disability [AHEAD] guidelines; see a later section for more on these).

Certain procedures are typical of what students will encounter at many colleges. Besides self-disclosing their disability, students must provide recent (within 3–5 years) professional (i.e., licensed or certified) documentation (i.e., comprehensive report) that includes objective indices to support a particular diagnosis. The diagnosis should be based on a comprehensive assessment that covers all diagnostic criteria and considers alternative explanations. In addition to diagnosis, the documentation should provide evidence of a substantial limitation in a major life activity, show how this limitation restricts access to learning and test taking, and state a rationale for specific accommodations and why each is needed. Implied in the guidelines, and an important point for potential applicants, is that a documented "record" of disability, impairment, and test accommodations is at least as important as a recent professional evaluation. Therefore, it is essential that students collect documentation from elementary school on up if at all possible.

Once students are approved for accommodations by the ODS, their work is not necessarily done. The ODS at many schools will notify instructors of the accommodation needs of each student. In some schools the procedure requires students to approach each instructor with a copy of an approved test accommodation plan. This makes the student become a self-advocate and assures that the student and instructor work together to implement a satisfactory plan. Although this system might seem burdensome on the student, we must keep in mind that instructors could have hundreds

---

[1]We do not refer directly to Section 504 since, at the postsecondary level, ADA covers the same ground.

of students in a class, and this includes athletes, commuters, parents, and fully employed students, all of whom might need certain considerations during a semester. The rule of thumb is that students discuss their personal needs with the instructor, a far cry from the elementary school teacher who notices a student needs more time to finish a test. In most cases, the self-advocacy approach with ODS documentation works fine. There are faculty that may be less than accommodating on occasion and need to be encouraged or assisted by the ODS. Also, there may be fewer options than what a student encountered in K–12. For example, a student receiving extended time may not be able to take the exam with other students because that classroom is booked as soon as the class ends. Many colleges use the ODS or an alternative location (e.g., tutoring center) as a place to take accommodated exams if other arrangements cannot be made. They often try to start the exam at the same time the class does, but this is not always possible. Students should be prepared for a different approach to accommodations at the college level.

As noted in the chapter on transition to postsecondary school, the percentage of students receiving accommodations in college is considerably lower than the number found in high school, in part because many students with disabilities do not continue to college (NLTS-2 reported by Newman et al., 2011). Another reason may be that students have to self-disclose their disability once they get to college. Many students want to succeed in college without help, either to prove their independence or because they realize they will not be accommodated in the workplace after graduation. And of course, some students who may have been accommodated since childhood without any questions being asked are now faced with having to provide evidence of a disability. They may not have the documentation or just choose to avoid the process completely. For whatever reason, fewer students seek and use test accommodations when they get to college. Yet, those who do self-disclose tend to be successful in acquiring test accommodations. Few statistics exist, but most ODS administrators admit to only small numbers of students who fail to qualify for test accommodations. From another perspective, most colleges that are charging students and their families for an education want students to stay and be successful. There is more incentive to treat the students well and provide desired support services than to deny students test accommodations, especially because the cost and effort involved are minimal and the mission of many schools includes promoting inclusivity and diversity. In fact, many schools provide services that go far beyond accommodations, such as specialized tutoring, study-skills training, assistive technology, and special programs that facilitate student success and school retention (Rath & Royer, 2002), even if the students admitted to these special programs do not meet formal criteria for having a disability (Sparks

& Lovett, 2013). In any case, students are most likely to be successful in obtaining accommodations in college if they keep good records, procure a recent professional evaluation, and are willing to self-advocate (see Madaus, Banerjee, & Merchant, 2011).

HIGH-STAKES EXAMS AND ACCOMMODATIONS PROCESSES

In this section, we discuss the processes and procedures confronted on admission tests to college and graduate schools (e.g., law, medicine, dentistry, business), as well as licensing exams for entry into various professions. Such exams have been termed *high stakes* because a pass or failure could mean the difference between achieving a career goal or not. Because the stakes are high, and in some cases the outcomes impact the quality of the profession itself, various testing bodies go to great lengths to protect the security, validity, and applicability of their exams. Therefore, these testing entities are less interested in pleasing customers (as may be the case at academic institutions). They tend to be interested in obtaining the most reliable and valid measurement of their intended constructs, while keeping the exam as fair and consistent as possible. Thus, the high-stakes test arena, in general, is more conservative when it comes to allotting test accommodations. One only has to look at court cases with regard to test accommodations and one will see a disproportionate number of test agencies being sued by unsuccessful accommodation applicants compared with suits against educational institutions for the same purpose.

Because the stakes are high and accommodations decisions are made quite carefully, most test agencies have a formal, thorough, and explicit set of guidelines and procedures that must be followed. These agencies realize that they must comply with laws governing test accommodations, and most have legal counsel that helps develop their guidelines in line with ADA requirements. As required by law, these guidelines are made public and typically cover the type of documents to be filed with an application and the procedures that are followed by the applicant and the agency. What are neither publicly posted nor made available to applicants are all the details of the documentation review proceedings and the decision-making process. All test agencies will notify applicants of the accommodation decision, but these agencies vary greatly in how much information they provide about the decision. Some may provide a lengthy rationale coupled with reports from outside consultants, whereas others only indicate that the documentation did or did not demonstrate a condition that rose to the level of a substantial limitation under ADA.

AHEAD PERSPECTIVE ON
ACCOMMODATION DOCUMENTATION

One organization that has developed various policy statements regarding disability issues, including test accommodations, is AHEAD (2012). According to AHEAD, acceptable sources of documentation for substantiating a student's disability and request for particular accommodations can take a variety of forms:

> Primary Documentation: Student's Self-Report. The student is a vital source of information regarding how he or she may be "limited by impairment." A student's narrative of his or her experience of disability, barriers, and effective and ineffective accommodations is an important tool which, when structured by interview or questionnaire and interpreted, may be sufficient for establishing disability and a need for accommodation.
>
> Secondary Documentation: Observation and Interaction. The impressions and conclusions formed by higher education disability professionals during interviews and conversations with students or in evaluating the effectiveness of previously implemented or provisional accommodations are important forms of documentation. Experienced disability professionals should feel comfortable using their observations of students' language, performance, and strategies as an appropriate tool in validating student narrative and self-report.
>
> Tertiary Documentation: Information From External or Third Parties. Documentation from external sources may include educational or medical records, reports and assessments created by health care providers, school psychologists, teachers, or the educational system. This information is inclusive of documents that reflect education and accommodation history, such as an IEP, Summary of Performance (SOP), and teacher observations. External documentation will vary in its relevance and value depending on the original context, credentials of the evaluator, the level of detail provided, and the comprehensiveness of the narrative. However, all forms of documentation are meaningful and should be mined for pertinent information.

Note that self-reported information is "primary," whereas objective, external information is merely "tertiary." In addition, the AHEAD guidance makes other comments that seem to discourage institutions from rigorously reviewing accommodations requests:

> Commonsense Standard. Disability and accommodation requests should be evaluated using a commonsense standard, without the need for specific language or extensive diagnostic evidence. Using diagnostic information as a tool in reviewing requests for accommodation is different than using it for treatment. Determining accommodations requires a more limited

range, level, and type of information. These two processes should not be conflated. No third party information may be necessary to confirm disability or evaluate requests for accommodations when the condition and its impact are readily apparent or comprehensively described. No specific language, tests, or diagnostic labels are required. Clinicians' training or philosophical approach may result in the use of euphemistic phrases rather than specific diagnostic labels. Therefore, reports that do not include a specific diagnosis should not be interpreted to suggest that a disability does not exist. The question is "Would an informed and reasonable person conclude from the available evidence that a disability is likely and the requested accommodation is warranted?"

Nonburdensome Process. Postsecondary institutions cannot create documentation processes that are burdensome or have the effect of discouraging students from seeking protections and accommodations to which they are entitled. This was clear even prior to the amendments to the ADA. The non-burdensome standard is applicable to initially establishing a relationship with the disability resource office and to setting up individual accommodations from institutional personnel, including course instructors. Students should not be required to bear responsibility for achieving access through cumbersome, time consuming processes.

Current and Relevant Information. Disability documentation should be current and relevant but not necessarily "recent." Disabilities are typically stable lifelong conditions. Therefore, historic information, supplemented by interview or self-report, is often sufficient to describe how the condition impacts the student at the current time and in the current circumstances. Institutions should not establish blanket statements that limit the age of acceptable external documentation. Determining accommodations in distinctly new contexts may require more focused information to illustrate a connection between the impact of the disability, the described barrier, and the requested accommodation.

AHEAD IN REVIEW

Officially, the guidance provided by AHEAD is informed by the amended ADA and the U.S. Department of Justice (DOJ) regulations that followed, but AHEAD clearly made its own interpretation of the meaning of the DOJ regulations. As noted from the focus of most comments, AHEAD seems to be addressing accommodations at institutions of higher education rather than testing agencies. Although much of this interpretive guidance seems reasonable, there are a couple of points that warrant additional consideration.

First, there seems to be considerable emphasis and excessive value placed on the self-report of the person seeking test accommodations. From an advocacy perspective, such an emphasis may seem like the natural thing to do, but from a scientific perspective, there has been too much research showing problems with validity of self-report information when incentives are in play (Green et al., 2001), including malingering during evaluations (Harrison, 2006; Harrison, Edwards, & Parker, 2007), as contrasted with the advantages of multi-informant, multimethod assessments. As noted in other parts of this book, the information contained in personal statements of applicants is often unverifiable and sometimes not even pertinent.

Second, there is an emphasis on the observations of clinicians who evaluate prospective applicants for test accommodations. Again from a scientific perspective, naturalistic or unsystematic observations, which is what clinicians tend to report, have been shown to be sometimes biased, situationally specific, and unreliable. If clinicians consistently used systematic and reliable observational systems, we would advocate for the use of this information. However, we would caution any decisions based on clinicians' informal observations of a client at one point in time.

A third issue with the AHEAD interpretations is the mention of a "commonsense standard" that would obviate the need for extensive diagnostic experience. Although this is likely the case for disabilities such as blindness, deafness, and various physical conditions, this standard would not easily apply to high incidence disorders such as learning disabilities (LD) and ADHD that are not easily verified and account for the bulk of accommodation requests. Further, LD and ADHD are developmentally based disorders. A person with substantial limitations from LD or ADHD should have a track record of impairment since childhood. If a commonsense standard includes a documented history of impairment from a childhood disorder, then there would be broad agreement on this concept.

Fourth, the AHEAD commentary suggests that documentation does not necessarily have to be recent, especially when historic evidence and self-report is sufficient to establish a condition that impacts a person's functioning. Although this might be true for a person with congenital blindness, it is misleading when it comes to high-incidence disorders such as LD, ADHD, anxiety, and concussion. These and other disorders are known to change and respond to interventions such that what appeared to be a significant limitation 20 years ago is no longer a limitation. Thus, we would encourage, in most cases, reliance on a current evaluation of a person's functional status. Students with ADHD, for example, do not necessarily have problems with reading, writing, or processing speed, and may have learned to manage their executive functioning problems (see Lewandowski, Gathje, Lovett, & Gordon, 2013; Miller et al., in press). Certainly, the same argument could be made about those who have experienced a mild head injury or periodic anxiety.

Last, we would add that an objective, data-based approach to the assessment of disability and impairment does not need to be any more time consuming, expensive, or burdensome than the types of diagnostic evaluations that focus largely on subjective interviews, observations, and self-report measures. We would ask that the government, advocacy associations, and testing agencies join together to advance the science of measuring impairment in persons with disabilities as well as determining the validity of various test accommodations. This would be preferred over the guidance that the DOJ and AHEAD have provided thus far that seems to lack an empirical basis.

THE DOCUMENTATION REVIEW PROCESS

We have spent most of this appendix discussing the guidelines provided by schools and test agencies on applying for test accommodations. We also have considered the types of documentation both required and suggested. What we have not discussed is documentation review by an external expert. As noted earlier, some agencies rely on a panel of experts to review documentation files. These consultants typically are credentialed; experienced; and in many cases, prominent professionals in various disability fields. Their job is to provide an objective, unbiased assessment of an applicant's application materials, addressing such questions as:

- Is there a recent evaluation performed by a licensed professional?
- Is the documentation sufficient to make an informed decision about the test accommodation request?
- Does the documentation provide adequate evidence to support the diagnosis?
- Does the evidence meet official criteria for the diagnosis?
- Did the evaluator make a differential diagnosis and examine alternative hypotheses?
- Is there evidence that the applicant is substantially limited in a major life activity compared with the general population?
- Is the limitation such that the applicant is restricted in access to all or part of the exam?
- Is there a rationale for the requested accommodations based on history or objective evidence?
- If the applicant is qualified as having a disability, are the requested test accommodations reasonable and appropriate or would other accommodations be advised?

The consultant typically writes a report for the test agency addressing these questions. Most consultants read the materials more than once, take notes, and answer the questions on the basis of the documentation and their knowledge of the disability. Consultants realize that their opinion is not binding on a test agency; it is merely suggestive. Most also report that they recommend accommodations in borderline cases. As one such reviewer wrote, "If in doubt, accommodate" (Gordon, 2012, p. 20). By the same token, the ultimate goal of consultants is fairness to all test takers, which means consistent, objective, fair, and evidence-based opinions. Clinical evaluators commissioned by accommodation applicants frequently state the purpose of their assessments as part of an application for test accommodations, even though many of them are not very familiar with some of the legal and measurement issues (Gordon et al., 2002). They may have an understandable bias toward assisting applicants in their quest for accommodations. External consultants, on the other hand, provide a "take it or leave it" recommendation to a test agency. Their approach is dispassionate and evidence based, much like that of a forensic assessment case. Their focus, regardless of the condition, is on documented evidence of a substantial limitation in a major life activity. This is what almost all contested accommodation decisions come down to.

CONCLUSION

This appendix provides examples of accommodation guidelines and documentation procedures that are followed by applicants, their evaluators, institutions of higher education, and test agencies. Although far from exhaustive, the illustrations should provide students with a roadmap for applying for test accommodations. We conclude by offering the following tips on what should be included in an accommodation application:

1. Submit a file of all school, medical, and clinical records from as early as possible.
2. Provide a documented history if possible; most disorders such as LD, ADHD, and autism are identified in childhood and cause impairment throughout one's life. Early diagnoses, IEPs, 504 plans, etc., are very helpful in establishing the disability.
3. Provide any and all objective evidence of functional impairment, including academic grades, standardized test scores, teacher notes, professional reports, and types of treatment attempted.
4. Obtain a comprehensive, recent evaluation from a competent evaluator who has experience with test accommodation procedures and knowledge of legal regulation.

5. Attempt exams with and without accommodations, if possible, to demonstrate potential need.
6. Use formally documented test accommodations rather than informally arranged ones.
7. Emphasize limitations in major life activities rather than focusing on the presence of symptoms or a diagnosis.
8. Make realistic accommodation requests based on demonstrated needs rather than a wish list of accommodations that would be nice to have.

APPENDIX B
PROFESSIONAL DEVELOPMENT
APPLICATIONS

Some of the readers of this book will be able to use the information here to influence testing accommodations decisions *directly*. For instance, a private evaluator may use the research reviewed in this book to make different recommendations about accommodations when writing evaluation reports. However, many readers will be able to amplify their influence through *indirect means, by influencing the views of other people who have a hand in test-ing accommodations decisions (e.g., teachers, school administrators). In this appendix, we provide suggestions to help psychologists, disability services specialists, and others with relevant expertise (i.e., readers of this book) to "spread the word" about appropriate accommodations practices.

Before starting in earnest, we note that teachers appear to be requesting more research-based information regarding accommodations. For instance, in multiple survey studies of teacher perceptions of accommodations, teachers' narrative comments have included a need for more training and staff development on the topic (Davis, 2012; Lazarus, Thompson, & Thurlow, 2006), and many teachers have expressed a lack of confidence in their own accommodations knowledge (W. M. Brown, 2007). In addition, other studies have found that this lack of confidence is warranted; teachers often do not know which accommodations are permitted on their states' exams (e.g., Hollenbeck et al., 1998), their recommendations for accommodations are poor predictors of actual student need (e.g., L. S. Fuchs & Fuchs, 2001), and they interpret and implement accommodations listed in individualized education programs (IEPs) inconsistently (e.g., Byrnes, 2008). We lack similar research of other relevant groups (e.g., postsecondary faculty members, disability services office staff), but we have no reason to think that they do not need additional training, especially because new research is always being published. In short, there is clearly a need for professional development for a wide variety of groups who deal with testing accommodations.

INFORMAL PROFESSIONAL DEVELOPMENT: CONSULTATION

Readers who seek to influence accommodations decisions indirectly can view themselves as consultants. Although the word *consultants* often denotes experts who are based outside of the setting where decisions are made, it also encompasses, for instance, a school psychologist who consults with teachers in the school where she works, or a disability services office administrator who consults with his college's vice president of student services.

Functions of Accommodations Consultants

In K–12 school settings, informal accommodations consultation can have several functions. The most obvious one involves deciding individual students' eligibility for accommodations. Consultants (such as a school psychologist) are often members of the IEP team anyway, and they are in a natural position to contribute to accommodations decisions here. At times, the psychologist–consultant will have administered assessments during the initial comprehensive evaluation that will bear on accommodation appropriateness. Even if this is not the case, the consultant can report the results of relevant research that applies to an individual student's case, offer predictions about the likelihood that a given student would benefit from an accommodation, and provide (if asked) a recommendation about each accommodations decision.

A second function involves monitoring the implementation of accommodations. Given that accommodations are implemented with varying degrees of fidelity, teachers and other exam proctors often need support to implement accommodations correctly. Consultants can verbally review how to administer a test with accommodations, model proper administration with the student, and give the teacher/proctor feedback as he or she tries implementing the accommodation. The importance of such support should not be underestimated; too often, when an accommodation decision is made, it is assumed that all parties know what the accommodation means and are capable of implementing it with integrity, despite research showing that this is often not the case.

A third function involves evaluating the effectiveness of accommodations. Consultants can show teachers how to easily collect, record, and display data showing whether a student benefits from having her tests read to her, or whether having additional time on her mathematics tests leads to increased performance. It is especially helpful for consultants to have forms on hand that teachers can use to write down and graph out student performance; school psychologists who are familiar with data displays associated with response-to-intervention (RTI) systems will find such displays similarly useful when evaluating accommodation efficacy.

Understanding Decision Makers' Constraints

To be effective, consultants must consider the role constraints of their consultees (Erchul & Martens, 2002), and this is certainly important in testing accommodations situations. More specifically, consultants must consider the set of incentives that accommodations decision makers work within. Because all decisions involve the possibility of error (denying accommodations when they are appropriate, or proffering them when they are inappropriate), decision makers often lean toward making one type of error at the expense of another. For instance, a decision maker may grant almost all accommodation requests to ensure that no accommodations are denied when they are appropriate, but this makes it more likely that inappropriate accommodations will be given as well. Alternately, a decision maker may set a very high threshold for allowing accommodations to ensure that inappropriate accommodations are never given, but this makes it more likely that accommodations will also be denied when they are appropriate. Incentives influence which type of error decision makers will work harder to avoid.

At the K–12 level, IEP team members have two large incentives to err on the side of granting accommodations. First, accommodations, even when inappropriate, are more likely to raise test scores than to lower them. Teachers and school administrators often have incentives to raise test performance, especially of students with disabilities. Under the No Child Left Behind Act, financial incentives are explicitly tied to student achievement levels, and in some districts, even teacher evaluation and compensation may be based in part on students' test scores (e.g., McCaffrey, Han, & Lockwood, 2009). In contrast, there are no financial incentives for ensuring that students with disabilities receive more *valid* test scores. Second, teachers and school administrators may believe that parents and students themselves will be less likely to complain about overaccommodation than underaccommodation. Indeed, in our own consulting experience, we have never encountered a case of a formal dispute where a parent requested that testing accommodations be removed and other members of the IEP team resisted this.

At the postsecondary level, the incentives for and against erring on the side of granting accommodations are more balanced. Here there are no explicit incentives for raising student test performance, although there may be pressures to increase retention of students with disabilities at colleges, and certainly students themselves are more likely to complain when accommodations are *not* granted than when they *are* granted. In addition, there are often significant logistical costs associated with testing accommodations in the postsecondary world; for instance, colleges and universities must hire staff to work at offices where students can take tests with accommodations under supervision of proctors, and testing agencies must pay the increased costs associated with using, for instance, a private room in a testing center with a separate proctor.

We review these incentives in part to encourage humility and sympathy in accommodations consultants. When we encounter consultees who seem unwilling to change their views and decisions, even after being confronted with relevant information, we should understand that they are typically working within constraints that we, being consultants, lack. Understanding the incentives that are present also suggests potential routes of consultant influence. For instance, teachers at a given high school may have concerns that students with visual disabilities are not being given sufficient appropriate accommodations, but the teachers may be under pressure from school administrators to not recommend costly technology-based accommodations. Speaking with administrators about the issue may lead to a removal of this pressure, thus allowing research-based recommendations to more freely influence decisions.

Starting Where Your Audience Is

Finally, successful consultants must adapt their style to consultees' prior perceptions and knowledge levels. In the case of accommodations, we have empirical research showing that teachers have relatively low levels of knowledge regarding the nature of accommodations, as we have noted before. In addition, research has found highly variable perceptions of testing accommodations among teachers. For instance, Davis (2012) asked secondary school teachers if accommodations "level the playing field" for students with disabilities, and the themes emerging from teachers' narrative responses ranged from claims that accommodations were an inappropriate "crutch" for students with mild disabilities to claims that accommodations were an appropriate way for students to demonstrate their knowledge (see also Lazarus et al., 2006). Other researchers have found teachers' perceptions to be internally inconsistent; for instance, Lang et al. (2005) found that teachers rated accommodations as generally being quite fair (an average rating of 4.64 on a 1–5 scale of fairness) but also as yielding test scores that were only "somewhat comparable" to other students' scores (an average rating of 3.3 on a 1–5 scale of comparability). Given these findings, consultants should be careful to assess individual consultees' prior attitudes and knowledge before developing a consultation strategy, because understanding and acknowledging consultees' concerns is a necessary first step toward addressing them.

FORMAL PROFESSIONAL DEVELOPMENT IN ACCOMMODATION DECISION MAKING

Consulting about individual accommodation decisions is helpful but inefficient. Professional development, instead, teaches others to become more knowledgeable about accommodation decision making so that they do not need consultation regarding individual decisions. Even though professional development programs do not have the same degree of impact on all participants, it can be gratifying to see at least some participants develop the ability to make research-based decisions. Readers of this book are in command of those skills and can pass the skills along to others efficiently by leading professional development activities.

Models of Professional Development Programming

Professional development programming varies widely, and research has suggested that some types of programming are far more effective than other types. Braden, Huai, White, and Elliott (2005) provided an excellent summary of best practice guidelines, including the following:

- Longer professional development trainings are more effective than briefer trainings.
- Trainings involving active learning, where participants simulate the actions that they are being trained to perform, are more effective than trainings that only involve watching and listening.
- Trainings that involve concrete applications and examples are more effective than trainings focused on abstract definitions and rules.

Unfortunately, as Braden et al. noted, traditional approaches to professional development rarely incorporate these guidelines, offering "little promise as a vehicle for improving educators' capacity to provide inclusive assessment for students with disabilities" (p. 64).

Building on these general best-practice guidelines, several formal models of professional development programming have been developed. Hodgson, Lazarus, and Thurlow (2011) reviewed three of these models. One model, *project-based learning*, involves participants producing tangible artifacts that show a problem-solving process. Classroom teachers might, for instance, be asked to create a checklist that would be used to determine if a testing accommodation were appropriate in a given case. In addition to the checklist, participants would need to create artifacts documenting earlier stages in the process, such as a definition of an appropriate accommodation.

In a second model, *case-based instruction*, participants are presented with concrete examples that they discuss, usually in small groups. This model has obvious relevance for accommodations training. Teachers, school administrators, independent evaluators, or other relevant professionals could be presented with typical (and atypical) cases of students where accommodations are being considered. After background training in the general ideas behind appropriate accommodations, participants would discuss each case and practice applying the ideas presented earlier. (In several chapters of the present book, we concluded with case studies to illustrate ideas.)

The final model, *communities of practice*, integrates elements of the two other models. A community of practice is an organized network of professionals (often teachers) who each have distinct, well-defined roles, although they share a common agenda and goals. Teachers with different amounts of experience share practices, and a set of common artifacts are produced in an organic fashion because of participants' genuine desires to document their knowledge and skills. Thus, teachers might share with each other how they decide which accommodations to recommend to IEP teams when a student's case is being reviewed, or how they measure and document students' needs for accommodations.

Hodgson et al. (2011) noted that Internet-based professional development is growing in popularity and can involve all three programming models. In online project-based learning, for instance, teachers might compose and submit journal entries detailing their problem-solving processes regarding accommodations decisions (or other practices). In online case-based instructions, participants can discuss presented cases using Internet applications such as written discussion forums or real-time chat rooms. Finally, in virtual communities of practice, teachers share practices with colleagues who are geographically distant but who face similar situations and challenges. In sum, several best practice-based models of professional development are available and can be adapted to Internet formats.

Efficacy of Accommodations Professional Development

Two studies have actually evaluated the efficacy of professional development programs aimed at improving teachers' and administrators' skills in the area of accommodations decision making. DeStefano, Shriner, and Lloyd (2001) evaluated the efficacy of a comprehensive program used to train teachers, subject area department heads, and special education directors of one Illinois school district. Seven training sessions were held, followed by additional observed meetings, and the training included instruction in relevant legal foundations (e.g., the 1997 Individuals With Disabilities Education Act guidelines), the nature of state content standards, the types of participation and accommodation available in state assessments, and the relationship between instructional and testing accommodations. Participants were given practice making accommodation decisions for the Illinois Standards Assessment Test by showing information from actual special education files of students in the district. The training program was shown to be effective in several ways. After training, instructional accommodations became more common, whereas testing accommodations became less common. In particular, teachers were less likely to give accommodations that altered the test's central constructs (e.g., giving a read-aloud accommodation on a test measuring reading skills). Finally, after training, almost all teachers (96%) reported being confident making accommodation decisions.

In a second study, Braden et al. (2005) reported on the development and evaluation of the Assessing One and All (AOA) program, an online professional development course provided through the Council for Exceptional Children. AOA comprises online instruction in basic assessment concepts; the nature and purpose of large-scale, high-stakes assessments; and participation options for students with disabilities (including accommodations as well as alternate assessments). Participants also viewed multimedia presentations of three cases of students and have access to a textbook and activity book. Study participants completed surveys that measured their knowledge/skills as well as their confidence with regard to accommodations decision making. Pre-post comparisons were large for both knowledge ($d = 0.73$) and confidence ($d = 0.94$). Other statistical analyses (including comparisons to a group who did not receive instruction) suggested even larger effects ($d > 1.0$).

The results of these two studies suggest that although designing effective professional development programming may be difficult, it can also be quite effective.

Other Resources for Professionals

In addition to formal professional development programming, a variety of other resources are available to help improve accommodations decision making. First, many state education departments have prepared manuals to guide accommodation decisions with regard to state tests, and they can improve decisions with regard to other tests as well. For instance, New York's manual (Office of Vocational and Education Services for Individuals With Disabilities, 2006) outlines state laws and guidelines, describes the role of different participants in the accommodation decision-making process, and shows how to implement and document various accommodations properly. Features such as a list of frequently asked questions help to address common concerns and confusions. We have been surprised at how few IEP team members in New York appear to be aware of this document, as it provides very useful information. Many states have similar manuals that educators can use to good effect. School districts may wish to develop their own guidance documents based on state manuals.

Professionals who are in states without comprehensive manuals might borrow from other states, or use manuals that have been developed by professional organizations; for instance, we heartily endorse the accommodations manual of the Council of Chief State School Officers (2005), which has helpful worksheets for teachers and others to use when making decisions. In addition to manuals, there are briefer articles and book chapters that serve as introductions to accommodations decision making. The most recent edition of *Best Practices in School Psychology* has a useful chapter (Braden & Joyce, 2008), and other introductions have been published elsewhere, some dealing with accommodations generally (e.g., Hollenbeck, 2002) and others focusing on specific accommodations or populations (e.g., Ofiesh, Hughes, & Scott, 2004). Finally, the National Center on Educational Outcomes has partnered with the state of Alabama to develop professional training tools, available on the web (http://nceo.umn.edu/alabama). Of course, we hope that the present book will serve as a comprehensive resource, although we understand that it may be *too* comprehensive (i.e., lengthy) to expect *all* relevant parties to read it!

CONCLUSION: RECOMMENDATIONS FOR PROFESSIONAL DEVELOPMENT

At the K–12 level, an optimal plan for improving accommodations decision making and implementation would have several elements that we have covered:

1. If a manual from the state education department is available, it should be distributed to all relevant parties: not just decision makers but other school administrators as well as those who proctor tests (in many schools, a variety of professionals and paraprofessionals administer accommodations). If a state manual is not available, consider distributing either a manual from a professional organization or an introductory article or book chapter (e.g., Edgemon, Jablonski, & Lloyd, 2006).

2. An in-person staff meeting should be held to cover the most relevant, foundational points regarding accommodations. Individual meetings should be held with certain staff members who have unique responsibilities. For instance, special educators who teach students with severe disabilities need expertise in deciding between accommodations and alternate assessments. Similarly, school administrators should be aware of the implicit messages that they send that can influence teachers' accommodations decisions. All of the meetings should be led or moderated by a school psychologist or administrator who understands accommodations in detail and who can provide research-based guidance like that in the present book. If no one in the school or school district has that capability, an external consultant should be sought. All of the meetings should address the three

areas of information suggested by Braden et al. (2005): (a) basic concepts of assessment, (b) the purposes of large-scale assessment, and (c) the nature and use of accommodations.

3. Either as part of the meetings described in #2, or after those meetings, staff members should analyze typical cases of students with disabilities to determine, with guidance, how to apply the principles of research-based accommodation decision making. Case analysis is a critical part of effective staff development and allows for practice of skills that are more likely to generalize to real-world decision making.

4. More comprehensive and advanced instruction in assessment should be available for interested teachers as part of a plan to increase the availability of expertise. This might be done through providing tuition for taking assessment courses (including online courses) at a college or university, by maintaining a library of resources on assessment, or by sending interested staff to conferences or workshops.

5. Consultants should be used for individual accommodation decisions whenever staff are unsure of which accommodations (if any) are appropriate. These kinds of cases will arise even in the context of good staff development; the key is a willingness to acknowledge them and get advice from a consultant.

RESOURCES FOR FURTHER READING

Beddow, P. A. (2011). Beyond universal design: Accessibility theory to advance testing for all students. In M. Russell & M. Kavanaugh (Eds.), *Assessing students in the margin: Challenges, strategies, and techniques* (pp. 381–406). Charlotte, NC: Information Age.

An interesting presentation on universal design principles that includes discussions of how individual test items can be developed to minimize the inclusion of any skills that are not the focus of the test. This book illustrates how the use of universal design can reduce the need for accommodations.

Bolt, S. E., & Roach, A. T. (2009). *Inclusive assessment and accountability: A guide to accommodations for students with diverse needs.* New York, NY: Guilford Press.

This is an excellent general text on deciding when and how to include students with disabilities and English language learners (ELLs) in K–12 assessment programs. A chapter is devoted to accommodations for students with disabilities, but the book also includes chapters on alternate assessments, ELLs, and related topics.

Cook, A. M., & Polgar, J. M. (2012). *Essentials of assistive technologies.* New York, NY: Mosby.

Increasingly, presentation and response accommodations are made possible, or at least logistically less demanding, through the use of technology. This textbook is a useful reference that describes specific products that may be worth obtaining for testing accommodations use.

Lee, D., Reynolds, C. R., & Wilson, V. L. (2003). Standardized test administration: Why bother? *Journal of Forensic Neuropsychology, 3*(3), 55–81.

An excellent review of research demonstrating that on cognitive, academic, and even personality tests, small changes in administration can lead to large differences in scores. More than anything else, this article shows how accommodations should never be granted thoughtlessly.

National Center on Educational Outcomes (http://www.cehd.umn.edu/NCEO/)

The National Center on Educational Outcomes website has a large number of resources pertaining to testing accommodations for students with disabilities, including technical research reports, statistics on accommodations usage, and practical guidelines for accommodations decisions.

Weigert, S. C. (2011). U.S. policies supporting inclusive assessments for students with disabilities. In S. N. Elliott, R. J. Kettler, P. A. Beddow, & A. Kurz (Eds.), *Handbook of accessible achievement tests for all students* (pp. 19–32). New York, NY: Springer.

An excellent, succinct history of recent education laws and their effects on testing accommodations and alternate assessments. Weigert does a wonderful job of integrating more obscure laws (well outside of IDEA) that school and clinical psychologists may not be familiar with into the discussion.

Wendling, B. J., & Mather, N. (2009). *Essentials of evidence-based academic interventions*. Hoboken, NJ: Wiley.

This book includes discussion of the implementation and research base for academic skills interventions, but the authors provide far more. They provide context that gives the reader a good background in the nature of key academic skills and the theory of instruction more generally. This is an important resource for psychologists, who often have little training in instruction.

REFERENCES

Abedi, J., Hofstetter, C. H., & Lord, C. (2004). Assessment accommodations for English language learners: Implications for policy-based empirical research. *Review of Educational Research, 74,* 1–28.

Abrams, S. J. (2005). Unflagged SATs: Who benefits from special accommodations? *Education Next, 5*(3), 42–44.

Ackerman, P. L., & Kanfer, R. (2009). Test length and cognitive fatigue: An empirical examination of effects on performance and test-taker reactions. *Journal of Experimental Psychology: Applied, 15,* 163–181. doi:10.1037/a0015719

ADA Amendments Act of 2008, Pub. L. No. 110–325, § 3406 (2008).

Alberto, P., & Troutman, A. C. (2009). *Applied behavior analysis for teachers* (8th ed.). Upper Saddle River, NJ: Merrill/Pearson.

American Educational Research Association, American Psychological Association, & National Council on Measurement in Education. (1999). *Standards for educational and psychological testing.* Washington, DC: Author.

American Psychiatric Association. (2000). *Diagnostic and statistical manual of mental disorders* (4th ed., text rev.). Washington, DC: Author.

American Psychiatric Association. (2013). *Diagnostic and statistical manual of mental disorders* (5th ed.). Washington, DC: Author.

American Psychological Association. (2010). *Ethical principles of psychologists and code of conduct (2002; amended June 1, 2010).* Washington, DC: Author. Retrieved from http://www.apa.org/ethics/code/principles.pdf

American Psychological Association. (2012). Guidelines for assessment of and intervention with persons with disabilities. *American Psychologist, 67,* 43–62.

Americans With Disabilities Act. (1990). Pub. L. No. 101–336, § 2, 104 Stat. 328 (1991).

Americans With Disabilities Act. (ADA) Amendments Act of 2008. Pub. L. No. 110–325. 42 USCA § 12101.

Amrein, A. L., & Berliner, D. C. (2002). High-stakes testing & student learning. *Education Policy Analysis Archives, 10*(18), 1–74.

Archer, K. (2013, April 15). Oklahoma school testing rules don't violate civil rights, feds rule. *Tulsa World.* Retrieved from http://www.tulsaworld.com/news/education/oklahoma-school-testing-rules-don-t-violate-civil-rights-feds/article_f24bd566-c27e-50d3-be57-ec964d8bdc14.html?mode=story

Arditi, A. (1999). *Making print legible.* New York, NY: Lighthouse.

Arnold, V., Legas, J., Obler, S., Pacheco, M. A., Russell, C., & Umbdenstock, L. (1990). *Do students get higher scores on their word-processed papers? A study of bias in scoring hand-written vs. word-processed papers* (ERIC Document Reproduction Service No. ED345818). Whittier, CA: Rio Hondo College.

261

Assistive Technology Act of 2004, Pub. L. No. 108–364.

Association on Higher Education and Disability. (2012). *Supporting accommodation requests: Guidance on documentation practices.* Huntersville, NC: Author. Retrieved from https://www.ahead.org/resources/documentation-guidance

Baer, D. M. (1999). *How to plan for generalization* (2nd ed.). Austin, TX: Pro-Ed.

Barkley, R. A. (2006a). ADHD in adults: Developmental course and outcome of children with ADHD, and ADHD in clinic-referred adults. In R. A. Barkley (Ed.), *Attention-deficit hyperactivity disorder: A handbook for diagnosis and treatment* (3rd ed., pp. 248–296). New York, NY: Guilford Press.

Barkley, R. A. (Ed.). (2006b). *Attention-deficit hyperactivity disorder: A handbook for diagnosis and treatment* (3rd ed.). New York, NY: Guilford Press.

Barkley, R. A., Cunningham, C. E., Gordon, M., Faraone, S. V., Lewandowski, L., & Murphy, K. R. (2006). ADHD symptoms vs. impairment: Revisited. *ADHD Report, 14*(2), 1–9. doi:10.1521/adhd.2006.14.2.1

Barkley, R. A., Murphy, K. R., & Fischer, M. (2010). *ADHD in adults: What the science says.* New York, NY: Guilford Press.

Barton, K. E. (2001). Stability of constructs across groups of students with different disabilities on a reading assessment under standard and accommodated administrations. *Dissertation Abstracts International: Section A. The Humanities and Social Sciences, 62,* 4136.

Barton, K. E., & Huynh, H. (2003). Patterns of errors made by students with disabilities on a reading test with oral reading administration. *Educational and Psychological Measurement, 63,* 602–614. doi:10.1177/0013164403256363

Beidel, D. C., Turner, S. M., & Taylor-Ferreira, J. C. (1999). Teaching study skills and test-taking strategies to elementary school students: The Testbusters Program. *Behavior Modification, 23,* 630–646. doi:10.1177/0145445599234007

Benderson, A. (1988). Testing, equality, and handicapped people. *Focus, 21,* 3–23.

Bennett, R. E., Braswell, J., Oranje, A., Sandene, B., Kaplan, B., & Yan, F. (2008). Does it matter if I take my mathematics test on computer? A second empirical study of mode effects in NAEP. *The Journal of Technology, Learning, and Assessment, 6*(9). Retrieved from http://ejournals.bc.edu/ojs/index.php/jtla/article/view/1639

Bennett, R. E., Rock, D. A., & Jirele, T. (1987). GRE score level, test completion, and reliability for visually impaired, physically handicapped, and nonhandicapped groups. *The Journal of Special Education, 21*(3), 9–21.

Berger, C., & Lewandowski, L. J. (2013). The effect of a word processor as an accommodation for students with learning disabilities. *Journal of Writing Research, 4,* 261–280.

Berkner, L., & Choy, S. (2008). *Descriptive summary of 2003–04 beginning postsecondary students: Three years later* (NCES 2008-174). Washington, DC: U.S. Department of Education, National Center for Education Statistics.

Bielinski, J., Thurlow, M., Ysseldyke, J. E., & Freidebach, J., & Freidebach, M. (2001). *Read-aloud accommodation: Effects on multiple-choice reading and math items* (Tech. Rep. No. 31). Minneapolis: University of Minnesota, National Center on Educational Outcomes.

Binder, C. (1996). Behavioral fluency: Evolution of a new paradigm. *The Behavior Analyst, 19*, 163–197.

Binder, C. (2003). Doesn't everybody need fluency? *Performance Improvement, 42*(3), 14–20. doi:10.1002/pfi.4930420304

Bird, H. R., Canino, G. J., Rubio-Stipec, M., Gould, M. S., Ribera, J., Sesman, M., . . . Moscoso, M. (1988). Estimates of the prevalence of childhood maladjustment in a community survey in Puerto Rico. *Archives of General Psychiatry, 45*, 1120–1126. doi:10.1001/archpsyc.1988.01800360068010

Bishop, D. V. M., & Snowling, M. J. (2004). Developmental dyslexia and specific language impairment: Same or different? *Psychological Bulletin, 130*, 858–886. doi:10.1037/0033-2909.130.6.858

Blaskey, P., Scheiman, M., Parisi, M., Ciner, E. B., Gallaway, M., & Selznick, R. (1990). The effectiveness of Irlen filters for improving reading performance: A pilot study. *Journal of Learning Disabilities, 23*, 604–612. doi:10.1177/002221949002301007

Board of Education of the Hendrick Hudson Central School District v. Amy Rowley, 458 U.S. 176 (1982). Retrieved from http://wrightslaw.com/law/caselaw/ussupct.rowley.htm

Bolt, S. E. (2004, April). *Using DIF analyses to examine several commonly-held beliefs about testing accommodations for students with disabilities*. Paper presented at the annual meeting of the National Council on Measurement in Education, San Diego, CA.

Bolt, S. E. (2011). Factors to consider in providing appropriate testing accommodations to individual students with disabilities. In M. Russell & M. Kavanaugh (Eds.), *Assessing students in the margin: Challenges, strategies, and techniques* (pp. 3–30). Charlotte, NC: Information Age.

Bolt, S. E., Decker, D. M., Lloyd, M., & Morlock, L. (2011). Students' perceptions of accommodations in high school and college. *Career Development for Exceptional Individuals, 34*, 165–175.

Bolt, S. E., & Roach, A. T. (2009). *Inclusive assessment and accountability: A guide to accommodations for students with diverse needs*. New York, NY: Guilford Press.

Bolt, S. E., & Thurlow, M. L. (2007). Item-level effects of the read-aloud accommodation for students with reading disabilities. *Assessment for Effective Intervention, 33*, 15–28. doi:10.1177/15345084070330010301

Borsboom, D. (2006). The attack of the psychometricians. *Psychometrika, 71*, 425–440. doi:10.1007/s11336-006-1447-6

Bottsford-Miller, N., Thurlow, M. L., Stout, K. E., & Quenemoen, R. F. (2006). *A comparison of IEP/504 accommodations under classroom and standardized testing conditions: A preliminary report on SEELS data* (Synthesis Report 63). Minneapolis: University of Minnesota, National Center on Educational Outcomes.

Bouck, E. C. (2009). Calculating the value of graphing calculators for seventh-grade students with and without disabilities: A pilot study. *Remedial and Special Education, 30,* 207–215. doi:10.1177/0741932508321010

Bouck, E. C., & Bouck, M. K. (2008). Calculators as accommodations for sixth-grade students with disabilities. *Journal of Special Education Technology, 23,* 17–32.

Braden, J. P., Huai, N., White, J. L., & Elliott, S. N. (2005). Effective professional development to support inclusive large-scale assessment practices for all children. *Assessment for Effective Intervention, 31,* 63–71. doi:10.1177/073724770503100106

Braden, J. P., & Joyce, L. B. (2008). Best practices in making assessment accommodations. In A. Thomas & J. Grimes (Eds.), *Best practices in school psychology* (5th ed., pp. 589–603). Bethesda, MD: National Association of School Psychologists.

Brennan, R. L. (2001). An essay on the history and future of reliability from the perspective of replications. *Journal of Educational Measurement, 38,* 295–317. doi:10.1111/j.1745-3984.2001.tb01129.x

Bridgeman, B., Lennon, M. L., & Jackenthal, A. (2003). Effects of screen size, screen resolution, and display rate on computer-based test performance. *Applied Measurement in Education, 16,* 191–205. doi:10.1207/S15324818AME1603_2

Bridgeman, B., Trapani, C., & Curley, W. E. (2003). *Effect of fewer questions per section on SAT I scores* (College Board Report No. 2003-2). New York, NY: College Entrance Examination Board.

Brigham, F. J., Gustashaw, W. E., III, & Brigham, M. S. (2004). Scientific practice and the tradition of advocacy in special education. *Journal of Learning Disabilities, 37,* 200–206. doi:10.1177/00222194040370030301

Brown, J. I., Fishco, V. V., & Hanna, G. (1993). *Nelson-Denny Reading Test, Forms G and H.* Itasca, IL: Riverside.

Brown, P. B., & Augustine, A. (2000). *Findings of the 1999–2000 Screen Reading Field Test.* Dover: Delaware Department of Education.

Brown, P. J. (1999). *Findings of the 1999 Plain Language Field Test.* Newark: Delaware Education Research and Development Center, University of Delaware.

Brown, W. M. (2007). *Virginia teachers' perceptions and knowledge of test accommodations for students with disabilities* (Unpublished doctoral dissertation). College of William and Mary, Williamsburg, VA.

Bruff, D. (2007). Clickers: A classroom innovation. *National Education Association Advocate, 25,* 5–8.

Bryant, B. R., Patton, J. R., & Dunn, C. (1991). *Scholastic Abilities Test for Adults.* Austin, TX: Pro-Ed.

Burgoyne, R. A., & Mew, C. M. (2011). New regulations under Titles II and III of the ADA: What has changed relative to the administration of licensing examinations? *Bar Examiner, 80,* 42–52.

Burk, M. (1999). *Computerized test accommodations: A new approach for inclusion and success for students with disabilities.* Washington, DC: A.U. Software.

Burns, E. (1998). *Test accommodations for students with disabilities*. Springfield, IL: Charles C. Thomas.

Burns, M., & Ysseldyke, J. (2009). Reported prevalence of evidence-based instructional practices in special education. *The Journal of Special Education, 43*, 3–11. doi:10.1177/0022466908315563

Bush, G., Valera, E. M., & Seidman, L. J. (2005). Functional neuroimaging of attention-deficit/hyperactivity disorder: A review and suggested future directions. *Biological Psychiatry, 57*, 1273–1284.

Byrnes, M. A. (2008). Educators' interpretations of ambiguous accommodations. *Remedial and Special Education, 29*, 306–315. doi:10.1177/0741932507313017

Cahalan, C., Mandinach, E. B., & Camara, W. J. (2002). *Predictive validity of SAT I: Reasoning test for test-takers with learning disabilities and extended time accommodations*. New York, NY: College Entrance Examination Board.

Cahalan-Laitusis, C., Cook, L. L., & Aicher, C. (2004, April). *Examining test items for students with disabilities by testing accommodation*. Paper presented at the annual meeting of the National Council on Measurement in Education, San Diego, CA.

Cahalan-Laitusis, C., King, T. C., Cline, F., & Bridgeman, B. (2006). *Observational timing study on the SAT reasoning test for test-takers with learning disabilities and/or AD/HD* (College Board Research Report 2006-4). New York, NY: College Board.

Calhoon, M. B., Fuchs, L. S., & Hamlett, C. L. (2000). Effects of computer-based test accommodations on mathematics performance assessments for secondary students with learning disabilities. *Learning Disability Quarterly, 23*, 271–282. doi:10.2307/1511349

Calvo, M. G., & Carreiras, M. (1993). Selective influence of test anxiety on reading processes. *British Journal of Psychology, 84*, 375–388. doi:10.1111/j.2044-8295.1993.tb02489.x

Calvo, M. G., & Eysenck, M. W. (1996). Phonological working memory and reading in test anxiety. *Memory, 4*, 289–306. doi:10.1080/096582196388960

Carlson, C. L., & Mann, M. (2002). Sluggish cognitive tempo predicts a different pattern of impairment in the attention deficit hyperactivity disorder, predominantly inattentive type. *Journal of Clinical Child and Adolescent Psychology, 31*, 123–129. doi:10.1207/S15374424JCCP3101_14

Carroll, J. B. (1993). *Human cognitive abilities: A survey of factor-analytic studies*. New York, NY: Cambridge University Press. doi:10.1017/CBO9780511571312

Casbarro, J. (2003). *Test anxiety and what you can do about it: A practical guide for teachers, parents, and kids*. Port Chester, NY: Dude Publishing, National Professional Resources.

Cawthon, S. W. (2006). National survey of accommodations and alternate assessments for students who are deaf or hard of hearing in the United States. *Journal of Deaf Studies and Deaf Education, 11*, 337–359. doi:10.1093/deafed/enj040

Cawthon, S. W. (2010). Science and evidence of success: Two emerging issues in assessment accommodations for students who are deaf or hard of hearing. *Journal of Deaf Studies and Deaf Education, 15*, 185–203. doi:10.1093/deafed/enq002

Ceci, S. J., & Papierno, P. B. (2005). The rhetoric and reality of gap closing: When the "have-nots" gain but the "haves" gain even more. *American Psychologist, 60*, 149–160. doi:10.1037/0003-066X.60.2.149

Centers for Disease Control and Prevention. (2012). *Autism spectrum disorders (ASDs): Data & statistics*. Retrieved from: http://www.cdc.gov/ncbddd/autism/data.html

Chappuis, S., & Chappuis, J. (2008). The best value in formative assessment. *Educational Leadership, 65*, 14–18.

Chard, D. J., Vaughn, S., & Tyler, B. (2002). A synthesis of research on effective interventions for building reading fluency with elementary students with learning disabilities. *Journal of Learning Disabilities, 35*, 386–406. doi:10.1177/00222194020350050101

Chermak, G. D., Tucker, E., & Seikel, J. A. (2002). Behavioral characteristics of auditory processing disorder and attention deficit hyperactivity disorder: Primarily inattentive type. *Journal of the American Academy of Audiology, 13*, 332–338.

Chickering, A. W., & Gamson, Z. F. (1987). Seven principles for good practice in undergraduate education. *AAHE Bulletin, 39*, 3–7.

Choi, S. W., & Tinkler, T. (2002, April). *Evaluating comparability of paper and computer based assessment in a K–12 setting*. Paper presented at the annual meeting of the National Council on Measurement in Education, New Orleans, LA.

Christensen, L. L., Braam, M., Scullin, S., & Thurlow, M. L. (2011). *2009 state policies on assessment participation and accommodations for students with disabilities* (Synthesis Report 83). Minneapolis: University of Minnesota, National Center on Educational Outcomes.

Cizek, G. J., & Burg, S. S. (2006). *Addressing test anxiety in a high-stakes environment: Strategies for classrooms and schools*. Thousand Oaks, CA: Corwin.

Clariana, R., & Wallace, P. (2002). Paper-based versus computer-based assessment: Key factors associated with the test mode effect. *British Journal of Educational Technology, 33*, 593–602. doi:10.1111/1467-8535.00294

Cohen, A. S., Gregg, N., & Deng, M. (2005). The role of extended time and item content on a high-stakes mathematics test. *Learning Disabilities Research & Practice, 20*, 225–233. doi:10.1111/j.1540-5826.2005.00138.x

Cohen, J. (1988). *Statistical power analysis for the behavioral sciences* (2nd ed.). Hillsdale, NJ: Erlbaum.

Colón, E., & Kranzler, J. (2006). Effect of instructions on curriculum-based measurement of reading. *Journal of Psychoeducational Assessment, 24*, 318–328. doi:10.1177/0734282906287830

Conderman, G., & Pedersen, T. (2010). Preparing students with mild disabilities for taking state and district tests. *Intervention in School and Clinic, 45*, 232–241. doi:10.1177/1053451209353446

Conners, C. K., & Multi-Health Systems Staff. (2000). *Conners Continuous Performance Test II (CPT II, V.5)*. North Tonawanda, NY: Multi-Health Systems Inc.

Cooper, J. O., Heron, T. E., & Heward, W. L. (2007). *Applied behavior analysis* (2nd ed.). Upper Saddle River, NJ: Pearson/Merrill/Prentice Hall.

Cortiella, C. (2011). *The state of learning disabilities*. New York, NY: National Center for Learning Disabilities.

Corwin, J., & Bylsma, F. W. (1993). Psychological examination of traumatic encephalopathy. *The Clinical Neuropsychologist, 7*, 3–21.

Costello, E. J., Angold, A., & Keeler, G. (1999). Adolescent outcomes of childhood disorders: The consequences of severity and impairment. *Journal of the American Academy of Child and Adolescent Psychiatry, 38*, 121–128.

Council of Chief State School Officers. (2005). *Accommodations manual*. Washington, DC: Author.

Covington, G. A., & Hannah, B. (1997). *Access by design*. New York, NY: Van Nostrand-Reinhold.

Crawford, L., & Ketterlin-Geller, L. R. (2013). Middle school teachers' assignment of test accommodations. *The Teacher Educator, 48*, 29–45.

Crawford, L., & Tindal, G. (2004). Effects of a read-aloud modification on a standardized reading test. *Exceptionality, 12*, 89–106.

Cronbach, L. J. (1951). Coefficient alpha and the internal structure of tests. *Psychometrika, 16*, 297–334. doi:10.1007/BF02310555

Cutting, L. E., & Scarborough, H. S. (2006). Prediction of reading comprehension: Relative contributions of word recognition, language proficiency, and other cognitive skills can depend on how comprehension is measured. *Scientific Studies of Reading, 10*, 277–299. doi:10.1207/s1532799xssr1003_5

Davis, J. E. (2012). *Secondary education teachers' perceptions related to their knowledge and effectiveness of accommodations for students with mild disabilities* (Unpublished doctoral dissertation). Texas Woman's University, Denton, TX.

Dawes, P., & Bishop, D. (2009). Auditory processing disorder in relation to developmental disorders of language, communication and attention: A review and critique. *International Journal of Language and Communication Disorders, 44*, 440–465.

DeStefano, L., Shriner, J. G., & Lloyd, C. A. (2001). Teacher decision making in participation of students with disabilities in large-scale assessment. *Exceptional Children, 68*, 7–22.

Dolan, R. P., Hall, T. E., Banerjee, M., Chun, E., & Strangman, N. (2005). Applying principles of universal design to test delivery: The effect of computer-based read-aloud on test performance of high school students with learning disabilities. *The Journal of Technology, Learning, and Assessment, 3*, 4–32.

Dombrowski, S. C., Kamphaus, R. W., & Reynolds, C. R. (2004). After the demise of the discrepancy: Proposed learning disabilities diagnostic criteria. *Professional Psychology: Research and Practice, 35*, 364–372.

Dotinga, W. (2014, January 14). Boost for disabled LSAT takers in CA revived. *Courthouse News Service.* Retrieved from http://www.courthousenews.com/2014/01/14/64529.htm

Driskell, J. E., Willis, R. P., & Copper, C. (1992). Effect of overlearning on retention. *Journal of Applied Psychology, 77,* 615–622. doi:10.1037/0021-9010.77.5.615

Dunn, L. M., & Dunn, D. M. (2007a). *Peabody Picture Vocabulary Test* (4th ed.). San Antonio, TX: Psychological Corporation.

Dunn, L. M., & Dunn, D. M. (2007b). *PPVT-4: Peabody Picture Vocabulary Test— Manual.* Bloomington, MN: NCS Pearson.

DuPaul, G. J. (2007). School-based interventions for students with attention deficit hyperactivity disorder: Current status and future directions. *School Psychology Review, 36,* 183–194.

Durham, G. (2007). *Teaching test-taking skills: Proven techniques to boost your student's scores.* Lanham, MD: Rowman & Littlefield Education.

Dweck, C. (2006). *Mindset: The new psychology of success* (1st ed.). New York, NY: Random House.

Earle, S., & Sharp, K. (2000). Disability and assessment in the UK: Should we compensate disabled students? *Teaching in Higher Education, 5,* 541–545. doi:10.1080/713699180

Edgemon, E. A., Jablonski, B. R., & Lloyd, J. W. (2006). Large-scale assessments: A teacher's guide to making decisions about accommodations. *Teaching Exceptional Children, 38*(3), 6–11.

Edmonds, M. S., Vaughn, S., Wexler, J., Reutebuch, C., Cable, A., Tackett, K. K., & Schnakenberg, J. W. (2009). A synthesis of reading interventions and effects on reading comprehension outcomes for older struggling readers. *Review of Educational Research, 79,* 262–300. doi:10.3102/0034654308325998

Elbaum, B. (2007). Effects of an oral testing accommodation on the mathematics performance of secondary students with and without learning disabilities. *The Journal of Special Education, 40,* 218–229. doi:10.1177/00224669070400040301

Elbaum, B., Arquelles, M., Campbell, Y., & Saleh, M. (2004). Effects of student reads-aloud accommodation on the performance of students with and without disabilities on a test of reading comprehension. *Exceptionality, 12,* 71–87. doi:10.1207/s15327035ex1202_2

Elkind, J. (1998). Computer reading machines for poor readers. *Perspectives, 24,* 9–13.

Elkind, J., Black, M., & Murray, C. (1996). Computer-based compensation of adult reading disabilities. *Annals of Dyslexia, 46,* 159–186. doi:10.1007/BF02648175

Elkind, J., Cohen, K., & Murray, C. (1993). Using computer-based readers to improve reading comprehension of students with dyslexia. *Annals of Dyslexia, 43,* 238–259. doi:10.1007/BF02928184

Elliott, S. N., Kratochwill, T. R., & Schulte, A. G. (1998). The assessment accommodation checklist: Who, what, where, when, why, how? *Teaching Exceptional Children, 31*(2), 10–14.

Elliott, S. N., & Marquart, A. M. (2004). Extended time as a testing accommodation: Its effects and perceived consequences. *Exceptional Children, 70*, 349–367.

Elliott, S. N., McKevitt, B. C., & Kettler, R. J. (2002). *Testing accommodations research and decision making: The case of "good" scores being highly valued but difficult to achieve for all students* (WCER Working Paper 2002-1). Madison: Wisconsin Center for Education Research.

Engelhard, G., Fincher, M., & Domaleski, C. S. (2010). Mathematics performance of students with and without disabilities under accommodated conditions using resource guides and calculators on high stakes tests. *Applied Measurement in Education, 24*, 22–38. doi:10.1080/08957347.2010.485975

Erchul, W. P., & Martens, B. K. (2002). *School consultation: Conceptual and empirical bases of practice* (2nd ed.). New York, NY: Kluwer Academic/Plenum.

Ergene, T. (2003). Effective interventions on test anxiety reduction: A meta-analysis. *School Psychology International, 24*, 313–328. doi:10.1177/01430343030243004

Etscheidt, S., & Curran, C. M. (2010). Reauthorization of the Individuals With Disabilities Education Improvement Act (IDEA, 2004): The peer-reviewed research requirement. *Journal of Disability Policy Studies, 21*, 29–39. doi:10.1177/1044207309360204

Feldman, E., Kim, J. S., & Elliott, S. (2011). The effects of accommodations on adolescents' self-efficacy and test performance. *The Journal of Special Education, 45*, 77–88. doi:10.1177/0022466909353791

Ferrier, D. E., Lovett, B. J., & Jordan, A. H. (2011). Construct-irrelevant variance in achievement test scores: A social cognitive perspective. In L. E. Madsen (Ed.), *Achievement tests: Types, interpretations, and uses* (pp. 89–108). Hauppauge, NY: Nova Science.

Finch, H., Barton, K., & Meyer, P. (2009). Differential item functioning analysis for accommodated versus nonaccommodated students. *Educational Assessment, 14*, 38–56. doi:10.1080/10627190902816264

Fletcher, J. M. (2006). Measuring reading comprehension. *Scientific Studies of Reading, 10*, 323–330. doi:10.1207/s1532799xssr1003_7

Fletcher, J. M., Francis, D. J., Boudousquie, A., Copeland, K., Young, V., Kalinowski, S., & Vaughn, S. (2006). Effects of accommodations on high-stakes testing for students with reading disabilities. *Exceptional Children, 72*, 136–150.

Frazier, T. W., Youngstrom, E. A., Glutting, J. J., & Watkins, M. W. (2007). ADHD and achievement meta-analysis of the child, adolescent, and adult literatures and a concomitant study with college students. *Journal of Learning Disabilities, 40*, 49–65.

Freedman, M. K. (2003). Disabling the SAT: How the College Board is undermining its premier test. *Education Next, 3*(4), 37–43.

Fuchs, D., & Fuchs, L. S. (2006). Introduction to response to intervention: What, why, and how valid is it? *Reading Research Quarterly, 41*, 93–99. doi:10.1598/RRQ.41.1.4

Fuchs, L. S. (2000). Helping schools formulate decisions about test accommodations for students with disabilities. *Assessment Focus, 9*(1), 3.

Fuchs, L. S., & Fuchs, D. (2001). Helping teachers formulate sound testing accommodation decisions for students with learning disabilities. *Learning Disabilities Research & Practice, 16*, 174–181. doi:10.1111/0938-8982.00018

Fuchs, L. S., Fuchs, D., Eaton, S. B., & Hamlett, C. (2003). *Dynamic assessment of test accommodations*. San Antonio, TX: Psychological Corporation.

Fuchs, L. S., Fuchs, D., Eaton, S. B., Hamlett, C., Binkley, E., & Crouch, R. (2000). Using objective data sources to enhance teacher judgments about test accommodations. *Exceptional Children, 67*, 67–81.

Fuchs, L. S., Fuchs, D., Eaton, S. B., Hamlett, C. L., & Karns, K. (2000). Supplementing teachers' judgments of mathematics test accommodations with objective data sources. *School Psychology Review, 29*, 65–85.

Fulk, B. M., Brigham, F. J., & Lohman, D. A. (1998). Motivation and self-regulation: A comparison of students with learning and behavior problems. *Remedial and Special Education, 19*, 300–309. doi:10.1177/074193259801900506

Furr, R. M., & Bacharach, V. R. (2008). *Psychometrics: An introduction*. Los Angeles, CA: Sage.

Gallaudet Research Institute. (2008). *Regional and national summary report of data from the 2007–08 annual survey of deaf and hard of hearing children and youth*. Washington, DC: Gallaudet Research Institute, Gallaudet University.

Gambrill, E. D. (2006). *Critical thinking in clinical practice: Improving the quality of judgments and decisions* (2nd ed.). Hoboken, NJ: Wiley.

Gartland, D., & Strosnider, R. (2007). The documentation disconnect for students with learning disabilities: Improving access to postsecondary disability services. *Learning Disability Quarterly, 30*, 265–274.

Gaster, L., & Clark, C. (1995). *A guide to providing alternate formats* (ERIC Document No. ED 405689). West Columbia, SC: Center for Rehabilitation Technology Services.

Goldberg, A. L., & Pedulla, J. J. (2002). Performance differences according to test mode and computer familiarity on a practice graduate record exam. *Educational and Psychological Measurement, 62*, 1053–1067.

Gordon, M. (1991). *Instruction manual for the Gordon Diagnostic System, Model III-R*. Dewitt, NY: Gordon Systems.

Gordon, M. (2009). *ADHD on trial*. Westport, CT: Praeger.

Gordon, M. (2012). How to optimize the use of outside consultants for ADA documentation reviews. *The Bar Examiner, 8*, 16–24.

Gordon, M., Antshel, K., Faraone, S., Barkley, R., Lewandowski, L., Hudziak, J. J., . . . Cunningham, C. (2006). Symptoms versus impairment: The case for respecting *DSM–IV*'s Criterion D. *Journal of Attention Disorders, 9*, 465–475. doi:10.1177/1087054705283881

Gordon, M., & Keiser, S. (1998). *Accommodations in higher education under the Americans With Disabilities Act (ADA)*. New York, NY: Guilford Press.

Gordon, M., Lewandowski, L., Murphy, K., & Dempsey, K. (2002). ADA-based accommodations in higher education: A survey of clinicians about documentation requirements of diagnostic standards. *Journal of Learning Disabilities, 35,* 357–363. doi:10.1177/00222194020350040601

Gormley, S., Hughes, C., Block, L., & Lendmann, C. (2005). Eligibility assessment requirements at the postsecondary level for students with learning disabilities: A disconnect with secondary schools? *Journal of Postsecondary Education and Disability, 18,* 63–70.

Graetz, B. W., Sawyer, M. G., Hazell, P. L., Arney, F., & Baghurst, P. (2001). Validity of DSM–IV ADHD subtypes in a nationally representative sample of Australian children and adolescents. *Journal of the American Academy of Child & Adolescent Psychiatry, 40,* 1410–1417. doi:10.1097/00004583-200112000-00011

Graham, S., Harris, K. R., & McKeown, D. (2013). The writing of students with learning disabilities, meta-analysis of self-regulated strategy development writing intervention studies, and future directions: Redux. In H. L. Swanson, K. R. Harris, & S. Graham (Eds.), *Handbook of learning disabilities* (2nd ed., pp. 405–438). New York, NY: Guilford Press.

Graham, S., & MacArthur, C. A. (1988). Improving learning disabled students' skills at revising essays produced on a word processor: Self-instructional strategy training. *The Journal of Special Education, 22,* 133–152. doi:10.1177/00224669880 2200202

Green, P. (2003). *Green's Word Memory Test for Windows: User's manual.* Edmonton, Alberta, Canada: Green's.

Green, P. (2007). The pervasive influence of effort on neuropsychological tests. *Physical medicine and rehabilitation clinics of North America, 18,* 43–68.

Green, P., Flaro, L., & Courtney, J. (2009). Examining false positives on the Word Memory Test in adults with mild traumatic brain injury. *Brain Injury, 23,* 741–750.

Green, P., Iverson, G. L., & Allen, L. (1999). Detecting malingering in head injury litigation with the Word Memory Test. *Brain Injury, 13,* 813–819.

Green, P., Rohling, M. L., Lees-Haley, P. R., & Allen, L. (2001). Effort has a greater effect on test scores than severe brain injury in compensation claimants. *Brain Injury, 15,* 1045–1060. doi:10.1080/02699050110088254

Greenhill, L. L., Halperin, J. M., & Abikoff, H. (1999). Stimulant medications. *Journal of the American Academy of Child & Adolescent Psychiatry, 38,* 503–512.

Gregg, N., Coleman, C., Davis, M., & Chalk, J. C. (2007). Timed essay writing: Implications for high-stakes tests. *Journal of Learning Disabilities, 40,* 306–318.

Gregory, M., & Poulton, E. C. (1970). Even versus uneven right-hand margins and the rate of comprehension in reading. *Ergonomics, 13,* 427–434.

Gregory, R. J. (2011). *Psychological testing: History, principles, and applications* (6th ed.). Boston, MA: Allyn & Bacon.

Gresham, F. M. (2002). Responsiveness to intervention: An alternative approach to the identification of learning disabilities. In R. Bradley, L. Danielson, & D. P. Hallahan (Eds.), *Identification of learning disabilities: From research to practice* (pp. 467–519). Mahwah, NJ: Erlbaum.

Gresham, F. M., MacMillan, D. L., & Bocian, K. M. (1996). Learning disabilities, low achievement, and mild mental retardation: More alike than different? *Journal of Learning Disabilities, 29,* 570–581. doi:10.1177/002221949602900601

Grise, P., Beattie, S., & Algozzine, B. (1982). Assessment of minimum competency in fifth grade learning disabled students: Test modifications make a difference. *The Journal of Educational Research, 76,* 35–40.

Guerin, B., & Innes, J. (2009). *Social facilitation.* Cambridge, England: Cambridge University Press.

Haertel, E. H. (2003, April). *Evidentiary argument and the comparability of scores from standard versus nonstandard test administrations.* Paper presented at the annual meeting of the National Council on Measurement in Education, Chicago, IL.

Haertel, E. H., & Lorié, W. A. (2004). Validating standards-based score interpretations. *Measurement: Interdisciplinary Research and Perspectives, 2,* 61–103. doi:10.1207/s15366359mea0202_1

Haertel, E. H., & Wiley, D. E. (2003, April). *Comparability issues when scores are produced under varying testing conditions.* Paper presented at the Psychometric Conference on Validity and Accommodations, University of Maryland, College Park.

Hagtvet, K. A., Man, F., & Sharma, S. (2001). Generalizability of self-related cognitions in test anxiety. *Personality and Individual Differences, 31,* 1147–1171. doi:10.1016/S0191-8869(00)00212-9

Haladyna, T. M., & Downing, S. M. (2004). Construct-irrelevant variance in high-stakes testing. *Educational Measurement: Issues and Practice, 23,* 17–27. doi:10.1111/j.1745-3992.2004.tb00149.x

Haladyna, T. M., Downing, S. M., & Rodriguez, M. C. (2002). A review of multiple-choice item-writing guidelines for classroom assessment. *Applied Measurement in Education, 15,* 309–333. doi:10.1207/S15324818AME1503_5

Halla, J. W. (1988). A psychological study of psychometric differences in Graduate Record Examinations General Test scores between learning disabled and non-learning disabled adults. *Dissertation Abstracts International: Section A. The Humanities and Social Sciences, 49*(11), 3341.

Hamill, D. D., & Larsen, S. C. (2009). *Test of Written Language* (4th ed.). Austin, TX: Pro-Ed.

Harris, K. R., Friedlander, B. D., Saddler, B., Frizzelle, R., & Graham, S. (2005). Self-monitoring of attention versus self-monitoring of academic performance effects among students with ADHD in the general education classroom. *The Journal of Special Education, 39,* 145–157. doi:10.1177/00224669050390030201

Harris, L. W. S. (2008). *Comparison of student performance between teacher read and CD-ROM delivered modes of test administration of English language arts tests* (Unpublished doctoral dissertation). University of South Carolina.

Harrison, A. G. (2006). Adults faking ADHD: You must be kidding! *The ADHD Report, 14*(4), 1–7. doi:10.1521/adhd.2006.14.4.1

Harrison, A. G., Edwards, M. J., & Parker, K. C. (2008). Identifying students feigning dyslexia: Preliminary findings and strategies for detection. *Dyslexia, 14*, 228–246.

Harrison, A. G., Edwards, M. J., & Parker, K. C. H. (2007). Identifying students faking ADHD: Preliminary findings and strategies for detection. *Archives of Clinical Neuropsychology, 22*, 577–588. doi:10.1016/j.acn.2007.03.008

Harrison, A. G., Green, P., & Flaro, L. (2012). The importance of symptom validity testing in adolescents and young adults undergoing assessments for learning or attention difficulties. *Canadian Journal of School Psychology, 27*, 98–113.

Hatzes, N. M., Reiff, H. B., & Bramel, M. H. (2002). The documentation dilemma: Access and accommodations for postsecondary students with learning disabilities. *Assessment for Effective Intervention, 27*(3), 37–52.

Heaney, K. J., & Pullin, D. C. (1998). Accommodations and flags: Admissions testing and the rights of individuals with disabilities. *Educational Assessment, 5*, 71–93. doi:10.1207/s15326977ea0502_1

Helwig, R., Rozek-Tedesco, M. A., Tindal, G., Heath, B., & Almond, P. (1999). Reading as an access to mathematics problem solving on multiple-choice tests for sixth-grade students. *The Journal of Educational Research, 93*, 113–125. doi:10.1080/00220679909597635

Helwig, R., & Tindal, G. (2003). An experimental analysis of accommodation decisions on large-scale mathematics tests. *Exceptional Children, 69*, 211–225.

Hembree, R. (1988). Correlates, causes, effects, and treatment of test anxiety. *Review of Educational Research, 58*, 47–77. doi:10.3102/00346543058001047

Henderson, C. (2001). *College freshman with disabilities: A statistical profile.* Washington, DC: HEATH Resource Center.

Hess, K., Burdge, M., & Clayton, J. (2011). Challenges to developing and implementing alternate assessments based on alternate achievement standards (AA-AAS). In M. Russell & M. Kavanaugh (Eds.), *Assessing students in the margin: Challenges, strategies, and techniques* (pp. 171–213). Charlotte, NC: Information Age.

Hetzroni, O. E., & Shrieber, B. (2004). Word processing as an assistive technology tool for enhancing academic outcomes of students with writing disabilities in the general classroom. *Journal of Learning Disabilities, 37*, 143–154. doi:10.1177/00222194040370020501

Hiebert, E. H., Samuels, S. J., & Rasinski, T. (2012). Comprehension-based silent reading rates: What do we know? What do we need to know? *Literacy Research and Instruction, 51*, 110–124.

Higgins, E. L., & Raskind, M. H. (1995). Compensatory effectiveness of speech recognition on the written composition performance of postsecondary students with learning disabilities. *Learning Disability Quarterly, 18*, 159–174. doi:10.2307/1511202

Higgins, E. L., & Raskind, M. H. (1997). The compensatory effectiveness of optical character recognition/speech synthesis on reading comprehension of post-secondary students with learning disabilities. *Learning Disabilities: A Multidisciplinary Journal, 8*, 75–87.

Higgins, E. L., & Raskind, M. H. (2005). The compensatory effectiveness of the Quicktionary Reading Pen II on the reading comprehension of students with learning disabilities. *Journal of Special Education Technology, 20*, 31–40.

Hill, G. A. (1984). Learning disabled college students: The assessment of academic aptitude. *Dissertation Abstracts International: Section B. The Sciences and Engineering, 46*(02), 642.

Hoagwood, K., & Johnson, J. (2003). School psychology: A public health framework: I. From evidence-based practices to evidence-based policies. *Journal of School Psychology, 41*, 3–21.

Hock, M. K., Brasseur, I. F., Deshler, D. D., Marquis, J. G., Stribling, J. W., Mark, C. A., & Catts, H. W. (2009). What is the reading component skill profile of adolescent struggling readers in urban schools? *Learning Disability Quarterly, 32*, 21–38.

Hodgson, J. R., Lazarus, S. S., & Thurlow, M. L. (2011). *Professional development to improve accommodations decisions—A review of the literature* (Synthesis Report 84). Minneapolis: University of Minnesota, National Center on Educational Outcomes.

Hoeft, F., Carter, J. C., Lightbody, A. A., Hazlett, H. C., Priven, J., & Reiss, A. L. (2010). Region-specific alterations in brain development in one- to three-year-old boys with fragile X syndrome. *Proceedings of the National Academy of Sciences, USA, 107*, 9335–9339. doi:10.1073/pnas.1002762107

Hoener, A., Salend, S. J., & Kay, S. (1997). Creating readable handouts, worksheets, overheads, tests, review materials, study guides, and homework assignments through effective typographic design. *Teaching Exceptional Children, 29*(3), 32–35.

Hollenbeck, K. (2002). Determining when test alterations are valid accommodations or modifications for large-scale assessment. In G. Tindal & T. M. Haladyna (Eds.), *Large-scale assessment programs for all students: Validity, technical adequacy, and implementation* (pp. 395–425). Mahwah, NJ: Erlbaum.

Hollenbeck, K., Rozek-Tedesco, M. A., Tindal, G., & Glasgow, A. (2000). An exploratory study of student-paced versus teacher-paced accommodations for large-scale math tests. *Journal of Special Education Technology, 15*, 27–36.

Hollenbeck, K., Tindal, G., & Almond, P. (1998). Teachers' knowledge of accommodations as a validity issue in high-stakes testing. *The Journal of Special Education, 32*, 175–183. doi:10.1177/002246699803200304

Holzer, M. L., Madaus, J. W., Bray, M. A., & Kehle, T. J. (2009). The test-taking strategy intervention for college students with learning disabilities. *Learning Disabilities Research & Practice, 24*, 44–56. doi:10.1111/j.1540-5826.2008.01276.x

Hoover, H. D., Dunbar, S. B., & Frisbie, D. A. (2001). *Iowa Tests of Basic Skills (ITBS) Forms A, B, and C.* Rolling Meadows, IL: Riverside.

Hoyt, C. S. (1990). Irlen lenses and reading difficulties. *Journal of Learning Disabilities, 23,* 624–626. doi:10.1177/002221949002301010

Huesman, R. L., & Frisbie, D. A. (2000, April). *The validity of ITBS reading comprehension test scores for learning disabled and non-learning disabled students under extended-time conditions.* Paper presented at the annual meeting of the National Council on Measurement in Education, New Orleans, LA.

Hughes, C. A., & Schumaker, J. B. (1991). Test-taking strategy instruction for adolescents with learning disabilities. *Exceptionality: A Research Journal, 2,* 205–221.

Hunsley, J., & Mash, E. J. (2011). Evidence-based assessment. In D. Barlow (Ed.), *The Oxford handbook of clinical psychology* (pp. 76–97). New York, NY: Oxford University Press.

Huynh, H., & Barton, K. E. (2006). Performance of students with disabilities under regular and oral administrations of a high-stakes reading examination. *Applied Measurement in Education, 19,* 21–39.

Huynh, H., Meyer, J. P., & Gallant, D. J. (2004). Comparability of student performance between regular and oral administrations for a high-stakes mathematics test. *Applied Measurement in Education, 17,* 39–57. doi:10.1207/s15324818ame1701_3

Individuals With Disabilities Education Act, 20 U.S.C. § 1400 *et seq.*

Individuals With Disabilities Education Improvement Act of 2004, Pub. L. No. 108–446.

Iowa Department of Education. (2013). *Iowa Alternate Assessment 2013–2014 Reading Rating Scale Grades 3–5.* Retrieved from https://www.educateiowa.gov/sites/files/ed/documents/Reading%203-5%20Rating%20Scale%202013-2014.pdf

Jachimowicz, G., & Geiselman, R. E. (2004). Comparison of ease of falsification of attention deficit hyperactivity disorder diagnosis using standard behavioral rating scales. *Cognitive Science Online, 2,* 6–20.

Jerger, J., & Musiek, F. (2000). Report of the consensus conference on the diagnosis of auditory processing disorders in school-aged children. *Journal of the American Academy of Audiology, 11,* 467–474.

Johnstone, C. J. (2003). *Improving validity of large-scale tests: Universal design and student performance.* Minneapolis: University of Minnesota, National Center on Educational Outcomes.

Johnstone, C. J., Thompson, S. J., Bottsford-Miller, N. A., & Thurlow, M. L. (2008). Universal design and multimethod approaches to item review. *Educational Measurement: Issues and Practice, 27,* 25–36.

Jordan, A. H., & Lovett, B. J. (2008). Self-theories of intelligence: Implications for school psychology. In D. H. Molina (Ed.), *School psychology: 21st century issues and challenges* (pp. 345–355). Hauppauge, NY: Nova Science.

Joy, J. A., Julius, J. R., Akter, R., & Baron, D. A. (2010). Assessment of ADHD documentation from candidates requesting Americans With Disabilities Act (ADA) accommodations for the National Board of Osteopathic Medical Examiners

COMLEX Exam. *Journal of Attention Disorders, 14*, 104–108. doi:10.1177/1087054710365056

Kameenui, E. J., & Carnine, D. J. (1998). *Effective teaching strategies that accommodate diverse learners.* Des Moines, IA: Prentice-Hall.

Kamei-Hannan, C. (2008). Examining the accessibility of a computerized adapted test using assistive technology. *Journal of Visual Impairment & Blindness, 102*, 261–271.

Kauffman, J. M., McGee, K., & Brigham, M. (2004). Enabling or disabling? Observations on changes in special education. *Phi Delta Kappan, 85*, 613–620.

Kavale, K. A. (2002). Discrepancy models in the identification of learning disability. In R. Bradley, L. Danielson, & D. P. Hallahan (Eds.), *Identification of learning disabilities: Research to practice* (pp. 369–426). Mahwah, NJ: Erlbaum.

Kavale, K. A., & Reese, J. H. (1992). The character of learning disabilities: An Iowa profile. *Learning Disability Quarterly, 15*, 74–94.

Keenan, W. R., & Shaw, S. F. (2011). The legal context for serving students with LD in postsecondary education. *Learning Disabilities, 17*, 55–61.

Ketterlin-Geller, L. R. (2005). Knowing what all students know: Procedures for developing universal design for assessment. *The Journal of Technology, Learning, and Assessment, 4*(2).

Ketterlin-Geller, L. R., Alonzo, J., Braun-Monegan, J., & Tindal, G. (2007). Recommendations for accommodations: Implications of (in)consistency. *Remedial and Special Education, 28*, 194–206. doi:10.1177/07419325070280040101

Ketterlin-Geller, L. R., & Jamgochian, E. M. (2011). Instructional adaptations: Accommodations and modifications that support accessible instruction. In S. N. Elliott, R. J. Kettler, P. A. Beddow, & A. Kurz (Eds.), *Handbook of accessible achievement tests for all students: Bridging the gaps between research, practice, and policy* (pp. 131–146). New York, NY: Springer. doi:10.1007/978-1-4419-9356-4_7

Ketterlin-Geller, L. R., Jamgochian, E. M., Nelson-Walker, N. J., & Geller, J. P. (2012). Disentangling mathematics target and access skills: Implications for accommodation assignment practices. *Learning Disabilities Research & Practice, 27*, 178–188.

Kettler, R. J., Braden, J. P., & Beddow, P. A. (2011). Test-taking skills and their impact on accessibility for all students. In S. N. Elliott, R. J. Kettler, P. A. Beddow, & A. Kurz (Eds.), *Handbook of accessible achievement tests for all students: Bridging the gaps between research, practice, and policy* (pp. 147–159). New York, NY: Springer. doi:10.1007/978-1-4419-9356-4_8

Kettler, R. J., Dickenson, T. S., Bennett, H. L., Morgan, G. B., Gilmore, J. A., Beddow, P. A., . . . Palmer, P. W. (2012). Enhancing the accessibility of high school science tests: A multistate experiment. *Exceptional Children, 79*, 91–106.

Kettler, R. J., Elliott, S. N., & Beddow, P. A. (2009). Modifying achievement test items: A theory-guided and data-based approach for better measurement of what students with disabilities know. *Peabody Journal of Education, 84*, 529–551. doi:10.1080/01619560903240996

Kettler, R. J., Rodriguez, M. C., Bolt, D. M., Elliott, S. N., Beddow, P. A., & Kurz, A. (2011). Modified multiple-choice items for alternate assessments: Reliability, difficulty, and differential boost. *Applied Measurement in Education, 24*, 210–234. doi:10.1080/08957347.2011.580620

Kieffer, M. J., Lesaux, N. K., Rivera, M., & Francis, D. J. (2009). Accommodations for English language learners taking large-scale assessments: A meta-analysis on effectiveness and validity. *Review of Educational Research, 79*, 1168–1201. doi:10.3102/0034654309332490

Kim, D.-H., & Huynh, H. (2010). Equivalence of paper-and-pencil and online administration modes of the statewide English test for students with and without disabilities. *Educational Assessment, 15*, 107–121. doi:10.1080/10627197.2010.491066

Kim, D.-H., Schneider, C., & Siskind, T. (2009). Examining the underlying factor structure of a statewide science test under oral and standard administrations. *Journal of Psychoeducational Assessment, 27*, 323–333. doi:10.1177/0734282908328632

Kim, J. (1999, October). *Meta-analysis of equivalence of computerized and P&P tests on ability measures*. Paper presented at the annual meeting of the Mid-Western Educational Research Association, Chicago, IL.

Kim, Y. S., Petscher, Y., Schatschneider, C., & Foorman, B. (2010). Does growth rate in oral reading fluency matter in predicting reading comprehension achievement? *Journal of Educational Psychology, 102*, 652–657.

Kingston, N. M. (2008). Comparability of computer- and paper-administered multiple-choice tests for K–12 populations: A synthesis. *Applied Measurement in Education, 22*, 22–37. doi:10.1080/08957340802558326

Kirkwood, M. W., Kirk, J. W., Blaha, R. Z., & Wilson, P. (2010). Noncredible effort during pediatric neuropsychological exam: A case series and literature review. *Child Neuropsychology, 16*, 604–618.

Klingner, J. K., Vaughn, S., & Boardman, A. (2007). *Teaching reading comprehension to students with learning difficulties*. New York, NY: Guilford Press.

Kochhar-Bryant, C. A., & Izzo, M. V. (2006). Access to post-high school services: Transition assessment and the summary of performance. *Career Development for Exceptional Individuals, 29*, 70–89.

Koretz, D. (2009). *Measuring up: What educational testing really tells us*. Cambridge, MA: Harvard University Press.

Koretz, D., & Barton, K. (2004). Assessing students with disabilities: Issues and evidence. *Educational Assessment, 9*, 29–60. doi:10.1080/10627197.2004.9652958

Kosciolek, S., & Ysseldyke, J. (2000). *Effects of a reading accommodation on the validity of a reading test* (Tech. Rep. No. 28). Minneapolis: University of Minnesota, National Center on Educational Outcomes.

Kretlow, A. G., Lo, Y. Y., White, R. B., & Jordan, L. (2008). Teaching test-taking strategies to improve the academic achievement of students with mild mental disabilities. *Education and Training in Developmental Disabilities, 43*, 397–408.

Kubina, R. M., Jr., & Morrison, R. S. (2000). Fluency in education. *Behavior and Social Issues, 10,* 83–99. doi:10.5210/bsi.v10i0.133

Kuhn, M. R. (2011). Interventions to enhance fluency and rate of reading. In R. Allington & A. McGill-Franzen (Eds.), *Handbook of reading disabilities research* (pp. 307–314). Mahwah, NJ: Erlbaum.

Kuhn, M. R., & Stahl, S. A. (2003). Fluency: A review of developmental and remedial practices. *Journal of Educational Psychology, 95,* 3–21. doi:10.1037/0022-0663.95.1.3

Kurzweil Educational Systems. (2013). *Firefly features.* Retrieved from http://www.kurzweiledu.com/kurzweil-3000-firefly-features.html

Laitusis, C. C. (2010). Examining the impact of audio presentation on tests of reading comprehension. *Applied Measurement in Education, 23,* 153–167.

Lancaster, P. E., Lancaster, S. J., Schumaker, J. B., & Deshler, D. D. (2006). The efficacy of an interactive hypermedia program for teaching a test-taking strategy to students with high-incidence disabilities. *Journal of Special Education Technology, 21*(2), 17–30.

Lancaster, P. E., Schumaker, J. B., Lancaster, S. J. C., & Deshler, D. D. (2009). Effects of a computerized program on use of the test-taking strategy by secondary students with disabilities. *Learning Disability Quarterly, 32,* 165–179.

Landau, S., Russell, M., Gourgey, K., Erin, J. N., & Cowan, J. (2003). Use of the Talking Tactile Tablet in mathematics testing. *Journal of Visual Impairment & Blindness, 97,* 85–96.

Lane, S., & Lewandowski, L. (1994). Oral versus written compositions of students with and without learning disabilities. *Journal of Psychoeducational Assessment, 12,* 142–153. doi:10.1177/073428299401200204

Lang, S. C., Elliott, S. N., Bolt, D. M., & Kratochwill, T. R. (2008). The effects of testing accommodations on students' performances and reactions to testing. *School Psychology Quarterly, 23,* 107–124. doi:10.1037/1045-3830.23.1.107

Lang, S. C., Kumke, P. J., Ray, C. E., Cowell, E. L., Elliott, S. N., Kratochwill, T. R., & Bolt, D. M. (2005). Consequences of using testing accommodations: Student, teacher, and parent perceptions of and reactions to testing accommodations. *Assessment for Effective Intervention, 31,* 49–62.

Larrabee, G. J. (2000). Forensic neuropsychological assessment. In R. D. Vanderploeg (Ed.), *Clinician's guide to neuropsychological assessment* (pp. 301–335). Mahwah, NJ: Erlbaum.

Lazarus, S. S., Thompson, S. J., & Thurlow, M. L. (2006, January). *How students access accommodations in assessment and instruction: Results of a survey of special education teachers* (Issue Brief No. 7). College Park, MD: Educational Policy and Reform Research Institute.

Lazarus, S. S., Thurlow, M. L., Lail, K. E., & Christensen, L. (2009). A longitudinal analysis of state accommodations policies: Twelve years of change, 1993–2005. *The Journal of Special Education, 43,* 67–80. doi:10.1177/0022466907313524

Lee, D., Reynolds, C. R., & Wilson, V. L. (2003). Standardized test administration: Why bother? *Journal of Forensic Neuropsychology, 3*(3), 55–81. doi:10.1300/J151v03n03_04

Lee, J., & Shute, V. J. (2010). Personal and social-contextual factors in K–12 academic performance: An integrative perspective on student learning. *Educational Psychologist, 45*, 185–202. doi:10.1080/00461520.2010.493471

Lee, K. S., Osborne, R. E., Hayes, K. A., & Simoes, R. A. (2008). The effects of pacing on the academic testing performance of college students with ADHD: A mixed methods study. *Journal of Educational Computing Research, 39*, 123–141.

Legge, G. E., Madison, C. M., & Mansfield, J. S. (1999). Measuring Braille reading speed with the MNREAD test. *Visual Impairment Research, 1*, 131–145. doi:10.1076/vimr.1.3.131.4438

Leong, C. K. (1995). Effects of on-line reading and simultaneous DECtalk aiding in helping below-average and poor readers comprehend and summarize text. *Learning Disability Quarterly, 18*, 101–116. doi:10.2307/1511198

Lerner, C. (2004). "Accommodations" for the learning disabled: A level playing field or affirmative action for elites? *Vanderbilt Law Review, 57*, 1041–1122.

Lewandowski, L., Cohen, J., & Lovett, B. J. (2013). Effects of extended time allotments on reading comprehension performance of college students with and without learning disabilities. *Journal of Psychoeducational Assessment, 31*, 326–336.

Lewandowski, L., Gathje, R. A., Lovett, B. J., & Gordon, M. (2013). Test-taking skills in college students with and without ADHD. *Journal of Psychoeducational Assessment, 31*, 41–52.

Lewandowski, L., Hendricks, K., & Gordon, M. (2012). Test-taking performance of high school students with ADHD. *Journal of Attention Disorders.* Advance online publication. doi:10.1177/1087054712449183

Lewandowski, L., Lambert, T. L., Lovett, B. J., Panahon, C. J., & Sytsma, M. R. (in press). College students' preferences for test accommodations. *Canadian Journal of School Psychology.*

Lewandowski, L. J., Codding, R. S., Kleinmann, A. E., & Tucker, K. L. (2003). Assessment of reading rate in postsecondary students. *Journal of Psychoeducational Assessment, 21*, 134–144. doi:10.1177/073428290302100202

Lewandowski, L. J., Lovett, B. J., Parolin, R. A., Gordon, M., & Codding, R. S. (2007). Extended time accommodations and the mathematics performance of students with and without ADHD. *Journal of Psychoeducational Assessment, 25*, 17–28. doi:10.1177/0734282906291961

Lewandowski, L. J., Lovett, B. J., & Rogers, C. L. (2008). Extended time as a testing accommodation for students with reading disabilities: Does a rising tide lift all ships? *Journal of Psychoeducational Assessment, 26*, 315–324. doi:10.1177/0734282908315757

Li, H., & Hamel, C. M. (2003). Writing issues in college students with learning disabilities: A synthesis of the literature from 1990 to 2000. *Learning Disability Quarterly, 26*, 29–46. doi:10.2307/1593683

Lichtenberg, J. (2004). How the academically rich get richer. *Philosophy & Public Policy Quarterly, 24*(4), 19–27.

Liebert, R. M., & Morris, L. W. (1967). Cognitive and emotional components of test anxiety: A distinction and some initial data. *Psychological Reports, 20,* 975–978. doi:10.2466/pr0.1967.20.3.975

Lilienfeld, S. O., Ammirati, R., & David, M. (2012). Distinguishing science from pseudoscience in school psychology: Science and scientific thinking as safeguards against human error. *Journal of School Psychology, 50,* 7–36.

Lilienfeld, S. O., Lynn, S. J., & Lohr, J. M. (2003). *Science and pseudoscience in clinical psychology.* New York, NY: Guilford Press.

Lindstrom, J. H., & Gregg, N. (2007). The role of extended time on the SAT for students with learning disabilities and/or attention-deficit/hyperactivity disorder. *Learning Disabilities Research & Practice, 22,* 85–95. doi:10.1111/j.1540-5826.2007.00233.x

Lindstrom, J. H., & Lindstrom, W. (2011). Assessment documentation considerations for postsecondary students with LD. *Learning Disabilities, 17,* 63–68.

Loncke, F. T. (2011). Communication disorders. In J. M. Kauffman & D. P. Hallahan (Eds.), *Handbook of special education* (pp. 221–232). New York, NY: Routledge.

Lovett, B. J. (2007). *Determinants of postsecondary students' performance on timed examinations: Implications for extended time testing accommodations* (Unpublished doctoral dissertation). Syracuse University, Syracuse, NY.

Lovett, B. J. (2010). Extended time testing accommodations for students with disabilities: Answers to five fundamental questions. *Review of Educational Research, 80,* 611–638. doi:10.3102/0034654310364063

Lovett, B. J. (2013, November). *Why give extended time accommodations? Why have time limits at all?* Paper presented at the Research Forum of the National Board of Osteopathic Medical Examiners, Conshohocken, PA.

Lovett, B. J. (in press). Testing accommodations under the amended ADA: The voice of empirical research. *Journal of Disability Policy Studies.*

Lovett, B. J., & Leja, A. (2013). Students' perceptions of testing accommodations: What we know, what we need to know, and why it matters. *Journal of Applied School Psychology, 29,* 72–89. doi:10.1080/15377903.2013.751477

Lovett, B. J., & Lewandowski, L. J. (2006). Gifted students with learning disabilities: Who are they? *Journal of Learning Disabilities, 39,* 515–527. doi:10.1177/00222 194060390060401

Lovett, B. J., Lewandowski, L. J., Berger, C. A., & Gathje, R. A. (2010). Effects of response mode and time allotment on college students' writing. *Journal of College Reading and Learning, 40*(2), 64–79.

Lovett, B. J., & Sparks, R. L. (2010). Exploring the diagnosis of "Gifted/LD": Characterizing postsecondary students with learning disability diagnoses at different IQ levels. *Journal of Psychoeducational Assessment, 28,* 91–101.

Lovie-Kitchin, J. E., Oliver, N. J., Bruce, A., & Leighton, M. S. (1994). The effect of print size on reading rate for adults and children. *Clinical and Experimental Optometry, 77*, 2–7.

Lu, Y., & Sireci, S. G. (2007). Validity issues in test speededness. *Educational Measurement: Issues and Practice, 26*(4), 29–37. doi:10.1111/j.1745-3992.2007.00106.x

Lustig, C., Hasher, L., & Tonev, S. T. (2006). Distraction as a determinant of processing speed. *Psychonomic Bulletin & Review, 13*, 619–625. doi:10.3758/BF03193972

Lyon, G. R., Fletcher, J. M., Fuchs, L. S., & Chhabra, V. (2006). Learning disabilities. In E. J. Mash & R. Barkley (Eds.), *Treatment of childhood disorders* (3rd ed., pp. 512–594). New York, NY: Guilford Press.

MacArthur, C. A. (1996). Using technology to enhance the writing process of students with learning disabilities. *Journal of Learning Disabilities, 29*, 344–354. doi:10.1177/002221949602900403

MacArthur, C. A., & Cavalier, A. (1999). *Dictation and speech recognition technology as accommodations in large-scale assessments for students with learning disabilities*. Newark: University of Delaware Education Research and Development Center.

MacArthur, C. A., & Cavalier, A. (2004). Dictation and speech recognition technology as test accommodations. *Exceptional Children, 71*, 43–58.

MacArthur, C. A., & Graham, S. (1987). Learning disabled students' composing under three methods of text production: Handwriting, word processing, and dictation. *The Journal of Special Education, 21*(3), 22–42.

MacCann, R., Eastment, B., & Pickering, S. (2002). Responding to free response examination questions: Computer versus pen and paper. *British Journal of Educational Technology, 33*, 173–188. doi:10.1111/1467-8535.00251

Mace, R. L., Hardie, G. J., & Place, J. P. (1991). *Accessible environments: Toward universal design*. Raleigh, NC: Center for Universal Design Press.

MacMillan, D. L., Gresham, F. M., & Bocian, K. M. (1998). Discrepancy between definitions of learning disabilities and school practices: An empirical investigation. *Journal of Learning Disabilities, 31*, 314–326. doi:10.1177/002221949803100401

Madaus, J. W. (2008). Employment self-disclosure rates and rationales of university graduates with learning disabilities. *Journal of Learning Disabilities, 41*, 291–299. doi:10.1177/0022219407313805

Madaus, J. W., Banerjee, M., & Hamblet, E. C. (2010). Learning disability documentation decision making at the postsecondary level. *Career Development for Exceptional Individuals, 33*, 68–79. doi:10.1177/0885728810368057

Madaus, J. W., Banerjee, M., & Merchant, D. (2011). Transition in postsecondary education. In J. M. Kauffman & D. P. Hallahan (Eds.), *Handbook of special education* (pp. 571–583). New York, NY: Routledge.

Madaus, J. W., Shaw, S. F., & Zhao, J. (2005). School district practices related to Section 504. *Journal of Special Education Leadership, 18*(2), 24–29.

Malouf, D. B. (2005). Accommodation research to guide practice: Comments on what we know and what we need to know. *Assessment for Effective Intervention, 31*, 79–83.

Mandinach, E. B., Cahalan, C., & Camara, W. J. (2002). *The impact of flagging on the admission process: Policies, practices, and implications* (College Board Research Report No. 2002-2). Retrieved from http://research.collegeboard.org/publications/content/2012/05/impact-flagging-admission-process-policies-practices-and-implications

Mangrum, I. I., Charles, T., Iannuzzi, P. A., & Strichart, S. S. (1998). *Teaching study skills and strategies in grades 4–8*. Boston, MA: Allyn and Bacon.

Martens, B. K., & Witt, J. C. (2004). Competence, persistence, and success: The positive psychology of behavioral skill instruction. *Psychology in the Schools, 41*, 19–30. doi:10.1002/pits.10135

Martin, G., & Pear, J. (2007). *Behavior modification: What it is and how to do it* (8th ed.). Upper Saddle River, NJ: Prentice Hall.

Mather, N., & Wendling, B. J. (2011). *Essentials of dyslexia assessment and intervention*. Hoboken, NJ: Wiley.

Mattson, S. N., & Riley, E. R. (1998). A review of the neurobehavioral deficits in children with fetal alcohol syndrome or prenatal exposure to alcohol. *Alcoholism: Clinical and Experimental Research, 22*, 279–294. doi:10.1111/j.1530-0277.1998.tb03651.x

Mayes, S. D., & Calhoun, S. L. (2007). Learning, attention, writing, and processing speed in typical children and children with ADHD, autism, anxiety, depression, and oppositional-defiant disorder. *Child Neuropsychology, 13*, 469–493. doi:10.1080/09297040601112773

Mazzeo, J., & Harvey, A. L. (1988). *The equivalence of scores from automated and conventional educational and psychological tests: A review of the literature* (College Board Report 88-8). New York, NY: College Entrance Examination Board.

McBurnett, K., Pfiffner, L., & Frick, P. (2001). Symptom properties as a function of ADHD type: An argument for continued study of sluggish cognitive tempo. *Journal of Abnormal Child Psychology, 29*, 207–213. doi:10.1023/A:1010377530749

McCaffrey, D. F., Han, B., & Lockwood, J. R. (2009). Turning student test scores into teacher compensation systems. In M. G. Springer (Ed.), *Performance incentives: Their growing impact on American K–12 education* (pp. 113–147). Washington, DC: The Brookings Institute.

McCallin, R. (2006). Test administration. In S. M. Downing & T. M. Haladyna (Eds.), *Handbook of test development* (pp. 625–652). Mahwah, NJ: Erlbaum.

McFall, R. M. (1991). Manifesto for a science of clinical psychology. *The Clinical Psychologist, 44*(6), 75–88.

McGraw-Hill. (1990). *Comprehensive Test of Basic Skills*. Monterey, CA: CTB Macmillan/McGraw-Hill.

McGuire, J. M., Scott, S. S., & Shaw, S. F. (2006). Universal design and its applications in educational environments. *Remedial and Special Education, 27,* 166–175. doi:10.1177/07419325060270030501

McKee, L. M., & Levinson, E. M. (1990). A review of the computerized version of the Self-Directed Search. *The Career Development Quarterly, 38,* 325–333. doi:10.1002/j.2161-0045.1990.tb00222.x

McKenna, M. C., & Stahl, S. A. (2003). *Assessment for reading instruction.* New York, NY: Guilford Press.

McKevitt, B. C., & Elliott, S. N. (2003). Effects and perceived consequences of using read-aloud and teacher-recommended testing accommodations on a reading achievement test. *School Psychology Review, 32,* 583–600.

McKevitt, B. C., Elliott, S. N., & Kettler, R. J. (2013). Testing accommodations for children with disabilities. In C. R. Reynolds (Ed.), *Oxford handbook of child psychological assessment* (pp. 722–734). New York, NY: Oxford University Press.

Mead, A. D., & Drasgow, F. (1993). Equivalence of computerized and paper-and-pencil cognitive ability tests: A meta-analysis. *Psychological Bulletin, 114,* 449–458. doi:10.1037/0033-2909.114.3.449

Melnick, D. E. (2011). Commentary: Balancing responsibility to patients and responsibility to aspiring physicians with disabilities. *Academic Medicine, 86,* 674–676. doi:10.1097/ACM.0b013e318217e956

Menlove, M., & Hammond, M. (1998). Meeting the demands of ADA, IDEA, and other disability legislation in the design, development, and delivery of instruction. *Journal of Technology and Teacher Education, 6,* 75–85.

Merrell, K. W., Ervin, R. A., & Peacock, G. G. (2012). *School psychology for the 21st century: Foundations and practices* (2nd ed.). New York, NY: Guilford Press.

Messick, S. (1989). Validity. In R. L. Linn (Ed.), *Educational measurement* (3rd ed., pp. 13–103). New York, NY: MacMillan.

Messick, S. (1995). Validity of psychological assessment: Validation of inferences from persons' responses and performances as scientific inquiry into score meaning. *American Psychologist, 50,* 741–749. doi:10.1037/0003-066X.50.9.741

Mick, L. B. (1989). Measurement effects of modifications in minimum competency test formats for exceptional students. *Measurement and Evaluation in Counseling and Development, 22,* 31–36.

Miller, L. A., Lewandowski, L. J., & Antshel, K. (in press). Effects of extended time for college students with and without attention deficit hyperactivity disorder. *Journal of Attention Disorders.*

Millman, J., Bishop, C. H., & Ebel, R. (1965). An analysis of test-wiseness. *Educational and Psychological Measurement, 25,* 707–726. doi:10.1177/00131644650 2500304

Mittenberg, W., Patton, C., Canyock, E. M., & Condit, D. C. (2002). Base rates of malingering and symptom exaggeration. *Journal of Clinical and Experimental Neuropsychology, 24,* 1094–1102.

Montali, J., & Lewandowski, L. (1996). Bimodal reading: Benefits of a talking computer for average and less skilled readers. *Journal of Learning Disabilities, 29,* 271–279. doi:10.1177/002221949602900305

Morgan, P. L., & Sideridis, G. D. (2006). Contrasting the effectiveness of fluency interventions for students with or at risk for learning disabilities: A multilevel random coefficient modeling meta-analysis. *Learning Disabilities Research & Practice, 21,* 191–210. doi:10.1111/j.1540-5826.2006.00218.x

Morsy, L., Kieffer, M., & Snow, C. (2010). *Measure for measure: A critical consumers' guide to reading comprehension assessments for adolescents* (Final Report from Carnegie Corporation of New York's Council on Advancing Adolescent Literacy). New York, NY: Carnegie Corporation of New York.

National Association of School Psychologists. (2010). *Principles for professional ethics.* Bethesda, MD: Author. Retrieved from http://www.nasponline.org/standards/2010standards/1_%20Ethical%20Principles.pdf

National Dissemination Center for Children with Disabilities. (2012). *Visual impairment, including blindness.* Washington, DC: Author.

National Institute on Deafness and Other Communication Disorders. (2010). *Quick statistics.* Retrieved from http://www.nidcd.nih.gov/health/statistics/Pages/quick.aspx

Nelson, J. S., Jayanthi, M., Epstein, M. H., & Bursuck, W. D. (2000). Student preferences for adaptations in classroom testing. *Remedial and Special Education, 21,* 41–52. doi:10.1177/074193250002100106

Newman, L., Wagner, M., Knokey, A. M., Marder, C., Nagle, K., Shaver, D., & Wei, X. (2011). *The post-high school outcomes of young adults with disabilities up to 8 years after high school: A report from the National Longitudinal Transition Study-2 (NLTS-2)* (NCSER 2-11-3005). Menlo Park, CA: SRI International.

No Child Left Behind Act of 2001, 20 U.S.C. § 16301 *et seq.*

Nunnally, J. C. (1978). *Psychometric theory* (2nd ed.). New York, NY: McGraw-Hill.

Office of Vocational and Education Services for Individuals With Disabilities (VESID). (2006). *Test access & accommodations for students with disabilities: Policy and tools to guide decision-making and implementation.* Albany, NY: New York State Department of Education.

Ofiesh, N. S., Hughes, C., & Scott, S. S. (2004). Extended test time and postsecondary students with learning disabilities: A model for decision making. *Learning Disabilities Research & Practice, 19,* 57–70. doi:10.1111/j.1540-5826.2004.00090.x

Ofiesh, N. S., & Hughes, C. A. (2002). How much time? A review of the literature on extended test time for postsecondary students with learning disabilities. *Journal of Postsecondary Education and Disability, 16,* 2–16.

Ofiesh, N. S., Mather, N., & Russell, A. (2005). Using speeded cognitive, reading, and academic measures to determine the need for extended test time among university students with learning disabilities. *Journal of Psychoeducational Assessment, 23,* 35–52. doi:10.1177/073428290502300103

Osterlind, S. J., & Everson, H. T. (2009). *Differential item functioning* (2nd ed.). Thousand Oaks, CA: Sage.

Outhred, L. (1989). Word processing: Its impact on children's writing. *Journal of Learning Disabilities, 22,* 262–264. doi:10.1177/002221948902200413

Owens, M., Stevenson, J., Hadwin, J. A., & Norgate, R. (2012). Anxiety and depression in academic performance: An exploration of the mediating factors of worry and working memory. *School Psychology International, 33,* 433–449. doi:10.1177/0143034311427433

Paek, P. (2005). *Recent trends in comparability studies* (PEM Research Report 05-05). Retrieved from http://www.pearsonemsolutions.com/downloads/research/TrendsCompStudies_rr0505.pdf

Pariseau, M. E., Fabiano, G. A., Massetti, G. M., Hart, K. C., & Pelham, W. F. (2010). Extended time on academic assignments: Does increased time lead to improved performance for children with attention-deficit/hyperactivity disorder? *School Psychology Quarterly, 25,* 236–248. doi:10.1037/a0022045

Parks, M. Q. (2009). *Possible effects of calculators on the problem solving-abilities and mathematical anxiety of students with learning disabilities or attention deficit hyperactivity disorder* (Unpublished doctoral dissertation). Walden University.

Pearson. (2009). *Wechsler Individual Achievement Test* (3rd ed.). San Antonio, TX: Author.

Pelham, W. E., Wheeler, T., & Chronis, A. (1998). Empirically supported psychosocial treatments for attention deficit hyperactivity disorder. *Journal of Clinical Child Psychology, 27,* 190–205. doi:10.1207/s15374424jccp2702_6

Pennington, B. F. (1995). Genetics of learning disabilities. *Journal of Child Neurology, 10,* 69–77.

Pepper, D. (2007, September). *Assessment for disabled students: An international comparison* (QCA Briefing Document). Carrickfergus, England: Qualifications and Curriculum Authority.

Petrill, S. A. (2013). Behavioral genetics, learning abilities, and disabilities. In H. L. Swanson, K. R. Harris, & S. Graham (Eds.), *Handbook of learning disabilities* (2nd ed., pp. 293–325). New York, NY: Guilford Press.

Phillips, S. E. (1994). High-stakes testing accommodations: Validity versus disabled rights. *Applied Measurement in Education, 7,* 93–120. doi:10.1207/s15324818ame0702_1

Phillips, S. E. (2011). U.S. legal issues in educational testing of special populations. In S. N. Elliott, R. J. Kettler, P. A. Beddow, & A. Kurz (Eds.), *Handbook of accessible achievement tests for all students: Bridging the gaps between research, practice, and policy* (pp. 33–67). New York, NY: Springer.

Piek, J. P., Dyck, M. J., Francis, M., & Conwell, A. (2007). Working memory, processing speed, and set-shifting in children with developmental coordination disorder and attention-deficit–hyperactivity disorder. *Developmental Medicine & Child Neurology, 49,* 678–683. doi:10.1111/j.1469-8749.2007.00678.x

Pitoniak, M., & Royer, J. (2001). Testing accommodations for examinees with disabilities: A review of psychometric, legal, and social policy issues. *Review of Educational Research, 71,* 53–104. doi:10.3102/00346543071001053

Pittman, A. L., Lewis, D. E., Hoover, B. M., & Stelmachowicz, P. G. (2005). Rapid word-learning in normal-hearing and hearing-impaired children: Effects of age, receptive vocabulary, and high-frequency amplification. *Ear and Hearing, 26,* 619–629. doi:10.1097/01.aud.0000189921.34322.68

Plake, B. S., Impara, J. C., & Fager, J. J. (1993). Assessment competencies of teachers: A national survey. *Educational Measurement: Issues and Practice, 12*(4), 10–12. doi:10.1111/j.1745-3992.1993.tb00548.x

Pliszka, S. R. (2007). Pharmacologic treatment of attention-deficit/hyperactivity disorder: Efficacy, safety and mechanisms of action. *Neuropsychology Review, 17,* 61–72.

Poggio, J., Glasnapp, D. R., Yang, X., & Poggio, A. J. (2005). A comparative evaluation of score results from computerized and paper & pencil mathematics testing in a large scale state assessment program. *The Journal of Technology, Learning, and Assessment, 3*(6), 1–31.

Pomplun, M., & Custer, M. (2005). The score comparability of computerized and paper-and-pencil formats for K–3 reading tests. *Journal of Educational Computing Research, 32,* 153–166. doi:10.2190/D2HU-PVAW-BR9Y-J1CL

Popham, W. J. (2001). *The truth about testing: An educator's call to action.* Alexandria, VA: Association for Supervision and Curriculum Development.

Popham, W. J., & Lindheim, E. (1980). The practical side of criterion-referenced test development. *NCME Measurement in Education, 10*(4), 1–8.

Popper, K. R. (1976). The logic of the social sciences. In G. Adey & D. Frisby (Eds.), *The positivist dispute in German sociology* (pp. 87–104). London, England: Heinemann.

Potter, K., Lewandowski, L., & Spenceley, L. (2013). *A comparison of multiple-choice test response formats: Circling is better than bubbling.* Manuscript submitted for publication.

Powell, R. A., Honey, P. L., & Symbaluk, D. G. (2013). *Introduction to learning and behavior* (4th ed.). Belmont, California: Wadsworth.

Pressley, M., Duke, N. K., Gaskins, I. W., Fingeret, L., Halladay, J., Hilden, K., . . . Collins, S. (2009). Working with struggling readers: Why we must get beyond the simple view of reading and visions of how it might be done. In T. B. Gutkin & C. R. Reynolds (Eds.), *The handbook of school psychology* (4th ed., pp. 522–546). Hoboken, NJ: Wiley.

Price, L. A., Gerber, P. J., & Mulligan, R. (2007). Adults with learning disabilities and the underutilization of the Americans With Disabilities Act. *Remedial and Special Education, 28,* 340–344. doi:10.1177/07419325070280060301

Psychological Corporation. (2001). *Wechsler Individual Achievement Test* (2nd ed.). San Antonio, TX: Author.

Putwain, D. W., Connors, L., & Symes, W. (2010). Do cognitive distortions mediate the test anxiety–examination performance relationship? *Educational Psychology, 30,* 11–26. doi:10.1080/01443410903328866

Quellmalz, E. S., & Pellegrino, J. W. (2009). Technology and testing. *Science, 323,* 75–79.

Quinn, C. A. (2003). Detection of malingering in assessment of adult ADHD. *Archives of Clinical Neuropsychology, 18,* 379–395.

Rakow, S. J., & Gee, T. C. (1987). Test science, not reading. *Science Teacher, 54*(2), 28–31.

Randall, J., & Engelhard, G. (2010). Performance of students with and without disabilities under modified conditions using resource guides and read-aloud test modifications on a high-stakes reading test. *The Journal of Special Education, 44,* 79–93.

Ransby, M. J., & Swanson, H. L. (2003). Reading comprehension skills of young adults with childhood diagnoses of dyslexia. *Journal of Learning Disabilities, 36,* 538–555. doi:10.1177/00222194030360060501

Raskind, M. H., & Higgins, E. L. (1999). Speaking to read: The effects of speech recognition technology on the reading and spelling performance of children with learning disabilities. *Annals of Dyslexia, 49,* 251–281. doi:10.1007/s11881-999-0026-9

Rath, K. A., & Royer, J. M. (2002). The nature and effectiveness of learning disability services for college students. *Educational Psychology Review, 14,* 353–381.

Rathvon, N. (1999). *Effective school interventions: Strategies for enhancing academic achievement and social competence.* New York, NY: Guilford Press.

Raue, K., & Lewis, L. (2011). *Students with disabilities at degree-granting postsecondary institutions: First look* (NCES 2011-018). Washington, DC: U.S. Department of Education, National Center for Education Statistics.

Rehabilitation Act of 1973, Section 504 Regulations, 34 C.F.R. § 104.1 *et seq.*

Reynolds, C. R. (1984). Critical measurement issues in learning disabilities. *Journal of Special Education, 18,* 451–476.

Richards, G. (2002). *Putting psychology in its place* (2nd ed.). New York, NY: Routledge.

Richlan, F., Kronbichler, M., & Wimmer, H. (2011). Meta-analyzing brain dysfunctions in dyslexic children and adults. *NeuroImage, 56,* 1735–1742. doi:10.1016/j.neuroimage.2011.02.040

Rickey, K. M. (2005). *Assessment accommodations for students with disabilities: A description of the decision-making process, perspectives of those affected, and current practices* (Unpublished doctoral dissertation). University of Iowa, Iowa City, IA.

Rindler, S. E. (1979). Pitfalls in assessing test speededness. *Journal of Educational Measurement, 16,* 261–270. doi:10.1111/j.1745-3984.1979.tb00107.x

Roach, A. T. (2005). Alternate assessment as the "ultimate accommodation": Four challenges for policy and practice. *Assessment for Effective Intervention, 31,* 73–78. doi:10.1177/073724770503100107

Rogers, W. T. (1983). Use of separate answer sheets with hearing impaired and deaf school age students. *BC Journal of Special Education, 7*, 63–72.

Rogers, W. T., & Yang, P. (1996). Test-wiseness: Its nature and application. *European Journal of Psychological Assessment, 12*, 247–259. doi:10.1027/1015-5759.12.3.247

Rourke, B. P. (1975). Brain-behavior relationships in children with learning disabilities. *American Psychologist, 30*, 911–920. doi:10.1037/0003-066X.30.9.911

Rovet, J., Netley, C., Keenan, M., Bailey, J., & Stewart, D. (1996). The psycho-educational profile of boys with Klinefelter syndrome. *Journal of Learning Disabilities, 29*, 180–196. doi:10.1177/002221949602900208

Royer, J. M., & Randall, J. (2012). Testing accommodations for students with disabilities. In K. R. Harris, S. Graham, T. Urdan, G. Adriana, S. Major, & H. L. Swanson (Eds.), *APA educational psychology handbook: Vol. 3. Application to learning and teaching* (pp. 139–158). Washington, DC: American Psychological Association.

Rozalski, M., Katsiyannis, A., Ryan, J., Collins, T., & Stewart, A. (2010). Americans With Disabilities Act Amendments of 2008. *Journal of Disability Policy Studies, 21*, 22–28. doi:10.1177/1044207309357561

Runyan, M. K. (1991a). The effect of extra time on reading comprehension scores for university students with and without learning disabilities. *Journal of Learning Disabilities, 24*, 104–108. doi:10.1177/002221949102400207

Runyan, M. K. (1991b). Reading comprehension performance of learning-disabled and non-learning disabled college and university students under timed and untimed conditions. *Dissertation Abstracts International: Section A. The Humanities and Social Sciences, 52*(08), 2875.

Salend, S. J. (2011). Addressing test anxiety. *Teaching Exceptional Children, 44*(2), 58–68.

Salthouse, T. A. (1996). The processing-speed theory of adult age differences in cognition. *Psychological Review, 103*, 403–428. doi:10.1037/0033-295X.103.3.403

Samson, G. E. (1985). Effects of training in test-taking skills on achievement test performance: A quantitative synthesis. *The Journal of Educational Research, 78*, 261–266.

Sarason, S. B., Davidson, K. S., Lighthall, F. F., Waite, R. R., & Ruebush, B. K. (1960). *Anxiety in elementary school children*. New York, NY: Wiley.

Scheuneman, J. D., Camara, W. J., Cascallar, A. S., Wendler, C., & Lawrence, I. (2002). Calculator access, use, and type in relation to performance in the SAT I: Reasoning test in mathematics. *Applied Measurement in Education, 15*, 95–112. doi:10.1207/S15324818AME1501_06

Schilling, S. G., Carlisle, J. F., Scott, S. E., & Zeng, J. (2007). Are fluency measures accurate predictors of reading achievement? *The Elementary School Journal, 107*, 429–448. doi:10.1086/518622

Schneider, W. J., & McGrew, K. S. (2012). The Cattell-Horn-Carroll model of intelligence. In D. Flanagan & P. Harrison (Eds.), *Contemporary intellectual assessment: Theories, tests, and issues* (3rd ed., pp. 99–144). New York, NY: Guilford Press.

Sciutto, M. J., Nolfi, C. J., & Bluhm, C. (2004). Effects of child gender and symptom type on referrals for ADHD by elementary school teachers. *Journal of Emotional and Behavioral Disorders, 12,* 247–253. doi:10.1177/10634266040120040501

Scott, S. S., McGuire, J. M., & Foley, T. E. (2003). Universal Design for Instruction: A framework for anticipating and responding to disability and other diverse learning needs in the college classroom. *Equity & Excellence in Education, 36,* 40–49. doi:10.1080/10665680303502

Scruggs, T. E., & Mastropieri, M. A. (1992). *Teaching test-taking skills: Helping students show what they know.* Cambridge, MA: Brookline Books.

Sena, J. D. W., Lowe, P. A., & Lee, S. W. (2007). Significant predictors of test anxiety among students with and without learning disabilities. *Journal of Learning Disabilities, 40,* 360–376. doi:10.1177/00222194070400040601

Shanahan, M. A., Pennington, B. F., Yerys, B. E., Scott, A., Boada, R., Willcutt, E. G., . . . DeFries, J. C. (2006). Processing speed deficits in attention deficit/hyperactivity disorder and reading disability. *Journal of Abnormal Child Psychology, 34,* 584–601. doi:10.1007/s10802-006-9037-8

Shapiro, E. S. (2010). *Academic skills problems: Direct assessment and intervention* (4th ed.). New York, NY: Guilford Press.

Sharp, K., & Earle, S. (2000). Assessment, disability and the problem of compensation. *Assessment & Evaluation in Higher Education, 25,* 191–199. doi:10.1080/713611423

Shaywitz, S. (2003). *Overcoming dyslexia.* New York, NY: Vintage.

Shinn, E., & Ofiesh, N. S. (2012). Cognitive diversity and the design of classroom tests for all learners. *Journal of Postsecondary Education and Disability, 25,* 227–245.

Shriner, J. G., & Ganguly, R. (2007). Assessment and accommodation issues under the No Child Left Behind Act and the Individuals With Disabilities Education Improvement Act: Information for IEP teams. *Assessment for Effective Intervention, 32,* 231–243. doi:10.1177/15345084070320040501

Siegel, L. S. (1992). An evaluation of the discrepancy definition of dyslexia. *Journal of Learning Disabilities 25,* 618–629.

Silva, M., Munk, D. D., & Bursuck, W. D. (2005). Grading adaptations for students with disabilities. *Intervention in School and Clinic, 41,* 87–98. doi:10.1177/10534512050410020901

Silver, P., Bourke, A., & Strehorn, K. C. (1998). Universal instructional design in higher education: An approach for inclusion. *Equity & Excellence in Education, 31,* 47–51. doi:10.1080/1066568980310206

Sireci, S. G. (2005). Unlabeling the disabled: A perspective on flagging scores from accommodated test administrations. *Educational Researcher, 34,* 3–12. doi:10.3102/0013189X034001003

Sireci, S. G., & Hambleton, R. K. (2009). Mission—Protect the public: Licensure and certification testing in the 21st century. In R. Phelps (Ed.), *Correcting fallacies about educational and psychological testing* (pp. 199–217). Washington, DC: American Psychological Association. doi:10.1037/11861-006

Sireci, S. G., Scarpati, S. E., & Li, S. (2005). Test accommodations for students with disabilities: An analysis of the interaction hypothesis. *Review of Educational Research, 75,* 457–490. doi:10.3102/00346543075004457

Siskind, T. G. (1993). Teachers' knowledge about test modifications for students with disabilities. *Diagnostique, 18,* 145–157.

Skiba, R. J., Simmons, A. B., Ritter, S., Gibb, A. C., Rausch, M. K., Cuadrado, J., & Chung, C. G. (2008). Achieving equity in special education: History, status, and current challenges. *Exceptional Children, 74,* 264–288.

Solis, M., Ciullo, S., Vaughn, S., Pyle, N., Hassaram, B., & Leroux, A. (2012). Reading comprehension interventions for middle school students with learning disabilities: A synthesis of 30 years of research. *Journal of Learning Disabilities, 45,* 327–340. doi:10.1177/0022219411402691

Sollman, M. J., Ranseen, J. D., & Berry, D. T. (2010). Detection of feigned ADHD in college students. *Psychological Assessment, 22,* 325–335.

Songlee, D., Miller, S. P., Tincani, M., Sileo, N. M., & Perkins, P. G. (2008). Effects of test-taking strategy instruction on high-functioning adolescents with autism spectrum disorders. *Focus on Autism and Other Developmental Disabilities, 23,* 217–228. doi:10.1177/1088357608324714

Sparks, R. L., & Lovett, B. J. (2009a). College students with learning disability diagnoses: Who are they and how do they perform? *Journal of Learning Disabilities, 42,* 494–510.

Sparks, R. L., & Lovett, B. J. (2009b). Objective criteria for classification of postsecondary students as learning disabled: Effects on prevalence rates and group characteristics. *Journal of Learning Disabilities, 42,* 230–239. doi:10.1177/0022219408331040

Sparks, R. L., & Lovett, B. J. (2013). Applying objective diagnostic criteria to students in a college support program for learning disabilities. *Learning Disability Quarterly, 36,* 231–241.

Spenceley, L. M. (2012, February). *The impact of incentives on neuropsychological test performance: An analog study.* Poster presented at the National Association of School Psychologists, Philadelphia, PA.

Spielberger, C. D., Gonzalez, H. P., Taylor, C. J., Anton, E. D., Algaze, B., Ross, G. R., & Westberry, L. G. (1980). *Test Anxiety Inventory.* Redwood City, CA: Consulting Psychologists Press.

Stanovich, K. E. (1999). The sociopsychometrics of learning disabilities. *Journal of Learning Disabilities, 32,* 350–361. doi:10.1177/002221949903200408

Sternberg, R. J., & Grigorenko, E. L. (2002). Difference scores in the identification of children with learning disabilities: It's time to use a different method. *Journal of School Psychology, 40,* 65–83. doi:10.1016/S0022-4405(01)00094-2

Stiggins, R. J. (1999). Evaluating classroom assessment training in teacher education programs. *Educational Measurement: Issues and Practice, 18*, 23–27. doi:10.1111/j.1745-3992.1999.tb00004.x

Stokes, T. F., & Baer, D. M. (1977). An implicit technology of generalization. *Journal of Applied Behavior Analysis, 10*, 349–367. doi:10.1901/jaba.1977.10-349

Story, M. F., Mueller, J. L., & Mace, R. L. (1998). *The universal design file*. Raleigh: North Carolina State University.

Sud, A., & Prabha, C. (2003). Academic performance in relation to perfectionism, test procrastination, and test anxiety of high school children. *Psychological Studies, 48*(3), 77–81.

Suen, H. K. (1990). *Principles of test theories*. Hillsdale, NJ: Erlbaum.

Suhr, J., Hammers, D., Dobbins-Buckland, K., Zimak, E., & Hughes, C. (2008). The relationship of malingering test failure to self-reported symptoms and neuropsychological findings in adults referred for ADHD evaluation. *Archives of Clinical Neuropsychology, 23*, 521–530.

Sullivan, B. K., May, K., & Galbally, L. (2007). Symptom exaggeration by college adults in attention-deficit hyperactivity disorder and learning disorder assessments. *Applied Neuropsychology, 14*, 189–207.

Sullivan, P. M. (1982). Administration modifications on the WISC–R Performance Scale with different categories of deaf children. *American Annals of the Deaf, 127*, 780–788.

Suskie, L. A. (2009). *Assessing student learning: A common sense guide* (2nd ed.). San Francisco, CA: Jossey-Bass.

Swanson, S., & Howell, C. (1996). Test anxiety in adolescents with learning disabilities and behavior disorders. *Exceptional Children, 62*, 389–397.

Szarko, J. E., Brown, A. J., & Watkins, M. W. (2013). Examiner familiarity effects for children with autism spectrum disorders. *Journal of Applied School Psychology, 29*, 37–51.

Tapper, J., Morris, D., & Setrakian, L. (2006). Does loophole give rich kids more time on SAT? Educators say more wealthy students get diagnosed with learning disabilities to get more time on test. *ABC News*. Retrieved from http://abcnews.go.com/Nightline/story?id=1787712

Taylor, M., & Houghton, S. (2008). Examination-related anxiety in students diagnosed with AD/HD and the case for an allocation of extra time: Perspectives of teachers, mothers and students. *Emotional & Behavioural Difficulties, 13*, 111–125. doi:10.1080/13632750802027663

Temple, C. M., & Marriot, A. J. (1998). Arithmetical ability and disability in Turner's syndrome: A cognitive neuropsychological analysis. *Developmental Neuropsychology, 14*, 47–67.

Temple, E., Deutsch, G. K., Poldrack, R. A., Miller, S. L., Tallal, P., Merzenich, M. M., & Gabrieli, J. D. E. (2003). Neural deficits in children with dyslexia ameliorated by behavioral remediation: Evidence from functional MRI. *Proceedings*

of the National Academy of Sciences of the USA, 100, 2860–2865. doi:10.1073/
pnas.0030098100

Texas Student Assessment Program. (2012). *2011–2012 accommodations manual.* Retrieved from http://www.tea.state.tx.us/student.assessment/taks/
accommodations/

Thompson, B., & Daniel, L. G. (1996). Factor analytic evidence for the construct
validity of scores: A historical overview and some guidelines. *Educational and
Psychological Measurement, 56,* 197–208. doi:10.1177/0013164496056002001

Thompson, S. J., Blount, A., & Thurlow, M. (2002). *A summary of research on the
effects of test accommodations: 1999 through 2001* (Tech. Rep. No. 34). National
Center on Educational Outcomes, University of Minnesota, Minneapolis.
Retrieved from http://education.umn.edu/NCEO/OnlinePubs/Technical34.htm

Thompson, S. J., Johnstone, C. J., & Thurlow, M. L. (2002). *Universal design applied
to large scale assessments* (NCEO Synthesis Report 44). Minneapolis: University of Minnesota, National Center on Educational Outcomes. Retrieved from
http://www.cehd.umn.edu/nceo/onlinepubs/Synthesis44.html

Thompson, S. J., Morse, A. B., Sharpe, M., & Hall, S. (2005). *Accommodations manual: How to select, administer, and evaluate use of accommodations for instruction
and assessment of students with disabilities.* Washington, DC: Council of Chief
State School Officers.

Thornton, A. E., Reese, L. M., Pashley, P. J., & Dalessandro, S. P. (2001). *Predictive
validity of accommodated LSAT scores* (Tech. Rep. No. 01-01). Newtown, PA:
Law School Admission Council.

Thurlow, M., & Bolt, S. (2001). *Empirical support for accommodations most often
allowed in state policy* (NCEO Synthesis Report 41). Minneapolis: University of
Minnesota, National Center on Educational Outcomes. Retrieved from http://
education.umn.edu/NCEO/OnlinePubs/Synthesis41.html

Thurlow, M. L., Elliott, J. L., & Ysseldyke, J. E. (2003). *Testing students with disabilities: Practical strategies for complying with district and state requirements* (2nd ed.).
Thousand Oaks, CA: Corwin Press.

Thurlow, M. L., McGrew, K. S., Tindal, G., Thompson, S. L., Ysseldyke, J. E., &
Elliott, J. L. (2000). *Assessment accommodations research: Considerations for
design and analysis* (Tech. Rep. No. 26). Minneapolis: University of Minnesota,
National Center on Educational Outcomes.

Thurlow, M. L., Moen, R. E., Lekwa, A. J., & Scullin, S. B. (2010). *Examination of a
reading pen as a partial auditory accommodation for reading assessment.* Minneapolis: University of Minnesota, Partnership for Accessible Reading Assessment.

Tindal, G. (2002). *Accommodating mathematics testing using a videotaped, read-aloud
administration.* Washington, DC: Council of Chief State School Officers.

Tindal, G., Heath, B., Hollenbeck, K., Almond, P., & Harniss, M. (1998). Accommodating students with disabilities on large-scale tests: An experimental study.
Exceptional Children, 64, 439–450.

Tolfa-Veit, D., & Scruggs, T. E. (1986). Can learning disabled students effectively use separate answer sheets? *Perceptual and Motor Skills, 63*, 155–160.

Tomlinson, C. A. (2008). Learning to love assessment. *Educational Leadership, 65*, 8–13.

Torgesen, J. K., & Barker, T. A. (1995). Computers as aids in the prevention and remediation of reading disabilities. *Learning Disability Quarterly, 18*, 76–87. doi:10.2307/1511196

Traxler, C. (2000). The Stanford Achievement Test, 9th edition: National norming and performance standards for deaf and hard-of-hearing students. *Journal of Deaf Studies and Deaf Education, 5*, 337–348.

Umpstead, R. R. (2009). Special education assessment policy under the No Child Left Behind Act and the Individuals with Disabilities Education Act. *Rutgers Journal of Law and Public Policy, 7*, 145–185.

U.S. Department of Education, Institute of Education Sciences, National Center for Special Education Research. (2002). *National Longitudinal Transition Study-2 (NLTS-2), Wave 1 student's school program survey, 2002*. Washington, DC: Author. Retrieved from http://ies.ed.gov/ncser/pubs/20073005/accommodations.asp

U.S. Department of Education, National Center for Education Statistics. (2010). *Digest of Education Statistics, 2009* (NCES 2010-013). Washington, DC: Author.

U.S. Department of Education, National Center for Education Statistics. (2012). *Digest of Education Statistics, 2011* (NCES 2012-001). Washington, DC: Author.

U.S. Government Accountability Office. (2011). *Higher education and disability: Improved federal enforcement needed to better protect students' rights to testing accommodations* (GAO Publication No. 12-40). Washington, DC: Author. Retrieved from http://www.gao.gov/assets/590/587367.pdf

VanDerHeyden, A. M., Witt, J. C., & Gilbertson, D. (2007). A multi-year evaluation of the effects of a Response to Intervention (RTI) model on identification of children for special education. *Journal of School Psychology, 45*, 225–256. doi:10.1016/j.jsp.2006.11.004

Vang, M., Thurlow, M., & Altman, J. (2012). *2008–2009 APR snapshot #2: Assessment accommodation use by special education students*. Minneapolis: University of Minnesota, National Center on Educational Outcomes.

Vernon, M., & Andrews, J. F. (1990). *The psychology of deafness: Understanding deaf and hard-of-hearing people*. New York, NY: Longman.

Vickers, M. Z. (2010). *Accommodating college students with learning disabilities: ADD, ADHD, and dyslexia*. Raleigh, NC: John William Pope Center for Higher Education Policy.

Von der Embse, N., Barterian, J., & Segool, N. (2013). Test anxiety interventions for children and adolescents: A systematic review of treatment studies from 2000–2010. *Psychology in the Schools, 50*, 57–71. doi:10.1002/pits.21660

Wachelka, D., & Katz, R. C. (1999). Reducing test anxiety and improving academic self-esteem in high school and college students with learning disabilities. *Journal* of Behavior Therapy and Experimental Psychiatry, 30, 191–198. doi:10.1016/S0005-7916(99)00024-5

Wadley, M. N., & Liljequist, L. (2013). The effect of extended test time for students with attention-deficit hyperactivity disorder. *Journal of Postsecondary Education and Disability, 26*, 263–271.

Wadsworth, S. J., DeFries, J. C., Olson, R. K., & Willcutt, E. G. (2007). Colorado longitudinal twin study of reading disability. *Annals of Dyslexia, 57*, 139–160.

Wainer, H., & Thissen, D. (1994). On examinee choice in educational testing. *Review of Educational Research, 64*, 159–195. doi:10.3102/00346543064001159

Wakeman, S. Y., Browder, D. M., Flowers, C., & Karvonen, M. (2011). Alternate achievement standards for alternate assessments: Considerations for policy and practice. In M. Russell & M. Kavanaugh (Eds.), *Assessing students in the margin: Challenges, strategies, and techniques* (pp. 149–169). Charlotte, NC: Information Age.

Walker, J. S. (2011). Malingering in children: Fibs and faking. *Child and Adolescent Psychiatric Clinics of North America, 20*, 547–556.

Walz, L., Albus, D., Thompson, S., & Thurlow, M. (2000). *Effect of a multiple day test accommodation on the performance of special education students* (Minnesota Report 34). Minneapolis: University of Minnesota, National Center on Educational Outcomes.

Wang, S., Jiao, H., Young, M. J., Brooks, T. E., & Olson, J. (2008). Comparability of computer-based and paper-and-pencil testing in K–12 assessments: A meta-analysis of testing mode effects. *Educational and Psychological Measurement, 68*, 5–24.

Wauters, L. N., Van Bon, W. H., & Tellings, A. E. (2006). Reading comprehension of Dutch deaf children. *Reading and Writing, 19*, 49–76. doi:10.1007/s11145-004-5894-0

Weaver, S. M. (1993). The validity of the use of extended and untimed testing for postsecondary students with learning disabilities. *Dissertation Abstracts International, 55*(03), 535.

Wechsler, D. (2003). *Wechsler Intelligence Scale for Children* (4th ed.). San Antonio, TX: Psychological Corporation.

Wechsler, D. (2008). *Wechsler Adult Intelligence Scale* (4th ed.). San Antonio, TX: Psychological Corporation.

Wendling, B. J., & Mather, N. (2009). *Essentials of evidence-based academic interventions*. Hoboken, NJ: Wiley.

Weston, T. J. (2003). *The validity of oral accommodation in testing: NAEP validity studies*. Washington, DC: National Center for Education Statistics. doi:10.1037/e313712005-001

Wexler, J., Vaughn, S., Edmonds, M., & Reutebuch, C. K. (2008). A synthesis of fluency interventions for secondary struggling readers. *Reading and Writing, 21*, 317–347. doi:10.1007/s11145-007-9085-7

Wiederholt, J. L., & Blalock, G. (2000). *Gray Silent Reading Tests*. Austin, TX: Pro-Ed.

Wiederholt, J. L., & Bryant, B. R. (2012). *Gray Oral Reading Tests* (5th ed.). Austin, TX: Pro-Ed.

Wilkins, A. J. (2003). *Reading through colour*. Chichester, England: Wiley.

Willcutt, E. G., Doyle, A. E., Nigg, J. T., Faraone, S. V., & Pennington, B. F. (2005). Validity of the executive function theory of attention-deficit/hyperactivity disorder: A meta-analytic review. *Biological Psychiatry, 57*, 1336–1346. doi:10.1016/j.biopsych.2005.02.006

Willingham, W. W. (1989). Standard testing conditions and standard score meaning for handicapped examinees. *Applied Measurement in Education, 2*, 97–103. doi:10.1207/s15324818ame0202_1

Wolf, J. (2007). *The effects of testing accommodations usage on students' standardized test scores for deaf and hard-of-hearing students in Arizona public schools* (Unpublished doctoral dissertation). University of Arizona.

Wood, W. M., Lewandowski, L., & Lambert, T. (2012, February). *A comparison of private versus group test taking*. Poster session presented at the National Association of School Psychologists convention, Philadelphia, PA.

Woodcock, R. W. (1987). *Woodcock Reading Mastery Tests—revised*. Circle Pines, MN: American Guidance Service.

Woodcock, R. W., McGrew, K. S., & Mather, N. (2001). *Woodcock-Johnson Tests of Achievement*. Itasca, IL: Riverside.

Wright, N., & Wendler, C. (1994, April). *Establishing timing limits for the new SAT for students with disabilities* (ERIC Document Reproduction Service No. ED375543). Paper presented at the annual meeting of the National Council on Measurement in Education, New Orleans, LA.

Yell, M. L. (2012). *The law and special education* (3rd ed.). Upper Saddle River, NJ: Pearson.

Yovanoff, P., Duesbery, L., Alonzo, J., & Tindal, G. (2005). Grade-level invariance of a theoretical causal structure predicting reading comprehension with vocabulary and oral reading fluency. *Educational Measurement: Issues and Practice, 24*(3), 4–12. doi:10.1111/j.1745-3992.2005.00014.x

Ysseldyke, J., Thurlow, M., Bielinski, J., House, A., Moody, M., & Haigh, J. (2001). The relationship between instructional and assessment accommodations in an inclusive state accountability system. *Journal of Learning Disabilities, 34*, 212–220.

Zachrisson, B. (1965). *Legibility of printed text*. Stockholm, Sweden: Almqvist & Wisell.

Zeidner, M. (1998). *Test anxiety: The state of the art*. New York, NY: Plenum Press.

Zeidner, M. (2007). Test anxiety in educational contexts: Concepts, findings, and future directions. In P. A. Schutz & R. Pekrun (Eds.), *Emotion in education* (pp. 165–184). San Diego, CA: Academic Press. doi:10.1016/B978-012372545-5/50011-3

Zuriff, G. E. (2000). Extra examination time for students with learning disabilities: An examination of the maximum potential thesis. *Applied Measurement in Education, 13*, 99–117.

INDEX

Computerized adaptive tests, 230n1
Computerized assessment, 138
Condit, D. C., 91
Confirmatory factor analysis, 64, 103
Connors, L., 182
Construct-irrelevant variance, 46–48
    with read-aloud accommodations, 154
    and test speededness, 96
Constructs, of tests. *See* Test constructs
Construct validity, 45, 49–50
Content validity (of tests), 44
Conwell, A., 83
Cook, L. L., 154
Cooper, J. O., 171
Council for Exceptional Children, 255
Council of Chief State School Officers,
    58, 255–256
Cowan, J., 149
Criterion-referenced construct-based
    interpretation, 52
Criterion-referenced direct sample
    interpretation, 51–52
Criterion-referenced expectancy table
    interpretation, 52
Criterion-referenced testing, 51
Criterion-related validity, 44–45, 64–65
Cronbach's alpha, 43
Curley, W. E., 215
Curriculum-based measurement (CBM),
    106–107

Dalessandro, S. P., 102
DATA (Dynamic Assessment of Test
    Accommodations), 58
Davis, J. E., 252
Davis, M., 126
DBH. *See* Differential boost hypothesis
Deafness, 74–77, 152–156
Decision procedures, 108–109
Decker, D. M., 125
Dempsey, K., 15, 17, 197
Deng, M., 104
Department of Justice, 191
Depression, and processing speed, 88
Deshler, D. D., 175
DeStefano, L., 254
Developmental disabilities, 73–74
Diagnoses
    of blindness and visual disabilities, 77
    commonsense standard vs., 242–244

of deafness and hearing disabilities,
    74–75
of disability conditions, 57–58
and functional impairment, 69–71
of learning disabilities, 78–79, 193
malingering in assessments for, 92
necessity of, for testing
    accommodations, 189–190
*Diagnostic and Statistical Manual of
    Mental Disorders (DSM)*, 67
*Diagnostic and Statistical Manual of
    Mental Disorders* (fourth ed., text
    rev.; *DSM–IV–TR*), 69
*Diagnostic and Statistical Manual of Mental
    Disorders* (fifth edition, *DSM–5*),
    69, 70, 78, 79, 82, 88, 193
Diagnosticians
    limitations of, 15
    reliability/validity of diagnoses from,
        57–58
Dictated-response recording, 128–132
Dictionary access, 136–137
DIF. *See* Differential item functioning
Differential benefits
    of calculator use, 133
    as ethical issue, 35
    as outcome-focused, 54n1
    and psychometrics, 52–54
    research on, 60–63
    of timing and scheduling
        accommodations, 104–106
    of word-processor use, 127
Differential boost hypothesis (DBH), 53
    and read-aloud accommodations, 153
    research on, 62, 63
Differential item functioning (DIF)
    and read-aloud accommodations, 154
    and score comparability, 65–66, 104
Digit-Symbol Coding, 112
Disability conditions, 67–92. *See also
    specific disabilities*
    attention-deficit/hyperactivity
        disorder (ADHD), 82–86
    autism spectrum disorder (ASD),
        88–89
    blindness and visual disabilities,
        77–78
    contribution of, to construct-
        irrelevant variance, 47
    deaf and hearing disabilities, 74–77

Incremental theory, 186
Individual case review, 39–40
Individualized education programs
        (IEPs), 23, 236
Individuals With Disabilities Education
        Act (IDEA), 22–24
    IEPs governed by, 236
    specific learning disabilities under,
        78
    transition planning required under,
        187
Individuals With Disabilities Education
        Improvement Act (IDEAIA), 24
    and ADAAA, 188–196
    impairment criteria under, 69
Instructional accommodations, 8
Instructional hierarchy (IH), 168–172
Instructors, college, 239–240
Intellectual disabilities, 73–74
Intelligence, 192
Interaction hypothesis, 53
Internal consistency, of test scores, 43
Internet-based professional
        development, 254
Interventions, 167–186
    accommodations provided for
        students accessing, 24
    based on instructional hierarchy
        (IH), 168–172
    for decreasing test anxiety, 181–185
    encouragement of, under IDEAIA, 24
    to increase test-taking skills, 226
    for increasing test-taking skills,
        172–177
    for reading comprehension, 179–181
    for reading fluency, 177–179
    to reduce need for accommodations,
        56
Intuitive use, of assessments, 214
iPads, for testing, 138
Irlen syndrome, 150
Item pacing, 94

Jachimowicz, G., 92
Jackenthal, A., 162
Jamgochian, E. M., 168
Jerger, J., 76
Jirele, T., 151
Johnstone, C. J., 218
Jordan, L., 176

Joy, J. A., 15
Joyce, L. B., 58, 256
Julius, J. R., 15

K–12 accommodations
    documentation and processes for,
        235–236
    incentives for granting, 251
    prevalence of, 10–11
    use of scribes, 129
    word-processor use, 125
Kamei-Hannan, C., 161–162
Karns, K., 153
Karvonen, M., 7
Katz, R. C., 183–184
Kehle, T. J., 175
Ketterlin-Geller, L. R., 168, 212
Kettler, R. J., 53–54, 122, 176, 212, 231
Kieffer, M. J., 137n2
Kim, D. H., 161
Kim, J., 161
King, T. C., 56–57, 107
Knowledge retrieval and use, fluency
        of, 110
Kosciolek, S., 12
Kranzler, J., 106–107
Kratochwill, T. R., 58
Kretlow, A. G., 176
Kubina, R. M., Jr., 99
Kuhn, M. R., 178
Kurzweil 3000 with Firefly, 159
Kurzweil Educational Systems, 159

Lail, K. E., 27
Laitusis, C. C., 157
Lambert, T. L., 35, 85, 145, 152
Lancaster, P. E., 175
Lancaster, S. J. C., 175
Landau, S., 149
Lane, S., 129
Lang, S. C., 252
Language and speech limitations
    and dictated-response recording
        accommodations, 131
    dictionary/thesaurus use for examinees
        with, 137
    of examinees, 124
Large-print test formats
    as format accommodations, 151–152
    state regulations related to, 28

ABOUT THE AUTHORS

Benjamin J. Lovett, PhD, is an assistant professor of psychology at the State University of New York College at Cortland, where his research focuses on conceptual and applied issues in psychoeducational assessment and psychiatric diagnosis. Dr. Lovett has over 50 publications that have appeared in peer-reviewed journals and edited books. He also serves as a consultant to a variety of educational institutions and testing agencies on the topics of disability diagnosis and testing accommodations.

Lawrence J. Lewandowski, PhD, is a professor of psychology at Syracuse University, holding distinction as a Laura J. and Douglas Meredith Professor for Teaching Excellence. Dr. Lewandowski has approximately 100 publications, most of which deal with the study of learning disabilities, attention disorders, and other pediatric neurological conditions. His recent research involves such topics as processing and reading speed in individuals with and without disabilities, extended-time accommodations for students with disabilities, assessment of clinical impairment in attention-deficit/hyperactivity disorder and learning disabilities, and the effects of concussion on children and adults.